Object-Oriented Programming in C++

T0181826

Object-Oriented Programming in C++

Nicolai M. Josuttis

Solutions in Time

JOHN WILEY & SONS, LTD

Other Wiley Editorial Offices

John Wiley & Sons Inc., 111 River Street, Hoboken, NJ 07030, USA

Jossey-Bass, 989 Market Street, San Francisco, CA 94103-1741, USA

Wiley-VCH Verlag GmbH, Boschstr. 12, D-69469 Weinheim, Germany

John Wiley & Sons Australia Ltd, 33 Park Road, Milton, Queensland 4064, Australia

John Wiley & Sons (Asia) Pte Ltd, 2 Clementi Loop #02-01, Jin Xing Distripark, Singapore 129809

John Wiley & Sons Canada Ltd, 22 Worcester Road, Etobicoke, Ontario, Canada M9W 1L1

Library of Congress Cataloging-in-Publication Data

Josuttis, Nicolai M.
   [Objektorientiertes Programmieren in C++. English]
   Object-oriented programming in C++/Nicolai M. Josuttis.
     p. cm.
   Includes bibliographical references and index.
   ISBN 0 470 84399 3
     1. Object-oriented programming (Computer science) 2. C++ (Computer program Language) I. Title.
   QA76.64. J6713 2002
   005.13'3–dc21   2002028094

British Library Cataloguing in Publication Data

A catalogue record for this book is available from the British Library

ISBN 0 470 84399 3
Produced from the author's LaTeX files

This book is printed on acid-free paper responsibly manufactured from sustainable forestry in which at least two trees are planted for each one used for paper production.

Contents

Preface

It took a long, long time to produce this book, but now it is done. I have used my experience with C++ and object-oriented programming, gained over several years of project and training work, as well as my experience as a member of the C++ standardization committee, to write a tutorial for C++ programmers consistent with the style in which C++ and its standard library should be used.

The result is a book for all beginners who want to learn and understand how to program in C++ as well as those programmers who want to get the overall picture and take advantage of the standardized C++ language and its standard library.

The first part (Chapters 2 and 3) introduces and clarifies how to use and combine classes to create a C++ program. Thus, it teaches from the *application programmers* point of view. The second part (Chapters 4 to 6) introduces all aspects for the design and implementation of classes and class hierarchies. It follows an extensive chapter about templates, which clarifies their advantages, also in the framework of object-oriented programming. To round the book off, there is a detailed introduction to certain aspects of the standard library (I/O, containers, etc.) and to additional special language features that are important for day-to-day use.

C++ is far too rich a language to explain everything in one book. (In fact, my other C++ books, which cover all aspects of the C++ standard library and templates respectively, are both over 500 pages.) However, this book contains a carefully planned introduction to programming, using the features that C++ currently offers.

I hope that all readers have as much fun in reading this book as I have had in writing it.

Thanks

The history of this book goes back to 1994 when the first edition was published in German. After the standardization of C++, a second German edition was published, which made use of all the features and advantages of the C++ standard and especially its library. Now, this English edition is a revised second edition, with some updates resulting from feedback and more experience. Because of this long history there is a long list of people who have given tremendous support to get this work done.

Firstly I should give special thanks to the staff at BREDEX (where I was working while writing the first edition). In particular, Achim Brede, Ulrich Obst, Achim Lörke, Bernhard Witte, and other employees have helped me a lot, devoting much of their time and effort.

Secondly, I'd like to thank all people who reviewed this book in its various editions over the years. They did an incredible job to give this book the quality it has now. Many thanks for the reviews of the German editions to Johannes Hampel, Peter Heilscher, Olaf Janßen, Jan Langer, Bernd Mohr, Olaf Petzold, Michael Pitz, André Pönitz, Daniel Rakel, Kurt Watzka, Andreas Wetjen, and Sascha Zapf. Many thanks for the reviews of the English edition to Jon Kalb, David Reynolds, Angelika Langer, Mark Radford, and Detlef Vollmann.

Thirdly, I'd like to thank all people of the publishing companies that were involved. I'd like to thank Susanne Spitzer, Judith Muhr, Margrit Seifert, and Friederike Daenecke from Addison-Wesley, Germany for their cooperation and their patience. And I'd also like to thank Gaynor Redvers-Mutton and Robert Hambrook from Wiley for giving me the opportunity to get this book published in English and helping to ensure that it speaks both C++ and English.

There are many more people who have given me feedback and valuable advice over the years. They have sent me e-mails or discussed various aspects of C++ at conferences or over the Internet. Thanks also go to all of them, although I can't list their names because this list would be far too long and I would probably forget some.

Finally, I naturally thank my family and friends, who, as always, have supported this project with a great deal of patience and understanding. Many thanks to Ulli, Lucas, Anica, and Frederic.

Nicolai Josuttis
Hondelage, September 2002

1

About this Book

This chapter explains why this book was written and the concepts that inspired it. A content overview is also provided.

1.1 Why Did I Write this Book?

'Object-oriented' is the buzzword associated with all good software nowadays. C++ has contributed to this breakthrough, yet it is not a purely object-oriented language. As a further development of C, C++ is a hybrid language, which enables object-oriented and non-object-oriented programming. This flexibility has its advantages and disadvantages. Using C++, one can react to almost every problem adequately, through the support of various programming paradigms. However, beginners find it difficult to get an overview of the many uses of C++.

This book introduces 'Object-Oriented Programming using C++'. C++ will be used with the full power of the object-oriented paradigm. In addition to the introduction of new language features, readers will also learn a new world of concepts and a new way of thinking. An explanation of the various object-oriented language features is provided by making reference to practical issues, and rounded off with the discussion of design aspects.

But there is more. This book also introduces the most important *non*-object-oriented features of C++. These are necessary in practice because not all problems require an object-oriented solution and C++ is a language that allows multi-paradigm programming. For instance, the language feature of templates represents a fundamental concept for generic problems. Such a language feature might also supplement object-oriented programming. For example, templates can also be used to implement polymorphism, which is an object-oriented concept. In addition, selected topics from the standard library are introduced to be able to benefit from the standard library from the beginning. All in all, the aim of this book is to introduce readers to the whole world of C++ gradually. Emphasizing the object-oriented point of view, the book teaches the language features, the library, and the actual way these should be used.

1.2   Prerequisites

The principal prerequisite for understanding this book is a degree of familiarity with the concepts of higher-level programming languages. It is assumed that the reader already knows terms such as *loop*, *procedure* or *function*, *statement*, *variable*, etc.

Knowledge of the concepts of object-oriented programming is not necessary. These concepts are introduced when we discuss language features that provide the basis for these concepts in C++. Some general knowledge of object-oriented concepts would be an advantage, however, as the book inevitably looks at these concepts mainly from the viewpoint of C++.

Readers who know C or Java will already be familiar with some of the fundamental language features. However, there are differences in details, and these will be explicitly pointed out where necessary.

1.3   Organization of the Book

The great advantage of C++ is its tremendous flexibility in allowing the implementation of almost any kind of data structure or type and functionality. This means that a suitable simple interface can be defined for almost every problem. This has the advantage that (partial) problems need only be solved once, and services only implemented once.

Application and System Programmers

The key elements of C++ are *classes*. These are types that provide a certain interface to store and retrieve data and/or to call operations. Their interface hides the details of a particular solution from the caller. For this reason, C++ can be viewed from different perspectives:

- On one hand, there is the perspective of the *application programmer* of a class. He *consumes* the class in various ways.
- On the other hand, there is the perspective of the *system programmer* of a class. He *produces* the classes that allows the application programmer to concentrate on the general task, while using the provided classes to solve particular problems of the task.

From the point of view of the system programmer, all details of the language must be known and mastered to provide an elegant, effective and high-quality interface. From the point of view of the applications programmer, knowledge of the interface and how to use it should be sufficient.

The book is organized according to these two points of view. For teaching purposes, the perspective moves from that of the application programmer (who consumes classes provided by the C++ standard library) to that of the system programmer (who implements classes by himself).

In practice, these two points of view cannot be completely separated. This is mainly because, when solving problems, modules (such as classes) and interfaces are always used to provide higher modules and interfaces. However, the book starts with the general concepts and the application view, so that existing classes and interfaces can be used. The flexibility underlying the classes and interfaces, which make C++ so valuable as a programming language, is explained step by step afterwards.

Language Version

It was a general goal of this book to concentrate on the general language C++ and not any special language extension such as 'Visual C++' or any language derivative such as 'managed C++'. C++ is taught according to the current ANSI/ISO standard (see [*Standard98*]), so that portability over all (standard-conforming) platforms is guaranteed.

Structure of the Book

The structure of the book is based on numerous training courses I gave over several years. In particular, the following topics are dealt with in the following chapters:

- Chapter 2: **Introduction: C++ and Object-Oriented Programming**
  Gives an introduction to the topic and introduces the basic terms required to understand C++.

- Chapter 3: **Basic Concepts of C++ Programs**
  Introduces the basic concepts of C++ from the point of view of the applications programmer. It also introduces fundamental types, functions, operators and control constructs. The most important members of the standard library are also introduced.

- Chapter 4: **Class Programming**
  Introduces the fundamental object-oriented concepts of classes and data encapsulation, with all related language features.

- Chapter 5: **Inheritance and Polymorphism**
  Introduces the fundamental object-oriented concepts of inheritance and polymorphism, with all related language features.

- Chapter 6: **Dynamic and Static Members**
  Introduces the special aspects that must be taken into account for programming complicated classes with dynamic and static members.

- Chapter 7: **Templates**
  Introduces aspects of generic programs using templates.

- Chapter 8: **The Standard I/O Library in Detail**
  Describes in detail the input and output aspect of the standard library. This includes an introduction to file access.

- Chapter 9: **Other Language Features and Details**
  Focuses on the remaining language features and standard components of C++.

- Chapter 10: **Summary**
  Contains a summarizing conclusion of C++.

- The **appendix** contains
  - a **bibliography**,
  - a **glossary**,
  - an **index**.

1.4   How Should You Read this Book?

As this book introduces all language features and their applications gradually, beginners should simply read the book from cover to cover. In some cases, forward references cannot be avoided, but should not present a major problem. For those just beginning to work with the material, a wealth of new terms are introduced and used, which first have to be understood and distinguished from each other. Unfortunately, there is a certain amount of confusion in object-oriented programming, and especially in C++. The glossary in the appendix should help clarify the situation.

Those who wish to start immediately with actual object-oriented programming with classes can begin with Chapter 4. This is the introduction from the standpoint of system programmers, and discusses the necessary language features from the perspective of their use. In this respect, the principal view of application programmers is explained, again with the corresponding background.

Anyone reading the book as a more-or-less experienced programmer can find introductory points for the topic areas in the index or table of contents. I have done my best to provide a detailed account in both.

How to Avoid Reading this Book?

This unexpected question is aimed at those who prefer to study facts by way of examples, rather than reading a book. (I am one of them.) I suggest that these readers work through the examples one after another. In addition, each section in which a new language feature is introduced has a short summary that can be used to decide whether the chapter should be read in detail.

1.5   Example Code and Additional Informations

You can access all example programs and find more information about this book from its Web site at http://www.josuttis.com/cppbook/.

1.6   Feedback

Something can always be improved upon. I would therefore welcome any suggestions and criticisms.

The best way to reach me is by e-mail:

cppbook@josuttis.com

Be sure to check the book's Web site for the currently known errata before submitting reports.

2

Introduction: C++ and Object-Oriented Programming

This chapter provides a general overview of C++ and introduces the basic terminology necessary to understand it. Following an introduction to the history and design aspects of C++, the most important language features are introduced in a brief overview, before going into them in more detail in the following chapters.

2.1 The C++ Language

C++ is an object-oriented language that has quickly become very widespread and is today a standard language for object-oriented programming.

One major property of C++ has contributed to this wide distribution: its compatibility with C. Developed by AT&T under the leadership of Bjarne Stroustrup, its aim was to provide an object-oriented extension of C that allowed existing C code to still be used whenever possible.

2.1.1 Design Criteria

C++ was designed as an object-oriented advancement to C. The C language was extended with object-oriented language features. As its compatibility with C had a very high priority, in principle, any C program can be compiled in C++ (except for small modifications, such as renaming due to naming conflicts with new keywords).

This means, however, that C++ is not a purely object-oriented language, but a *hybrid*. One can program with C++ in both a data- or control-flow-oriented, as well as object-oriented, manner. Programmers must therefore make sure that they use C++ as an object-oriented language. On the other hand, where problems occur for which there are no object-oriented solutions, C++ can still be used.

2.1.2   History of the Language

C++ is a standardized language. In 1998, an ANSI/ISO (American National Standard Institute/ International Organization for Standardization) committee adopted a worldwide uniform language specification (see [*Standard98*]). In 2002, a second version of the Standard, amended by a first technical corrigendum, was adopted (see [*Standard02*]). The Standard is available on the Internet as PDF file under the document number 14882 in the Electronic Standards Store (ESS) at http://www.ansi.org for $18.

Because it takes a bit of time until a compiler vendor implements the latest specification of a language, even five years later there are still compilers that do not conform to the standard. This can lead to restrictions in some cases. However, it can safely be assumed that, in principle, all programs introduced in this book can be compiled with the latest versions of the different compilers.

2.2   C++ as an Object-Oriented Programming Language

The term 'object-oriented' has become a mark of quality, although it is not always clear what it means. There are also various interpretations of the term, and its meaning is occasionally abused when providing software with this claim of quality.

The question of whether and when something is object-oriented is also as controversial as the term itself. There are various features of object-oriented languages, but it is not explicitly established whether all features, or only a selection, need to be present.

C++ supports all language features that, according to widespread opinion, are typical for object-oriented languages. These concepts are:

* **classes (abstract data types)**,
* **data encapsulation**,
* **inheritance**,
* **polymorphism**.

Despite the question, which features define object-orientation, there are some discussions as to whether C++ is a true object-oriented language. This is because, in contrast to languages such as Smalltalk or Java, C++ is not a purely object-oriented language. C++ supports object-oriented programming, but, as it is backward compatible with C, it enables C++ programs to be written that do not use object-oriented language features. In fact, C++ is a multi-paradigm language that allows structured, procedural, object-oriented, and generic programming.

2.2.1 Objects, Classes, and Instances

One way of reducing complexity is abstraction. Features and processes are reduced to the essentials, summarized, or are combined by a common term. In this way, complex features become manageable.

An example of an abstraction in multiple ways is the term *car*:

- A *car* is the combination (or *composition*) of various parts, such as engine, bodywork, four wheels, etc.
- A *car* is also a common term for different types of cars. They might differ in the vendor (such as Volkswagen, Ford, and Jaguar) or in the category (such as sports car, limousine, and all-terrain vehicle).

If the members of cars or differences of individual cars are not relevant, the term *car* is used. One builds *car* transporters, or uses a *car* to get from A to B.

Structures

A fundamental progress in the history of programming languages was the ability to combine several items of data together, and therefore to bundle various properties in one type. These kinds of *structures* or *records* enable one variable to contain all data belonging to the circumstances represented by the variables.

Structures therefore provide one way of abstraction in programs, namely the combination (or *composition*) of different parts or elements (or so-called *members*). A structure for the type Car consists of members such as engine, bodywork and four wheels.

Objects

The object lies at the center of object-oriented programming. An object is *something* that is viewed, used and plays a role. If one programs in an object-oriented way, one tries to discover and then implement the objects that play a role in the problem domain of the program. The internal structure and behavior of an object therefore do not have priority. It is important that an object such as a car plays a role.

Depending on the problem, various aspects of an object are relevant. A car can be assembled from members such as engine and bodywork, or can be described using properties such as mileage and speed. These *attributes* indicate the object. Accordingly, a person can also be regarded as an object, of which various attributes are of interest. Depending on the problem definition, these can be first name, address, personal number, hair color, and/or weight.

An object does not necessarily have to be something concrete or tangible. It could be totally abstract and can also describe a process. A football match could be regarded as an object. The attributes of this object could be the players, the score, and the time elapsed.

Structures enable objects to be managed within programs. Ultimately, they enable an object to be broken down into individual attributes, and to get managed using fundamental types supported by the programming language.

Abstract Data Types

In structures or records, the individual properties of objects can be stored in the members. For objects, it is not only of interest *how* they are organized, but also *what* you can do with them. That is, the operations that form the interface of an object are also important.

The term *abstract data type* (or *ADT*) comes into effect here: an abstract data type describes not only the attributes of an object, but also its behaviors (the operations). This could also include a description of the states the object could have.

In the example of the football match, an object is not only described via the players, the score, and the time that has elapsed. There are also the operations that can be carried out with the object (substitution of a player, scoring a goal, blowing the final whistle) and the constraints (the game starts with the score 0:0 and lasts 90 minutes[1]).

The ability to program these semantics is insufficiently supported in traditional non-object-oriented programming languages. There is support for the fact that an object is composed from attributes. There is, however, no support for the fact that operations and constraints are a part of it. This has to be programmed separately as an addition.

Classes

For the production of abstract data types, the term *class* has been introduced in object-oriented programming. A class is the implementation of an abstract data type. As opposed to a structure, it not only describes the attributes (data) of an object, but also its operations (behavior).

For example, a Car class defines that a car consists of an engine, bodywork and four wheels *and* that one can get into a car, drive it and get out of it.

A class can therefore be regarded as a realization of the term 'abstract data type'. However, in doing so, the exact difference is controversial. Sometimes the terms are used as synonyms; sometimes a distinction is made between them, as, in contrast to an abstract data type, properties of a class are derivable by other classes. In the C++ world in particular, the term *abstract data type* is also used as a separation from the term *fundamental data type* (or *FDT*), and therefore means the same as a (user-defined) class.

Instances

A class describes an object. It is also actually a *type* in the sense of programming. Several variables can be created from this type. In object-oriented programming, these are called *instances*.

Instances are therefore the realization of the objects described in a class. These instances consist of data or attributes described in the class, and can be manipulated with the operations defined within.

The terms *object* and *instance* are frequently used synonymously (particularly in C++). If a variable of the Car type is declared, a Car object (an instance of the class Car) is created. In

---

[1] Of course, I talk about the European 'football' game, here, which you might know as being called 'soccer.'

some languages, a distinction is made between *object* and *instance*, because a class can also be regarded as an object. *Object* is then the common term for *class* and *instance*.

Methods

In object-oriented terminology, the operations defined for objects are called *methods*. Every operation called for an object is interpreted as a *message* to the object, which uses a particular method to process it.

An object-oriented program is ultimately produced via messages to objects, which can then produce more messages for other objects. If the operation 'drive' is called for a car, the message 'drive' is sent to the car, which is then processed using the appropriate method.

This approach focuses on the object rather than the operation. During object-oriented design, one thinks about the objects available in the problem area. Their construction and behavior are described depending on their roles. The concrete program is then 'only' a simple sequence of operations provided by these objects.

2.2.2 Classes in C++

With the implementation of object-oriented concepts in C++, we should always remember that C++ is not a purely object-oriented language, but a language hybrid. This is also reflected in the naming: *methods* are also described as *functions* (any *procedure* or *subroutine* is called a *function* in C++), and *instances* are merely described as concrete *objects*. The terminology babel, prevalent in the object-oriented world, is perfect in C++ (I will discuss this in more detail in Section 2.4 on page 20).

In C++, a class is a structure that can also contain functions (methods) as members. This is demonstrated in the following example of the Car class.

A Car as a C++ Class

In C++, a car may be defined as follows:

```
class Car {
    int yearOfManufacture;        // year of manufacture as integral value
    float mileage;                // current mileage as floating-point values
    string licensePlate;          // current license plate

    int getYearOfManufacture();   // query year of manufacture
    void drive(float m);          // drive m miles
    float getMileage();           // query mileage
    ...
    void Car();                   // automatic initialization
    void ~Car()                   // automatic clean-up on destruction
};
```

Both the construction and the behavior, including initialization and destruction, are parts of the class structure:

- Internally, a car has the following attributes:
    - `yearOfManufacture` defines the year of manufacture of the car. The type used for this `int` is available for integer values in C++.
    - `mileage` defines the current mileage of the car. The type used for this `float` is available for floating-point values in C++.
    - `licensePlate` defines the actual license plate of the car. The type used for this `string` is available for strings (character sequences) in C++.
- The following operations are defined:
    - `getYearOfManufacture()` is used to query the year of manufacture and return it as an integer value.
    - `drive()` is used to cover a distance submitted as a floating-point value m with the car.
    - `getMileage()` is used to query the current mileage of the car and return it as a floating-point value.
- There are also special functions that can be used to influence the behavior of a car during creation and destruction:
    - `Car()` defines what will happen automatically during the creation of a car. For example, the year of manufacture, mileage and license plate will be initialized appropriately.
    - `~Car()` defines what will happen during the destruction of a car. For example, it can be defined here that specially created internal memory space is automatically released.

This kind of definition has several advantages:

- The operations (functions/methods) do not fill (or 'pollute') the global namespace. The only global type is the `Car` type.
- Operations on a car object do not require the `Car` object as a parameter. The object invokes the operation (rather than the other way around); thus an appropriate car is always automatically available within the operation.
- Neither initialization nor clean-up operations have to be called explicitly. As a result, objects always have a useful initial state and the user of a class (its *application programmer*) does not have to (and cannot forget to) call a clean-up function when a car leaves its scope.

A corresponding application program in C++ looks as follows:

```
void cartest()
{
    Car c;          // create car c and initialize it

    c.drive(77);                             // drive 77 miles
    ...
    float mileage = c.getMileage();          // query mileage
    ...
    if (c.getYearOfManufacture() < 1900) {   // query year of manufacture
```

```
    ...
  }
    ...
}                         // automatic clean-up and destruction at the end of the block
```

Using the declaration of c, an instance (a concrete object) is created as a Car *and* initialized automatically. Access is then carried out using the functions (or methods) defined for Cars. This is done by calling the function for the car c using the dot character. At the end of the block, when the object leaves its scope, a function defined for cleaning-up is called automatically.

2.2.3 Data Encapsulation

A problem with conventional structures is that all members of them can be accessed at any time. Each part of the program therefore enables all application programmers to change the status of the data in the structure arbitrarily. If we use this model for objects of a class, there is a danger of producing inconsistencies and errors. A car application program could, for example, easily change the year of manufacture or reduce the mileage.

From this comes the idea of *data encapsulation*, or just *encapsulation*[2]: In order to prevent any application programmer from doing anything they want with an object, access to an object is simply restricted via a well-defined interface. Every application programmer working with an object will only be able to carry out the functions for which the designer of the corresponding class (its *system programmer*) granted *public* access. Further access to internal affairs, which are used for the management of the object and its data, is forbidden.

In C++, access to the members of a class structure can be defined using special access keywords[3]:

```
class Car {
  private:
      int yearOfManufacture;      // year of manufacture as an integral value
      float mileage;              // current mileage as a floating-point value
      string licensePlate;        // current license plate

  public:
      int getYearOfManufacture(); // query year of manufacture
      void drive(float m);        // drive m miles
      float getMileage();         // query mileage
      ...
```

---

[2] Sometimes the term *information hiding* is used instead of *data encapsulation*. However, this is incorrect, at least as far as C++ is concerned, because the internal data is only prevented from being accessed from the outside, and is not actually hidden.

[3] Without access keywords, none of the members of a class can be accessed from outside (private is the default). In this respect, the applications program introduced only compiles with this version of class Car.

```
        void Car();                    // automatic initialization
        void ~Car()                    // automatic clean-up on destruction
};
```

The members declared after `private:` are protected from being accessed by the application programmer of a class. The application programmer can only access the members and call the functions declared after `public:`.

In this case, it is not possible for an application programmer who uses this class to access `yearOfManufacture` or `mileage` directly. Access is only given to the functions declared in the class structure.

Access to attributes is typically only possible using functions. This enables every access attempt to be verified as to whether this kind of access is valid in the actual situation and with the actual parameters.

Separation of Interfaces and Implementation

The concept of data encapsulation is ultimately based on the idea that the internal organization and behavior of an object is not relevant to the application programmer of the object. It is only important that the object behaves correctly.

In the `Car` example, the way in which the year of manufacture and the mileage are managed are of no interest to the application programmer. It is decisive that a car can be created, can be driven, and that certain attributes can be requested. Figure 2.1 shows the car interface graphically. The figure uses the Unified Modeling Language (UML) notation, which is the de facto standard for object-oriented modeling and programming.

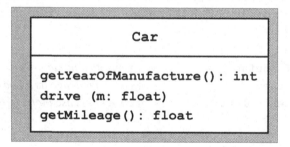

Figure 2.1. Public interface of `Cars`

For the application programmer, only the *WHAT* is of interest: the public interface establishes *what* can be done with an object. The *HOW* is only of interest to the implementer of the class. From the application programmer's point of view, this is just a 'black box'. As long as the public interface is stable, implementation can be changed in any way without the application code being affected. An implementation of a class can therefore be optimized later in order to increase the performance without the need to update all uses of a class.

2.2.4 Inheritance

If the behavior of objects is described, there are often properties that different objects have in common. In natural language use, *common terms* are used for this[4]. A blue car manufactured in 1984 with a diesel engine simply becomes a car, as long as its details are not relevant. It can even be regarded simply as a vehicle, if the fact that it is a car is irrelevant.

For example, this kind of generalization occurs with a car transporter. It is unimportant which cars are transported; only size and weight may be relevant. Nevertheless, various types of car may be transported and their differences may very well be relevant again once they have been unloaded.

There is no equivalent data model in conventional programming for this means of abstraction of generalization and specialization. In object-oriented programming, the concepts of inheritance and polymorphism are used for this purpose.

Different classes can be connected to each other hierarchically. A *derived* class is always a specialization or *concretion* of its *base class*. The reverse of this is that the base class is the generalization of the derived class. This means that all properties (attributes and operations) of the base class are inherited by the derived class, usually supplemented with additional properties.

Figure 2.2 shows an appropriate example (again we use the UML notation). The `Vehicle` class describes the properties of a vehicle as a base class. For example, these include the attribute `yearOfManufacture` or the operation `getYearOfManufacture()`. For all classes derived from this, such as `Bike`, `Car` or `Truck`, these properties are also valid. The `Vehicle` class is therefore the common term under which the common properties come.

The different properties of special vehicles are then implemented in the respective derived classes. Vehicles with speedometers (`VehicleWithSpeedo`), for example, also have the additional attribute `mileage`, as well as the `drive()` and `getMileage()` operations. Trucks also have the additional `load()` and `unload()` operations. In this way, a *class hierarchy* arises where common terms become more and more concrete. The fundamental characteristic of inheritance is the *is-a* relationship. A truck *is a* 'vehicle with a speedometer'; a 'vehicle with a speedometer' *is a* vehicle.

What are the advantages of inheritance? First, it is used for consistency and to reduce code. Common properties of various classes only need to be implemented once and only need to be changed in one place if necessary. The other advantage is that the means of abstraction of the common functionality is supported. This will be clarified in Section 2.2.5 on page 16, with an introduction to polymorphism.

In practice, it may also be necessary to change inherited properties. This is possible but has its limitations. The inheritance is, of course, meaningless if no property still applies. In this case, a separate class should be implemented.

---

[4] *Generic term* is probably a better phrase for *common term*. However, as *generic* has a special meaning in C++, I decided to use *common term* here.

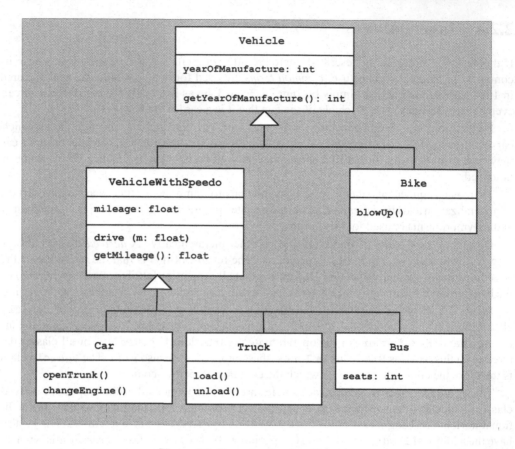

Figure 2.2. Example of a class hierarchy

2.2.5 Polymorphism

Concerning the advantages that arise from inheritance, only consistency and code reduction have been mentioned so far. However, inheritance is also an important prerequisite in facilitating polymorphism. Work with common terms is only useful if objects can be accessed using this common term.

Let us assume that a collection of cars is to be viewed for a garage. These could be completely different cars, different brands, different models, different types. It is therefore a 'heterogenous collection' of cars. If the engine is to be changed in different cars, the same thing is done in principle, but, depending on the car, it may look very different. The request used in everyday language '*change the engine of the cars*' will therefore lead to various different actions.

In order to reflect this, a separate version of the engine change can be implemented for every class that describes a kind of car. The specialty of polymorphism is that even for such a heterogenous collection of different cars, the general `changeEngine()` operation can be called, which *automatically* results in the respective function being called according to the actual type of car.

Ultimately, polymorphism means the ability for an operation to be interpreted only by the object itself. This might happen at run time, because during compilation it is not known what kind of car is used and therefore what operation has to be called.

There are different ways of implementing polymorphism[5]. In C++, inheritance is normally used for the implementation of polymorphism[6]. If similar classes implement the same operation differently, these can be declared in a common base class first, without them necessarily having to be implemented there. If a heterogeneous collection of objects of different classes is used, this collection is declared with the type of the common base class. If an operation is then called for an element in the collection, this results in code that at run time finds out what class the object actually belongs to to call the appropriate function.

An applications program can declare an appropriate heterogeneous collection of cars, assign various objects and call the `changeEngine()` function for all objects. In each case, the correct function is called automatically, according to the class of the actual car at run time:

```
CarCollection cars;    // collection of Cars
VW            v;        // Object of the class VW (Volkswagen)
Ford          f;        // Object of the class Ford

cars.insert(v);        // collection of cars contains a VW
cars.insert(f);        // collection of cars contains a Ford

for (i=0; i<cars.number(); ++i) {
    /* change engine of all cars
     * - calls according to the actual object type:
     *     changeEngine() for VW,
     *     changeEngine() for Ford,
     *     ...
     */
    cars[i].changeEngine();
}
```

It should be taken into account that it doesn't matter what derived classes exist for Car. There is no code for a selection of a fixed set of classes. If one decides to implement a new car class as a derived class from Car, cars can also contain its objects without having to be recompiled.

---

[5] The prototype of all object-oriented languages, Smalltalk, works in the most radical way. Variables are not bound to a type and can therefore represent any kind of object. If an operation is called for a variable, at run time the actual class of the object is evaluated. Depending on this, either a corresponding operation of the class is called or you get an error message that the operation is not possible.

[6] In C++, polymorphism can also be implemented using templates. This is discussed in Section 7.5.3 on page 457.

2.3   Other Concepts of C++

In C++, there are three other basic concepts to supplement or support object-oriented language features: *exception handling*, *templates*, and *namespaces*.

2.3.1   Exception Handling

Unexpected problems can occur with abstract data types. For example, a declaration of a collection may not be successful, because there is not enough memory space available. However, declarations have no return value.

In this case, the program may exit with an error message, or output an appropriate warning before continuing. Whether and to what extent this is useful very often depends on the situation, and cannot usually be defined. For this reason, a concept for dealing with exceptions was integrated into C++. This is known as *exception handling*. If an unexpected situation arises, a corresponding *exception* is raised, which can be intercepted and evaluated by the application program. In this way, the detection of an exceptional situation is separated from the handling of this situation. The detection of an exception is implemented by the system programmer of a class or function. The reaction is implemented by the application programmer, who knows the situation in which the exception arose and can react to it accordingly.

As the concept of exception handling does not use parameters and return values, there is another advantage to this method of error handling: the normal data flow is separated from error handling. In conventional programs, return values often need to be checked for errors and are therefore not only used for normal data flow. The result is that normal data flow is constantly 'polluted' by statements for error cases. Using exception handling, a clear separation can be made between normal data flow and error handling.

As we find ourselves in an object-oriented language environment, it is only consistent to define an exception as an object. Accordingly, there are classes that define similar objects, and therefore similar exceptions with similar properties. They can even be connected in a hierarchy in which different types of exception are generalized or specialized. Thus we can use inheritance and polymorphism to work with hierarchies of exceptions.

2.3.2   Templates

Many object-oriented languages have freedom of type. This means that a variable is not of a particular type, but can stand for all possibilities. For example, a variable can first be assigned an integral value, then a collection and then a string.

This freedom of type does not exist in C++. Variables in C++ always have a particular type. This is not necessarily a disadvantage, as, during compilation, it is always guaranteed that types are not mixed, and no operation can be called for an object that is not provided by its class.

However, type binding can also be very restrictive, as shown in the example of the car collection. For all possible types for which a collection is needed, an appropriate collection class must also be implemented. That is, as we have to implement a class `CarCollection` to manage a set of Cars (see page 17), we would have to implement a class WindowCollection to handle Windows, etc.

To avoid these disadvantages of type binding, *templates* were introduced to C++. Using these templates, individual functions or whole classes can be implemented without a particular type being defined. A template is implemented for arbitrary types. When types become clear, code is generated for these types. That is, template code is just pseudo code that produces different code for different types (in contrast to polymorphism, where the same code is used for different types because the common term is used).

For instance, a class collection can be implemented for the management of all possible kinds of objects[7]:

```
template <typename T>        // template for the adopted type T
class Collection {
  private:
    T*        elems;         // elements have type T
    unsigned num;           // actual number of elements

  public:
    void insert(T);          // insert object of type T
    T    operator[](int);    // define index operator to return an element of type T
    int  number();          // return number of elements

    void Collection();       // automatic initialization
    void ~Collection()       // automatic clean-up on destruction
};
```

Users can then define for which type they want to use a collection:

```
Collection<Car> cars;    // collection of Cars
VW              v;        // object of the class VW
Ford            f;        // object of the class Ford

cars.insert(v);          // collection of cars contains a VW
cars.insert(f);          // collection of cars contains a Ford

for (i=0; i<cars.number(); ++i) {
    // change engine of all cars
    cars[i].changeEngine();
}
```

The advantage of templates is that data structures and algorithms must only be implemented once, even if they are used for different types. Other collections can also be used:

---

[7] The implementation shown here leaves out some details that are necessary to be able to compile this code.

```
Collection<Car>     cars;        // collection of cars
Collection<int>     intcoll;     // collection of integral values
Collection<string> stringcoll;  // collection of strings
```

This not only reduces code, but also supports reusability. With every new implementation, there is the danger of implementing new errors. If an existing, tested collection implementation is reused, this danger does not exist.

2.3.3   Namespaces

Symbols can be grouped symbolically using the concept of namespaces. This avoids name conflicts and also clarifies what symbols logically belong together (i.e. constitute a *package* or *component*).

For example, all symbols of the standard library are defined in the std namespace. In order to use a string from the standard library, the type must therefore be qualified accordingly:

```
std::string s;      // string of the standard library
```

All custom symbols should be defined in their own namespaces.

2.4   Terminology

In the object-oriented-language world, there is a certain terminological chaos. One and the same features are named with different terms, while identical terms have different meanings. In C++, this chaos is made even worse by the fact that object-oriented terms are mixed with terms borrowed from conventional procedural programming, especially with C terms. I will therefore list the most important terms used in this book.

In C++, a class is a description of a type. In this respect, it is often formulated so that an object has a particular *type*, which means the same as *class*. This might lead to the consequence that we avoid the term *type* and use only *class* instead. However, in C++, there are also types that are not classes (for example, fundamental types such as float). If something in C++ applies to 'different types', then this means not only classes, but also fundamental types. For this reason, I will use the term *type* in the sense of 'any type', which can also be a class. However, note that the class keyword, which is usually used to define a class, sometimes stands for *any type*, including fundamental types.

An *instance* is often just simply described as an *object*, as it is a concrete object of a class. This, however, contradicts the fact that an *object* is sometimes understood as a generic term, which means more. A class can also be regarded as an object. However, in C++, there is no difference between the terms *instance* and *object*. In the language specification, the term instance is not used at all. However, it is confusing that the term *instantiate* is used in connection with templates. This does *not* relate to the creation of an object of a class, but to the generation of the actual code to be compiled from template code. For this reason, I follow the current terminology of C++ and describe instances of a class simply as *objects* of the class.

The largest confusing mixture of terms occurs with the elements of classes. In the context of object-oriented programming and in the context of C++, they are called *elements, members, attributes, data,* etc. The operations that can be called for objects are described as *methods, member functions* or just *functions*. As it is common in the C++ community, I will use the term *member* as a generic term for class elements,and make use of the distinction *data member* and *member function* when needed.

These naming choices can be argued over indefinitely. A reader familiar with the world of object-oriented languages may well ask, for example, why *member function* is used instead of *method* and why *object* is used instead of *instance*. I have chosen C++ terminology, as the use of the language of C++ from an object-oriented point of view is more prominent than the concept of object-oriented programming from the point of view of C++.

3

Basic Concepts of C++ Programs

There are many ways of looking at C++ code. We can look at it from the point of view of the *applications programmer*, who combines the types and the classes to create programs using functions and control constructs. Or we can look at it from the point of view of the *system programmer*, who provides new types and classes, which are abstractions of concepts. In practice, programmers usually take on both roles. This is especially true because, when abstracting problems, types and classes are repeatedly used to program higher levels and classes.

In this chapter we will only deal with the basic concepts that are relevant from the point of view of the *applications programmer*. That is, we will 'only' use existing types and classes to write C++ programs. Doing this, we learn the syntax of functions and function calls, the use of fundamental types, the division of programs into modules, and the use of the most important types and classes from the standard library.

In the following chapters, we will then see how to implement specific types and classes.

3.1 The First Program

This section contains our first C++ program. This will introduce us to some basic language features.

3.1.1 'Hello, World!'

The following program simply outputs the string 'Hello, World!' [1]:

```
// progs/hello.cpp

/* the first C++ program
 * - just outputs 'Hello, World!'
 */

#include <iostream>        // declarations for I/O

int main()                 // main function main()
{
    /* print 'Hello, World!' on standard output channel std::cout
     * followed by an endline (std::endl)
     */
    std::cout << "Hello, World!" << std::endl;
}
```

Roughly speaking, the program works as follows:

- Using

  ```
  #include <iostream>
  ```

  all necessary declarations for input and output are included. This consists of access to special input/output symbols and corresponding operations. A statement such as this can typically be found in all programs that use input and output.

- The program behavior is defined in the main() function:

  ```
  int main()
  {
      ...
  }
  ```

---

[1] If this program cannot be compiled, this could be the result of using a C++ compiler that does not conform to the current standard. In this case, a modified form of this program might work, which is shown in Section 3.1.5 on page 28.

A function with this name must be present in all C++ programs. This function is called automatically when the program starts.

- Within main(), there is only one statement, which ends with a semicolon (as all statements do):

  ```
  std::cout << "Hello, world!" << std::endl;
  ```

  This statement writes the string "Hello, World!", followed by the symbol std::endl, to the standard output channel std::cout. The symbol std::endl stands for 'end of line'. It makes sure that a line break is issued and the output buffer is flushed.

The program is supplemented by different comments, which are either enclosed by /* and */ or reach from // to the end of a line.

The following sections explain in more detail the language features introduced by this example.

3.1.2 Comments in C++

Two ways of commenting are possible in C++:

- The first way (adopted from C) allows a comment of any number of lines. They are bound by the character sequences '/*' and '*/':

  ```
  /*  This is a comment
      over numerous lines */
  ```

- The other way (which was newly introduced in C++) allows comments on the rest of a line. Two slashes '//' (as long as they are not part of a string) start a comment, which goes on to the end of the line:

  ```
  //  This is a comment that lasts to the end of the line
  ```

Both forms of comment are independent of each other. A comment beginning with '//' does not end with '*/':

```
//  This comment */ lasts to the end of the line
```

```
/*  This comment with // inside
    ends here  */
```

Comments cannot be nested:

```
/*  The comment beginning here
    /* therefore stops exactly here  */
```

The different possibilities for comments naturally beg the question as to which kind should be used, and for what purpose. This is essentially a matter of taste. As a guideline, I would advise you to limit /* and */ for multi-line comments and to use // for single-lined comments. For a multi-line comment, I also recommend that you begin it with an additional asterisk at every additional comment line:

```
/* first comment line
 * additional comment line
 * ...
 * last comment line
 */
```

This makes it stands out from the rest of the code.

3.1.3   Function `main()`

A C++ program is made up of various *functions*. The term function is used for every type of 'sub program' (*subroutine*, *procedure*, or whatever name you are familiar with from other programming languages). A function can pass parameters as arguments and can (but does not have to) return a value. That is, even operations that return no value (often called *procedures* in other languages) are called *functions* in C++. They just return nothing (i.e. have return type `void`).

There is a special function in every C++ program: the `main()` function. This function must be present once in a C++ program. It is called automatically at the start of the program. Leaving `main()` ends the program.

According to the `main()` example, you can see the general structure of functions:

- The *function head* consists of
  - the *return type* (the type of the return value),
  - the *function name*,
  - the *parameter list*, enclosed by parentheses.

- The *function body* consists of a *block of statements*. This block is enclosed by braces. The block consists of statements that all end with a semicolon (including the last one). The block itself does not have a semicolon at the end.

The return type of `main()` is always `int`. `int` stands for 'integer' and represents an integral value type (see the list of types in Section 3.2 on page 33). The corresponding return value is returned by the program to the calling environment (e.g. the operating system). Thus `main()` returns an integral value to the calling environment. This feature is used to give the calling environment the ability to evaluate whether the program has run properly. According to operating system conventions, a return value of 0 for `main()` indicates that the program has run properly. Any other value means that the program has not run properly. The exact meaning of values other than zero are up to the programmer.

Normally, every function that declares a return type must have an accompanying return statement. `main()` is an exception here. At the end of `main()` you will always find an implicit statement that returns 0:

```
return 0;
```

That is, every C++ program by default indicates that it has run correctly. You can also write the statement explicitly[2]:

```
#include <iostream>        // declarations for I/O

int main()                 // main function main()
{
    std::cout << "Hello, World!" << std::endl;
    return 0;              // not actually required in main()
}
```

C++ differs from C in this way. In C, there is no implicit `return 0` at the end of `main()`. This means that C programs that do not contain a return statement in `main()`, in contrast to C++ programs, will return an undefined value (in the sense of 'any given' value) to the calling environment of the program.

A program can also be passed arguments from the caller, which appear in `main()` as parameters. This is discussed in Section 3.9.1 on page 120.

3.1.4   Input and Output

The input/output (I/O) functionality is not an actual language feature in C++, but an application of components that are implemented using language features and provided as a standard library. To avoid explaining all these language features now, we only describe the basic I/O concept and the way in which simple I/O can be achieved.

From the point of view of the application programmer, the I/O mechanism is relatively simple. First, the standardized language features of C++ for input and output must be made known to the program. This is done by a so-called *include* statement:

```
#include <iostream>
```

An include statement is processed by a *preprocessor*, which is able to modify the source code before the actual compilation starts. The `#include` statement asks that all code found in `iostream` be inserted into the program, as it would have been had it been manually written there. The included code is usually a file that has a corresponding name. Such a file is called a *header file*. Thus `<iostream>` is the general header file for I/O.

With the inclusion of the declarations from `iostream` (data streams for input and output) the symbols listed in Table 3.1 are defined.

Input is made through a standard channel, which is generally assigned to the keyboard. Output is made through another standard channel, which is generally assigned to the screen. Both can be 'redirected' by the operating system or by using system functions, so that, for example, standard output is written to a file.

---

[2] If your compiler finds that a corresponding return statement is missing at the end of `main()`, it means that it does not conform to the standard.

Symbol	Meaning
std::cin	standard input channel (typically the keyboard)
std::cout	standard output channel (typically the screen)
std::cerr	standard error output channel (typically the screen)
std::endl	symbol for the output of a line break (newline) and the actual flushing of the output

Table 3.1. Fundamental symbols of the standard I/O library

There is also a standard error output channel for error messages, which is also generally assigned to the screen. By separating normal outputs and error outputs, error messages can be treated differently by the environment in which the program runs. This allows operating systems, for example, to write error messages to a log file, while normal output is still written to the screen.

In order to output data, it simply has to be 'sent' to the output channel using the << operator. Doing this, multiple outputs can be chained. For example:

```
#include <iostream>
...
std::cout << "now a number: " << 42 << std::endl;
```

The integer 42 is automatically converted into the character sequence '4' followed by '2' and written to the standard output channel std::cout. After this, std::endl ends the line by appending a newline character and flushing the whole output (which might be buffered) to the corresponding output device.

In a similar way, you can read from a channel using the operator >>. Further examples of this will follow.

3.1.5   Namespaces

Both symbols of the input and output library begin with std::. This prefix determines that cout and endl are both defined in the std namespace. This namespace is used for all symbols of the C++ standard library.

Using the namespace concept, symbols can be grouped logically (defining a *package* or *component*). Thus, writing std::cout means that we use the cout symbol of the std component, which is the standard library.

The namespace concept was introduced during the standardization of C++. There was no such concept in previous versions of C++. As a consequence, the way standard symbols are defined and used changed during the standardization. You might still see (or even have to use) the old style, which looks slightly different. For our example program, an earlier version might look as follows:

```
// progs/helloold.cpp

/* the first C++ program
 * - version for systems that are not standard conforming
 */
```

```
#include <iostream.h>    // declarations for I/O

int main()               // main function main()
{
    /* print 'Hello, World!' on standard output channel cout
     * followed by an endline (endl)
     */
    cout << "Hello, World!" << endl;
}
```

The following differences exist:

- All symbols of the standard library are defined globally, rather than in a specific namespace. The standard output is therefore represented with cout instead of std::cout.
- Header files have the .h ending. Thus, instead of
    ```
    #include <iostream>
    ```
  we have
    ```
    #include <iostream.h>
    ```

Nevertheless, you should not use the old style anymore, because it does not conform to the standard and may no longer be compilable or portable.

3.1.6 Summary

- C++ programs have the main function main(). This function is automatically called at the start of the program, and the program ends when this function is exited.
- main() can return an integral value with return, which indicates whether or not the program has run properly. The statement
    ```
    return 0;
    ```
  indicates the end of a program, after the program has run successfully; every other value denotes an unsuccessful program run.
- main() ultimately has an implicit
    ```
    return 0;
    ```
- Every statement must end with a semicolon.
- The variables std::cout and std::endl are defined using #include <iostream>, which enable output using the << operator.
- All symbols of the standard library are located in the std namespace. As a consequence, they have to get qualified by std::.

3.2   Types, Operators, and Control Constructs

This section introduces the elementary language features of C++, which are provided in every high-level programming language: fundamental types, operators and control constructs. These features are motivated by a new example program. After discussing this program, the language features are discussed in detail.

3.2.1   A First Program that Actually Calculates Something

A simple program will be useful for introducing elementary language features. This program calculates the following: if you split a four-digit number into two parts, one having the first two digits and the other having the last two digits, and add the square of these two numbers, you get the original four-digit number. This is true, for example, for 1233:

$$1233 \text{ is the same as } 12^2 + 33^2.$$

Consider the following program:

```
// progs/fourdigits.cpp

#include <iostream>        // C++ header file for I/O

int main()
{
    int counter = 0;       // current number of found four-digit numbers

    // for every number from 1000 to 9999
    for (int number=1000; number<10000; ++number) {

        // separate the first and last two digits
        int front = number/100;     // the first two digits
        int back  = number%100;     // the last two digits

        // if the sum of the squares produce the original number,
        // output number and increment counter
        if (front*front + back*back == number) {
            std::cout << number << " == "
                      << front << "*" << front << " + "
                      << back << "*" << back << std::endl;
            ++counter;
        }
    }

    // output number of four-digit numbers found
    std::cout << counter << " numbers found" << std::endl;
}
```

Again, the behavior of the program is defined in the `main()` function:

```
int main()
{
    ...
}
```

Inside `main()`, a variable is defined that counts how many four-digit numbers were found with the required property:

```
int counter = 0;
```

The type `int` stands for integer. `counter` is the name of the variable. A variable is defined from the point of its declaration to the end of the block in which it was declared. A block is enclosed by braces. `counter` is therefore defined until the end of the `main()` function.

`counter` is initialized with the value zero. If this initialization does not occur, the initial value of this variable is not defined! In fact, for all fundamental types, initial values for local variables are not defined. For this reason, you should always explicitly specify the initial value of a variable that has a fundamental type.

The most interesting part of `main()` is covered by a `for` loop:

```
// for every number from 1000 to 9999
for (int number=1000; number<10000; ++number) {
    ...
}
```

`for` loops are a generalized mechanism in C++ for loops that iterate over certain values. A `for` loop is nothing more than a combination of three statements:

1. The first statement is executed once at the beginning:

   `int number=1000`   // *initialize loop variable* number *with 1000*

2. The middle statement defines the condition under which the loop works:

   `number<10000`   // *as long as* number *is less than 10 000*

3. The last statement is carried out after every loop run:

   `++number`   // *increment* number *(increase by one)*

You could also write the loop as follows:

```
{
    int number=1000;
    while (number<10000) {
        ...
        ++number;
    }
}
```

The loop initializes a loop variable `number` with the value 1000 and allows this variable to carry out statements in the loop for every value smaller than 10 000. The loop is therefore called for all values from 1000 to 9999, while the actual value is always located in `number`.

Within the loop, it is checked whether the square of the two digits produces the same value as before. To do this, the first and last two digits are separated:

```
int front = number/100;    // the first two digits
int back  = number%100;    // the last two digits
```

The / operator is the division operator, which divides `number` by 100 here. The % operator is the modulo operator, which yields the remainder of an integer division.

An `if` statement then checks whether the sum of the squares of these two numbers produces the original number:

```
if (front*front + back*back == number) {
    ...
}
```

The * operator is the multiplication operator and + is the addition operator. The use of two equals signs to compare two values might look unusual. The reason is that the single equal sign is used for assignments:

```
a = b;      // a is assigned the value of b
```

The designers of C had chosen one equal sign for assignments because this is by far the most frequent operation and therefore using a two-character notation such as : = is a waste of time and space.

If the condition inside the loop is satisfied, an appropriate message is written to the standard output channel:

```
std::cout << number << " == "
          << front << "*" << front << " + "
          << back << "*" << back << std::endl;
```

In this multi-lined statement, the values of `number`, followed by the characters '==', followed by the value of `front`, followed by the '*' character, followed by the value of `front`, and so on, are written. An output line looks as follows:

```
1233 == 12*12 + 33*33
```

Finally, if the condition is true, the counter is increased by one using the increment operator:

```
++counter;
```

The corresponding value is then output at the end of the loop:

```
std::cout << counter << " numbers found" << std::endl;
```

The following sections focus on the language features used here, such as variables, fundamental types and control constructs.

3.2.2 Fundamental Types

C++ has the *fundamental data types* (sometimes abbreviated as FDTs or just called *fundamental types*) listed in Table 3.2. Apart from bool, these types are all adopted from C. The following subsections provide some notes on the individual types.

Type	Meaning
int	integer (typical word size of the machine)
float	floating-point value with single precision
double	floating-point value with double precision
char	character (can also be used as an integral value)
bool	Boolean number (true or false)
enum	for enumeration types (names that represent integral values)
void	'nothing' (for functions without a return value and empty parameter lists in ANSI-C)

Table 3.2. List of fundamental types

Numeric Types

The numeric types (int, float, double) can have different sizes and therefore different value ranges. The actual size of the numeric types is therefore *not* determined in C++. Behind this is the concept adopted from C that int has the typical size of the underlying hardware, so that it performs best. On machines with a 32-bit processor, int would typically have 32 bits; with a 64-bit processor, it would have 64 bits.

This size and the question as to whether we are dealing with a signed or unsigned type can be qualified by the attributes listed in Table 3.3.

Type Attribute	Meaning
short	possibly smaller than 'normal'
long	possibly larger than 'normal'
unsigned	unsigned
signed	signed

Table 3.3. Qualifying attributes of fundamental types

If you enter a qualifying attribute, the actual fundamental type does not need to be entered. int is assumed in this case:

```
int x1;         // integer with a normal value range
long int x2;    // integer, possibly with a larger value range
long x3;        // ditto
unsigned x4;    // unsigned integer with a normal value range
```

In standard C++, the smallest sizes listed in Table 3.4 can be processed.

Types	Minimum Size
char	1 byte (8 bits)
short int	2 bytes (16 bits)
int	2 bytes (16 bits)
long int	4 bytes (32 bits)
float	6 digits up to $10^{\pm37}$
double	10 digits up to $10^{\pm37}$
long double	10 digits up to $10^{\pm37}$

Table 3.4. Minimum size for fundamental types

The precise sizes are defined using `numeric_limits` in the `<limits>` header files, along with further information on the type (see Section 9.1.4 on page 531).

Characters

The char type is used for individual characters. Character literals are enclosed in single quotes. 'a' therefore stands for the character 'a'. Any given character can be located between the quotes, apart from a line break. Some special characters must be masked with a backslash (see Table 3.5). The literal '\n' stands for a line break, the literal '\'' stands for a single quote and the literal '\\' stands for the backslash itself.

Literal	Meaning
\'	single quote
\"	double quotes
\\	backslash
\n	line break/newline
\t	tab
\oct-digits	character with octal value of one to three digits
\xhex-digits	characters with hexadecimal values
\b	backspace
\f	form feed
\r	carriage return

Table 3.5. Special characters

These special characters can also be used in string literals. Using an ASCII character set, the string

```
"A few special characters: \"\t\'\n\\\100\x3F\n"
```

stands for the following character sequence (in ASCII, '@' has an octal value of 100, and the question mark has a hexadecimal value 3F):

```
A few special characters: "     '
\@?
```

Characters are managed internally as integral values. More precisely, '\n' is merely another representation for the value of the newline character in the current character set. You can also use the char type for integral values that are 1 byte in size. The qualifying attribute signed or unsigned can be used to determine whether the value area ranges from -128 to 127 or 0 to 255[3]. Without qualification, it is undefined whether type char is signed or unsigned.

With this knowledge, we can write a simple program that outputs the current character set. The following program issues all characters with values ranging from 32 to 126 (values under 32 and the value 127 are special characters in the ASCII character set):

```cpp
// progs/charset.cpp

/* output character set
 */

#include <iostream>       // declarations for I/O

int main()
{
    // for every character c with a value of 32 to 126
    for (unsigned char c=32; c<127; ++c) {
        // output value as number and as character:
        std::cout << "Value: " << static_cast<int>(c)
                  << " Character: " << c
                  << std::endl;
    }
}
```

Inside the program, c is used as an integral value that iterates values above 32. Within the loop, c is written once as a number and once as a character:

```cpp
std::cout << ... << static_cast<int>(c) << ... << c << ... ;
```

Because c has the char type, it is written as a character by default. Using the expression

```cpp
static_cast<int>(c)
```

c is converted to the int type. static_cast is an operator that can be used for logical type conversion, provided type conversion is valid. This type conversion guarantees that the value of c is output as its integral value. The output of the program is (provided an ASCII character set is used) as follows:

---

[3] Because only the minimum value of char is determined by the standard, the actual value ranges may exceed this.

```
Value: 32 Character:
Value: 33 Character: !
Value: 34 Character: "
Value: 35 Character: #
Value: 36 Character: $
Value: 37 Character: %
Value: 38 Character: &
...
Value: 120 Character: x
Value: 121 Character: y
Value: 122 Character: z
Value: 123 Character: {
Value: 124 Character: |
Value: 125 Character: }
Value: 126 Character: ~
```

Boolean Values

For a long time, in both C++ and C, there were no special types for Boolean values. They were managed using integers, with 0 denoting `false` and all other values `true`.

Later in C++, the `bool` type was introduced with the literals `true` and `false`. To guarantee backwards compatibility, integers can be used alongside the constants `true` and `false`. Zero therefore stands for `false`, and every other value for `true`. Conditions in control constructs are always satisfied if the expression inside has the value `true` or an integer value other than zero.

3.2.3 Operators

C++ provides an unusually large number of operators. The basic operators, taken from C, are outlined below. A complete list of all C++ operators can be found in Section 10.1 on page 569.

Basic Operators

Table 3.6 lists the basic operators, found in every programming language, for combining values.

It is worth noting that the equality test is carried out with *two* equals signs. A single equals sign is used as the assignment operator.

Caution: if you inadvertently use only one equals sign, this is still valid code, but it will not do what it is supposed to. For example, the line

```
if (x = 42)          // correct code, wrong semantics
```

does not test whether x has the value 42, but assigns 42 to x, and the condition is viewed as being satisfied. This is because an assignment returns the assigned value. Thus the expression 'x = 42' yields the value 42, which is not equal to zero and is therefore interpreted as `true`. In this

Operator	Meaning
+	addition, positive sign
−	subtraction, negative sign
*	multiplication
/	division
%	modulo operator (remainder according to division)
<	less than
<=	less or equal to
>	greater than
>=	greater than or equal to
==	equal to
!=	not equal to
&&	logical AND (evaluation up to the first `false`)
||	logical OR (evaluation up to the first `true`)
!	logical negation

Table 3.6. Fundamental operators

respect, we are dealing with correct code, which always assigns the value 42 to x, and where the condition is always satisfied, regardless of the previous value of x.

This feature is even used by some users in order to write concise code, which, however, is rarely legible. It is unusual to formulate the following conditions:

```
if (x = f())      // assigns the return value of f() to x and
                  // simultaneously tests whether this value is equal to 0
```

This kind of code is probably the reason why C and C++, for some people at least, have a somewhat dubious reputation. We can formulate very concisely, but the resulting code may well be quite illegible. You should wait until you feel more comfortable with C++ before writing this kind of code. However, this does not mean that you need to be familiar with everything. The most important thing is being able to read the code.

Note that always placing literals to the left of a comparison helps to avoid some of these errors, because a statement such as 42 = x is illegal.

Assignments

As explained in the last paragraph, an assignment is an operator that is formulated by an equals sign[4]. C++, like C, defines more than one assignment operator. In addition to the ordinary assignment, a variable can be modified relative to its current value by using a combined assignment operator. Table 3.7 lists all assignment operators.

---

[4] The designers of C believed that there was no point in giving the most commonly used operator a name, which, as in other programming languages, usually consists of two characters (such as :=).

Operator	Meaning
=	simple assignment
*=	
/=	
%=	
+=	
-=	'a *op*= b' usually corresponds to 'a = a *op* b'
<<=	
>>=	
&=	
^=	
|=	

Table 3.7. Assignment operators

It is true of all assignment operators that an assignment can be part of a larger expression. An expression with the assignment operator yields the value of the variable to which a new value was assigned. This makes chained assignments possible:

```
x = y = 42;        // 42 is assigned to both x and y
```

The expression is evaluated as

```
x = (y = 42);
```

Inside the parentheses, y is assigned a value of 42. The expression inside the parentheses then yields y, which is finally assigned to x. In this way, x is also given the value 42.

In the same way, you can make an assignment part of a larger expression:

```
if ((x = f()) < 42)     // assign the return value of f() to x and
                        // compares this value with 42
```

The other assignment operators are abbreviations for a combination of two operators: the operator situated before the equals sign and the assignment, i.e.

```
x op= y       corresponds to      x = x op y
```

These operators were introduced because compilers were not optimized at the time C was invented, and C was developed for a time-critical operating system (UNIX). Instead of

```
x = x + 7;      // increase x by 7
```

you could write the following:

```
x += 7;         // increase x by 7
```

This did shorten the running time, because the compiler knew, without special code analysis, that the value to which seven was added would be at the same address to which the result of the addition is to be stored. Compilers nowadays should be able to cope with these kinds of trivial optimizations. However, the style is still used, as it is more concise, without being illegible.

Increment and Decrement Operators

In C, special operators for incrementing (increasing by one) and decrementing (decreasing by one) were introduced (see Table 3.8). Again, the reason for the introduction of these operators was to support special processor commands for non-optimizing compilers.

Operator	Meaning
++	Postfix increment ('a++')
--	Postfix decrement ('a--')
++	Prefix increment ('++a')
--	Prefix decrement ('--a')

Table 3.8. Increment and decrement operators

There are two versions of the increment and decrement operators, a prefix and a postfix version. Both versions increase or decrease the value of a variable by one, respectively. The difference lies in what the expression yields as a whole. The prefix version (the version in which the operator precedes the variable) returns the value of the variable after the increase:

```
x = 42;
std::cout << ++x;        // writes 43 (first increase, then yield the value of x)
std::cout << x;          // writes 43
```

The postfix version (the version in which the operator follows the variable) returns the value of the variable it had before the increase:

```
x = 42;
std::cout << x++;        // writes 42 (first yield the value x, then increase)
std::cout << x;          // writes 43
```

It is from this operator that the name of C++ originated: 'one step further than C'[5].

As long as increment and decrement operators are not used as part of a larger expression, you should stick to using the prefix version, i.e. ++x. The other version may lead to a temporary value being created for the value of x before the increase, which is less efficient.

Bit Operators

The low-level nature of C++ can be recognized by the fact that there are special operators that operate bitwise. These are listed in Table 3.9.

The >> and << operators should be familiar from I/O operations discussed previously. That usage of them can be considered as a misappropriation of the shift operators for special types, namely the *I/O stream* types. In the meantime, this frequent (ab)use of << and >> leads to the fact

---

[5] An interesting question is why the language was not called '++C'. If you use C++ as part of a larger expression, this expression returns the old value, i.e. C :-).

Operator	Meaning
<<	left shift
>>	right shift
&	bit-wise AND
^	bit-wise XOR (exclusive or)
|	bit-wise OR
~	bit complement

Table 3.9. Bit operators

that these operators are being called *input* and *output operators*[6]. As a consequence, the exact semantics of these operators depend on the operands:

- Provided both operands have an integral type, it is a shift operation:

  ```
  int x;
  x << 2;              // left-shifts the bits in x
  ```

  The right operand must not be negative.

- If the first operand is an I/O stream, such as std::cout, it is an input or output operation:

  ```
  std::cout << 2;   // write the number 2
  ```

Special Operators

Three further operators require special attention. They are listed in Table 3.10.

Operator	Meaning
?:	conditional evaluation
,	sequence of expressions
sizeof (...)	storage size

Table 3.10. Special operators

- **Conditional evaluation**

  The operator ?: enables a *conditional evaluation*. Depending on the condition, one of two possible values is returned. This is the sole three-digit operator of C++.

  The expression

  condition ? *expression1* : *expression2*

  yields *expression1* if the condition is satisfied, otherwise *expression2*.

  Using this operator, if a value is manipulated in the then-case as well as in the else-case, then if statements can be shortened. Instead of

---

[6] The discussion of the input and output techniques of C++ in Section 4.5 on page 195 will discuss the motivation of this 'misuse'.

```
if (x < y) {     // assign the minimum of x and y to z
    z = x;
}
else {
    z = y;
}
```

you can write the following:

```
z =    x < y  ?  x  :  y;
```

If x is less than y, x is assigned, otherwise y is assigned.

Another example would be

```
std::cout <<  (x==0 ? "false" : "true")  << std::endl;
```

If x has a value of zero, 'false' is written, otherwise 'true' is written. Because this operator has a very low precedence (higher than assignments but lower than almost any other operators), it has to be placed in parentheses here (see Section 10.1 on page 569 for a list of all operators, including their precedence).

- **Comma operator**

The comma operator enables two statements to be combined into one. Instead of

```
x = 42;
y = 33;
```

one could also write

```
x = 42, y = 33;
```

This whole expression yields the result of the expression after the (last) comma.

This operator is very useful if you wish to execute multiple statements, but only one statement can be given. A typical example of this is a for loop (see Section 3.2.4 on page 44). Besides this special case, this operator should not normally be used.

- **sizeof operator**

The sizeof operator returns the size of an object or type in bytes. This operator is used, particularly in C, to calculate memory for objects in programs at run time. In C++, this operator is hardly ever required.

Operator Precedence

The previous operators, and all others introduced during the course of the book, have different precedences and evaluation orders. The table of all operators on page 569 lists these. The usual arithmetic rules apply, such as 'point calculation comes before line calculation'.

The precedence and evaluation order can be changed by using parenthesis. Two examples are listed below:

```
(x + y) * z             // without parentheses, first y is multiplied by z
while ((x += 2) < 42 )  // without parentheses, x is increased by 1 (which is the
                        // numeric value of true, which is the result of 2 < 42)
```

3.2.4   Control Constructs

All types of control constructs in C++ are adopted from C. There are single and multiple selections, different loops and the facility to combine several statements in one block.

Selections

The following control constructs for selections exist in C++:

- **if**

  This is used for a single selection:

  ```
  if (x < 7) {
      std::cout << "x is less than 7" << std::endl;
  }
  else {
      std::cout << "x is greater than or equal to 7" << std::endl;
  }
  ```

  The `else` branch can be omitted.

- **switch**

  This is used to select between multiple constant values:

  ```
  switch (x) {
    case 7:
      std::cout << "x is 7" << std::endl;
      break;
    case 17:
    case 18:
      std::cout << "x is 17 or 18" << std::endl;
      break;
    default:
      std::cout << "x is neither 7 nor 17 nor 18" << std::endl;
      break;
  }
  ```

The `case` labels define the places where a case begins. If the expression evaluated by `switch` has this value, all statements starting from the corresponding case label are executed until a `break` is found. Multiple case labels can be positioned as a case entry.

The `break` statement is used within a switch statement to end a case and continue with the statement after the switch statement. If a case is not ended by a `break` statement, the following statements are executed, even if there is another `case` label in between.

The optional `default` label indicates 'all other cases'. This default case can be located anywhere. If no default case is executed and none of the given cases apply, no statement inside the switch statement is executed and the program continues after the closing brace.

Loops

The following control constructs for iteration exist in C++:

- **While loop**
  The while loop is a *pre-test* loop. Thus the loop condition, which must be satisfied to continue the loop, is tested *before* every run:

  ```
  while (x < 7) {
      std::cout << "x is (still) smaller than 7" << std::endl;
      ++x;            // increase x by 1
  }
  std::cout << "x is greater than or equal to 7" << std::endl;
  ```

- **Do-while loop**
  The do-while loop is a *post-test* loop. Thus the loop condition, which must be satisfied to continue the loop, is tested *after* every run. As a result, this loop runs at least once.

  In contrast to the repeat-until loop of Pascal, the condition must be satisfied for the loop to continue; it is not an abort condition:

  ```
  // x is incremented at least once and output
  do {
      ++x;
      std::cout << "x: " << x << std::endl;
  } while (x < 7);
  ```

- **For loop**
  All the conditions for a loop to continue are determined in the head of the for loop:

  ```
          for (initialization; condition; reinitialization)
  ```

  Initialization occurs once at the beginning. Provided the condition is satisfied, the statements will be (re)executed in the loop body. At the end of every loop, reinitialization occurs before the condition is re-evaluated.

  This loop can typically be used to iterate via a value sequence:

  ```
  // loop in which i executes all values from 0 to 6
  for (i=0; i<7; ++i) {
      std::cout << "i has the value: " << i << std::endl;
  }
  ```

  At the beginning of the loop, i is initialized with 0. The loop runs as long as i has a value less than 7. With the increment operator ++, i is increased by 1 every time in the body of the loop.

  Because the expressions in the loop head of the for loop can be arbitrary, a loop run can also be defined in a more complex fashion:

```
/* loop that will run for every second value from 100 to 0
 * (100, 98, 96, 94, ... , 0)
 */
for (i=100; i>=0; i-=2) {
    std::cout << "i has the value: " << i << std::endl;
}
```

Here, i starts with the value 100 and is decreased by 2 after each iteration. The loop runs as long as i is greater than or equal to 0.

The individual expressions in the head of a for loop can also be skipped. If no condition is specified, this means that the condition is always satisfied:

```
// endless loop
for (;;) {
    std::cout << "this goes on like this forever" << std::endl;
}
```

Using the comma operator (see Section 3.2.3 on page 41), initialization or reinitialization can consist of numerous statements. For example, with an array, two indices can run to each other (although arrays are not introduced until Section 3.7.2 on page 106, this code should still be comprehensible):

```
// swapping values in an array
int array[100];        // array of 100 whole integral values

// the i and j indices run in the loop from the outside in
// and swap the values, respectively
for (int i=0, int j=99;  i<j;  ++i, --j) {
    int tmp  = array[i];
    array[i] = array[j];
    array[j] = tmp;
}
```

At the beginning of the loop, i is assigned the value 0 (the index of the first elements) and j is assigned the value 99 (the index of the last elements). As long as i is less than j, the statements in the loop body are executed. After each iteration, i is increased by one and j is decreased by one.

Two further special statements can also be located in the loops:

- **break**
  Aborts a loop immediately (as it aborts a switch statement). This statement can be considered as a jump out of (or right after) a loop, and should only be used under special circumstances.

- **continue**
  Starts a new loop iteration immediately. This statement can be considered as a jump to the position where the loop is re-evaluated (or reinitializes in the case of for loops). Again, it should only be used under special circumstances.

Blocks

The bodies of all control constructs are enclosed by braces in the examples. These brackets are used to combine several statements into a single block of statements. This is usually required with control constructs, because the body may only comprise one statement or a block of statements. If two individual statements are written, only the first one belongs to the control construct. The second statement is considered as the first statement after the control construct:

```
if (x < 7)
    std::cout << "x is smaller than 7" << std::endl;
std::cout << "this statement is executed in every case" << std::endl;
```

Even though it is unnecessary, I would recommend using braces even if the body of a control construct consists of only one statement:

```
if (x < 7) {
    std::cout << "x is less than 7" << std::endl;
}
std::cout << "this statement is executed in every case" << std::endl;
```

Not only is it more legible, but it also prevents the brackets from being forgotten when a second statement is inserted in the loop body.

3.2.5 Summary

- C++ provides various different types for characters, integrals, floating-point numbers and Boolean values.
- The exact value range of the numeric types is system specific.
- C++ has many operators. This includes operators for incrementing and decrementing, as well as for modifying assignments.
- The = operator is the assignment operator; the == operator is the equality test.
- C++ has all the usual control constructs (selections, loops).
- The for loop allows us to iterate values flexibly.
- Several statements can be combined, using braces, into one statement block.

3.3   Functions and Modules

A C++ program is made up of a structured sequence of statements. At the lowest level, these statements are grouped using control constructs and blocks. The term *function* stands for every type of operation. Other possible descriptions for *function* in other contexts could be *procedure* or *subroutine*.

There are two ways of grouping functions: physical or logical groupings. For a physical grouping, functions are divided into various *translation units* or *modules*. These are merely various files, compiled independently of each other. This grouping has the advantage that we do not need to recompile the whole code when there is a change inside a function. The resulting compiled file is then combined with the other compiled files using a *linker*. This grouping also has the advantage that the functions form a special entity, a so-called *library*, that can be reused in other programs. In his way, a physical grouping implies a logical grouping.

As well as this physically based grouping (adopted from C), there are other types of logical groupings in C++. There is the option of labelling related code independently from physical boundaries using a namespace. The object-oriented paradigm is another option. This assigns a common type to functions (a *class*). All operations that can be called for objects of this class logically belong to the class. These sorts of functions are also called *member functions* or, according to object-oriented language terminology, *methods*. This kind of logical grouping is, in principle, independent of the physical grouping. However, all functions of a class are usually physically managed in the same file.

In this section, first a facility for dividing functions (which have not yet been assigned to a class) physically into different modules is presented. Afterwards, we will look at a logical structuring facility using a namespace. Logical grouping using a class will be discussed in Chapter 4.

3.3.1   Header Files

C++ is a language with type checking. This means that, at compile time, you can see whether operations such as function calls are meaningful, at least as far as type is concerned. If you divide functions into different modules that are compiled separately, the question arises as to how we can ensure this kind of type check.

For the passing of data between functions of different modules to be successful, the interface of a function is declared in a separate header file. This file is then included by the module that implements the function, as well as all modules that call the function.

The following program shows an example of this. It consists of three files, which, as shown in Figure 3.1, have the following roles:

- In cross.hpp, the crosssum() function is declared. It is therefore known and can be called in all modules that include this file.
- In cross.cpp, the crosssum() function declared in cross.hpp is implemented. By including cross.hpp, we ensure that declaration and implementation do not contradict each other.

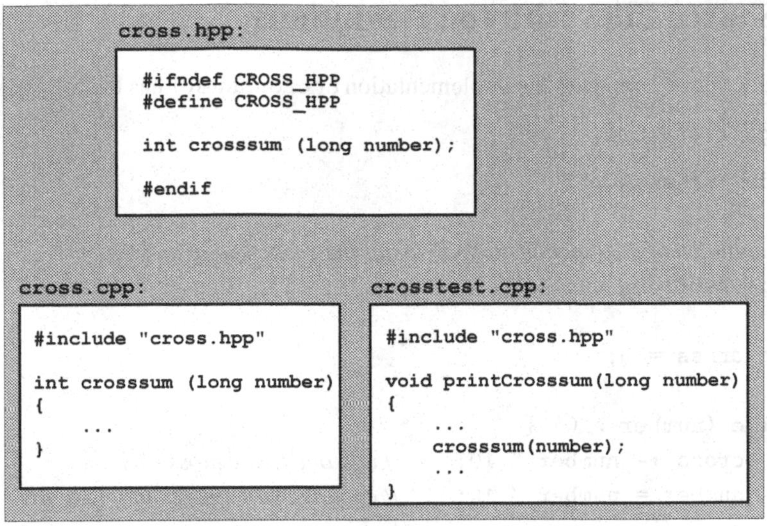

```
cross.hpp:

        #ifndef CROSS_HPP
        #define CROSS_HPP

        int crosssum (long number);

        #endif
```

```
cross.cpp:                          crosstest.cpp:

#include "cross.hpp"              #include "cross.hpp"

int crosssum (long number)       void printCrosssum(long number)
{                                {
    ...                              ...
}                                    crosssum(number);
                                     ...
                                 }
```

Figure 3.1. Declaration, implementation, and calling of crosssum()

- In crosstest.cpp, the crosssum() function declared in cross.hpp is called. By including cross.hpp, we ensure that the function is known when it is called.

The precise contents of the header file is as follows:

// progs/cross.hpp

```
#ifndef CROSS_HPP
#define CROSS_HPP
```

// declaration of a function that calculates the cross sum of an integer
```
int crosssum(long number);
```

```
#endif
```

The header file is enclosed by preprocessor instructions that ensure that the contents of the file are processed only once, even if the file is included more than once by a translation unit:

```
#ifndef CROSS_HPP        // is only satisfied in the first run, because
#define CROSS_HPP        // CROSS_HPP gets defined in the first run

    ...
#endif
```

The uppercase filename is typically used as a symbol. Every header file should be enclosed by this sort of 'guard'. The precise reasons are discussed in Section 3.3.7 on page 52.

3.3.2   Source Files with the Definitions

The source file `cross.cpp` with the implementation of `crosssum()` has the following structure:

```
// progs/cross.cpp

#include "cross.hpp"


// implementation of the function that calculates the cross sum of an integer
int crosssum(long number)
{
    int cross = 0;

    while (number > 0) {
        cross += number % 10;        // add one to the cross sum
        number = number / 10;        // continue with the remaining digits
    }

    return cross;
}
```

In this file,

```
#include "crosscross.hpp"
```

is used to include the file with the declaration. By doing this, the compiler can determine whether there are contradictions between declaration and implementation.

3.3.3   Source Files with the Calls

Every file that calls `crosssum()` includes the header files with its declaration, as every function must be declared before being called:

```
// progs/crosstest.cpp

// include header file with the declaration of crosssum()
#include "cross.hpp"

// include header file for I/O
#include <iostream>

// forward declaration of printCrosssum()
void printCrosssum(long);
```

```
// implementation of main()
int main()
{
    printCrosssum(12345678);
    printCrosssum(0);
    printCrosssum(13*77);
}


// implementation of printCrosssum()
void printCrosssum(long number)
{
    std::cout << "the cross sum of " << number
              << " is " << crosssum(number) << std::endl;
}
```

In this case, the test program contains two functions, `main()` and `printCrosssum()`. Within `main()`, the `printCrosssum()` function is called three times. As this function is implemented after having been called, it also has to be declared before `main()`. Otherwise an error message occurs, warning that the function called is unknown. As we can see, you can omit the parameter names when declaring a function. These names are nevertheless often written because the name documents what the parameter is for (see, for example, the declaration of `crosssum()` in the header file `cross.hpp`).

Every time `printCrosssum()` is called, a number is passed whose crosswise sum should be output. Within the function, the number itself and the crosswise sum calculated by `crosssum()` are output. The parameter is usually passed 'by value'. This means that the parameter `number` in `printCrosssum()` is a *copy* of the argument passed. Thus it could be changed inside `crosssum()` without any consequences for the argument passed by the caller.

3.3.4 Compiling and Linking

The compilation scheme displayed in Figure 3.2 is produced for this program. The header file `cross.hpp`, which declares `crosssum()`, is included both by the source file with the implementation of the function and by the application source file. These source files are also called *dot-C files*. Both dot-C files are then converted into object files by the C++ compiler (these files typically have the extension `.o` or `.obj`). The object files are then linked to the executable program `crosstest` or `crosstest.exe` by a linker (or 'binder').

Once the executable program has been created, the program can be started. Its output is as follows:

```
The cross sum of 12345678 is 36
The cross sum of 0 is 0
The cross sum of 1001 is 2
```

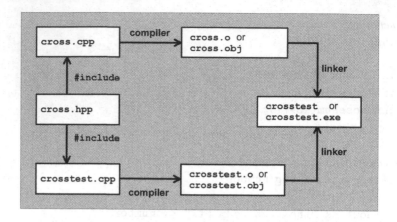

Figure 3.2. Compiling and linking

3.3.5   Filename Endings

Two types of file are used in C++:

- **Header files** (also called *include files*, *H files*, or *dot-H files*) are used to manage declarations for different translation units centrally. They typically contain the declarations of global constants, variables, functions, and types, and are included by files in which these declarations are required.
- **Dot-C files** (or sometimes just called *source files*) serve as actual *modules* or *translation units* that are individually compiled. They contain the 'real' source of the program; that is, the implementation of types and functions.

Unfortunately, there is no standardized file ending in C++:

- The ending for the dot-C files is usually `.cpp`. Sometimes, however, `.cc`, `.C`, or `.cxx` is used[7].
- Similarly, the ending for the header files is typically `.hpp`. In a similar way to the endings of the dot-C files, `.hh`, `.H`, or `.hxx` can also be used.

Things get worse though, because, for the first versions of C++, the system files had the ending `.h`. This means that we were unable to distinguish between C and C++. After the standardization, however, system files of C++ no longer have any ending[8]. This, however, is a bad example, and you should not follow this policy. Clear and unique endings such as `.cpp` and `.hpp` are strongly recommended for efficient management of C++ files.

---

[7] Although, there is no standard ending specified, all endings start with `.c`; which is why these files are called *dot-C files*.

[8] In fact, these system header files do not even need to exist as files. The standard only requires that `#include <iostream>` makes all required I/O declarations available. The way this is done is up to the C++ environment. However, in practice, you can find corresponding files without endings in a system directory.

3.3.6   System Files and Libraries

When linking, not just the characteristic modules are combined. In addition to these, other modules that provide additional functions and symbols are also linked. One typical example is the modules of the standard library.

In this case, for example, a module is linked that implements the standard I/O interface of C++. These sort of modules are typically linked from libraries, which can manage numerous related modules. Depending on the system, they have endings such as `.a`, `.so`, `.lib`, or `.dll`.

As always in C++, to use functions and symbols of the I/O library, they have to be declared. For this reason, the `<iostream>` has be get included by the test program. For the include statements two thjings are remarkable:

- As a system header file, the filename in the include command has no ending.
- By using angled brackets, the file is not searched for in the local directory, but only in the system directories.

3.3.7   The Preprocessor

A preprocessor is contained in C++ with which the source code can be modified before being compiled. Using this preprocessor, for example, files can be included or specific parts of the code can be ignored.

The commands for the preprocessor all begin with the # character, which must be the first character in the line that is neither a space nor a tab.

Including Other Files

As previously explained, the contents of another file can be included by the preprocessor using `#include`. The required filenames can be enclosed by double quotes or angled brackets:

```
#include <header1.hpp>
#include "header2.hpp"
```

In both cases, these files are searched in the system directories for header files. Their exact location is system specific. In many systems, you can influence the path for the system directories when compiling by making use of the `-I` option.

If you use double quotes, the files are additionally searched for in the local directory before the system directories.

Conditional Compilation

The preprocessor can also be used to influence what parts of a file should actually be compiled. For example:

```
void f()
{
    ...
#ifdef DEBUG
    std::cout << "x has the value: " << x << std::endl;
#endif
    ...
}
```

Here, the output statement is only compiled if the DEBUG constant is defined. The constant can be defined both inside the source code and when calling the compiler (typically by passing the compiler option −D*constant*).

Because specific constants are defined for each system, we can also handle system differences if necessary. For example:

```
#if defined __GNUC__
    // special treatment for the GNU compiler
#   if __GNUC__ == 2 && __GNUC_MINOR__ <= 95
        // up to Version 2.95
        ...
#   else
        // afterwards
        ...
#   endif
#elif defined _MSC_VER
    // special treatment for the Microsoft Visual C++ compiler
    ...
#endif
```

Conditional Compilation of Header Files

Another example of the use of conditional compilation are the guards around the code in header files:

```
#ifndef CROSS_HPP        // is only satisfied in the first run, because
#define CROSS_HPP        // CROSS_HPP gets defined in the first run
    ...
#endif
```

If a file includes this header file, the statements of this file are adopted. Therefore, from

```
#include "cross.hpp"
```

we get

```
#ifndef CROSS_HPP          // is only satisfied in the first run, because
#define CROSS_HPP          // CROSS_HPP gets defined in the first run
    ...
#endif
```

This causes all lines of `cross.hpp` to be processed only if the constant `CROSS_HPP` is not yet defined (`#ifndef` stands for 'if not defined'). This is the case with the first run through the file. However, consider the file is then included a second time. Thus, from

```
#include "cross.hpp"
#include "cross.hpp"
```

we get

```
#ifndef CROSS_HPP          // is only satisfied in the first run, because
#define CROSS_HPP          // CROSS_HPP gets defined in the first run
    ...
#endif
#ifndef CROSS_HPP          // is only satisfied in the first run, because
#define CROSS_HPP          // CROSS_HPP gets defined in the first run
    ...
#endif
```

In this case, the contents of `cross.hpp` are only taken into consideration with the first inclusion. During the second inclusion, all characters from `cross.hpp` are ignored, because the first run defines `CROSS_HPP` and so the second condition does not apply. In this way, error messages regarding double definitions are avoided.

You might argue that the same header file is rarely included twice, one directly after the other. However, this often happens indirectly, when two included header files include the same header file. So, because it is always possible that header files are included more than once for the same translation unit, the enclosing guards should always be part of a header file.

Definitions

Definition commands of the preprocessor can be used to define your own constants in the code:

```
#define DEBUG
```

Values can also be defined:

```
#define VERSION 13
```

These constants can then be evaluated in the code:

```
void foo()
{
#ifdef DEBUG
    std::clog << "foo() called" << std::endl;
#endif
    ...
```

```
#if VERSION < 10
    ...
#else
    ...
#endif
}
```

In old C programs, preprocessors were also used for defining constants:

```
#define NUM 100                    // BAD
...
int array[NUM];                    // create an array with NUM elements
for (int i=0; i<NUM; ++i) {        // iterate over the array
    ...
}
```

This kind of preprocessor misuse for the actual data flow can and should be avoided in C++. We are dealing with 'dumb' text replacement, which is neither subject to the rules of type checking nor takes scope into consideration. C++ uses the concept of constants for this:

```
const int num = 100;               // OK
...
int array[num];                    // create an array with num elements
for (int i=0; i<num; ++i) {        // iterate over the array
    ...
}
```

Using `#define` you can even pass parameters. These so-called *preprocessor macros* should also be avoided. There are also suitable language features in C++, such as inline functions (see Section 4.3.3 on page 173) and function templates (see Section 7.2 on page 429).

3.3.8   Namespaces

As explained in Section 3.1.5 on page 28, the concept of the namespace is used in C++ for the logical grouping of types and functions. All symbols can be assigned a namespace. If a symbol is used outside the namespace, it must be qualified. By doing this, name conflicts are avoided and it is made clear what symbols logically belong together (form a logical package or component).

The following example demonstrates the use of namespaces:

```
namespace A {
    typedef ... String;            // define type A::String
    void foo (String);             // define A::foo(A::String)
}
```

```
namespace B {
    typedef ...  String;           // define type B::String
    void foo (String);             // define B::foo(B::String)
}
```

The `namespace` keyword assigns the symbols defined within to the scope of this namespace. These symbols can no longer clash with symbols of other namespaces or global symbols that have the same name.

When using these symbols outside the namespace, the namespace has to be qualified:

```
A::String s1;        // create a string of namespace A
B::String s2;        // create a string of namespace B

A::foo(s1);          // call foo() of namespace A
B::foo(s2);          // call foo() of namespace B
```

Qualification of the function calls can often be omitted. If arguments are passed to a function, the function is also automatically searched for in all namespaces of the arguments passed:

```
A::String s1;        // create a string from the namespace A
B::String s2;        // create a string from the namespace B

foo(s1);             // OK, finds A::foo(), because s1 belongs to A
foo(s2);             // OK, finds B::foo(), because s1 belongs to B
```

More information and other ways of omitting the qualification of namespaces are discussed later in Section 4.3.5 on page 175.

3.3.9 The `static` Keyword

C++ adopted the `static` keyword from C. This keyword can have two different purposes:

1. It can influence the lifespan of local variables, insofar as their lifespan is extended to the entire lifespan of the program.
2. It can limit the visibility of symbols to one module.

Static Local Variables

Normally, all local variables and objects of a function are created when the corresponding point of definition is reached at run time. If the block or function is left, the local variables and objects are automatically destroyed:

```
void foo()
{
    int x;              // is created with an undefined value each time this point is reached

    ...
    std::string s;      // is created using a empty string as its value each time this
    ...                 //  point is reached
}   // each leaving of foo() destroys x and s
```

Using `static`, we can establish that a local variable is initialized the first time the definition is reached and destroyed at the end of the program. In this case, the variable keeps its value even after leaving the function. This value can then be reused the next time the function is called. In other words, this is a global variable that can only be accessed locally within a function:

```cpp
void foo()
{
    static int numberOfCalls = 0;    // is initialized with the first call and
                                     // destroyed at the end of the program

    ++numberOfCalls;                          // increment value with each call of foo()
    std::cout << "The function is called " << numberOfCalls
              << " times" << std::endl;
    ...
}
```

The `numberOfCalls` variable is initialized with the value passed for initialization purposes when `foo()` is first called. It remains valid for the duration of the program. Once the value is initialized, the initial value is no longer important. The value of the variable is increased by one with every function call. The number of calls of this function is therefore counted in this variable. This number is then output with each call.

These kinds of static variables or objects are useful if we wish to keep a status between two function calls, without explicitly passing data from one call to another. However, it is better to avoid these kinds of variables altogether. One reason is that there are considerable problems if you can access these variables in a parallel manner, such as in multi-threading programs.

Module-Specific Variables and Functions

Another application of the `static` keyword is used to limit the visibility of a variable or a function to one module. By doing so, you can program auxiliary variables or functions whose names cannot conflict with symbols of other modules.

In the following example, a `status` variable and an `auxiliaryFunction()` function are declared, which are only accessible within the module:

```cpp
static std::string status;        // only known in this module

static void auxiliaryFunction();  // only known in this module

void foo()                        // known globally
{
    ...
    ++status;
    ...
}
```

```
static void auxiliaryFunction()
{
    ...
    if (status == 17) {
        auxiliaryFunction();
    }
    ...
}
```

Calling auxiliaryFunction() or accessing status outside the module causes an error. Only foo() can be called from outside this module.

There is a new language feature for this kind of use of static in C++: *anonymous namespaces*. This is a namespace for which no name is assigned. Using it, the above example reads as follows:

```
namespace {      // everything here is only known in this module
  std::string status;
  void auxiliaryFunction();
}


void foo()       // known globally
{
    ...
    ++status;
    ...
}


namespace {      // everything here is only known in this module
  void auxiliaryFunction()
  {
      if (status == 17) {
          auxiliaryFunction();
      }
      ...
  }
}
```

The use of anonymous namespaces has the advantage that static is now only useful in influencing the lifespan of the variables. The semantics for limiting visibility is omitted for other language features. In this respect, the use of anonymous namespaces is preferable to using static; static should only be used in influencing the lifespan of variables in C++.

3.3.10   Summary

- Two types of files are used in C++: *header files* for declarations and *dot-C files* (or sometimes just called *source files*) for actual implementations. The header files are included by the dot-C files for compilation.
- Header files typically have the ending `.hpp`.
- Dot-C files typically have the ending `.cpp`.
- Using the preprocessor, header files can be included before the actual compilation of a dot-C file.
- Using the preprocessor, code can be written that is only compiled under certain conditions.
- Header files should essentially be enclosed by preprocessor guards that avoid errors by including them more than once.
- There are better ways of defining constants and macros in C++ than using the preprocessor.
- Symbols can be logically grouped using *namespaces*.
- Using `static`, local variables can be defined whose lifespan is the duration of the program.
- Using *anonymous namespaces*, the visibility of variables and functions can be limited to modules.

3.4   Strings

In C++, there are no built-in types for the use of strings. However, in contrast to C, there is a `string` type, provided by the standard library. More precisely, we are dealing with a *class* that defines the capabilities and properties of strings. This class is implemented in such a way that we can work with strings in the same way as with fundamental types. We can therefore assign strings using =, compare them using == and concatenate them using +.

The fact that a string class exists, which provides this type as a fundamental type, is a great advantage. Modern data processing is, by and large, string processing. Names, data and texts are recorded, passed and processed as character sequences. In languages in which there are no simple string types (for example, in C or Fortran), strings are often a source of trouble, which is no longer the case in C++.

3.4.1   A First Simple Sample Program with Strings

The following example shows what operations can be executed for strings:

```cpp
// progs/string1.cpp

#include <iostream>      // C++ header file for I/O
#include <string>        // C++ header file for strings

int main()
{
    // create two strings
    std::string firstname = "bjarne";
    std::string lastname = "stroustrup";
    std::string name;

    // manipulate strings
    firstname[0] = 'B';
    lastname[0] = 'S';

    // chain strings
    name = firstname + " " + lastname;

    // compare strings
    if (name != "") {
        // output strings
        std::cout << name
                  << " is the founder of C++" << std::endl;
    }
```

```
// determine number of characters in a string
int num = name.length();
std::cout << "\"" << name << "\" has " << num
          << " characters" << std::endl;
}
```

First, in addition to the standard header file for I/O, the standard header file for string processing is included:

```
#include <iostream>        // C++ header files for I/O
#include <string>          // C++ header file for strings
```

Three strings are then created:

```
std::string firstname = "bjarne";
std::string lastname = "stroustrup";
std::string name;
```

The first two strings are initialized with `"bjarne"` and `"stroustrup"`. The third string has no value for initialization. Its initial default value is the empty string.

What happens here can be described in two different ways:

- From the point of view of traditional programming, *variables* of *type* std::string are defined.
- From the point of view of object-oriented programming, *objects* or *instances* of the *class* std::string are created.

In object-oriented terminology, types are called *classes*. If concrete variables of a class are created, these variables are described as *objects* or *instances*. The effect is basically the same: something is created that represents a character sequence under a particular name.

The strings are manipulated in the following statement:

```
firstname[0] = 'B';
lastname[0] = 'S';
```

The first characters in the two initialized strings are corrected appropriately. As you can see, we can access the ith character of a string using an index operator. As always in C and C++, the first character has the index 0.

Finally, both initialized strings are concatenated with a space in between and are assigned to the name string:

```
name = firstname + " " + lastname;
```

We can therefore use the + operator to concatenate two strings.

A test is carried out in the following if-query to see whether the name string is empty:

```
if (name != "") {
    ...
}
```

As you can see, we can use the usual comparison operators != and == for strings.

Strings can be output like any other types:

```
std::string name;
...
std::cout << name
          << " is the founder of C++" << std::endl;
```

Finally, the number of characters in the string name is queried:

```
name.length();
```

These lines may appear a little unusual. Without any knowledge of object-oriented programming, we might expect a call such as getLength(name). For the first time, we see the object-oriented syntax for operations that are defined for objects. We use the object name to call the length() function for it. This kind of function is called a *member function* in C++, because it is a member of the class std::string.

In object-oriented terminology, we are dealing with a *method* call. The *message* length is sent to the object name without arguments. This object then has a method, which will react to the message.

The effect of this call depends on the implementation of this operation in the std::string class. In this case, the reaction to the message will be such that the object returns its length (i.e. the number of characters).

The program produces the following output:

```
Bjarne Stroustrup is the founder of C++
"Bjarne Stroustrup" has 17 characters
```

Strings and String Literals

Strings can be used as fundamental types:

- Using the operators == and !=, strings can be compared.
- Using the operator +, strings can be concatenated.
- Using the operator =, strings can be assigned to one another.

This may seem obvious. For C programmers, however, this is not the case because in C you cannot program with strings in this way (see also Section 3.7.3 on page 110). In Java, you also cannot simply compare a string with an empty string using ==[9].

You can also use string literals such as "bjarne" or "" as one operand of string operators. This is worth mentioning because string literals have a type different from std::string[10]. For

---

[9] In Java, the operator == exists for strings but it compares whether two strings are identical (i.e. have the same address), instead of whether their values are equal. This is often a source of trouble and confusion.

[10] The actual type of string literals is const char*. An explanation and the precise consequences of this type are given in Section 3.7.3 on page 109.

this reason, we cannot use string literals as both operands. For example, we cannot simply concatenate only string literals:

```
"hello" + " " + "world"                                            // ERROR
```

In this case, we must convert at least one of the first operands explicitly into a string. This is easily done (cf. page 35, where we converted a char into an int):

```
static_cast<std::string>("hello") + " " + "world"   // OK
```

Value Semantics

Especially for those programmers coming from languages such as Java or Smalltalk, the following hint is important: C++ has value semantics for every type. That means that when a variable is declared, memory is created for the necessary data.

This is an important difference from languages with (partial) reference semantics such as Java and Smalltalk. In these, a variable declaration simply creates a reference, which at first refers to nothing (NIL or null). Only when new is called is a real object created with memory for the necessary data.

In C++, there is also a new keyword. However, this is only required for creating objects that have to be managed independently from block boundaries (this will be discussed in Section 3.8 on page 114). Thus, usually there is no need to use new in C++.

3.4.2   Another Sample Program Using Strings

The following program demonstrates additional capabilities and functionality of string types. It extracts and returns HTML links from the lines entered:

```
// progs/html.cpp

#include <iostream>        // C++ header file for I/O
#include <string>          // C++ header file for strings

int main()
{
    const std::string start("http:");            // start of an HTML link
    const std::string separator (" \"\t\n<>");   // characters that end the link
    std::string line;                            // current line
    std::string link;                            // current HTML link
    std::string::size_type begIdx, endIdx;       // indices

    // for every line read successfully
    while (getline(std::cin,line)) {
        // search for first occurence of "http:"
        begIdx = line.find(start);
```

```
                   // as long as "http:" was found in the line,
                   while (begIdx != std::string::npos) {
                       // find the end of the link
                       endIdx = line.find_first_of(separator,begIdx);

                       // extract the link
                       if (endIdx != std::string::npos) {
                           // extract from the start to the end
                           link = line.substr(begIdx,endIdx-begIdx);
                       }
                       else {
                           // no end found: use remainder of the line
                           link = line.substr(begIdx);
                       }

                       // output link
                       // - ignore "http:" without further characters
                       if (link != "http:") {
                           link = std::string("Link: ") + link;
                           std::cout << link << std::endl;
                       }

                       // search for another link in the line
                       if (endIdx != std::string::npos) {
                           // search for an additional occurence of "http:" from the found end
                           begIdx = line.find(start,endIdx);
                       }
                       else {
                           // end of link was the line end: no new start index
                           begIdx = std::string::npos;
                       }
                   }
               }
           }
```

On entering the following input:

```
    Various links are embedded in this text.
    The link "http://www.josuttis.com/cppbook" belongs to this book.
    My homepage can be found under:
    http://www.josuttis.de and http://www.josuttis.com
```

the following output is produced:

```
Link: http://www.josuttis.com/cppbook
Link: http://www.josuttis.de
Link: http://www.josuttis.com
```

Types

In `main()`, variables are declared and objects are created as follows:

- An unchangeable `start` string as a search criterion for the start of an HTML link:
  ```
  const std::string start("http:");          // start of an HTML link
  ```
  All strings that start with `http:` are therefore searched for. To make sure that this object cannot be manipulated, it is declared as being `const`.

- A constant string in which all characters that end an HTML link are given:
  ```
  const std::string separator(" \"\t\n<>");   // characters that end the link
  ```
  In this case, a link is ended by a space, the `"` character, a tabulator, or a newline (which is unnecessary because we operate line by line), as well as the `<` and `>` characters (see the table of special characters on page 34).

- Two variables for the current line and the current link:
  ```
  std::string line;                          // current line
  std::string link;                          // current HTML link
  ```

- Two variables for the start index and the end index of a link:
  ```
  std::string::size_type begIdx, endIdx;     // indices
  ```

Here, two different types are used, `std::string` and `std::string::size_type`. Type `std::string` is the string type of the standard library `std`. `std::string::size_type` is an auxiliary type of this string class. This special type is used for indices because there is a special value representing 'no index': `std::string::npos` ('no position').

Reading Line by Line

The main part of the program comprises a loop that reads from the standard input line by line:

```
std::string line;
...
// for every line read successfully
while (getline(std::cin,line)) {
    ...
}
```

The lines are read from `std::cin` and stored in `line`. The character for the line break, '\n', is read, but not stored.

`while` tests the return value of `getline()` to decide whether to continue the loop. The return value is the input stream, `std::cin`, passed as the first argument. This stream can be used as a condition in a status query. This is possible due to some language features that will be introduced later in this book. Thus, without trying to understand why, it is enough for the moment to understand that it is possible to read a line and check whether the read was successful this way.

String Operations

Different string operations are called within the loop. They all have the syntax of a member function, i.e. `line.`*operation()*. An operation is called for the current `line`, which processes this line in any form.

First, `find()` is used to search for the first occurrence of the start of a link:

```
const std::string start("http:");        // start of an HTML link
std::string line;                         // current line
std::string::size_type begIdx;            // index
...

    // search for first occurrence of "http:"
    begIdx = line.find(start);
```

This operation finds the first occurrence of the argument string inside the string for which this operation is called. In this case, the first occurrence of `http:` is searched for in `line`. The return value is the index of the first character of the string found. If the string is not found, the `std::string::npos` constant is returned. This is checked in the next line:

```
    // as long as "http:" is found in the line,
    while (begIdx != std::string::npos) {

        ...

    }
```

Provided the search for the beginning of an HTML link is successful in the current line, the inner loop will be entered. An additional occurrence of `http:` in the line is then searched for inside the inner loop.

Once the start index has been found, the end of the HTML link is searched for inside the inner loop. The `find_first_of()` operation enables you to search for a number of characters at the same time. As soon as one of the characters passed as a parameter is found, its index is returned. Again, `std::string::npos` is returned if none of the characters are found.

In this case, the separator characters defined above are searched for in `line`:

```
const std::string separator(" \"\t\n<>");    // characters that end the link
std::string line;                             // current line
std::string::size_type begIdx, endIdx;        // indices
...

    endIdx = line.find_first_of(separator,begIdx);
```

The optional second parameter determines the point from which the separator characters are searched for. In order that the characters before the start of this HTML link play no role, we only begin looking after the start of the HTML link.

In the next statement, the actual HTML link is extracted from the line. Depending on whether a trailing character was found or not, all characters from the first index to the last index, or to the end of the line, are extracted:

```
// extract link
if (endIdx != std::string::npos) {
    // extract from the start to the end
    link = line.substr(begIdx,endIdx-begIdx);
}
else {
    // no end found: use remainder of the line
    link = line.substr(begIdx);
}
```

When called with a parameter, substr() finds the substring of all characters from the passed index to the end of the string. An optional second parameter is used as the maximum number of characters to be extracted. In this case, this is the difference between the end index and the start index.

The next statement outputs the link. But, before, it checks whether any characters follow http:

```
// output link
// - ignore "http:" without further characters
if (link != "http:") {
    link = string("Link: ") + link;
    std::cout << link << std::endl;
}
```

The fundamental operators for strings (!=, + and =), which were introduced in the first string example, are again used here.

All that remains to be done is to find an additional available HTML link on the same line, which can, of course, only be the case if the end of the previous link was not the end of the line:

```
// search for another link in the line
if (endIdx != std::string::npos) {
    // search for an additional occurrence of "http:" from the found end
    begIdx = line.find(start,endIdx);
}
else {
    // end of link was the line end: no new start index
    begIdx = std::string::npos;
}
```

As long as begIdx does not have the value std::string::npos, the inner loop continues by processing the current line.

3.4.3   An Overview of String Operations

These examples give a good idea of the capabilities of the standard string type. Table 3.11 lists the most important operations again.

Operation	Effect
`=`, `assign()`	assign new value
`swap()`	swap values between two strings
`+=`, `append()`, `push_back()`	append characters
`insert()`	insert characters
`erase()`	erase characters
`clear()`	erase all characters (empty string)
`resize()`	change number of characters (erase or add characters at the end)
`replace()`	replace characters
`+`	create sum string
`==`, `!=`, `<`, `<=`, `>`, `>=`, `compare()`	compare sum string
`length()`, `size()`	return number of characters
`empty()`	test whether a string is empty
`[]`, `at()`	access a single character
`>>`, `getline()`	feed in string
`<<`	output string
find functions	search for a part string or character
`substr()`	issue a part string
`c_str()`	use string as C-string
`copy()`	copy a character into a character buffer

Table 3.11. Most important string operators

For a more precise description of the operations (parameters, return value, semantics), the reader is referred to the appropriate reference handbooks for the C++ class library (such as my book, *The C++ Standard Library*; see [*JosuttisStdLib*]).

In Section 3.6 on page 93, we discuss another important general aspect of the string class: behavior in the event of an error. Behavior in the event of an error plays a particular role in accessing a single character of the string. When using the index operator, using an invalid index leads to undefined behavior. If we use the member function `at()` instead, an *exception* is thrown in the case of an invalid index, which automatically leads to proper error handling in the program. More information on error handling when accessing a character of a string is given in Section 3.6.4 on page 96.

3.4.4   Strings and C-Strings

The `string` class encapsulates the fact that characters are managed internally by arrays and pointers. In C, the `char*` type must be used instead, which is a source of trouble. Unfortunately, we cannot avoid this type in C++ because string literals have a corresponding type (string literals have the type `const char*`). For clarification, I will name all strings of the `char*` or `const char*` types as *C-strings* in the remainder of the book. These C-strings are discussed in detail in Section 3.7.3 on page 109.

For the moment, we concentrate on two things about C-strings:

1. To use the old C-string interfaces from C (which are unfortunately also often still used in C++), special converting functions are provided:

   ```
   void cfunction(const char*);      // forward declaration of C-style function
   ...
   std::string s;
   ...
   cfunction(s.c_str());             // pass string s converted into a C-string
   ```

   If the parameter in the C function is mistakenly declared without `const`, despite the string not being changed in the called function, we must write the following:

   ```
   void cfunction(char*);            // ugly forward declaration of C-style function
   ...
   std::string s;
   ...
   // pass string s as a non-constant C-string
   cfunction(const_cast<char*>(s.c_str()));
   ```

   `const_cast<`*type*`>`(*value*) is provided to remove constness from a value. You have to pass the non-constant version of its current type as a new *type*. This operator should be used with caution, as it enables write access to objects that should not be changed as far as their type is concerned. It should then only be used in exceptional cases such as this.

2. `strings` can contain any characters, including special characters. In contrast to the C-string, the '\0' character in `strings` is not an end indicator (end-of-string character). The conversion to a C-string using `c_str()` automatically appends an end-of-string character.

3.4.5   Summary

- The C++ standard library provides the `std::string` type for strings.
- Strings can be used as fundamental types.
- Several search functions allow you to search for characters or substrings in strings.
- The `std::string::size_type` type is used for string indices.
- The `std::string::npos` value stands for 'no index'.
- `c_str()` allows strings to be converted to C-strings.
- Strings can contain any characters (including special characters).

- In object-oriented terminology, types are described as *classes* and variables as *objects* or *instances*.
- All types of C++ have value semantics.

Further aspects and internal details of the string class are demonstrated in the example of the implementation of the standard string class in Section 6.1 on page 352 and Section 6.2.1 on page 373.

3.5   Collections

Modern data processing involves not only single data values, variables or objects being processed, but collections of these. In many conventional programming languages, appropriate data structures such as arrays, linked lists, trees or hash tables must be programmed to manage collections. This is not necessary in C++.

The C++ standard library offers an individual framework for working with collections: the *Standard Template Library* (STL). This framework provides mechanisms in which different data structures (so-called *containers*) can be used for collection processing by using single type declarations. There are also mechanisms with which you can apply operations (so-called *algorithms*) to these types of collections, independently of the underlying data structure.

The main advantage of the STL is that it provides an interface, which means that you no longer need concern yourself with the details of the data structures and the necessary memory management when processing collections. These details are abstracted. This abstraction was done while paying careful consideration to performance issues. As a result, using the STL is just as fast as manually programming data structures and algorithms.

A complete introduction to the STL would be too much information for this book [11]. However, the use of the STL for simple collection management is explained in this section.

3.5.1   A Sample Program with Vectors

The first example shows the use of the simplest type for processing collections: a *vector*. The description 'vector' has nothing to do with the mathematical expression, but is used in the STL for a *container* that manages its elements as a dynamic array. For example, this means that elements can be accessed using the index operator, and inserting and erasing elements is quicker if these elements are located at the end of the collection (otherwise the following elements must be moved accordingly).

The following example defines a vector of whole numbers as the collection, inserts six elements into this and then outputs all elements of the collection:

```
// stl/vector1.cpp

#include <iostream>
#include <vector>

int main()
{
    std::vector<int> coll;      // vector container for ints
```

---

[11] I would recommend my book *The C++ Standard Library – A Tutorial and Reference*, published by Addison-Wesley.

```
// insert elements with the values 1 to 6
for (int i=1; i<=6; ++i) {
    coll.push_back(i);
}

// output all elements followed by a space
for (unsigned i=0; i<coll.size(); ++i) {
    std::cout << coll[i] << ' ';
}

// finally output a newline
    std::cout << std::endl;
}
```

The header file for the vector type is included using

```
#include <vector>
```

By using this type, we are dealing with a *class template*. This means that this is a class in which not all details are fixed. The type of the elements managed in the collection must be indicated in angled brackets. The declaration

```
std::vector<int> coll;
```

creates this kind of container. In this case, this is a vector that contains elements of the int type. The newly created container is initially empty.

By calling push_back() for the container, elements can be added to the end of it:

```
coll.push_back(i);
```

In the loop for outputting elements, the current number of elements in the container is queried using size():

```
for (unsigned i=0; i<coll.size(); ++i) {
    ...
}
```

An unsigned integral type is used as a running variable i. If i is simply declared as int, then comparing it to coll.size() may cause a warning that an unsigned value is being compared with a value that is signed.

Inside the loop, the element with the index i is output. Here, the typical array syntax can be used:

```
std::cout << coll[i] << ' ';
```

As usual, the first element has the index 0 and the last element has the index $size() - 1$.

The program produces the following output:

```
1 2 3 4 5 6
```

Looks easy, doesn't it? Pay attention though—STL containers are not 'idiot proof'. The containers are programmed so that you see nothing of the underlying data structure. However, good performance was a design goal. As a consequence, when accessing an element with [i], as with strings, no test is made to determine whether the index is correct. This must be determined by the programmer. The test is omitted because it takes time. When weighing up the advantages and disadvantages (faster versus safer), it should be remembered that this behavior could be wrapped at any time by a checking collection type. However, you cannot wrap a checking type that then does not do any checking.

3.5.2   A Sample Program with Deques

The previous example can easily be changed. The following program should demonstrate this. It creates a collection, inserts six elements and outputs all elements again. In contrast to the previous example, the elements are strings in this case, a deque (pronounced 'deck') is used as a container and the elements are inserted into it at the front:

```
// stl/deque1.cpp

#include <iostream>
#include <deque>
#include <string>

int main()
{
    std::deque<std::string> coll;       // deque container for strings

    // insert elements at the front
    coll.push_front("often");
    coll.push_front("always");
    coll.push_front("but");
    coll.push_front("always");
    coll.push_front("not");

    // output all elements followed by a space
    for (unsigned i=0; i<coll.size(); ++i) {
        std::cout << coll[i] << ' ';
    }

    // finally output a newline
    std::cout << std::endl;
}
```

In this case, the header file for the deque is included using

```
#include <deque>
```

The declaration

```
std::deque<std::string> coll;
```

creates an empty collection of string elements.

The elements are inserted using push_front():

```
coll.push_front("often");
...
coll.push_front("not");
```

Because the elements are inserted at the front, the sequence of elements is reversed. The word that was inserted last comes right at the front. The program therefore has the following output:

```
not always but always often
```

3.5.3 Vectors versus Deques

In the previous examples, two different STL containers are used: a vector and a deque. How differ these types?

The description 'deque' is an abbreviation of 'double-ended queue'. This is a rather tricky data structure, which, in principle, has the properties of a dynamic array, but can grow in both directions.

If you add a new element at the front of a vector, all previous elements must be pushed back one slot. This is not the case with a deque. The internal implementation typically manages an array of arrays, on which both ends can grow and shrink (see Figure 3.3).

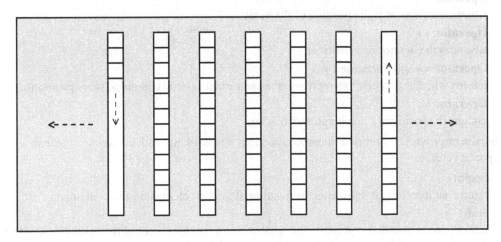

Figure 3.3. Typical internal structure of a deque

A vector is fast if you insert or erase elements only at the end. A deque, however, is fast at both ends (though it may be a little slower than vectors, due to the internal structure). In both containers, the insertion and deletion of elements in the middle is relatively slow, as elements must be moved to one side.

This difference in capabilities is also mirrored in the interfaces of the two classes. The deque offers functions for inserting and removing at both ends. As with vectors, elements can be inserted using `push_back()` with deques. However, the `push_front()` function is not provided for vectors.

STL containers generally offer special functions that mirror the special capabilities of the container and have a good running time. This helps prevent programmers using functions or containers with a poor performance. However, elements can be inserted into both containers at any position using a common insertion function (this is explained later in Section 3.5.7 on page 84).

3.5.4   Iterators

STL containers are generally accessed using *iterators*. Iterators are objects that can 'iterate' containers. Every iterator object represents a position in a container.

The advantage of iterators is that they allow all containers to use the same interface when accessing the elements. The increment operator always advances an iterator one position. This is independent of whether the underlying data structure is an array, a linked list or a binary tree. This is possible because the actual iterator types for a container are provided by the container itself. Thus it is implemented such that the iterator does the right thing according to the underlying data structure.

The following fundamental operations define the behavior of an iterator:

* **Operator ***
  returns the element at the position of the iterator.
* **Operator ++**
  advances the iterator one position.
* **Operator ==** and **operator != **
  returns whether two iterators represent the same object (same container, same position).
* **Operator =**
  assigns the position of one iterator to another.

Containers provide appropriate member functions for working with iterators. The two most important are:

* **begin**()
  returns an iterator that represents the position of the first element in the container;
* **end**()
  returns an iterator that represents the 'past-the-end' position behind the last element of the container.

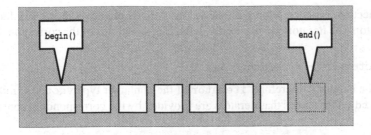

Figure 3.4. begin() and end() for containers

The range from begin() to end() is therefore a *half-open* range (see Figure 3.4). This has the advantage that a simple end condition can be defined for iterators that iterate over containers: The iterators run until end() is reached. If begin() is equal to end(), the collection is empty.

The following sample program outputs all the elements in a vector container with iterators. This is the example of page 70, transposed for use with iterators:

```cpp
// stl/vector2.cpp

#include <iostream>
#include <vector>

int main()
{
    std::vector<int> coll;      // vector container for ints

    // insert elements with the values 1 to 6
    for (int i=1; i<=6; ++i) {
        coll.push_back(i);
    }

    // output all elements followed by a space
    // - iterator iterates over all elements
    std::vector<int>::iterator pos;
    for (pos = coll.begin(); pos != coll.end(); ++pos) {
        std::cout << *pos << ' ';
    }

    // finally output a newline
    std::cout << std::endl;
}
```

After the collection has been filled with the values 1–6, all elements in the `for` loop are output using an iterator. The iterator `pos` is initially defined as an iterator of the corresponding container class:

```
std::vector<int>::iterator pos;
```

The type of the iterator is therefore 'iterator of the container type `vector<int>` of the standard library `std`'. This shows that iterators are provided by the corresponding container class.

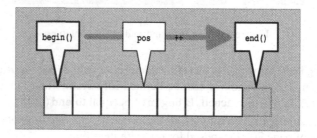

Figure 3.5. Iterator pos iterating over a vector

Inside the `for` loop, the iterator is initialized with the position of the first element, and then iterates over all elements until it reaches the end (i.e. the position after the last element; see Figure 3.5):

```
for (pos = coll.begin(); pos != coll.end(); ++pos) {
    cout << *pos << ' ';
}
```

In the body of the loop,

```
*pos
```

is used to access the actual element.

Instead of `iterator`, `const_iterator` can be used as the type for the iterator:

```
std::vector<int>::const_iterator pos;
```

This type ensures that elements cannot be modified when they are accessed via the iterator. This type also has to be used if the container is non-modifiable (that is, declared as being `const`). In Section 7.5.1 on page 453, a `const_iterator` is used in a generic function that can output elements of any given STL container.

3.5.5   A Sample Program with Lists

Containers for which the index operator is not provided can also be accessed using iterators. This applies to all containers whose elements are managed as nodes, with references to successors and predecessors. One example of such a container is the list container.

A list container, or 'a list' for short, is implemented as a doubly linked list of elements. This means that every element in the collection refers to one predecessor and one successor.

Selection-free access is therefore no longer possible. In order to access the tenth element, you must navigate through the first nine elements. A step to neighboring elements is possible in both directions in a constant time. Accessing a particular element takes a linear time (it is proportional to the distance from the actual position). Inserting and removing elements in all positions takes the same amount of time. Only the appropriate links have to be changed.

The following example defines a list of characters, inserts the characters 'a' to 'z' and outputs them using an iterator:

```cpp
// stl/list1.cpp

#include <iostream>
#include <list>

int main()
{
    std::list<char> coll;        // list container for chars

    // insert elements with the values 'a' to 'z'
    for (char c='a'; c<='z'; ++c) {
        coll.push_back(c);
    }

    // output all elements followed by a space
    // - iterator iterates over all elements
    std::list<char>::iterator pos;
    for (pos = coll.begin(); pos != coll.end(); ++pos) {
        std::cout << *pos << ' ';
    }

    // finally output a newline
    std::cout << std::endl;
}
```

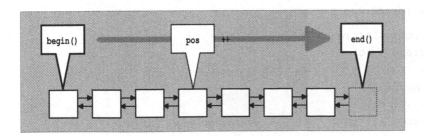

Figure 3.6. Iterator pos iterating over a list

The loop that outputs all the elements looks exactly the same as before. Only the type of the iterator has been changed. Because this type belongs to a list, it knows that it has to traverse a link, rather than increment an index, to get to the next element (see Figure 3.6).

3.5.6 Sample Programs with Associative Containers

The iterator loop can be used for all containers (if the iterator type is modified accordingly). This is the case for all containers introduced so far: vectors, deques, and lists. These containers are also described as *sequential containers* because the elements form a sequence in which the order is defined by the application programmer while he inserts and removes elements.

There are also *associative containers*. Elements are automatically sorted in these containers. The value of the element also determines its position. The following types of associative containers exist:

- **Set**
  A set container, or 'a set', is a collection in which each element can only occur once. The elements are sorted automatically according to their value.

- **Multiset**
  A multiset container, or 'a multiset', is a collection in which multiple elements with the same value can occur. The elements are also sorted according to their value.

- **Map**
  A map container, or 'a map', manages a key/value pair. Every element has an identifying key by which it is sorted inside the container, and an appropriate value. Each key can only appear once.

- **Multimap**
  A multimap container, or 'a multimap', corresponds to a map, with the difference that the key can occur more than once.

All these containers use a binary tree as an internal data structure. Two examples of these containers are outlined below.

A Sample Program with Sets

The first example shows the use of a set:

```
// stl/set1.cpp

#include <iostream>
#include <set>

int main()
{
    std::set<int> coll;     // set container for ints
```

```
// insert seven unordered elements with the values 1 to 6
coll.insert(3);
coll.insert(1);
coll.insert(5);
coll.insert(4);
coll.insert(6);
coll.insert(2);
coll.insert(1);

// output all elements followed by a space
std::set<int>::iterator pos;
for (pos = coll.begin(); pos != coll.end(); ++pos) {
    std::cout << *pos << ' ';
}

// finally output a newline
std::cout << std::endl;
}
```

The header file for sets is included using

```
#include <set>
```

An empty set is created for elements of type int using

```
std::set<int> coll;
```

In this case, we could also specify a sort criterion. As this is not the case, the elements are sorted by default in ascending order using the < operator.

An element is inserted using the insert() member function, which inserts the elements into the position according to the actual sorting criterion:

```
coll.insert(3);
coll.insert(1);
...
coll.insert(1);
```

After the values have been inserted, the condition displayed in Figure 3.7 is produced. The elements are sorted in the internal tree structure of the container, so that elements with a smaller value are found on the left and elements with a larger value on the right. Because a set is used rather than a multiset, the element that is inserted twice, the value 1, only exists once in the set. It would have been available twice in a multiset.

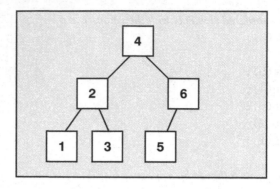

Figure 3.7. A set with six elements

The output of all elements works according to the same pattern, as in the previous example. An iterator traverses all elements and outputs them:

```
std::set<int>::iterator pos;
for (pos = coll.begin(); pos != coll.end(); ++pos) {
    std::cout << *pos << ' ';
}
```

The increment operator of this iterator is defined in such a way that it finds the correct successor element by taking into account the tree structure of the container. From the third element, we move up to the fourth element, and then down again to the fifth element (see Figure 3.8).

The output of the program is as follows:

```
1 2 3 4 5 6
```

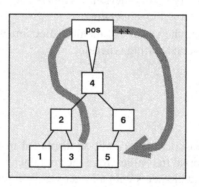

Figure 3.8. Iterator pos iterating over a set

A Sample Program with Maps

When using maps, we must ensure that an element of the collection is a key/value pair. This impacts the way declarations, insertions and element access is carried out:

```
// stl/mmap1.cpp

#include <iostream>
#include <map>
#include <string>

int main()
{
    // datatype of the collection
    typedef std::multimap<int,std::string> IntStringMMap;

    IntStringMMap coll;        // multimap container for int/string value pairs

    // insert some unordered elements
    // - two elements have the key 5
    coll.insert(std::make_pair(5,"heavy"));
    coll.insert(std::make_pair(2,"best"));
    coll.insert(std::make_pair(1,"The"));
    coll.insert(std::make_pair(4,"are:"));
    coll.insert(std::make_pair(5,"long"));
    coll.insert(std::make_pair(3,"parties"));

    /* output the values of all elements
     * - an iterator iterates over all elements
     * - using second, the value of the element is accessed
     */
    IntStringMMap::iterator pos;
    for (pos = coll.begin(); pos != coll.end(); ++pos) {
        std::cout << pos->second << ' ';
    }
    std::cout << std::endl;
}
```

Because the type of the container is required in many places, it is defined once as a type:

```
    typedef std::multimap<int,std::string> IntStringMMap;
```

Instead of with

```
    std::multimap<int,std::string> coll;
```

the collection can now be created with

```
IntStringMMap coll;
```

In general, `typedef` is used to define symbols that represent a certain type. This can be used to replace complicated type names by a simple name or to get more flexibility (depending on the platform, a type might be defined differently). In any case, this type definition is no distinct type, but an alias that might be mixed with the original type.

The type defined here is a multimap, whose elements have the `int` type as the key and the `string` type as the value.

Because the elements are value pairs, they are inserted using `make_pair()`:

```
coll.insert(std::make_pair(5,"heavy"));
coll.insert(std::make_pair(2,"best"));
...
```

`make_pair()` creates objects of the type `std::pair`, which is provided to represent value pairs.

We cannot simply output the elements. If we access an element using `*pos` via an iterator, we get the type `std::pair<int,std::string>`. With a value pair such as this, you can access the first part of the value pair (in this case, the key) using `.first`, and the second part (in this case, the value belonging to the key) using `.second`. The following could be written to output the key and value:

```
std::cout << (*pos).first << ' ';      // output the key of the element
std::cout << (*pos).second << ' ';     // output the value of the element
```

You should ensure that the expression with the operator `*` is inside parentheses, because it has a lower precedence than the dot operator. For this combination of operators, the `->` operator is provided as an abbreviation, which is why the value of the element here in the example can be output using

```
std::cout << pos->second << ' ';       // output the value of the element
```

The output of the program could be as follows:

```
The best parties are: heavy long
```

There are two elements with the value 5. Depending on the implementation of the standard library, the following output is also possible:

```
The best parties are: long heavy
```

3.5.7 Algorithms

As the examples seen above indicate, the actual data structures of STL containers are encapsulated. There may be some special operations (such as the index operator for vectors and deques), but there are also common ways to access elements, such as using iterators.

We can use these common interfaces to write functions that can operate on any container (and therefore on any data structure). The STL offers a collection of functions of this kind. They are called *algorithms*. There are algorithms for finding, swapping, sorting, copying, combining and modifying elements.

The example below shows a few algorithms and their use:

```cpp
// stl/algo1.cpp

#include <iostream>
#include <vector>
#include <algorithm>

int main()
{
    std::vector<int> coll;            // vector container for ints
    std::vector<int>::iterator pos;   // iterator

    // insert elements 1 to 6 into the collection, unsorted
    coll.push_back(2);
    coll.push_back(5);
    coll.push_back(4);
    coll.push_back(1);
    coll.push_back(6);
    coll.push_back(3);

    // output minimum and maximum element
    pos = std::min_element(coll.begin(), coll.end());
    std::cout << "min: " << *pos << std::endl;
    pos = std::max_element(coll.begin(), coll.end());
    std::cout << "max: " << *pos << std::endl;

    // sort all elements elements in ascending order
    std::sort(coll.begin(), coll.end());

    // reverse order of elements
    std::reverse(coll.begin(), coll.end());

    // output all elements
    for (pos=coll.begin(); pos!=coll.end(); ++pos) {
        std::cout << *pos << ' ';
    }
    std::cout << std::endl;
}
```

In this example, a collection with six unsorted integers is created first:

```
std::vector<int> coll;

coll.push_back(2);
...
```

First of all, the two algorithms `std::min_element()` and `std::max_element()` are called. As a parameter, they are assigned a range defined by two iterators, in which the minimum or maximum element should be searched. An iterator for the position of this element is returned. With the assignment of

```
pos = std::min_element(coll.begin(), coll.end());
```

`min_element()` therefore produces an iterator for the smallest element in the entire collection (if there are more than one, the first is taken) and assigns it to the iterator `pos`. This element is then output:

```
std::cout << "min: " << *pos << std::endl;
```

Of course, this could all have been achieved in one step:

```
std::cout << *std::max_element(coll.begin(), coll.end())
          << std::endl;
```

The next algorithm to be applied is `std::sort()`. It sorts the elements of the range that is passed by two iterators. As the range encompasses all elements of the container, all its elements are sorted:

```
std::sort(coll.begin(), coll.end());
```

The last algorithm used in this example is `std::reverse()`. It reverses the sequence of all the elements in the given range:

```
std::reverse(coll.begin(), coll.end());
```

The output of the program is:

```
min: 1
max: 6
6 5 4 3 2 1
```

This example shows how easy it is to use different data structures. By using other types, you can easily swap the data structures around. The same example works if you swap `vector` with either `deque` or `list`. There is only a problem if a set is used. Because a set determines the sequence of the elements itself, `sort()` and `reverse()` cannot be called. The attempt is stopped by a cryptic error message from the compiler. In addition, `push_back()` has to be replaced by `insert()`.

Finding and Inserting

A further example demonstrates how elements can be inserted in front of certain other elements using algorithms and operators. The program has the following structure:

```cpp
// stl/algo2.cpp

#include <iostream>
#include <vector>
#include <algorithm>
#include <string>

int main()
{
    std::vector<std::string> coll;              // container for strings
    std::vector<std::string>::iterator pos;     // iterator

    // insert various city names
    coll.push_back("Hamburg");
    coll.push_back("Munich");
    coll.push_back("Berlin");
    coll.push_back("Braunschweig");
    coll.push_back("Duisburg");
    coll.push_back("Leipzig");

    // sort all elements
    std::sort(coll.begin(), coll.end());

    /* insert 'Hannover' in front of 'Hamburg'
     * - search for position of 'Hamburg'
     * - insert 'Hannover' before it
     */
    pos = find(coll.begin(), coll.end(),        // range
               "Hamburg");                      // search criteria
    if (pos != coll.end()) {
        coll.insert(pos,"Hanover");
    }
    else {
        std::cerr << "oops, Hamburg is not available" << std::endl;
        coll.push_back("Hanover");
    }

    // output all elements
    for (pos=coll.begin(); pos!=coll.end(); ++pos) {
        std::cout << *pos << ' ';
    }
    std::cout << std::endl;
}
```

At first, different city names are inserted in a vector and sorted. The most interesting part is the assignment with which we attempt to insert Hanover in front of Hamburg. The find algorithm is called first, in order to find the position of Hamburg:

```
pos = find(coll.begin(), coll.end(),     // range
           "Hamburg");                    // search criteria
```

As is usually the case with algorithms, the beginning and end of the range to be searched are passed to find(). The third parameter is the value that is being searched for. It is then compared to all elements using the == operator.

If a corresponding element is found, its position is returned in the form of an iterator. If no suitable element is found, the end of the collection is returned, which is checked:

```
if (pos != coll.end()) {
    ...
}
```

If Hamburg is found, its position is used to insert Hanover in front of it. For this purpose, the member function insert() is used. An iterator for this position is passed as a first parameter and the value to get inserted is submitted as a second parameter:

```
coll.insert(pos,"Hanover");
```

The output of the program is as follows:

```
Berlin Braunschweig Duisburg Hanover Hamburg Leipzig Munich
```

3.5.8   Algorithms with Multiple Ranges

With most algorithms that process multiple ranges, only for the first range does the beginning *and* the end have to be passed. For all other ranges, entering just the beginning is sufficient. The end then follows from the context of the operation.

This is particularly true for algorithms that copy modified elements into other collections. However, be careful: **You must make sure that the destination range is large enough!** The following program clarifies the problem:

```
// stl/copy1.cpp

#include <iostream>
#include <vector>
#include <list>
#include <algorithm>

int main()
{
    std::list<int>   coll1;
    std::vector<int> coll2;
```

```
    // insert elements 1 to 6 in the first collection
    for (int i=1; i<=6; i++) {
        coll1.push_back(i);
    }

    /* RUNTIME ERROR:
     * - copy elements into the second collection
     */
    std::copy(coll1.begin(), coll1.end(),    // source range
              coll2.begin());                // destination range
}
```

The `std::copy()` algorithm gets the beginning and the end of the source range and the beginning of the destination range in which the elements of the source range are to be copied. It *assumes* that the destination range is big enough to include all the elements. If the destination range is empty (as in this example), unavailable memory is being accessed, which causes the program to crash (hopefully, because then you see that something has gone wrong).

There are two ways to avoid this type of error:

1. We must make sure that the destination range is large enough.
2. We must use insert iterators.

Setting the Size of a Container

To ensure that the destination range is large enough, it must either be initialized with the correct size or explicitly set to the right size. Both are only possible with sequential containers (vectors, deques, lists).

The following program shows this:

```
// stl/copy2.cpp

#include <iostream>
#include <vector>
#include <list>
#include <deque>
#include <algorithm>

int main()
{
    std::list<int>   coll1;
    std::vector<int> coll2;
```

```
// insert elements 1 to 6 in the first collection
for (int i=1; i<=6; i++) {
    coll1.push_back(i);
}

// create space for the elements for being copied
coll2.resize(coll1.size());

// copy elements into the second collection
std::copy(coll1.begin(), coll1.end(),        // source range
          coll2.begin());                     // destination range

/* define a third collection sufficiently large
 * - the start size is passed as a parameter
 */
std::deque<int> coll3(coll1.size());

// copy elements into the third collection
std::copy(coll1.begin(), coll1.end(),        // source range
          coll3.begin());                     // destination range
}
```

Note that when passing an initial size to the container, the initial elements are initialized by their default value.

Insert Iterators

The other method, using insertion iterators, is shown in the following example:

```
// stl/copy3.cpp

#include <iostream>
#include <vector>
#include <list>
#include <deque>
#include <algorithm>

int main()
{
    std::list<int>   coll1;
    std::vector<int> coll2;
    std::deque<int>  coll3;
```

```
// insert elements 1 to 6 in the first collection
for (int i=1; i<=6; i++) {
    coll1.push_back(i);
}
```

```
// copy elements inserting at the back of the second collection
std::copy(coll1.begin(), coll1.end(),      // source range
          std::back_inserter(coll2));      // destination range
```

```
// copy elements inserting at the front of the third collection
std::copy(coll1.begin(), coll1.end(),      // source range
          std::front_inserter(coll3));     // destination range
}
```

Two special predefined iterators are used here (so-called *iterator adapters*):

- **Back inserters**
  A back inserter inserts the elements at the end of a container (i.e. appends them). Each element is inserted in the container, which is passed at initialization time using push_back(). By calling

  ```
  std::copy(coll1.begin(), coll1.end(),      // source range
            std::back_inserter(coll2));      // destination range
  ```

  all elements of coll1 are inserted at the end of coll2.

  The operation can only be called for destination containers in which the push_back() member function is available. These are vectors, deques and lists.

- **Front inserters**
  A front inserter inserts the elements at the beginning of a passed container by calling the push_front() function. This causes the sequence of the elements to be inserted in reverse order. By calling

  ```
  std::copy(coll1.begin(), coll1.end(),      // source range
            std::front_inserter(coll3));     // destination range
  ```

  all elements of coll1 are inserted at the beginning of coll3.

  The operation can only be called for destination containers for which the push_front() member function is available. These are deques and lists.

3.5.9   Stream Iterators

An additional form of iterator adapter is the *stream iterator*. These are iterators that read from or write to a stream. Keyboard input or screen output form the 'collection' or the 'container', whose elements are then processed. The following example shows how this may look:

```
// stl/ioiter1.cpp

#include <iostream>
#include <vector>
#include <algorithm>
#include <string>

int main()
{
    using namespace std;       // all symbols in std are global

    vector<string> coll;       // vector container for strings

    /* read strings from the standard input up until the end of the data
     * - copy from the 'input collection' cin, inserting into coll
     */
    copy(istream_iterator<string>(cin),      // start of source range
         istream_iterator<string>(),         // end of source range
         back_inserter(coll));               // destination range

    // sort elements in coll
    sort(coll.begin(), coll.end());

    /* output all elements
     * - copy from coll to the 'output collection' cout
     * - every string on its own line (separated by "\n")
     */
    copy(coll.begin(), coll.end(),                   // source range
         ostream_iterator<string>(cout,"\n"));       // destination range
}
```

At first, a special using directive is used:

```
using namespace std;
```

This directive means that, in the current scope, all the symbols from std can be accessed without qualifying them with std::. That is, they are considered to be in the global scope. Caution: this sort of directive should only be used in a context where it is known that no conflicts or side effects are caused. In this respect, using directives should never be used in header files.

In the statement

```
copy(istream_iterator<string>(cin),      // start of source range
     istream_iterator<string>(),         // end of source range
     back_inserter(coll));               // destination range
```

two special iterators are created:

- The expression

    ```
    istream_iterator<string>(cin)
    ```

    creates a iterator that reads `string` elements from the input stream `cin`. These elements are read by the iterator, calling the `>>` input operator.

- The expression

    ```
    istream_iterator<string>()
    ```

    creates a special *end-of-stream iterator*, as no parameter is passed. It stands for a input stream from which it is no longer possible to read.

The `copy()` algorithm lets the first passed iterator operate as long as it is not equal to the second iterator. This means that the algorithm reads from `cin` until no more data exists, or no more data can be read. The submitted range therefore defines 'all the `string`s read from `cin`'. These are inserted by `copy()`, with the help of a back inserter, into `coll`.

After the elements read into the collection have been sorted, all the elements are copied to the destination range `cout`:

```
copy(coll.begin(), coll.end(),            // source range
     ostream_iterator<string>(cout,"\n"));  // destination range
```

The expression

```
ostream_iterator<string>(cout,"\n")
```

creates an iterator for the output stream `cout`, which outputs `string` elements. Any type can be passed here in angled brackets, for which the respective output operator `<<` is called. The optional second parameter defines what character sequence is inserted between two elements. In this case, it is a line separator, which ensures that each string is written on an individual line.

To summarize, the program reads all the strings from the standard default input `cin`, sorts them and outputs them to `cout`, with each string on its own line.

This example shows how concisely things can be programmed in C++ when making use of the STL. In addition, by changing the types, we can easily check whether other data structures accomplish the task faster as vectors. For example, we could try to use a set container instead. Because a set sorts automatically, we no longer need to call `sort()`. Try it!

3.5.10   Endnotes

As mentioned previously, this was a short general introduction to the STL. Many details, background information and supplementary techniques were not explained. However, these examples should be sufficient to start programming with collections.

Much use of STL containers is made in the remainder of this book. In Chapter 9, further details and helpful techniques for working with the STL are discussed:

- In Section 9.1.1 on page 518, all the operations of vectors are discussed in more detail.
- In Section 9.1.3 on page 526, all standard algorithms are listed.

- Section 9.2.1 on page 536 shows how to manage references to objects in STL containers with the help of smart pointers.
- Section 9.2.2 on page 540 explains how we can define processing criteria for STL algorithms using helper functions and function objects.

For further details, the reader is referred to special books on the C++ standard library and the STL (see [*JosuttisStdLib*]).

3.5.11   Summary

- The STL framework of the C++ standard library provides different containers, iterators, and algorithms, which can be used to manage collections in different data structures.
- In particular, the following types exist (listed with their typical data structure):

Container	Typical Data Structure
vector	dynamic array
deque	dynamic array, open at both ends
list	doubly linked list
set	binary tree without duplicates
multiset	binary tree with duplicates
map	binary tree for key/value pairs without duplicates
multimap	binary tree for key/value pairs with duplicates

- Iterators provide access to the elements of the containers. Their interface is independent of the underlying data structure.
- Different algorithms for access to and operations on collections are predefined.
- Inserters are special iterators that perform insertion operations with algorithms.
- Without inserters, we must ensure that destination collections of algorithms are large enough.
- Stream iterators enable the use of standard input and output as collections or containers.
- The STL prefers performance over safety. Thus, you have to be careful when using the STL.
- typedef can be used to define your own name for types.
- With

      using namespace std;

  we can make the symbols of the standard library globally available. This feature should never be used in header files.

3.6 Exception Handling

This section discusses *exception handling*. Exception handling makes possible a new type of error handling and the controlled treatment of exceptional situations. In contrast to conventional languages, in which error handling occurs via normal interfaces, parameters and output values, this is a language feature with which errors and exceptions are treated with a separate mechanism, parallel to the data flow. This separation makes program behavior more readable and secure.

In this section, after a conceptional introduction, we focus on the handling of exceptions by application programmers. Further details of exception handling are given in Section 4.7 on page 234, particularly those of classes in which exceptions are recognized and thrown.

3.6.1 Motivation for the Concept of Exception Handling

In every program, situations may arise that are not expected. As not all cases are considered or tested during implementation, users can input nonsensical values, connections to other processes can be interrupted, memory can be used and simple mistakes can occur.

To avoid programs crashing or behaving unexpectedly, an appropriate error handling has to be implemented. This is particularly important when calling functions that have contact with 'the outside world': a user may enter an invalid value; a system function may not perform as it is supposed to. However, errors may also be caused during internal function calls or when program data are being accessed.

In order to deal with errors or unforeseen situations, status flags, error handlers and return values are used in conventional programming languages. These error cases have to be tested and treated in the program code. There is therefore no clear distinction between normal data flow and error handling. With function calls, the normal data flow and error handling are dealt with through the same interface (i.e. parameters and return values).

For example, special return values typically exhibit error cases. As a consequence, special handling always has to be implemented for the processing of return values. If this special handling is omitted, the program may run into an undefined condition, which can have a fatal effect. Sometimes, the value range of the return value is extended to include special error values. One example of this is the C function getchar(), which reads and returns characters. Instead of returning a char, it returns an int, which might have the value of any char or a special value that indicates an error.

In object-oriented languages such as C++, many operations cannot even have a return value with which an error can be displayed. The creation of objects through a simple declaration is an example of this. For example, if memory is required during initialization for objects, arguments have to get processed, or files have to get opened. This can go wrong:

```
std::string s("hello");    // can fail
```

Access using an index operator can also lead to failure:

```
s[20] = 'q';              // can fail
```

These sorts of errors can only be poorly tested and processed (if at all) by conventional language features. How is one supposed to test whether everything has gone right when creating a temporary object in the middle of an expression?

The problem here is that the error can be detected, but not handled appropriately. The only possibility that remains with conventional languages is to issue a warning and to continue as best as possible, or to end the program with an error message.

The basic problem is this: error cases can be detected, but not properly dealt with, because the context from which the error originated is not known. Often the error cannot be reported back to the caller because return values are either not defined or else used for other purposes.

We therefore require a mechanism that allows a distinction between error detection and error handling, and allows the passage of information between both without using parameters or return values. This could separate error handling from the normal data flow.

Exception handling provides this mechanism: errors can be detected at any given position in the code and reported to the corresponding caller using a mechanism designed for this purpose. The error can then be intercepted and processed according to the situation. If this does not occur, the error is not just simply ignored, but leads to a clean program exit (rather than a program abort).

To prevent a possible wrong interpretation, it is noted that exception handling in C++ means that errors or situations are handled that appear during the normal processing of a program. It is not a mechanism for interrupts or signals; thus it is not a mechanism for messages that interrupt the running program from the outside, resulting in a jump to another place in the program. The exceptions I talk about here are explicitly triggered by special C++ statements inside the program, and are processed in the current scope.

It should also be noted that the mechanism is called 'exception handling' rather than 'error handling'. The exceptions do not necessarily have to be errors, and not every error is an exception (input errors are more likely the normal data flow). The mechanism can and should be used to react flexibly in unusual situations that do not correspond to the bandwidth of a 'normal' program run. This does not include incorrect user input.

3.6.2   The Concept of Exception Handling

Exceptions are processed in C++ according to the following concept:

- If an unusual situation occurs in a function, this is communicated to the caller with a special statement. We switch from normal data flow to exception handling. This exception handling leaves all blocks or functions called until a block is found in which an exception can be handled.

- When executing statements, we can define what happens if an exception situation occurs. An individual block of statements can then determine how to deal with the situation.

Exception Classes

C++ adopts an object-oriented approach for handling exceptions:

- Exceptions are regarded as objects. If an exception occurs, a corresponding object is created that describes the exception.
- Exception classes define the properties of this object. Properties of an exception can be defined as attributes (i.e. an incorrect index or an explanatory message). Operations can be used to query further information of an exception. For different types of exceptions, there is also the ability to provide different corresponding classes. Every exception class describes a particular kind of exception.

If an exception occurs, an object of the corresponding exception class is created. Like all other objects, these can possess members that describe the exceptions and the conditions in which they occur. They are therefore parameters of the exception.

Hierarchies of exception classes can be formed using inheritance. For example, 'mathematical errors' can be divided into special classes for 'division by 0' or the 'square root of a negative number'. An application program can then handle mathematical errors in general, or divisions by zero in particular.

Keywords

Three keywords are introduced for exception handling:

- **throw** is used to 'throw' a corresponding exception object into the program area. In this way, we switch from normal data flow to exception handling.
- **catch** is used to 'catch' an exception object and to react to the exception situation. It is used to implement what will happen when the normal data flow no longer works.
- **try** indicates a scope in which exceptions are intercepted and handled using `catch`. An *attempt* is made to execute the statements without errors. Using `try`, the scope for an exception handling is therefore defined.

3.6.3 Standard Exception Classes

As previously explained, exceptions are represented by objects. The necessary types have to be defined from the classes or the libraries that trigger these exceptions. In C++, a collection of standard exception classes is defined, which are displayed in Figure 3.9.

All exception classes have the same basic class, `std::exception`. This is a type that can be used to represent all standard exceptions. Only one operation is defined for objects of these classes: `what` returns an implementation-specific message.

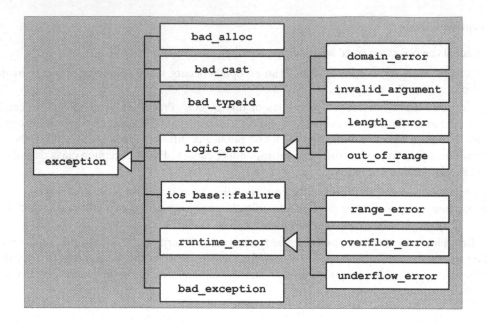

Figure 3.9. Hierarchy of the standard exception classes

3.6.4   An Example of Exception Handling

When handling an exception, the area in which we are to react to exceptions is enclosed by a `try` block. The reaction to the exception is then defined directly after the `try` block by one or more `catch` blocks. The following example shows exactly how this works:

```cpp
// progs/eh1.cpp

#include <iostream>      // header file for I/O
#include <string>        // header file for strings
#include <cstdlib>       // header file for EXIT_FAILURE
#include <exception>     // header file for exceptions

int main()
{
    try {
        // create two strings
        std::string firstname("bjarne");        // may trigger std::bad_alloc
        std::string lastname("stroustrup");     // may trigger std::bad_alloc
        std::string name;
```

```
        // manipulate strings
        firstname.at(20) = 'B';                    // triggers std::out_of_range
        lastname[30] = 'S';                        // ERROR: undefined behaviour

        // concatenate strings
        name = firstname + " " + lastname;   // may trigger std::bad_alloc
    }
    catch (const std::bad_alloc& e) {
        // special exception: no more memory
        std::cerr << "no more memory" << std::endl;
        return EXIT_FAILURE;       // exit main() with error status
    }
    catch (const std::exception& e) {
        // other standard exceptions
        std::cerr << "standard exception: " << e.what() << std::endl;
        return EXIT_FAILURE;       // exit main() with error status
    }
    catch (...) {
        // all other exceptions
        std::cerr << "other unexpected exception" << std::endl;
        return EXIT_FAILURE;       // exit main() with error status
    }

    std::cout << "OK, everything was alright until now" << std::endl;
}
```

Using try, an area is set aside in which a common exception handling is defined. An 'attempt' is made to execute the statements found in the try block:

```
try {
    // create two strings
    std::string firstname("bjarne");       // may trigger std::bad_alloc
    std::string lastname("stroustrup");    // may trigger std::bad_alloc
    std::string name;

    // manipulate strings
    firstname.at(20) = 'B';                // triggers std::out_of_range
    lastname[30] = 'S';                    // ERROR: undefined behavior

    // concatenate strings
    name = firstname + " " + lastname;     // may trigger std::bad_alloc
}
```

If an exception occurs, the whole `try` block is exited immediately. In this example, if an exception is triggered in one of the declarations, the following statements are *no longer executed*. Here, the `try` block is left by calling

```
firstname.at(20) = 'B';
```

as an attempt is made to access the character with index 20 in `firstname`, and this character does not exist. In contrast to the index operator, `at()` checks strings to find out whether the index is correct and, if necessary, triggers a corresponding exception. When using the index operator, checking is avoided for performance reasons (the following line would therefore not trigger an exception, but would lead to the system crashing or some other undefined behavior).

The appearance of a reaction to an exception is defined via the `catch` blocks that follow the try block:

```
catch (const std::bad_alloc& e) {
    // special exception: no more memory
    std::cerr << "no more memory" << std::endl;
    return EXIT_FAILURE;      // exit main() with error status
}
catch (const std::exception& e) {
    // other standard exceptions
    std::cerr << "standard exception: " << e.what() << std::endl;
    return EXIT_FAILURE;      // exit main() with error status
}
catch (...) {
    // all other exceptions
    std::cerr << "other unexpected exception" << std::endl;
    return EXIT_FAILURE;      // exit main() with error status
}
```

Reactions to exceptions of `std::bad_alloc` type (i.e. memory shortage), `std::exception` type (i.e. all standard exceptions) and reactions to all other exceptions are defined in sequence. The last `catch` block demonstrates a special facility to react to any given exception:

```
catch (...) {
    // all other exceptions
    ...
}
```

A sequence of three dots in a catch statement stands for 'any given exception'. As we do not know anything about the type of the exception, we can only react very generally here.

This sequence of `catch` blocks is no coincidence. When an exception occurs in a `try` block, the following `catch` blocks are searched in the sequence in which they are given, in accordance with a suitable handling technique. The statements from the first suitable handler are used. As a consequence, the sequences of the `catch` blocks have to be defined so that special classes come before general exception classes. A `catch` block for any given exception, which is defined by

```
catch (...) {
     ...
}
```

should therefore always be the last catch block.

Any statements can be enclosed in a catch block. In this case, an error message is issued to the standard error output channel std::cerr and the function main() is exited with an error status using return:

```
std::cerr << ... << std::endl;
return EXIT_FAILURE;      // exit main() with an error status
```

The constant EXIT_FAILURE defined in <cstdlib> is used as the return value of main() to indicate an incorrect run of the program (see Section 3.9.3 on page 122).

Provided that an exception object is defined as a parameter of a catch clause, this object can be accessed to gain further information about the exception. With standard exceptions, a simple call of what() is possible:

```
catch (const std::exception& e) {
     ... e.what() ...
}
```

The return value of what() is an implementation-specific string. As an exception is triggered by the call of at() in this example, and it is a standard exception of the std::out_of_range type, this second block is found to be the suitable handler of exceptions. For example, implementation-specific output can look as follows:

```
standard exception: pos >= length ()
```

Provided the function is not exited in the catch block, the program continues after the last catch block. In this example, without the return statements, the following output statement would be called after an exception.

It should be noted that the exception object in the catch block is declared in the form 'const type&'. This is a so-called *constant reference*, which ensures that no unnecessary copies of the exception object are made. The necessary language features are explained in detail in Section 4.4 on page 181.

As previously mentioned, all the blocks located between detection and handling are left bottom-up. This process is called *stack unwinding*. While doing this, all local objects of these blocks are destroyed. If these are class objects for which clean-up operations (so-called *destructors*) are defined, then these are also called.

The following example clarifies the scenario once more:

```
// progs/eh2.cpp

char f1 (const std::string s, int idx)
{
     std::string tmp = s;      // local object that is destroyed
     ...                       // if there is an exception
     char c = s.at(idx);       // could trigger an exception
```

```
    ...
    return c;
}

void foo()
{
    try {
        std::string s("hello");   // is destroyed if there is an exception
        f1(s,11);        // triggers an exception
        f2();            // is not called if there is an exception in f1()
    }
    catch (...) {
        std::cerr << "Exception, but we will go on" << std::endl;
    }

    // program continues here after the exception in f1()
    ...
}
```

From foo(), f1() is called with the string 'hello' and the index 11. In f1(), this triggers an exception when at() is called. In this case, f1() is immediately exited, and the local object tmp is cleaned up. The try block in foo() is also exited immediately. f2() is no longer called. If a suitable catch block exists, its statements are executed and it continues after the last catch block. If a suitable catch block does not exist, then foo() is exited immediately. This happens until a suitable catch block is found.

3.6.5   Handling of Unexpected Exceptions

In a commercial program, all exceptions should be handled. If this is not the case, an uncaught exception usually leads to the program being terminated. In this case, the function std::terminate() is called, which, in turn, calls std::abort().

The std::abort() function causes a program to abort as if it were an emergency. Run-time information such as core dumping is typically issued dependent on the operating system (see also Section 3.9.3 on page 122).

In order to avoid std::terminate() calling std::abort(), an alternative terminating function can be defined using the std::set_terminate() function. The present terminating function is returned. A terminating function submitted by set_terminate() has neither a parameter nor a return value.

3.6.6   Auxiliary Functions for Exception Handling

In practice, it is often useful to handle exceptions in different situations in the same way. Implementing the same `catch` blocks every time can be tedious. Instead, we could handle all exceptions by an auxiliary function. There is only one problem: how do we pass the exceptions to be handled to this function? There is no common type for all exceptions.

A little trick helps in this case:

```cpp
// progs/eh3.cpp

#include <iostream>      // header file for I/O
#include <string>        // header file for strings
#include <cstdlib>       // header file for EXIT_FAILURE
#include <exception>     // header file for exceptions

void processException()
{
    try {
        throw;      // rethrow the exception again so that it
                    // can be handled here
    }
    catch (const std::bad_alloc& e) {
        // special exception: no more memory
        std::cerr << "no more memory" << std::endl;
    }
    catch (const std::exception& e) {
        // other standard exception
        std::cerr << "standard exception: " << e.what() << std::endl;
    }
    catch (...) {
        // all other exceptions
        std::cerr << "other exception" << std::endl;
    }
}

int main()
{
    try {
        // create two strings
        std::string firstname("bjarne");      // may trigger std::bad_alloc
        std::string lastname("stroustrup");   // may trigger std::bad_alloc
        std::string name;
```

```
        // manipulate strings
        firstname.at(20) = 'B';                    // triggers std::out_of_range
        lastname[30] = 'S';                        // ERROR: undefined behaviour

        // chain strings
        name = firstname + " " + lastname;   // may trigger std::bad_alloc
    }
    catch (...) {
        // deal with all exceptions in auxiliary function
        processException();
        return EXIT_FAILURE;       // exit main() with error status
    }

    std::cout << "OK, everything was alright up until now"
            << std::endl;
}
```

Inside main(), a catch block is defined for all exceptions, which calls the auxiliary function processException() for the actual handling of the exception:

```
try {
    ...
}
catch (...) {
    ...
    processException();
    ...
}
```

Within processException(), throw is called (without parameters) in a try block. This causes the exception that is currently being dealt with to be triggered again. In this way, all blocks are then exited in sequence until a suitable catch block is found. By means of the catch blocks that follow in processException(), the handling is done inside this function.

3.6.7 Summary

- Exception handling is a language feature for the treatment of errors and exceptions that appear in the normal processing of the program.
- It provides a facility to separate normal data flow from error handling.
- Because no return values have to be used with this mechanism, the concept is especially useful for error handling when creating objects.
- Exceptions are objects whose types are defined in corresponding classes.

- If an exception is triggered, a corresponding object is created and all superior blocks are dismissed in sequence until the object is intercepted for exception handling. This is called *stack unwinding*.

- If an exception is not handled, a program error is triggered, which causes an abnormal termination using `std::terminate()` and `std::abort()`.

- Several standard exception classes are defined in C++. `what()` returns an implementation-specific string for the corresponding exception objects.

- Using `throw`, we can trigger exceptions that have just been dealt with. In this way, we can implement general functions for exception handling.

- Exceptions should always be declared in the '`const` *type&*' form (i.e. as constant references).

- If strings or vectors are accessed with the index operator, we must ensure that the index is valid. If we use `at()` for access purposes, an exception is triggered whenever an index is invalid.

3.7 Pointers, Arrays, and C-Strings

This chapter introduces the elements of C that led to the commonly held belief that C++ is a complicated language. It is true that only those who understand pointers and arrays will be able to successfully program in C, and it is equally true that the concept of each is sometimes difficult to comprehend.

These language features are still provided in C++ by default. However, there are several components in the standard library that make the use of pointers and arrays superfluous. Skilful programming encapsulates the 'low-level' aspects of arrays and pointers, producing new types that can be used without prior knowledge of pointers and arrays.

The subject of strings is a classic example of this. In C, strings are arrays of characters managed by pointers. This is a source of much confusion. In C++, the `string` type is used to encapsulate this problem and thus allows intuitive programming with strings (see Section 3.4 on page 59).

In this respect, anybody who fails to fully understand the subjects discussed in this chapter needs not worry. When we come across them later in the book, we will give them a little more attention.

3.7.1 Pointers

Understanding *pointers* is a prerequisite for understanding C. Pointers are references to data. By having an address of memory as their value, they 'point' to other variables, objects or even functions.

The & and * operators are provided for using pointers:

- The unary operator & yields the address of a value or a pointer to a value.
- The unary operator * dereferences a pointer, which means that it returns whatever the pointer refers to or whatever is located at its address.

Consider the following example:

- After the following declarations:

      int x = 42;   // integer
      int* xp;   // pointer to integer

  a variable x exists with the initial value 42 and a pointer xp with an undefined value:

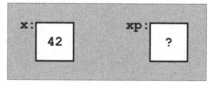

- With the statement

      xp = &x;   // xp now points to x

  the address of x is assigned to xp. In this way, xp refers to x:

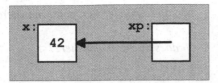

- Having this situation, the expression *xp stands for x because it yields whatever xp points to. Using this pointer, x can, for example, receive a new value:

  `*xp = 7;`   // *that to which* xp *points (i.e.* x*) gets the value* 7

  In this way, the following situation occurs:

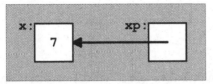

- We can also output the value x with the help of xp:

  `std::cout << *xp << std::endl;`   // *output that to which* xp *points*

Declaration of Pointers

Pointers are declared by placing an asterisk in front of the name. Because C++ is a format-free language, there are different ways of defining pointers. The following methods are equivalent:

```
int *xp;        // K&R notation
int * xp;
int*xp;
int* xp;        // typical C++ notation
```

The first form, which was introduced by Kernighan and Ritchie, the founders of C, and is normally used in C.

I prefer the latter notation (as many in the C++ community do), which may confuse one or two readers at first. It has the advantage that the type (pointer to `int`) is clearly separated from the name (`xp`). However, it also has one severe disadvantage: It cannot be used for the declaration of more than one pointer because, when declaring

```
int* p1, p2;      // NO, not two pointers, so avoid!
```

the asterisk only belongs to the first variable. `p1` is declared as a pointer to an `int`, but `p2` is declared as an `int`, which becomes clearer when using the K&R notation:

```
int *p1, p2;      // pointer and simple variable
```

The Constant NULL

The special constant NULL denotes a pointer that points nowhere. This is in contrast to a non-initialized pointer, which points to any place, a defined state. NULL can be assigned and queried:

```
int* xp = NULL;          // xp is a pointer that points nowhere
...
if (xp != NULL) {        // does xp point anywhere?
    ...
}
```

NULL is defined as the value 0. Zero is the only integer value that can be assigned to pointers. Thus the value 0 can simply be used instead of NULL:

```
int* xp = 0;             // xp is a pointer that points nowhere
...
if (xp != 0) {           // does xp point anywhere?
    ...
}
```

As 0 corresponds to the value `false` and all other values correspond to `true`, we can also test pointers logically:

```
if (xp) {                // does xp point anywhere?
    ...
}
...
if (!xp) {               // does xp point nowhere?
    ...
}
```

3.7.2 Arrays

An array is a collection of several elements of the same type, arranged in sequence. The number of elements has to be indicated when an array is created. Element access is done via the operator [ ]:

```
int values[10];          // array of ten ints

values[0] = 77;          // initialize first element
values[9] = values[0];   // last element receives the value of the first

for (int i=0; i<10; ++i) {    // initialize all elements
    values[i] = 42;
}
```

The index area always ranges from 0 to $size - 1$. A programmer must ensure that arrays are not accessed using invalid indices. This is not checked in the program for performance reasons. The result of invalid access is not defined and is random.

Arrays and Pointers

Arrays can be accessed using pointers. This mirrors the fact that an array variable inside the program is actually a pointer to the first element (and therefore contains the address of the first element in the array). By means of the declaration

```
int values[10];          // array of ten ints
```

the condition displayed in Figure 3.10 is created.

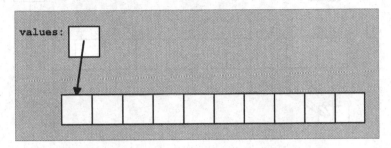

Figure 3.10. Status after the creation of the values[] array

In this respect, we can also access arrays using pointer notation:

```
int* vp = values;        // corresponds to vp = &values[0]
*values = 88;            // changes values[0]
```

By assigning values to vp, vp is assigned to the address of the first element in the array. vp therefore points to values[0]. By assigning 88 to what values points to, 88 is assigned to values[0].

Pointer Arithmetic

The analogy between arrays and pointers extends further, in that pointers can move around all elements of an array. It is also possible for pointers to call arithmetic operations:

- If an integer n is added to the pointer, the pointer is increased by n elements. The ++ operator increases the pointer by one element.
- If we process the sum of a pointer and an integer n, the result points to the nth value after the pointer.
- If we subtract two pointers, we get the distance between the elements to which they point.

The following loop outputs all elements of an array:

```
int values[10];          // array of ten ints

for (int* p=values; p<values+10; ++p) {
    std::cout << *p << std::endl;
}
```

At the beginning, p is initialized as a pointer to the first element of values. Provided this pointer is before (less than) a pointer that points to the position of ten elements after the beginning of values, the current element is accessed using *p, and the pointer is increased, with ++p, by one element (see Figure 3.11).

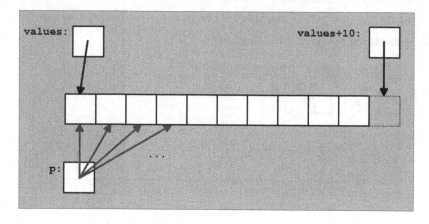

Figure 3.11. Pointer p iterating over the array values[]

If you process the difference of p and values inside the loop, you get the distance between the elements from the beginning, which corresponds to the current index:

```
std::cout << "index: " << p-values
         << " value: " << *p << std::endl;
```

According to these rules, it is totally irrelevant whether we access the elements of an array using the index operator or pointer notation. Instead of

```
values[5]
```

we can access the sixth element of the values array using

```
*(values+5)
```

Pointers and Iterators

Does the way pointers iterate over arrays look familiar? The interface corresponds to the iterator interface (see Section 3.5.4 on page 74). This is no coincidence. The behavior of arrays and pointers was abstracted when designing the STL: Iterators can access containers using the same interface with which pointers can access arrays. Iterators can therefore be described as 'smart pointers' (see Section 9.2.1 on page 536). On the surface, they behave like pointers, but are intelligent in converting the operations suitably for the data structure on which they operate.

3.7.3   C-Strings

The standard string types of C++ encapsulate the details of the low-level string processing with fundamental types, which is adopted from C. In C, strings are managed as arrays of characters. To signify the end, C-strings use the character '\0' (again, this is nothing else but the value 0). The length of a C-string is therefore the number of characters until '\0' appears.

String literals have this low-level format. That is, they are arrays of characters in C++, suffixed with '\0'. The string constant

```
"hello"
```

is stored as displayed in Figure 3.12.

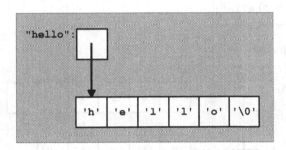

Figure 3.12. Internal representation of a string literal "hello"

The type of a string literal is `const char*`; thus, it is a pointer to non-changeable characters. However, many (old) C functions do not use `const` (for C-strings). For this reason, we are allowed also to use a string literal as type `char*`. However, we are still not allowed to modify the characters of a string literal in this case.

If you use strings in C++, you usually do not see the underlying management adopted from C. The `std::string` type hides the fact that strings are arrays of characters. By declaring

```
std::string s = "hello";
```

one object of the standard `std::string` type is initialized with a value of the `const char*` type. Instead of this, we can also write the following:

```
std::string s("hello");
```

If we (for whatever reason) use the `const char*` type, we can access all characters of a C-string by allowing a pointer to iterate over these characters:

```
// loop that outputs each character of a C-string s character by character
const char* s = "hello";

for (const char* p=s; *p != '\0'; ++p) {
    std::cout << *p << std::endl;
}
```

p is initially assigned to the C-string s, which means that p points to the first character of the string. As long as p does not point to the string-ending character '\0', the statements in the loop body are executed and the pointer is advanced by one character using ++p.

Problems with C-Strings

Without using a type that encapsulates C-strings, the problem of arrays and pointers arises. By managing strings as an array, they cannot be treated as fundamental types. If a string is assigned to another string using an assignment operator, the addresses are copied, rather than the elements (as arrays are actually pointers to the first element, these pointers are assigned to one another).

For example, if two strings are declared as follows:

```
const char* s = "hello";
const char* t = "Nico";
```

the following situation arises:

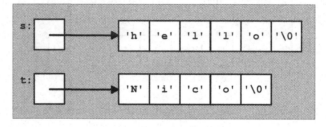

By assigning

```
s = t;                // CAUTION: pointers are assigned
```

we get:

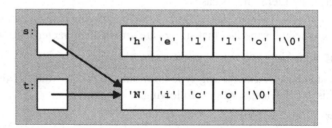

The pointers (addresses of the C-strings) are therefore assigned rather than the characters. Because of this, s and t represent the same C-string afterwards.

In order to copy the C-strings properly, the individual characters have to be copied. In addition to this, C programmers must always ensure that sufficient memory is available for the strings themselves. For this reason, C programs that operate with strings nearly always turn out badly. For example:

```
// progs/cstring.cpp

// C header file for I/O
#include <stdio.h>

// C header file for the string treatment
#include <string.h>

void f()
{
    const char* c = "input: ";   // string constant
    char        text[81];        // string variable for 80 characters
    char        s[81];           // string variable for the input (up to 80 characters)

    /* read string s
     * - because of limited memory, no more than 80 characters
     */
    if(scanf("%80s", s) != 1) {
       // read error

       ...
    }


    // compare string with empty string
    if(strcmp(s,"") == 0) {
       /* assign string literal to string text
        * - CAUTION: text has to be big enough
        */
       strcpy(text, "no input");
    }
    else {
       /* assign string constants c, followed by read string, to text
        * - CAUTION: text has to be big enough
        */
       if(strlen(c)+strlen(s) <= 80) {
          strcpy (text, c);
          strcat (text, s);
       }
    }
    ...
}
```

The problems displayed by this small program should be familiar to all C programmers:

- For an assignment, the `strcpy()` function has to be used. The programmer must ensure that the string memory to which a new value is assigned is large enough.
- In order to append one string to another, the `strcat()` function is useful. Sufficient memory also has to be provided in this case.
- The `strcmp()` function has to be used to compare two strings.
- When entering a string, it has to be specified that space is only available for a certain number of characters.

String processing in C is therefore not only tedious, but also dangerous. Special functions have to be called for all operations (the most important ones are listed in Table 3.12), and we need to worry about memory management.

Function	Meaning
strlen()	returns the number of characters in a string
strcpy()	assigns one C-string to another
strncpy()	assigns up to n characters of one string to another
strcat()	appends one C-string to the other
strncat()	appends up to n characters of one string to another
strcmp()	compares two C-strings
strncmp()	compares up to n characters from two strings
strchr()	searches for a certain character in a C-string

Table 3.12. Most important functions for C-strings

All these problems no longer occur in C++. By using the standard `string` type introduced in Section 3.4 on page 59, we can use standard operators and need not worry about memory management. In C++, the above C program would look as follows:

```
// progs/string2.cpp

#include <iostream>       // C++ header file for I/O
#include <string>         // C++ header file for strings

int main()
{
    const std::string c = "input: ";   // string constant
    std::string text;                  // string variable
    std::string s;                     // string variable for the input

    // read string s
    if (! (std::cin >> s)) {
        // read error
        ...
    }
```

```
    // compare string with empty string
    if (s == "") {
        // assign string literal to string text
        text = "no input";
    }
    else {
        /* assign string constant c, followed by read string, to text
        */
        text = c + s;
    }
    ...
}
```

The handling of dynamic arrays in C has the same complications. C++ has the advantage that the standard library makes classes available with STL containers that encapsulate these difficulties. For this reason, you should also use vectors instead of dynamic arrays.

3.7.4 Summary

- Pointers are variables that refer to other variables. Their values are the addresses of these variables.
- The unary operators * and & are used in the processing of pointers.
- If a pointer has the value 0 (NULL), it does not refer to anything. This is different from a non-initialized pointer, which can point anywhere.
- Arrays are created with brackets. Their index ranges from 0 to $size - 1$.
- The type and value of an array variable corresponds to a pointer to the first element.
- Pointers can move around arrays using arithmetic operators.
- C-strings are arrays of characters.
- The difficulties associated with C-strings are eliminated by using the C++ type for strings, std::string.

3.8   Memory Management Using new and delete

This section introduces the concept of explicit memory management. The new and delete operators in C++ are introduced and their uses are explained.

Variables usually have a clearly defined scope. The variables become invalid as soon as the block in which these variables are declared is exited. In this way, the necessary memory is automatically freed and the data stored within become invalid. If the variables are complex objects, the necessary clean-up work is carried out (if, for example, a variable represents an open file, it is automatically closed).

Sometimes it is necessary that variables or objects remain valid outside block limits. A global variable does not necessarily help here, as it is initialized at the start of the program. However, the data may not even exist at this point. We therefore need to create explicit objects for run time and destroy them again later. We also require a facility to request and free memory for these objects.

Operators for Memory Management

The new and delete operators are available in C++ for dynamic memory management and the explicit creation and deletion of objects. With new, memory is requested and a new object is explicitly created; with delete, this object is removed and any reserved memory is released.

The objects managed with new and delete can belong to a class or can have a fundamental type. Arrays of objects of any given type can also be created.

Demarcation of C Functions

The new operations replace the memory-management functions familiar from C, malloc() and free(). This has many advantages:

- As operators, new and delete are part of the C++ language and do not belong to a standard library.
- For this reason, the types of object to be created can be given directly as operands, and do not have to be bracketed as a parameter or be provided with sizeof.
- In addition, new, in contrast to malloc(), returns a pointer to the correct type. Thus, its return value does not have to be explicitly converted into the correct type.
- Provided that new creates objects, these are initialized. When requesting memory for fundamental types, the memory of local variables may not be initialized.
- The return value does not necessarily have to be tested for NULL because a standard error handling is installed that throws exceptions if it is not possible to allocate memory or create objects.
- Finally, the new operator can itself be implemented for individual types. By doing so, any kind of optimization is possible for memory management, without changing the interface for the caller.

Much code can be spared using these methods. C code such as

```
personPointer = (Person*) malloc(sizeof(Person));
if (personPointer == NULL) {
    // ERROR
    ...
}
initPerson(personPointer,"Nicolai","Josuttis");
```

becomes, in C++,

```
personPointer = new Person("Nicolai","Josuttis");
```

We only indicate in C++ what kind of object should be created and, optionally, submit initializing arguments.

3.8.1   The new Operator

Memory can be allocated explicitly for an object of a certain type using the new operator. As an operand, the type of object that is to be explicitly created is written right after new. A pointer to this object is returned:

```
float* fp = new float;              // creates a floating-point value
std::string* sp = new std::string;  // creates a string
```

Provided the type is a class, the created object is initialized immediately (a *constructor* of the class is called). Optional arguments can be passed in parentheses:

```
std::string* sp1;
sp1 = new std::string;             // create a string initialized with the default value
std::string* sp2;
sp2 = new std::string("hello"); // create a string initialized with "hello"
```

3.8.2   The delete Operator

The delete operator is used to free memory allocated by new. As an operand, the pointer returned by new is passed to the object (the address of the object to be freed):

```
float* fp = new float;              // create floating-point value
std::string* sp = new std::string;  // create string
...
delete fp;                          // release floating-point value
delete sp;                          // release string
```

```
std::string* p1 = new std::string("hello");  // create string (p1 points to it)
...
std::string* p2 = p1;                        // p2 points to it now, too
...
delete p2;                                   // release string
```

The call of `delete` for an object not created by `new` is not defined, and can cause fatal results. It is an error to free memory allocated by `malloc()` with `delete`, or memory allocated by `new` with `free()`. However, this sometimes works, because `new` and `delete` are often implemented via `malloc()` and `free()`. However, note that this kind of programming is not portable, because `new` and `delete` can also be defined in various other ways.

`delete` can be called for 0 (or `NULL`). This can be used to avoid special handling of pointers that might or might not refer to allocated memory:

```
Person* ptr = NULL;
...

if (condition-which-may-be-achieved) {
    ptr = new Person;
}
...

delete ptr;       // OK (whether or not memory was allocated)
```

Note that local pointers have an undefined value without being initialized. Without the explicit initialization of `ptr` with `NULL` in this example, this would be invalid code, because `delete` is called for any address `ptr` has by random.

3.8.3   Dynamic Memory Management for Arrays

Using array brackets, `new` and `delete` can also be used to allocate and release (memory for) arrays. When using `new[]`, a pointer is returned to the first object:

```
char*        s = new char[len+1];          // len+1 chars
std::string* strings = new std::string[42];  // 42 strings
float**      values = new float*[10];       // ten pointers to floats
```

Again, if objects are allocated, then they are initialized with their default value. Thus the 42 strings are all initialized with the empty string. Fundamental types (such as `char`, `float`, etc.) get an undefined initial value by default. With arrays created by `new`, it is not possible to submit arguments for initialization.

There is a corresponding `delete` operator syntax for releasing arrays, which requires that array brackets also be given:

```
char*        s = new char[len+1];          // len+1 chars
std::string* strings = new std::string[42]; // 42 strings
float**      values = new float*[10];       // ten pointers to floats
...
delete [] s;                                // release chars
delete [] strings;                          // release strings
delete [] values;                           // release float pointer
```

A programmer must pay attention to whether a pointer refers to an individual object or to an array of objects, so that the correct syntax is used in the release:

```
void release (std::string* sp)
{
    // what is meant?:
    delete sp;          // only OK with sp = new std::string
    delete [] sp;       // only OK with sp = new std::string[10]
}
```

If the wrong syntax is used, the C++ standard states that this results in undefined behavior.

This somewhat unappealing property of the language is due to the fact that, in C++, no distinction can be made between a pointer to an object and an array of objects (a result of the backwards compatibility with C). However, the difference is important because different operations can be called under different conditions. A call of delete or delete[] may result in different functions being called, which can even be replaced by user-defined functions (this is discussed in Section 9.3.4 on page 552). As the compiler cannot decide on the type, nor on the context as to whether an individual object or an array of objects should be deleted (new and delete can be called by different translation units), this has to be specified by the programmer.

Multi-Dimensional Arrays

Multi-dimensional arrays can also be created using new. Again, a pointer to the first object of the array is returned:

```
std::string(*twodim)[7] = new std::string[10][7];   // 10 * 7 strings
...
delete [] twodim;                                    // release strings
```

By calling new, 70 strings are created and initialized with the default value of the class. The delete statement then releases these strings.

Note that by calling

```
new std::string[num][7]
```

a pointer of num elements of the type 'array of seven strings' is returned:

```
std::string(*twodim)[7]
```

This is not the same as an array of num multiplied by seven strings:

```
std::string* p = new std::string[num*7];                    // (num * 7) strings
```

Due to the fact that every further dimension is part of the returned type, all but the first dimension have to be passed as a constant value:

```
new std::string[num][7];    // OK
new std::string[10][num]    // ERROR
```

Because of the complicated types of multi-dimensional arrays, programmers usually use a one-dimensional array and manage the dimension themselves.

Arrays without Elements

The new operator can create arrays with no elements. This avoids special handling for empty arrays:

```
int size = 0;
...
// size can still be 0
int* numbers = new int[size];
...
delete [] numbers;        // OK
```

3.8.4   Error Handling for new

The call of new could always fail, because, for example, no memory is available, which may happen in ordinary multi-user operating systems. If new gets no memory, a *new handler* is called. The default new handler throws an *exception* of the type std::bad_alloc.

We can interfere with this default handling in various different ways:

1. This kind of error can be intercepted and dealt with in the program using exception handling. This is discussed in Section 3.6.4 on page 96.
2. We can install new handlers that try to request further memory or open the 'reserve memory' with an appropriate warning. This is discussed in Section 9.3.3 on page 547.
3. We can call new in such a way that, in case of an error, no new handler is called and NULL is returned instead. This is discussed in Section 9.3.1 on page 546.
4. We can implement the new operator in a completely different way. This is discussed in Section 9.3.4 on page 552.

Note that a lack of memory usually indicates that it is fairly pointless to allow the program to continue running. In this respect, a global reaction is normally defined in exception handling that ends the program with a suitable error message (see, for example, Section 3.6.4 on page 96).

3.8.5 Summary

- The new and delete operators are introduced in C++ for memory management.
- For arrays, new[] and delete[] are provided.
- The memory management of C++ using new and delete should *never* be confused with the C functions malloc(), free(), etc.
- If no memory can be allocated by new, an exception of the type std::bad_alloc is usually thrown. Programs should handle exceptions of this type appropriately.

3.9   Communication with the Outside World

To conclude the application programmer's view of C++, this chapter introduces facilities to 'communicate with the outside world' of a program. This includes handling arguments from the caller, working with system variables, starting other programs and returning exit codes.

Most of the concepts and interfaces provided here are adopted from C. Thus higher types in C++, such as `string`, are unfortunately not used here.

3.9.1   Arguments from the Program Call

The `main()` function can be declared in two different ways:

- On one hand, without parameters:
  ```
  int main() {
      ...
  }
  ```

- On the other hand, with two parameters:
  ```
  int main(int argc, char* argv[]) {
      ...
  }
  ```

In the second case, `argv` contains the arguments from the call of the program, passed as an array of C-strings. The number of elements in this array is located in `argc`. The array always contains the program name as the first element; the other elements are program parameters (if any).

A simple example showing the processing of program parameters is shown in the following program:

```
// progs/argv.cpp

#include <iostream>      // C++ header file for I/O
#include <string>        // C++ header file for strings

int main(int argc, char* argv[])
{
    // output program name and number of parameters
    std::string progname = argv[0];
    if (argc > 1) {
        std::cout << progname << " has " << argc-1 << " parameters: "
                << std::endl;
    }
    else {
        std::cout << progname << " was called without parameters"
                << std::endl;
    }
```

```
// output program parameters
for (int i=1; i<argc; ++i) {
    std::cout << "argv[" << i << "]: " << argv[i] << std::endl;
}
}
```

If the program is simply called using the name argv and without any parameters, it has the following output:

```
argv was called without parameters
```

If the program is called like this:

```
argv hello "two words" 42
```

the output is as follows:

```
argv has 3 parameters:
argv[1]: hello
argv[2]: two words
argv[3]: 42
```

3.9.2 Access to Environment Variables

With the getenv() function defined in <cstdlib> or <stdlib.h>, values can be requested from environment variables:

```
#include <cstdlib>
#include <string>

std::string path;
const char* path_cstr = std::getenv("PATH");
if (path_cstr == NULL) {
    ...
}
else {
    path = path_cstr;
}
```

The value of the environment variable is either returned as a C-string or as NULL. Note that NULL cannot be assigned to C++ strings. For this reason, the return value has to be checked before being used as a C++ string.

3.9.3 Aborting Programs

A C++ program is ended either by exiting `main()` or by calling a function to abort the program.

Three functions, adopted from C, which are declared in `<cstdlib>` or `<stdlib.h>`, are important in this context (see Table 3.13). A C++ program can be interrupted at any time by calling `exit()` or `abort()`. In addition, using `atexit()`, we can register functions that are automatically called when the program is exited.

Function	Meaning
`exit()`	interrupts a program in an 'orderly' manner
`atexit()`	installs a function that is called at the end of the program
`abort()`	interrupts a program in a 'disorderly' manner

Table 3.13. Functions to force a program termination

We can terminate a C++ program at run time anywhere using `exit()`. This is not an ordered ending to the program, because the program is exited while still running. Certain clean-up work is still carried out (for example, output buffers are usually flushed), but temporary files are not removed.

More precisely, all global objects are cleaned up, but local objects are not. This can lead to undesirable side effects, which is why calling `exit()` should be avoided whenever possible.

`exit()` receives an integer value as a parameter, which is passed to the caller of the program. This can be used to indicate whether the program ran successfully (the so-called *exit code*). These values correspond to the return value of `main()`. If 0 or the `EXIT_SUCCESS` constant is passed, it is a 'successful' program end. The `EXIT_FAILURE` constant indicates an 'unsuccessful' program end:

```
#include <cstdlib>

if (fatal-problem) {
    std::exit(EXIT_FAILURE);      // abort with partial clean-up
}
```

The constants `EXIT_SUCCESS` and `EXIT_FAILURE` can also be used as return values of `main()`. Using `EXIT_FAILURE` is particularly helpful, as this clearly indicates that something has failed:

```
int main()
{
    ...
    if (error) {
        return EXIT_FAILURE;      // end program with an error status
    }
    ...
}
```

A function can be defined using `atexit()`, which is automatically called directly before the program terminates via `exit()`. This is typically used to end a program in case of an error. In the installed function, opened files can be closed, buffers flushed or connections to other processes closed in an orderly manner. These functions are not only called when a program is terminated by `exit()`, but also with the regular ending of `main()`.

`abort()` is used to abort a program immediately, without any additional cleaning up, in case of a fatal error. The precise reaction is system specific, and a core dump is typically created. `abort()` is called without parameters:

```
#include <cstdlib>

if (every-further-operation-is-no-longer-useful) {
    std::abort();      // abort with core dump
}
```

3.9.4   Calling Other Programs

By using the `system()` function defined in `<cstdlib>` or `<stdlib.h>`, another program can be started. The name of the program and all arguments are passed as one C-string. The exit status of the program is returned:

```
#include <cstdlib>

int status;
if (is-unix-system) {
    status = std::system("ls -l");      // list files under UNIX
}
else {
    status = std::system("dir");        // list files under Windows
}

if (status == EXIT_SUCCESS) {
    ...
}
```

The return value of `system()` is the exit code of the program, or an error code if the program is unable to be called at all.

3.9.5   Summary

- A C++ program can be called with arguments that can be evaluated as parameters of `main()`.
- Environment variables can be accessed using `getenv()`.

- Programs can be terminated using exit() and abort(). These functions should normally be avoided.
- Other programs can be called using system().
- If a C-string has the value NULL, then you cannot simply assign it to a std::string. The value has to be treated as a special value.

4

Class Programming

This chapter introduces two basic concepts of object-oriented programming: programming with *classes* and *data encapsulation*.

The various language features and programming techniques required in C++ for the use of classes are introduced and explained with the help of examples.

As an introductory example, a class Fraction is used. As the name implies, this class describes objects that represent fractions. These rather simple objects are used deliberately so that the example itself does not pose a problem when different languages features are introduced.

4.1 The First Class: Fraction

In this section, the Fraction class will be implemented and used as our first C++ class. The Fraction class provides a small and easy-to-understand example. Knowledge of fractions can be assumed. Nevertheless, there are some traps that require the use of non-trivial language features in subsequent versions of the implementation.

Readers already familiar with C++ will be a little surprised by this first version. With advanced knowledge of the language, the class would surely be implemented differently. However, you will agree that all the properties of the language cannot be introduced simultaneously. During the course of the book, the Fraction class will be improved from version to version. Several fundamental programming techniques introduced here will then be questioned on the basis of the knowledge acquired, or will be replaced by other mechanisms.

4.1.1 Food for Thought Before Implementation

As with every class, before the Fraction class is implemented, two issues must be clarified:

- What should we be able to do with objects of the class?
- Which data represent objects of this class?

The first question regards the application of the class, and therefore defines the look and feel of its external interface. This is described in a corresponding specification, according to the requirements made of the class.

The second question concerns the internal structure of the class and its objects (instances). In some way, the data must be managed as attributes. This question mainly applies to the implementation of the class, and must be answered in such a way that the requirements resulting from the first question are solved as skillfully as possible.

Requirements of the Fraction Class

For our first example, the requirements on the Fraction class will be kept to a minimum. We are only interested in clarifying the principles. For this reason, we will require only one single operation:

- The output of a fraction.

In the following sections, further operations will be added that will be used, for example, to multiply or input fractions.

Nevertheless, we should remember that, in order to execute an operation with fractions, fraction objects must exist in the first place. In addition, a fraction should be able to be deleted if it is no longer needed. Therefore, two additional operations are required:

- The creation (and initialization) of a fraction.
- The destruction of a fraction.

The resulting life-cycle of a fraction is displayed in Figure 4.1.

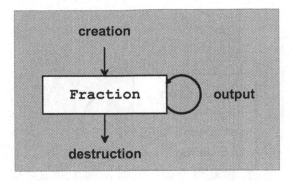

Figure 4.1. Life-cycle of the `Fraction` class

Design of Fractions

Trying to find the attributes and internal structure of an object involves transform this kind of abstract construct directly or indirectly to already available types. The information content and state of the object must be described by several individual members that have types already available.

Initial questions that may be asked are as follows:

- What kind of data describes the fundamental state of the object?
- What does the object represent?
- What are the 'parts' of the object?

These questions often lead to the first members of an object. During the implementation of a class, supplementary members may be added that represent an internal object state and therefore make the implementation process easier, or shorten the running time.

It is fairly easy to say what a fraction represents or what it is made up of: A fraction consists of a numerator and a denominator. We can use fundamental types such as `int` for these members. As a result, the two essential members of a fraction are as follows:

- An `int numer` for the numerator.
- An `int denom` for the denominator.

Further auxiliary members may well be required. For example, a member can determine internally whether the numerator and denominator can be reduced. Thus the members essential for information content, the numerator and denominator, do not need to remain the only members.

Ultimately, the diagram shown in Figure 4.2 is the result: a fraction consists of a numerator and a denominator, and can be created, output, and destroyed.

Terminology

In object-oriented terminology, the numerator and denominator are the *data* or *attributes* from which an instance of the `Fraction` class is created. The creation, output, and destruction operations are the *methods* that are defined for the class.

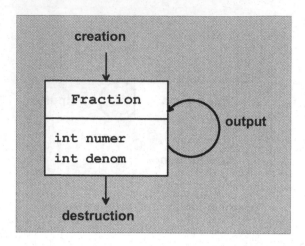

Figure 4.2. Design of the Fraction class

In C++ terminology, this means that a Fraction class is needed that consists of the *members* numerator and denominator, as well as functions for creating, outputting, and destroying instances. The methods, i.e. the operations, defined in a class are called *member functions* in C++, which are special kinds of *member*. Those members that are not member functions are called *data members* in C++. Thus, in C++, we generally speak of *members* of a class, which might be *member functions* or *data members*. The members of the Fraction class could therefore be categorized into the numerator and denominator data members, and the member functions for creation, output, and destruction.

Encapsulation

Fractions have a fundamental property: Their denominator cannot be zero because division by zero is not allowed (at least without introducing semantics for infinite numbers). This constraint should, of course, also be valid for the Fraction class.

If unlimited access is available to all members of the Fraction class for all users, the denominator could inadvertently be set to zero. For this reason, it is useful to prevent direct access to the denominator when using a fraction. Provided that access is only possible using functions, attempting to assign zero to the denominator could result in an error message.

In general, it is recommended that access to objects only be permitted using operations that were specifically designed for this purpose. By implementing these carefully, errors can be handled and inconsistencies prevented. For example, if, in an auxiliary member, we store internally whether a fraction can be reduced, an appropriate adjustment can be made, once the contents have been changed externally by assigning a new numerator.

In the case of fractions, it is therefore reasonable to allow access only to the numerator and denominator members via functions belonging to the Fraction class. This gives an additional advantage: the internal behavior of a fraction can be modified without changing the external interface.

4.1.2 Declaration of the `Fraction` Class

A class must be declared before it can be used in C++. This is done by declaring a *class structure* in which the principal properties of the class are listed. For the `Fraction` class, these properties contain the data members for the numerator and denominator, as well as the member functions that make up the interface.

To compile all modules in which the `Fraction` class is used, the declaration is placed in a header file. The file name should usually be indicative of the class, so that `frac.hpp` would be an appropriate filename.

The first version of the header file `frac.hpp` is as follows:

```
// classes/frac1.hpp

#ifndef FRACTION_HPP
#define FRACTION_HPP

// **** BEGIN namespace CPPBook *******************************
namespace CPPBook {

/* Fraction class
 */
class Fraction {

  /* private: no access from outside
   */
  private:
    int numer;
    int denom;

  /* public interface
   */
  public:
    // default constructor
    Fraction();

    // constructor from int (denominator)
    Fraction(int);

    // constructor from two ints (numerator and denominator)
    Fraction(int, int);

    // output
    void print();
  };
```

```
} // **** END namespace CPPBook *******************************

#endif     /* FRACTION_HPP */
```

Preprocessor Statements

The complete header file is enclosed by preprocessor statements. These prevent the declaration being executed multiple times when the file is included more than once:

```
#ifndef FRACTION_HPP        // is only fulfilled with the first #include because
#define FRACTION_HPP        // FRACTION_HPP gets defined then

    ...

#endif
```

If the FRACTION_HPP constant is not already defined, the #ifndef ('if not defined') statement processes the following lines until the corresponding #endif is reached. Because the constant is defined on the first pass, subsequent attempts to define it again (due to other direct or indirect #includes) will be ignored.

As header files may be included by other source files in various ways, declarations in header files should always be enclosed by these kinds of statement (see Section 3.3.7 on page 52).

4.1.3   The Class Structure

Classes are declared using a *class structure*. All members of the class are declared here (i.e. both attributes and operations).

The Keyword `class`

The declaration starts with the `class` keyword. This is followed by the name of the class and then the class body, in which the class members are declared, enclosed by braces and separated by semicolons:

```
class Fraction {

    ...

};
```

If a library consisting of several classes is defined, every class name represents a global symbol that can be used anywhere. This may lead to name conflicts when various libraries are used. For this reason, the Fraction class is declared within a *namespace*:

```
namespace CPPBook {      // start of namespace CPPBook

class Fraction {

    ...

};


}                        // end of namespace CPPBook
```

The CPPBook symbol is therefore the only symbol found in the global scope. Strictly speaking, we define 'Fraction in CPPBook'. In C++, the notation used to access this class is CPPBook::Fraction.

All classes and other symbols should always be assigned to a namespace. This both avoids conflicts and clarifies what members of a program logically belong together. This kind of grouping is described as a *package* in object-oriented modeling.

Further details on namespaces can be found in Section 3.3.8 on page 54 and Section 4.3.5 on page 175.

Access Keywords

The class structure contains access keywords that group the individual members together. This enables us to determine which members of the class are internal and which can also be accessed externally.

The members numer and denom are declared as private:

```
class Fraction {
  private:
    int numer;
    int denom;
    ...
};
```

By using the private keyword, all the following members are declared as private. Though this is the default setting in classes, it should be stated explicitly in order to make the code more readable.

The fact that the members are private means that access is only granted within the implementation of the class. Any code using a fraction has no direct access to them. Only indirect access can be granted by making appropriate member functions available.

The user of the Fraction class only has access to the public members. These are declared with the public keyword. Obvious candidates for public members are the functions that form the interface of the objects of this class with the outside:

```
class Fraction {
    ...
  public:
    void print();
};
```

It is not compulsory for all member functions to be public and all data members to be private. Larger classes often have auxiliary internal functions, declared as private member functions.

Data members can also be provided for public access. However, this is generally not recommended because you lose control when somebody accesses data members directly. Providing access to data members only through member functions ensures that you have a clear separation of internal state and external interface and that you can always intervene when data members are set or queried.

Access declarations can occur in a class declaration any number of times, and access to the members can be changed repeatedly:

```
class Fraction {
  private:
    ...
  public:
    ...
  private:
    ...
};
```

Structures versus Classes

From the point of view of a C programmer, a class can be regarded as a C structure endowed with additional properties (e.g. access control and member functions). In fact, in C++, structures are classes. You can do everything with structures that you can with classes. Thus, instead of the class keyword, the struct keyword can also be used to define a class. The only difference is that with the struct keyword, all members are public by default. Therefore, from a C++ point of view, each C structure is a class with only public members.

Nevertheless, I would recommend using class and struct in a way that helps clarify the semantics. That is, class should be used when we define objects that have data members and member functions with different access levels, while struct should be used if we only need a data structure (a composition of values) with public access to all data. A type that can be defined without certain C++ features is also called a *POD*, which stands for 'plain old data (type)'. Thus, every ordinary C struct is a POD and you should use struct only for PODs.

Unfortunately, the semantic difference between class and struct is not made in much of the literature. Thus you may often find examples where the struct keyword is used just to avoid the need to put a public declaration in front of the first member.

4.1.4 Member Functions

One member declared in the Fraction class structure is the print() function:

```
class Fraction {
    ...
    void print();          // output of a fraction
    ...
};
```

This is used to output fractions (that is, write the value of a fraction to the standard output channel). As no value is returned, it has the void return type.

Note that, although we have a fraction to write, it is not passed as a parameter. For member functions, there is always an implicit parameter, which is the object for which the function is called:

```
CPPBook::Fraction x;
...
x.print();          // member function print() called for object x
```

The print() function is called for a fraction by using the dot operator. Additional arguments (if any) can be passed in the parentheses. In object-oriented terminology, by calling x.print(), the *message* print (without a parameter) is sent to the *object* x, which is an *instance* of the Fraction class.

4.1.5 Constructors

The first three functions declared in the Fraction class are special functions. They determine how a fraction is created ('constructed'). The *constructor* bears the name of the class as a function name:

```
class Fraction {
    ...
    // default constructor
    Fraction();

    // constructor from int (numerator)
    Fraction(int);

    // constructor from two ints (numerator and denominator)
    Fraction(int, int);
    ...
};
```

A constructor is always called if a concrete object (instance) of the corresponding class is created. For example, this happens when a variable of this type gets defined. Once the memory required for the object has been allocated, the statements in the constructor are executed. They are typically used to initialize the created object by assigning sensible initial values to the data members of the object.

Having three constructors means that a fraction can be created in three different ways:

1. A fraction can be created without an argument.

    This constructor is called if an object of the Fraction class is defined without any other parameters:

    ```
    CPPBook::Fraction x;          // initializing with the default constructor
    ```

A constructor without parameters is called a *default constructor*.

2. A fraction can be created with an integer as an argument. As we will see in the implementation of the constructors, this parameter gets interpreted as whole number, with which the
fraction is initialized.

This kind of constructor is called when, for example, a fraction is defined with an initial
integral value:

```
CPPBook::Fraction y = 7;        // initializing with the int constructor
```

This manner of initialization was adopted from C.

However, a new notation was introduced in C++ for initializing an object, which can be
used instead:

```
CPPBook::Fraction y(7);         // initialization with int constructor
```

3. A fraction can be created with two integer arguments. These parameters are used to initialize
the numerator and denominator.

The new notation for initializing an object can be used to call this kind of constructor, as
it enables several arguments to be passed:

```
CPPBook::Fraction w(7,3);       // initialization with the int/int constructor
```

Constructors have an unusual feature: they have no return type (not even void). They are therefore not functions or procedures in the ordinary sense.

Classes without Constructors

If no constructors are defined for a class, concrete objects (instances) of the class can still be
created. However, these objects are not initialized. For each class, there is a predefined default
constructor that does nothing.

You should always try to avoid creating objects with undefined states. If it is required that an
object has the state '*not initialized*', a Boolean member should be introduced that manages this
status. The constructor can then initialize the object as '*not initialized*' and, when operations are
called, a check can be performed to see whether the data members have been initialized in the
meantime.

As soon as constructors are defined, objects can only be created using them [1]. If a constructor
but no default constructor is defined, the creation of an object without parameters is not possible.
In this way, the passing of values for initialization can be forced.

4.1.6   Function Overloading

As in the case of constructors, the fact that multiple functions can have the same name is a basic
feature of C++. We say that functions (not only member functions) may be *overloaded*.

Overloaded functions have the same name but different parameters. The number and type of
parameters passed determine which of the overloaded functions is called. Distinction through
return type alone is not permitted.

---

[1] It is still possible to create a copy, which is discussed in Section 4.3.7 on page 179.

The following example shows the overloading of the global function `square()`. One version calculates the square of an integer, the other the square of a floating-point value:

```
// declaration
int    square(int);          // square of an int
double square(double);       // square of a double


void foo()
{
    // function call
    square(713);             // computes the square of an int
    square(4.378);           // computes the square of a double
}
```

In addition, functions can be overloaded for user-defined types such as `Fraction`:

```
// declaration
int                square(int);                 // square of an int
double             square(double);              // square of a double
CPPBook::Fraction square(CPPBook::Fraction);   // square of a Fraction


void foo()
{
    CPPBook::Fraction f;
    ...
    // function call
    square(f);                      // computes the square of a Fraction
}
```

When overloading functions, we need to ensure that each of the overloaded functions do the same thing. As every function is implemented separately, this is up to the programmer.

Parameter Prototypes

For a distinction to be made between overloaded functions, they must be declared with parameter prototypes. This means that the parameter type must be given with the declaration, and is included in the list of parameters when a function is defined:

```
// declaration
int square(int, int);

// definition
int square(int a, int b)
{
    return a * b;
}
```

Parameter prototypes can also be defined in ANSI-C. However, in C, the parameters did not necessarily have to be included on declaration. There is therefore a fundamental difference between C and C++. In C, the declaration

```
void foo();
```

defines a function with as many parameters as desired. In C++, this means that the function does not have *any* parameters. The ANSI-C notation of declaring a function without parameters

```
void foo(void);
```

can also be used in C++, but is not very common.

If a function has a variable number of arguments, these can be indicated in the declaration using three points (with or without a comma):

```
int printf(char*, ...);
```

This kind of notation is called an *ellipsis*.

4.1.7 Implementation of the `Fraction` Class

The member functions included in the declaration of the `Fraction` class must be implemented. This typically occurs in a separate dot-C file created for the class. A suitable filename would be `frac.cpp`.

Using a separate dot-C file for every class is an advantage because programs only have to bind in the modules of the class to be used. This approach also supports the object-oriented programming concept, as all types of objects should rather be independent of each other (although, there are also good reasons for deviating from this rule, such as when two classes are closely linked both logically and technically).

The first dot-C file for the `Fraction` class looks as follows:

```
// classes/frac1.cpp

// include header file with the class declaration
#include "frac.hpp"

// include standard header files
#include <iostream>
#include <cstdlib>

// **** BEGIN namespace CPPBook ********************************
namespace CPPBook {

/* default constructor
 */
```

```
Fraction::Fraction()
  : numer(0), denom(1)        // initialize fraction with 0
{
      // no further statements
}

/* constructor for whole number
 */
Fraction::Fraction(int n)
  : numer(n), denom(1)        // initialize fraction with n
{
      // no further statements
}

/* constructor for numerator and denominator
 */
Fraction::Fraction(int n, int d)
  : numer(n), denom(d)        // initialize numerator and denominator as passed
{
      // 0 as denominator is not allowed
      if (d == 0) {
            // exit program with error message
            std::cerr << "error: denominator is 0" << std::endl;
            std::exit(EXIT_FAILURE);
      }
}

/* print
 */
void Fraction::print()
{
      std::cout << numer << '/' << denom << std::endl;
}

} // **** END namespace CPPBook *******************************
```

First, the declaration of the class is included:

```
#include "frac.hpp"
```

This inclusion is necessary because it lets the compiler know what members the Fraction class has. Otherwise the compiler would have no chance to detect invalid member access or function calls at compile time.

Then various other header files are included that declare the types and functions being used by the class. In this case, there are two files:

```
#include <iostream>
#include <cstdlib>
```

The first statement includes all declarations of C++ for input and output (see page 27 and page 195). The second statement includes a header file in which various standard functions are declared, which are also available in C (see Section 3.9 on page 120). In general, all standard functions from C are also available for use in C++. The corresponding header files have a c prefix instead of the .h extension. With this modification, the symbols declared in the header file belong to the namespace std instead of the global namespace.

In this program, <cstdlib> is included so that we can make use of std::exit() function and the EXIT_FAILURE constant. As explained in Section 3.9.3 on page 122, std::exit() can be used to terminate a program in the event of an error.

The include statements have two different forms:

```
#include "frac.hpp"
#include <iostream>
```

The second form, with the angled brackets, is intended for external files. The associated files are searched for in the directories seen by the compiler as system directories[2]. The files indicated between double quotes are first searched for in the local directory. If they are not found, the system directories are also searched (see page 51).

The Scope Operator

The expression

```
Fraction::
```

prefixes all function names. The :: operator is the *scope operator*, which assigns a symbol according to scope of the class preceding it. It is the operator with the highest precedence.

In this case, it is made clear that a member function of the Fraction class is involved, which, in turn, implies that there exists a Fraction object, for which the function will be called and its members accessed.

Implementation of the Constructors

The constructors are the first functions that are implemented. As mentioned already, their name is the same as the class name, i.e. Fraction::Fraction.

---

[2] In Unix systems, these directories can usually be defined with the -I option. Microsoft Visual C++ also provides a facility for indicating 'additional include directories'.

The default constructor initializes the fraction with 0 (more precisely, with $\frac{0}{1}$):

```
Fraction::Fraction()
  : numer(0), denom(1)      // initialize fraction with 0
{
      // no further statements
}
```

This constructor is called every time a fraction is created without arguments. This ensures that a fraction created without arguments for initialization does not have an undefined value.

A special feature of the constructors becomes apparent at this point. As they are used in the initialization of the objects, they are able to determine the initial values of the members before the actual statements of the function body. The initial values can be set for every attribute in a list, separated from the constructor name by a colon. This is known as an *initializer list*. It has the same effect as if the fractions had been declared with initial values for each member:

```
int numer(0);
int denom(1);
```

Alternatively, values could also be assigned using ordinary statements:

```
Fraction::Fraction()
{
      numer = 0;
      denom = 1;
}
```

This has the same effect but is not quite the same. It is similar to the difference between

```
int x = 0;    // create x and immediately initialize it with 0
```

or

```
int x(0);     // create x and immediately initialize it with 0
```

and

```
int x;        // create x
x = 0;        // assign 0 in a separate step
```

These differences are not important here; however, for more complicated members, the difference may matter. Thus you should familiarize yourself with the syntax of the direct initialization used with the initializer list.

The second constructor is called when an integer is passed. This parameter is interpreted as whole number, which is used to initialize the fraction. Thus the numerator is initialized with the parameter passed and the denominator with 1:

```
Fraction::Fraction(int n)
  : numer(n), denom(1)      // initialize fraction with n
{
      // no further statements
}
```

The third constructor contains two parameters, which are used to initialize the numerator and denominator. The constructor is always called if two integers are passed when a fraction is created. However, if the denominator is passed as 0, the program will exit and display an error message:

```
Fraction::Fraction(int n, int d)
  : numer(n), denom(d)      // initialize numerator and denominator as passed
{
    // 0 is not permitted as denominator
    if (d == 0) {
        // exit program with error message
        std::cerr << "Error: denominator is 0" << std::endl;
        std::exit(EXIT_FAILURE);
    }
}
```

Error Handling in Constructors

It is very radical that, in this example, the program exits due to a faulty initialization. It would have been better to report the error and then react accordingly. The only problem is that constructors are not ordinary functions that can be explicitly called and return a value: they are called implicitly when an object of the class gets created and cannot return anything to the caller.

The program therefore exits for lack of any better alternatives. To prevent a program from exiting in this way, we must ensure that the denominator is not passed as 0 in all programs in which this class is used.

You may consider alternatives to exiting. The fraction could, perhaps, also receive a default value. However, this is far from ideal, as it 'hides' an obvious error (i.e. the numerator cannot be 0), so that it might (by accident) simply be ignored. This goes against the guideline that you should always notify an error (or at least have a chance to notify it).

You could also introduce additional auxiliary members that maintain the state of whether or not the fraction has been initialized correctly. However, these members would then have to be evaluated and taken into account with each operation. This has the effect of simply postponing the problem. We still need to know what to do if someone attempts to use a fraction that was initialized with zero as the denominator.

The best way to deal with these kinds of errors is to use the concept of exception handling, introduced in Section 3.6 on page 93. This would enable errors to be handled during a declaration, which would not necessarily lead to a program exit. Instead, the program could intercept the error and treat it accordingly. We will modify the Fraction class to incorporate this mechanism later (see Section 4.7 on page 234).

Implementation of Member Functions

After the constructors follows the definition of the `print()` member function, which outputs a fraction. In this case, the function simply writes the numerator and the denominator to the standard output channel, `std::cout`, in the format '*numerator/denominator*':

```
void Fraction::print()
{
    std::cout << numer << '/' << denom << std::endl;
}
```

As this is a member function, it must always be called for a particular object. Therefore, the data members `numer` and `denom` can freely be used in the function's implementation. They belong to the object the member function was called for. This means that there is a new type of scope for member functions, which is taken into account when assigning symbols: the scope of the class to which the function belongs. The declaration of a symbol used in a member function is first searched for in the local scope of the function, then in the class declaration, and finally in the global (or namespace) scope.

Using `w.print()`, the `print()` function is called for the object `w`. In this case, it follows that the numerator of object `w` is output (i.e. `w.numer`), along with the character '/' and `w`'s denominator. Likewise, `x.print()` would output `x.numer` and `x.denom`.

Notice that the `numer` member cannot be accessed in the application program directly, as it is declared as private within the `Fraction` class. Only the member functions of a class have access to the private members of this class.

4.1.8   Application of the `Fraction` Class

The first version of the `Fraction` class introduced above can already be used in an application program. To do this, the header file of the class must be included in the dot-C file. Due to the type binding of C++, the declaration of a variable of the `Fraction` type is otherwise forbidden. In addition, the compiler requires information on the members of a fraction, so that it can allocate memory when a `Fraction` object gets created. The class declaration is also used to verify what (if any) members of the `Fraction` class may be accessed.

Assuming that the application program is called `ftest.cpp`, Figure 4.3 how source files are used to create the executable program. The `frac.hpp` header file, which contains the class declaration, is included by the dot-C file with the class implementation and the dot-C file of the application program. Both dot-C files are converted into object files by the C++ compiler (the resulting files usually have the extensions `.o` or `.obj`). The object files are then combined by a linker to form an executable program `ftest` (or `ftest.exe`). On most systems, compiling, and linking can usually be performed in a single step.

The following program is the first sample application of the first version of the `Fraction` class, and shows what can be achieved using fractions:

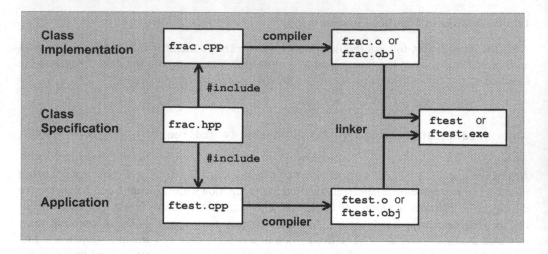

Figure 4.3. Compiling and linking for the Fraction class

```
// classes/ftest1.cpp
```

// include header files for the classes that are being used
```
#include "frac1.hpp"

int main()
{
    CPPBook::Fraction x;          // initialisation using the default constructor
    CPPBook::Fraction w(7,3);     // initialisation using the int/int constructor

    // output fraction w
    w.print();

    // fraction w is assigned to fraction x
    x = w;

    // convert 1000 to a fraction and assign the result to w
    w = CPPBook::Fraction(1000);

    // output x and w
    x.print();
    w.print();
}
```

The output of the program is as follows:

```
7/3
7/3
1000/1
```

Declarations

First, the variables x and w are defined:

```
CPPBook::Fraction x;          // initialization using the default constructor
CPPBook::Fraction w(7,3);     // initialization using the int/int constructor
```

This process has two different names:

- In non-object-oriented terminology, two *variables* of *type* CPPBook::Fraction are created.
- In object-oriented terminology, two *instances* (concrete objects) of the *class* Fraction are created.

Memory is allocated and the appropriate constructors are called for both x and w. This happens for x in the following steps:

- First, memory is allocated for the object. The state is initially undefined:

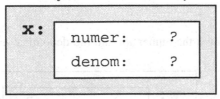

- As x is defined without a value for initialization, the default constructor will then be called:

```
Fraction::Fraction()
  : numer(0), denom(1)      // initialize fraction with 0
{
    // no further statements
}
```

By using the initializer list, the fraction x is initialized with the value 0 (i.e. $\frac{0}{1}$):

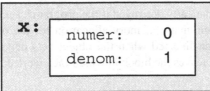

Similarly, w is initialized using the following steps:

- First, memory for the object is allocated. Its status is initially undefined:

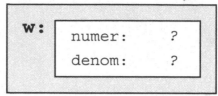

- Because w is initialized with two arguments, the constructor for two integer parameters is called:

```
Fraction::Fraction(int n, int d)
  : numer(n), denom(d)      // initialize numerator and denominator as passed
{
    // 0 is not permitted as a denominator
    if (d == 0) {
        // exit program with error message
        std::cerr << "Error: denominator is 0" << std::endl;
        std::exit(EXIT_FAILURE);
    }
}
```

The constructor initializes the numerator and the denominator with the parameters passed, creating the fraction $\frac{7}{3}$:

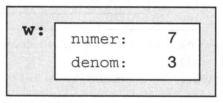

Finally, it is checked whether the denominator is 0.

Destruction of Objects

The object created is automatically destroyed if the program leaves the scope of the surrounding block. According to the automatic memory allocation for the object during its creation, this memory is automatically deallocated when the object gets destroyed. For local objects, this happens when the program leaves the block in which they were defined:

```
void foo()
{
    CPPBook::Fraction x;            // creation and initialization of x
    CPPBook::Fraction w(7,3);       // creation and initialization of w

    ...

}                                   // automatic destruction of x and w
```

It is possible to define functions that are called immediately before the memory of the object is released. These counterparts to the constructors are called *destructors*. They can be used, for example, to output the destruction or to decrement a counter for the number of existing objects. Explicitly releasing allocated memory belonging to an object is also typical. As destructors are not needed by the Fraction class, they will be introduced later (see Section 6.1 on page 352).

Static and Global Objects

Static or global objects exist once for the whole lifetime of a program. You can consider them as objects that are created at the beginning of the program and destroyed at the end. This has an important consequence: the main() function is not the first function of a program to be called. All constructors for static objects are called first, which, in turn, can call any auxiliary functions. In the same way, once main() has been exited or exit() is called, destructors for static and global objects can also be called.

For example, for a global fraction twoThirds, the constructor of the Fraction class is called *before* main() is called:

```
/* global fraction
 * - creating and initializing (via constructor) at program start
 * - automatic destruction (via destructor) at program end
 */
Fraction twoThirds(2,3);

int main()
{
    ...
}
```

As constructors can call any auxiliary functions, much can happen with complex classes before main() is called. One example of this would be a class for objects that represent opened files. If a global object of this class is declared, a corresponding file is opened by calling the constructor before calling main(). However, as this may cause problems (for example, the general settings for error handling may not yet have been set), global and static objects in general should be avoided.

Arrays of Objects

Constructors are called for any created object of a class. If an array of ten fractions is declared, the default constructor is called ten times:

```
CPPBook::Fraction values[10];        // array of ten fractions
```

You can also define values for the initialization of the array elements, as the following example shows:

```
CPPBook::Fraction fc[5] = { CPPBook::Fraction(7,2),
                            CPPBook::Fraction(42),
                            CPPBook::Fraction(),
                            13 };
```

Five fractions are initialized for the array (fc[0] through fc[4]): fc[0] is initialized using the int/int constructor because two parameters are passed. fc[1] and fc[3] are both initialized using the int constructor because one integer is passed. fc[2] and fc[4] are initialized using the default constructor because no arguments are passed (fc[2] because of the empty brackets, and fc[4] because no value was defined for initialization).

These five fractions are also destroyed, when the scope in which they were created is left.

Call of Member Functions

The

```
w.print()
```

statement calls the print() member function for w. The member function then outputs the fraction. The dot operator is, in general, the operator that accesses members for an object. If the member is a member function, this member function is called for it.

A pointer (see Section 3.7.1 on page 104) to a fraction can also be defined in C++. In this case, a member, or call to a member function, can be accessed using the -> operator:

```
CPPBook::Fraction  x;      // fraction
CPPBook::Fraction* xp;     // pointer to fraction

xp = &x;                   // xp points to x

xp->print();               // call print() for what xp points to
```

Assignments

The statement

```
x = w;
```

assigns the fraction w to the fraction x.

This kind of assignment is possible, despite not having been declared in the class specifications. A *default assignment operator* is automatically predefined for every class. It is implemented so that it assigns member-wise. This means that the numerator of w is assigned to the numerator of x and the denominator of w is assigned to the denominator of x.

The assignment operator can itself be defined for a class. This is required if a member-wise assignment is not what is wanted. This is typically the case if a pointer is used as a member. Section 6.1.5 on page 362 discusses this in detail, with the String class as an example.

4.1.9 Creation of Temporary Objects

In the following assignment, the value of 1000, converted to a fraction, is assigned to the fraction w:

```
// convert 1000 to a fraction and assign the result to w
w = CPPBook::Fraction(1000);
```

The expression

```
CPPBook::Fraction(1000)
```

creates a temporary object, in which the corresponding one-parameter constructor is called. This is essentially an explicit type conversion of the integer constant 1000 to a Fraction type.

The statement

```
w = CPPBook::Fraction(1000);
```

therefore creates a temporary object of the Fraction class, initialized with $\frac{1000}{1}$ using the appropriate constructor, assigns the temporary object to the w object, and destroys the temporary object then.

In general, to create temporary objects of a class, corresponding constructors have to be defined. In this case, a temporary fraction can be created with none, one or two arguments:

```
CPPBook::Fraction()        // creating temporary fraction with the value 0/1
CPPBook::Fraction(42)      // creating temporary fraction with the value 42/1
CPPBook::Fraction(16,100)  // creating temporary fraction with the value 16/100
```

4.1.10 UML Notation

When modeling classes, the UML defines a de facto standard for graphical representations. Figure 4.4 displays the UML notation of the Fraction class.

In UML notation, classes are represented by rectangles. These contain the class name, attributes and operations, separated by horizontal lines. Leading minus signs in attributes and operations indicate that these are private. Leading plus signs indicate public access. If an operation has a return type, it is given after the operation, separated by a colon.

Depending on the status of the modeling, details can be omitted. For example, you could skip the package name (the namespace), the leading sign for visibility, the types of the attribute or the parameters of the operations. You could also omit attributes and operations as a whole. Therefore, the shortest form of a UML notation for the Fraction class is a rectangle, containing only the word Fraction.

4.1.11 Summary

- *Classes* are declared by a class structure with the class keyword.
- As with all other global symbols, classes should be declared in a namespace.

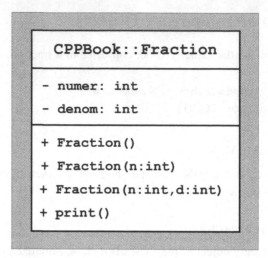

Figure 4.4. UML notation of the Fraction class

- The *members* of a class have *access restrictions*, denoted by the public and private keywords. The default access is private.

- Classes can have *data members* and *member functions*. Member functions typically form the public interface for the data members, which define the state of the object. However, private auxiliary functions may also exist. Member functions have access to all members of their class.

- *Constructors* are special member functions, called when objects of a class are created, in order to initialize these objects. They adopt the name of the class as their function name, and have neither a return value nor a return type.

- For every class, there is a predefined *default assignment operator*, which assigns memberwise.

- All functions must be declared with *parameter prototypes*.

- Functions can be *overloaded*. This means that the same function name may be used for different functions, provided they have differing parameter counts or types. A difference in return types only is not allowed.

- The *scope operator* '::' assigns the scope of a certain class to a symbol. This operator has the highest precedence.

- A structure is the same as a class in C++. The only difference (besides using the struct keyword instead of class) is that the default access for a struct is public. However, you should only use struct if you define a plain data structure (a composition of public values).

- A type that can be defined without certain C++ features is called a *POD* ("plain old data (type)").

- To model classes, the UML notation is usually used.

4.2   Operators for Classes

In C++, operators can be defined for classes. This enables fractions, for example, to be treated in the same way as other numbers:

```
CPPBook::Fraction a, b, c;
...
if (a < c) {
    c = a * b;
}
```

A new version of the fraction class is introduced in this section that enables operators to be used when working with fractions.

In addition, the `this` keyword is introduced. In a member function, `this` can be used to refer to the object for which the member function was called.

4.2.1   Declaring Operator Functions

We define three operators of the `Fraction` class to demonstrate the use of operators for classes:

- The operator `*`, used to multiply two fractions
- The operator `*=`, used for the multiplicative assignment of a fraction
- The operator `<`, used to see if one fraction is less than the other.

With the inclusion of these operators, the class structure of the `Fraction` class now looks as follows:

```
// classes/frac2.hpp

#ifndef FRACTION_HPP
#define FRACTION_HPP

// **** BEGIN namespace CPPBook ********************************
namespace CPPBook {

/* fraction class
 */
class Fraction {
  /* private: no access from outside
   */
  private:
    int numer;
    int denom;
```

```
/* public interface
 */
public:
    // default constructor
    Fraction();

    // constructor from int (denominator)
    Fraction(int);

    // constructor from two ints (numerator and denominator)
    Fraction(int, int);

    // output
    void print();

    // new: multiplication with other fraction
    Fraction operator * (Fraction);

    // new: multiplicative assignment
    Fraction operator *= (Fraction);

    // new: comparison with different fraction
    bool operator < (Fraction);
};


} // **** END namespace CPPBook ********************************

#endif      // FRACTION_HPP
```

The declarations for the operators have been added. These are declared using the `operator` keyword.

Note that although we added binary operators (operators that have two operands), they are declared with one parameter only. This is because, for operator functions of a class, as for all member functions, one object is passed implicitly when the operation is called. This is always the first operand, or in the case of a unary operator, the only operand. The parameter passed (explicitly) is therefore the *second* operand (if any).

It should be understood that in the declaration

```
class Fraction {
    ...
    Fraction operator * (Fraction);
    ...
};
```

the * operator is declared so that the first operand is a fraction (as the declaration takes place in the class Fraction), and that the second operand is also a fraction (as Fraction is used as parameter type). The Fraction before 'operator *' is the return type and indicates that a new fraction is returned as result.

The fact that only the second operand is explicitly passed as a parameter is the consequence of adopting the object-oriented approach, which says that every operation is merely a message to a recipient, which may have parameters. In the object-oriented world, the multiplication of two fractions is not globally understood; instead, the message 'compute the product with the passed fraction' is sent to an existing fraction. In C++, the message is the function, and the recipient of the message is the object for which the function is called. In other words,

```
a * b
```

is interpreted as

```
a.operator*(b)
```

We will see that, in fact, you can also use the second form to call the operator function.

Accordingly, the declaration

```
class Fraction {
    ...
    bool operator < (Fraction);
    ...
};
```

means that the < operator is declared so that both the first and second operands are fractions (as it is declared within the Fraction class and has Fraction as a parameter type). A Boolean value is returned.

As C++ is a format-free language, blank spaces can be omitted in the declarations of operator functions:

```
class Fraction {
    ...
    Fraction operator*(Fraction);
    bool operator<(Fraction);
    ...
};
```

Overloading Operators

Operators can also be overloaded. For example, the multiplication of a fraction can be declared with different types for the second operand:

```
class Fraction {
    ...
    // compute product, with Fraction as second operand
    Fraction operator * (Fraction);
```

```
      // compute product, with int as second operand
      Fraction operator * (int);
      ...
};
```

However, this is only possible if at least one operand is not a fundamental type. Operations where only fundamental types (`char`, `int`, `float`, etc.) are involved are predefined by C++ (as in C) and cannot be extended in this way.

4.2.2   Implementation of Operator Functions

Operator functions also have to be implemented. The first version of the `Fraction` class definition must therefore be extended to include the implementation of the operator functions:

```
// classes/frac2.cpp

// include header file with the class declaration
#include "frac.hpp"

// include standard header files
#include <iostream>
#include <cstdlib>

// **** BEGIN namespace CPPBook ****************************
namespace CPPBook {

/* default constructor
 */
Fraction::Fraction()
  : numer(0), denom(1)       // initialize fraction with 0
{
    // no further instructions
}


/* constructor for integer
 */
Fraction::Fraction(int n)
  : numer(n), denom(1)       // initialize fraction with n
{
    // no further instructions
}
```

```cpp
/* constructor for numerator and denominator
 */
Fraction::Fraction(int n, int d)
{
    // 0 is not allowed as a denomiator
    if (d == 0) {
        // exit program with error message
        std::cerr << "error: denominator is 0" << std::endl;
        std::exit(EXIT_FAILURE);
    }

    /* new: move a negative sign of the denominator to the numerator
     * this prevents, among other things, special treatment with the operator <
     */
    if (d < 0) {
        numer = -n;
        denom = -d;
    }
    else {
        numer = n;
        denom = d;
    }
}

/* print
 */
void Fraction::print()
{
    std::cout << numer << '/' << denom << std::endl;
}

/* new: operator *
 */
Fraction Fraction::operator * (Fraction f)
{
    /* simply multiply numerator and denominator
     * - this is quicker
     */
    return Fraction(numer * f.numer, denom * f.denom);
}
```

```
/* new: operator *=
 */
Fraction Fraction::operator *= (Fraction f)
{
      // 'x *= y' => 'x = x * y'
      *this = *this * f;

      // return object for which the operation was called (first operand)
      return *this;
}

/* new: operator <
 */
bool Fraction::operator< (Fraction f)
{
      /* simply mulitply inequality by numerator
       * - since the numerator cannot be negative, the comparison cannot be reversed
       */
      return numer * f.denom < f.numer * denom;
}

} // **** END namespace CPPBook ********************************
```

As mentioned before, for all three operators, two fractions are involved because binary operators are defined. By qualifying them for the Fraction class using the scope operator (Fraction::), it is determined that the operator function is called for a fraction as the first operand. The Fraction parameter type determines the type of the second operand.

Thus, the first operator is available automatically because the function is called for it. This means that its members can be addressed directly. Therefore, using numer and denom, you can access data members of the first operand. Every other numerator and denominator must be accessed by qualifying the name of the appropriate object. Thus the numerator and the denominator of the second operand are accessed using the name of the parameter, i.e. f.numer and f.denom.

Note that this means that private access is interpreted type-wise, and not object-wise, in C++. In a member function, you not only have access to the object for which the function was called, but also for any other object that has the same type. Other object-oriented languages such as Smalltalk handle this differently, and allow access to objects other than the one for which the function was called via the public interface only.

Detailed discussions of the implementation of each of the three operator functions follow.

Multiplication Using the * Operator

The * operator multiplies a fraction object by another fraction object. The first operand is the object for which the operation is called, and the second operand is passed as a parameter. The resulting fraction is returned. Its value has the product of both numerators and denominators as numerator and denominator, respectively. Reduction is not performed.

As a first attempt, the function might be implemented as follows:

```
Fraction Fraction::operator * (Fraction f)
{
    Fraction result;            // create fraction result

    // assign products of numerators and denominators
    result.numer = numer * f.numer;
    result.denom = denom * f.denom;

    // return result
    return result;
}
```

This implementation will work fine. However, it has a running-time disadvantage: an additional local `result` fraction object is used unnecessarily. This object will have to be created and then destroyed. In addition, the default constructor for `result` is called when it gets defined. This constructor initializes the object 'incorrectly' with $0/1$. The 'correct' value is assigned afterwards.

In the actual implementation,

```
Fraction Fraction::operator * (Fraction f)
{
    return Fraction(numer * f.numer, denom * f.denom);
}
```

the 'incorrect' initialization of the local object is omitted. A new temporary fraction is created instead, which is also used directly as the return value.

This avoidance of the unnecessary creation of objects may save a considerable amount of time. It would not be noticeable if you were to just multiply two fractions together, but would become apparent if you were to perform the operation thousands of times. Note that you are providing the implementation of a class that may well be used a lot in commercial code. Thus you should definitely take time to consider code optimizations of the kind highlighted above. However, always remember that performance is only one aspect of quality of code. Readability is another.

Comparisons Using the < Operator

The < comparison operator determines whether the fraction for which the operation was called (i.e. the first operand) is smaller than the passed parameter (i.e. the second operand). At this point, we face a minor pitfall: To be able to do the computation as pure integer computation we may reformulate the computation by multiplying the inequalities with both denominators. However, for inequalities, comparison signs must be reversed when multiplied by a negative value. The following rule applies:

$$\frac{a}{b} < \frac{c}{d} \Leftrightarrow \begin{cases} a*d < c*b & \text{if } b \text{ and } d \text{ are of the same sign} \\ a*d > c*b & \text{if } b \text{ and } d \text{ have different signs} \end{cases}$$

Therefore, the implementation of the operation should differentiate between the two cases:

```
bool Fraction::operator < (Fraction f)
{
    if (denom * b.denom > 0) {
        // multiplication by the denominators is OK
        return numer * f.denom < f.numer * denom;
    }
    else {
        // multiplication by the denominators reverses the comparison
        return numer * f.denom > f.numer * denom;
    }
}
```

However, this check can be avoided altogether by ensuring that the denominator of a fraction is never negative. This is possible because all operations for fractions, including the initialization of new fractions, are under our control.

The only place where a fraction with a negative denominator can exist (namely in the `int/int` constructor) is therefore rewritten, so that the negative sign is shifted from denominator to numerator:

```
Fraction::Fraction(int n, int d)
{
    if (d < 0) {
        numer = -n;
        denom = -d;
    }
    else {
        numer = n;
        denom = d;
    }
    ...
}
```

The reversal of the comparison if the denominator is negative can therefore be omitted, and the comparison operator can then be implemented as follows:

```
bool Fraction::operator < (Fraction f)
{
    return numer * f.denom < f.numer * denom;
}
```

This is a good example of the advantage of data encapsulation: provided the interface is not changed, the internal management of a fraction in the class can be implemented and optimized in different ways. If the user of a fraction has direct access to the numer and denom members, this would not be possible.

Multiplicative Assignment Using the *= Operator

C++ has numerous assignment operators. In addition to the ordinary assignment with the = operator, there are value-changing assignments of the form +=, *=, and so on (see Section 3.2.3 on page 37). These value-changing assignments can also be defined for classes.

There is no default behavior that when an operator * is defined, the corresponding operator *= is also defined. In contrast, the programmer of a class must alsways define all operators (except the assignment operator) himself, and it is also up to the programmer to ensure that the usual rules of operators for fundamental types apply:

x *op*= y   corresponds to   x = x *op* y

In other words, there is no guarantee that this analogy is valid for non-fundamental types. However, if this does not apply to a class, it definitely contradicts the purpose of readable code and intuitive interfaces.

On the basis of these initial thoughts, we can now look at the implementation of the multiplicative assignment. It is implemented as though it contains a multiplication with an assignment:

```
Fraction Fraction::operator *= (Fraction f)
{
    // 'x *= y' ==> 'x = x * y'
    *this = *this * f;

    // return object for which the operation was called (first operand)
    return *this;
}
```

Here, the this keyword is used. In all member functions, *this denotes the object for which the function or operation was called.

In every member function, this is automatically defined as a *pointer* to the object for which the function is called (pointers are introduced in Section 3.7.1 on page 104). The expression

*this

dereferences this pointer and returns the object to which it was pointing. The whole expression therefore represents the object for which the member function was called. In an operator function, *this thus describes the first operand. So, if the operation

x *= y

is called, then *this denotes the first operand x, while the second operand y is submitted as the parameter f.

*this is also used in the return statement at the end of the operation. This means that the *= operation returns the object to which the new value was assigned as a return value. A call such as

```
x *= y
```

is not an entirely closed statement, but returns something, and can therefore be part of a larger expression. For example, we can formulate the condition

```
if ((x *= 2) < 10)        // tests if x is less than 10 after duplication
```

The fact that the object for which the statement was called is then returned is a property that applies to all fundamental types in C++, as well as in C. This is used mainly by the assignment operator, making expressions like

```
x = y = 10;                    // assigns the value 10 to y, and then y (i.e. 10) to x
```

or

```
// assigns return value from fopen() to fp and then tests for NULL
if ((fp = fopen(... )) != NULL) {
    ...
}
```

possible.

The default assignment operators of classes also return the object to which something is assigned. This can be used to implement the *= operator more concisely:

```
Fraction Fraction::operator *= (Fraction f)
{
    // 'x *= y' ==> 'x = x * y' and x returned
    return  *this = *this * f;
}
```

The readability of such expressions can, of course, be scrutinized. For some people, this is the elegance of C++; for others, it is the ugliness.

Anyway, in C++, the programmer is able to define whether the object should be returned by the assignment operator or not, and thus controls the elegance, or ugliness, of the code.

If you are undecided, you can simply define the multiplicative assignment so that no return value is defined:

```
void Fraction::operator *= (Fraction f)
{
    // 'x *= y' ==> 'x = x * y'
    *this = *this * f;
}
```

However, this is rather unusual in C++. Users of this class would usually assume that assignment operators can form part of a larger expression.

Running Time versus Consistency

In the version introduced above, the *= operator is implemented so that it uses the = and * operators. It is therefore guaranteed that the statement 'x *= a' always does the same as the statement 'x = x * a'. However, this implementation has a possible running-time disadvantage: another function for multiplication is called that creates a temporary object for the return value, which can then be assigned.

The semantics of the operator can also be directly implemented:

```
Fraction Fraction::operator *= (Fraction f)
{
    // numerator and denominator multiplied directly
    numer *= f.numer;
    denom *= f.denom;

    // return object for which the operation was called
    return *this;
}
```

However, this may lead to inconsistencies. If the definition of multiplication is changed (for example, because it is reduced), the definition of this operation must also be changed.

Both implementation methods are feasible, and both have their advantages and disadvantages. In practice, the risk of inconsistency has to be weighed up against the running-time considerations. This kind of trade-off frequently occurs in the design of classes (and software in general).

However, if you decide to implement the operator directly, you must ensure that the multiplicative assignment corresponds to the assignment of the multiplication. This includes the fact that the *= operator changes the value of the object for which it is called. The * operator does not do this.

4.2.3   Using Operator Functions

Now that it is possible to multiply and compare fractions, we can modify our application program accordingly. The following program shows one possible use of the new version of the Fraction class:

```
// classes/ftest2.cpp

// include header files for the classes that are being used
#include "frac.hpp"

int main()
{
    CPPBook::Fraction x;              // declare fraction x
    CPPBook::Fraction w(7,3);         // declare fraction w
```

```
// output fraction w
w.print();

// x assign the square of w
x = w * w;

// as long as x is less than 1000
while (x < CPPBook::Fraction(1000)) {

    // multiply x by a
    x *= w;

    // and output
    x.print();
}
}
```

Using the statement

```
x = w * w;
```

fraction x is assigned the square of fraction w.

There are two operations:

- First of all, the * operation is called, with two fractions (both w) as operands. The operation returns a new temporary fraction as a result.
- This returned fraction is then assigned to the fraction x. The default assignment operator is used again in this case, which assigns member-wise.

The operator notation is merely a simple means of calling operator functions as they are declared. In fact, the following call is made:

```
x.operator = (w.operator * (w));        // corresponds to: x = w * w;
```

For w, the operator* member function is called using w as a parameter. Therefore, in accordance with the principles of object-oriented programming, the first operand is the object that is the recipient of a request for an operation that passes the second operand as a parameter. The product is therefore not globally created from two values. Instead, it is left to the first operand to calculate and return the product of itself and the passed operand. The result is used as a parameter, which is passed when operator= is called for the object x. We therefore use x, with the request to take on the value of the second operand passed as a parameter.

The notation with the explicit writing of the keyword operator can also be used to call operator functions in C++ programs. Thus, writing

```
x.operator = (w.operator * (w));        // corresponds to: x = w * w;
```

is valid code. You can consider the fact that you can write w * w instead of w.operator * (w) as a 'convenience feature' for the programmer because he is familiar with this syntax.

4.2.4 Global Operator Functions

As with other functions, operator functions do not have to be defined in the object-oriented way (i.e. as members of a class). They can also be defined as global functions. If the compiler comes across the statement

```
x * y
```

there are two ways this could be interpreted:

- As a procedural interpretation, i.e. operator * (x,y).
- As an object-oriented interpretation, i.e. x.operator * (y).

The object-oriented interpretation has the advantage that it directly belongs to a class, and therefore has access to private members of x and y (provided that y belongs to the same class).

The procedural interpretation does not belong to a class. In this case, the first or only operand is *not* the object for which the operation is called. Instead, all operators are parameters. this is therefore not defined within the operator function.

As these kinds of operator-function implementation do not belong to a class, they can be provided as 'auxiliary functions' later on by the application programmer. For example, the following operator function might be defined by the user of the Fraction class as an addition:

```
/* product of int with Fraction
 * - globally defined
 */
CPPBook::Fraction operator * (int i, CPPBook::Fraction f)
{
    return CPPBook::Fraction(i) * f;
}
```

As this is *not* a member function (because there is no Fraction:: in front of operator), both operands must be given as parameters. Thus this is a binary * operation, defining multiplication of an integer (the first operand) and a fraction (the second operand).

As the operation does not belong to the Fraction class, there is no access to private members of the second operand. Therefore, the numerator of f cannot easily be multiplied by i. Instead, the first operand i is converted into a fraction, and the operand defined for the multiplication of two fractions in the Fraction class is called.

Another example is shown by the following definition:

```
/* negation
 * - globally defined
 */
CPPBook::Fraction operator - (CPPBook::Fraction f)
{
    return f * CPPBook::Fraction(-1);
}
```

As this is also *not* a member function (i.e. `Fraction::` is missing), the given parameter is the only operand. Therefore, we define a unary operator for -, namely negation, rather than a binary subtraction.

Again, as this operation does not belong to a class, there is no access to the private members of the operand. The numerator of `f` cannot simply be multiplied by -1. Therefore, the integer -1 is converted into a fraction, which is then multiplied by `f`.

Both globally defined operators could be used, for example, as follows:

```
CPPBook::Fraction x, y;
...
y = 3 * -x;
```

The fraction `x` is negated with the globally defined negation, and the result is then multiplied by the integer 3 using the globally defined multiplication operator. This result is then assigned to the fraction `y` using the predefined assignment operator of the `Fraction` class.

4.2.5   Limitations in Defining Operators

The examples displayed up to this point demonstrate the possibilities for defining operators. However, there are limitations. For example, it is not possible to define all C++ operators for custom classes.

When defining operators, the following rules apply:

- The collection of available operators is predetermined and cannot be extended. For example, it is not possible to define a new operator '`**`' for exponentiating.

  There are many reasons for this limitation. First, it simplifies the work of compilers. Second, handling additional rules for determining the priority, etc., of new operators (which is not a trivial task) is avoided.

- The priority, syntax and evaluation order of the operators are fixed and cannot be changed. Multiplication always has a higher priority than addition, and these operators are evaluated from left to right. A unary operator for = cannot be defined.

  This is a great advantage because it makes the program code readable even if user-defined operators are involved. Compiler requirements are also simplified.

- The operations predefined for fundamental types are not automatically transferred to abstract types. For example, by defining multiplication and assignment, the `*=` operator is not automatically defined, but must be defined explicitly, as shown in the example of the `Fraction` class.

  This means that the default property '`x *= a` equals `x = x * a`', which applies to fundamental types, does not automatically apply to classes because operators can be implemented differently. However, this should be avoided at all costs for reasons of readability.

- The operators for the fundamental types (`int`, `char`, pointer etc.) are predetermined and can neither be redefined nor extended. However, the combination of an abstract type and a fundamental type can easily be defined with the limitations given here, using a global function or a member function.

- The following operators and all cast operators cannot be overloaded:

```
.
::
sizeof
.*
?:
```

Overloading them is mainly not permitted because the operators already have a predefined meaning for all objects, which serves as a fundamental base for the whole syntax of C++. For the ?: operator, overloading is not considered to be worthwhile (?: is the only ternary operator).

The .* operator is introduced in Section 9.4 on page 557.

On page 569 there is a list of all the C++ operators.

4.2.6 Special Features of Certain Operators

Some special operators have unusual features, as shown below.

The Assignment Operator =

A default assignment operator is defined for every class. It assigns member-wise and returns the object to which the new value is assigned. If the default behavior does not make sense for a user-defined class, an assignment operator can (and should) be defined.

If no assignment is possible, the assignment operator should be declared `private`. For example, the following declaration will make an assignment impossible for two fractions [3]:

```
class Fraction {
    ...
  private:
      // assignment forbidden, as operator is declared private
      Fraction operator = (Fraction);
};
```

Because a member-wise assignment is usually a problem for classes with pointers as members, the assignment operator must be defined for such classes. Detailed informations and examples of this can be found in Section 6.1.5 on page 362.

---

[3] The assignment operator should actually be defined with a slightly different syntax; however, the necessary language feature, a *reference*, is not introduced yet. The correct syntax can be found in Section 6.1.5 on page 362.

Increment and Decrement Operators

The unary increment and decrement operators ++ and -- have both a prefix and a postfix notation (see also Section 3.2.3 on page 39). In the prefix notation

    ++x

for fundamental types, the expression ++x returns the value of x *after* the incrementing it (i.e. the value is increased, then returned). In the postfix notation

    x++

for fundamental types, the expression x++ returns the value x has *before* it is incremented (i.e. the value is returned, then increased).

For example, this difference is often used when accessing elements of an array:

    x = elems[i++];

In this statement, the index i is incremented, but x gets the value of the element with the index i has *before* it is incremented.

This distinction can also be implemented for classes. As both involve unary operators, the differentiation is determined by declaring a dummy parameter to the declaration of the postfix operator, while the prefix version has no such parameter. For example, the following declarations define a prefix and a postfix increment operator for class X:

    class X {
        ...
      public:
        operator ++ ();   // prefix notation, called for ++x
        operator ++ (int);   // postfix notation, called for x++
    };

Again, it is up to the programmer to ensure that the operators behave as expected. That is, both increment an object (whatever this means), while the first returns the value of the object before it is incremented and the second returns the object after it was incremented.

The same applies to the decrement operator.

The Index Operator [ ]

The *index operator*, [ ] (sometimes also called the *array operator* or *subscription operator*), can also be defined for classes. This gives objects array-like characteristics, even though they may not be arrays. Such objects then receive array characters.

The index operator is a binary operator, in which the index passed is the second operand. For member functions, the index is therefore passed as parameter.

Typical examples of the implementation of index operators are collection classes, in which the *i*th member can be accessed using operator [ ]. One example application is the standard vector class (see Section 3.5.1 on page 71). As another example, the following declaration defines operator [ ] for a class whose concrete objects (instances) are members of a collection of Persons:

```
class CollOfPersons {
   ...
   public:
      // return idxth member from the collection (a person)
      Person operator [] (int idx);
   ...
};
```

A person of an CollOfPersons can then be accessed as follows:

```
void foo (CollOfPersons allEmployees)
{
    Person p;

    // assign first member of the collection allEmployees to p
    p = allEmployees[0];
    ...
}
```

Note that the parameter of the index operator can have an arbitrary type. Because of overloading, the operator can even be implemented differently for different index types. So-called *associative arrays* can be implemented in this way. For example, when accessing the collection of Persons using the [ ] operator, it is also possible to pass the name of the person as an index rather than an integer. To be able to do this, we can declare the operators as follows:

```
class CollOfPersons {
   ...
   public:
      // return ith member of the collection (a person)
      Person operator [] (int i);

      // return member of the collection that has the passed name
      Person operator [] (std::string name);
   ...
};
```

The following call can then be made:

```
void foo (CollOfPersons allEmployees)
{
    Person p;

    // assign element 'nico' of collection allEmployees to person p
    p = allEmployees["nico"];
    ...
}
```

In Section 6.2.1 on page 373, an additional example of the definition of an index operator is given.

The Pointer Operators * and ->

Just as it can be useful to define objects that behave like arrays, it can also be useful to define objects that behave like pointers. As the semantics of the operations can be defined freely, pointer-like objects can be assigned a certain degree of intelligence. For this reason, such objects will be called *smart pointers*. This will be discussed in more detail in Section 9.2.1 on page 536.

The Call Operator ()

The function call is also an operator, which can be defined for classes. By doing this, we can let objects behave like functions. This sounds strange, I know, but can be useful.

Its declaration looks as follows:

```
class X {
  ...
  public:
    void operator () ();     // declare operator () without parameters
}
```

This kind of declaration enables the following call to be made:

```
X a;        // create object a of class X

a();        // no, not calling function a(), but
            // calling operation () for object a
```

It looks as though a global function a() is called, but, in fact, a[] is the call of operator () for object a.

This is probably so confusing that it does not seem worth defining at all. However, it can sometimes be useful to define objects that behave like functions. These kind of objects are called *function objects*, or *functors*. They are also used in the C++ standard library. This is discussed in Section 9.2.2 on page 540.

4.2.7   Summary

- *Operators* can be defined for objects of a class. They are declared as *operator functions* with the keyword `operator`.
- Operators can be *overloaded* for classes.
- The collection of possible operators, their priority, syntax and evaluation order, is predefined and cannot be changed.
- Operators should always be implemented so that they perform in a way that you would expect. This usually corresponds to how they behave for fundamental types.

For example, if operators are defined for classes, the following relationships should apply:

x + y	neither changes x nor y		
x - y	corresponds to x + (-y)		
x *op=* y	corresponds to x = x *op* y		
x = x + 1	corresponds to x += 1	corresponds to ++x	
p->k	corresponds to (*p).k	corresponds to p[0]	

- In an member function, `this` describes a pointer to the object for which the function was called. `*this` is therefore always the (dereferenced) object for which a member function was called. In the case of operators defined as member functions, `this` is the first or only operand.

A list of all C++ operators can be found on page 569.

4.3 Running Time and Code Optimization

In previous sections, it has been shown how a class can be implemented to meet specific requirements (creation, multiplication, outputting, etc.). The 'what' (i.e. *what service does a class provide?*) was the main reason for the considerations that led to the first versions. In this and the following sections, we will discuss the 'how' (i.e. *how is the class implemented in order to provide its service?*).

There was one aspect which played a significant role in the distribution of C: performance. In C++, performance still has a high priority. There are some language features that are not required from an object-oriented point of view, and whose only function is to improve performance. Their use might even contradict object-oriented concepts.

In this section, we will discuss inline functions and declarations in blocks, and how their use can lead to improved performance. Another language feature that considerably improves running time is then introduced in Section 4.4 on page 181: references.

Default arguments and `using` statements will also be introduced in this section. However, both language features are used less to improve performance (rather the opposite), and more to reduce source code.

4.3.1 The `Fraction` Class with Initial Optimizations

The following things have changed in the latest version of the `Fraction` class:

- The three constructors are combined into one function that uses default arguments for the numerator and denominator.
- Two functions (`print()` and `operator*()`) are implemented as *inline functions* in the header file. By doing this, the compiler can and is indicated to generate code that substitutes a function call by the statements of the function called. This can save running time because function calls are time-consuming and for short functions the replacement of the call by the function body means no space overhead.
- As there are no name conflicts, all symbols of the `CPPBook` namespace are defined globally. This means that `CPPBook::` does not have to be entered every time.

Header File

The header file for the `Fraction` class with the new language features is as follows:

```
// classes/frac3.hpp

#ifndef FRACTION_HPP
#define FRACTION_HPP

// include standard header files
#include <iostream>
```

```
// **** BEGIN namespace CPPBook ******************************
namespace CPPBook {

/* Fraction class
 */
class Fraction {

  private:
    int numer;
    int denom;

  public:
    /* new: default constructor and one- and two-parameter
     * constructors combined into the one function
     */
    Fraction(int = 0, int = 1);

    /* output
     * - new: defined inline
     */
    void print() {
        std::cout << numer << '/' << denom << std::endl;
    }

    // multiplication
    Fraction operator * (Fraction);

    // multiplicative assignment
    Fraction operator *= (Fraction);

    // comparison
    bool operator < (Fraction);
};

/* operator *
 * - new: defined inline
 */
inline Fraction Fraction::operator * (Fraction f)
{
    /* simply multiply numerator and denominator
     * - no reducing yet
```

```
        */
        return Fraction(numer * f.numer, denom * f.denom);
}

} // **** END namespace CPPBook ******************************

#endif      // FRACTION_HPP
```

Before discussing the changes in detail, we give the new dot-C file.

Dot-C File

According to the changes in the header file, the dot-C file of the Fraction class now only has one constructor. In addition, the definition of the two inline operations are omitted:

```
// classes/frac3.cpp

// include header file of the class
#include "frac.hpp"

// include standard header files
#include <cstdlib>

// **** BEGIN namespace CPPBook ******************************
namespace CPPBook {

/* new: default constructor and one- and two-parameter
 * constructors combined into the one function
 * - default for n: 0
 * - default for d: 1
 */
Fraction::Fraction(int n, int d)
{
    /* initialize numerator and denominator as passed
     * - 0 is not allowed as a denominator
     * - move negative sign of the denominator (if present) to the numerator
     */
    if (d == 0) {
        // exit program with error message
        std::cerr << "error: denominator is 0" << std::endl;
        std::exit(EXIT_FAILURE);
    }
    if (d < 0) {
        numer = -n;
```

```
            denom = -d;
        }
        else {
            numer = n;
            denom = d;
        }
}


/* operator *=
 */
Fraction Fraction::operator *= (Fraction f)
{
        // 'x *= y' ==> 'x = x * y'
        *this = *this * f;

        // object (first operand) is returned
        return *this;
}


/* operator <
 */
bool Fraction::operator < (Fraction f)
{
        // since the numerator cannot be negative, the following is sufficient:
        return numer * f.denom < f.numer * denom;
}


} // **** END namespace CPPBook *******************************
```

The changes of the Fraction class are explained in the following sections.

4.3.2 Default Arguments

In the new version of the Fraction class, the three constructors that have been used until now
are combined into one function. If the second parameter (the denominator) is not passed, the
default value of 1 is used; if the first parameter (the numerator) is not passed, 0 is used:

```
class Fraction {
    ...
    Fraction(int = 0, int = 1);
    ...
};
```

The default value is automatically provided by the compiler if too few parameters are passed. As this happens during the call, the origin of the parameters is irrelevant in the implementation of the function. The implementation therefore declares both parameters with no default values:

```
Fraction::Fraction(int n, int d)
{
    ...
}
```

In order to ensure a clear assignment, default values may only be defined at the end of a parameter list. On a function call, the passed arguments are assigned to the leading parameters in the same order. Thus the first argument becomes the first parameter, and so on. If all arguments are exhausted, the remaining parameters are assigned their default values. It is therefore clearly defined that if only one argument is passed, it is always the first parameter.

Global functions can also have default values. For example, the following global function, `max()`, returns the maximum of two, three or four unsigned integers:

```
unsigned max(unsigned, unsigned, unsigned = 0, unsigned = 0);
```

When calling the function with two arguments, the default value 0 is used for the final two parameters.

When using default arguments, you must ensure that a blank space is placed before the assignment operator if it is a parameter or a pointer:

```
void f(const char* = "hello");        // OK
```

Otherwise, it is assumed that the `*=` operator is used, which is an error:

```
void f(const char*= "hello");        // ERROR
```

Default arguments cannot be redefined in a second declaration. It is also not possible to use default arguments with operator functions.

It should be noted that the type of a function is not affected by some parameters having default values. A pointer to the `max()` function must be declared as a pointer to a function that has four `unsigned`s passed to it:

```
unsigned (* funcpointer)(unsigned, unsigned, unsigned, unsigned);
```

To use default values here, you must again define them:

```
unsigned (* funcpointer)(unsigned, unsigned,
                         unsigned = 0, unsigned = 0);
```

If a function can also be called via a function pointer, different default values can be used. However, you should never do this. If calling `max()` directly with two parameters leads to a different result than if it is called via a function pointer, this will be very confusing.

Default Arguments Can Increase Running Time

One issue should be taken into account: default arguments combine multiple functions, reduce program code and improve consistency (changes must only be carried out at one place). However, running time can be prolonged by using default arguments. For example, if the `max()`

function for two, three or four arguments is called with only two arguments, all four parameters are compared.

The new version of the Fraction class provides an example of this. If the constructor is called with less than two arguments, the default value for the denominator is set to 1. However, inside the function, it is checked (unnecessarily) whether 0 is negative. To avoid this kind of running-time cost, only two constructors of the Fraction class need be combined:

```
class Fraction {
    ...
    public:
        /* default constructor and one-parameter constructor combined
         * - defined as an inline function
         */
        Fraction(int n = 0)
          : numer(n), denom(1)
        {
        }

        /* two-parameter constructor
         * - with special treatment for denominator less than zero
         */
        Fraction(int, int);
        ...
};
```

4.3.3 Inline Functions

Functions can be declared as being *inline*. The inline specifier indicates that inline substitution of the function body at the point of call is preferred over the usual function call mechanism. That is, a function call may be replaced by the statements of the called function body without changing the semantics. To be able to do this, the function body needs to be known when the function is called. Therefore, the whole function is implemented in the header file.

Inline functions can be defined in two different ways:

- Either the function is defined in the header file with the inline keyword:

```
class Fraction {
    ...
    bool operator < (Fraction);
};

inline bool Fraction::operator < (Fraction f)
{
    return numer * f.denom < f.numer * denom;
}
```

- Or the function is directly implemented in the class structure:

```
class Fraction{
    ...
    void print() {
        std::cout << numer << '/' << denom << std::endl;
    }
    ...
};
```

In both cases, the compiler is given the ability of generating code to execute the statements directly, instead of generating a function call. Thus, a call such as

```
b.print()
```

can be translated into

```
std::cout << b.numer << '/' << b.denom << std::endl;
```

by the compiler, as it knows that this has the same semantics.

Inline functions replace the usual macros in C and have an important advantage: inline functions are not 'blind' text replacements. From the point of view of semantics, they are no different from normal functions. As with functions, a type checking occurs and the same scopes exist. There are no side effects caused by a missing bracket or by a double substitution of a parameter such as n++. As far as the semantics of a program are concerned, it makes no difference whether functions are declared inline or not. Only running time is influenced.

However, the compiler has the last word. Every compiler is free to generate inline functions in a non-inline way, or to generate non-inline functions inline. A good compiler can decide whether it is worth generating code for a function call that carries out the call, or to execute the statements of the function directly. This can often be influenced by compiler options.

In order to carry out a substitution, the implementation of the function must be known when the function call is compiled. Inline functions that are used in more than one source file must therefore be implemented in the header file. This explains why it is necessary to have the inline keyword: It prevents an error being raised that says that a function is defined multiple times in different translation units.

However, the implementation of inline functions in header files also has its disadvantages. For example, as inline functions are part of a header file, it is easy to see and manipulate their implementation. This is not possible for an implementation that is part of a compiled object file. The running-time advantage in C++ may be at the expense of the strict adherence of object-oriented concepts. From a purely object-oriented point of view, placing implementation details in the class specification is questionable. This is an issue that always leads to intense discussions. For some people, C++ disqualifies itself as an object-oriented language by allowing such behavior; for others, the ability to directly affect the running time is one of the things that makes C++ so powerful.

4.3.4 Optimizations from the User's Point of View

The changes to the implementation of the Fraction class introduced in this chapter are not relevant to an application program. The interface does not change. As an example application program, the version introduced on page 159 can still be used.

Nevertheless, a slightly modified application program will be introduced here, showing the facility for making declarations within blocks, and only having to mention a namespace once:

```
// classes/ftest3.cpp

// include header files for the classes that are being used
#include "frac.hpp"

int main()
{
    using namespace CPPBook;    // new: all symbols of the namespace CPPBook
                                //      are considered global in this scope

    Fraction w(7,3);           // declare fraction w

    w.print();                 // output fraction w

    // new: declare and initialize x with the square of w
    Fraction x = w*w;

    // as long as x is less than 1000
    while (x < Fraction(1000)) {
        // multipy x by w and output result
        x *= w;
        x.print();
    }
}
```

4.3.5 Using Statements

Namespaces are introduced in order to avoid name conflicts, and to make it clear that a set of symbols belong together. These symbols can also be defined in different files. However, the repetitive statements of the namespace can be avoided with the using keyword. There are two options:

- A *using declaration.*
- A *using directive.*

Using Declarations

A symbol of a namespace can be accessed *locally* by using a *using declaration*. The statement

```
using CPPBook::Fraction;
```

causes Fraction to become a local synonym for CPPBook::Fraction in the current scope.

These declarations correspond to a declaration of local variables, and can also hide global variables. For example:

```
namespace N {                // namespace N
    int x, y, z;
}


int z;                       // global z


void usingDeclarations()
{
    int y = 0;
    using N::x;              // symbol x of namespace N is locally accessible
    using N::y;              // ERROR: y is declared twice in usingDeclarations()
    using N::z;              // hides global z


    ++x;                    // N::x
    ++z;                    // N::z
}
```

Using Directives

A using directive enables all names of a namespace to be accessed without qualification. Throughout the current scope, all symbols in that namespace are considered to be defined globally. This might cause ambiguities with existing global symbols. If the

```
using namespace CPPBook;
```

directive is used, all symbols of the CPPBook namespace will be considered as global variables in the current scope.

If there is already a symbol in the global scope, which is also in the global namespace, its usage causes an error. For example:

```
namespace N {                // namespace N
    int x, y, z;
}


int z;                       // global z
```

```
void usingDirective()
{
    int y = 0;
    using namespace N;      // symbols of namespace N globally accessible
    ++x;                    // N::x
    ++y;                    // local y
    ++z;                    // ERROR: N::z or global z?
}
```

Using directives should never be used in a context where it is not clear what symbols are known. Otherwise, a using directive can change the visibility of other symbols, leading to ambiguity and different behavior (a function call suddenly finds a completely different function than it did without the directive). Using directives should therefore be used with caution. In fact, they should never be part of a header file.

Koenig Lookup

Without the use of using, it is not always necessary to enter the namespace of a symbol. Provided an operation with arguments is called, the operation is also searched for in all namespaces of the arguments passed. This is commonly known as *Koenig lookup*. For example:

```
#include "frac.hpp"

// definition of a function in the namespace CPPBook
namespace CPPBook {
    void auxiliaryFunction(Fraction);
}
...

CPPBook::Fraction x;
...
auxiliaryFunction(x);      // OK, CPPBook::auxiliaryFunction() is found
```

4.3.6 Declarations Between Statements

In the new version of the application program, it should be noted that the definition of x does not occur at the beginning, but in the middle of the block, after some statements have been carried out:

```
w.print();              // statement

Fraction x = w*w;       // declaration with initialization
```

In C++, variables may be declared anywhere in a block. Its scope then covers the declaration up to the end of the block.

This feature was introduced to avoid variables having to be declared at a time when they cannot be initialized. If a parameter that has yet to be processed is needed to create an object, the declaration can be postponed until the appropriate statements have been carried out.

The alternative would be an 'incorrect' initialization, such as with the default constructor. The object may well be initialized, but would have to be corrected again later. This takes time with larger objects. In addition, classes can be defined for which you cannot modify the value once it is initialized. For these objects, it should be possible to create them later when all initial values are prepared.

This freedom of point-of-declaration runs the risk of creating hard-to-read programs. The declaration of variables is no longer restricted to the beginning of blocks, but can occur anywhere in the code. For this reason, declarations after the beginning of a block should only be used if it is necessary or improves readability. They should always be done at the beginning of a logical section.

Declarations Inside the `for` Loop

One frequent application of declarations in the middle of the code are declarations inside a `for` loop. Values used to iterate over the loop are a typical example. You can define them just inside the head of a `for` loop:

```
for (int i=0; i<num; ++i) {
    ...
}
```

Here, `i` is only known within the `for` loop. A second loop with a further declaration of `i` would be valid. The `for` loop shown above is equivalent to the following implementation:

```
{ int i;
    for (i=0; i<num; ++i) {
        ...
    }
}
```

However, in practice, this kind of declaration presents another small problem: in older versions of C++, `i` declared as above would be known until the end of the block that contains the complete `for` loop. `i` would therefore still be declared after the `for` loop. The loop head was not considered to be part of the same block that contains the loop body. Therefore, a second `for` loop in the same block could not be implemented:

```
for (int i=0; i<num; ++i) {
    ...
}
...
for (int i=0; i<num; ++i) {        // ERROR: i defined for the second time
    ...
}
```

This behavior was corrected during the standardization of C++. In the conditions of if, switch, while and for statements, declarations can appear that are only valid for the scope of the statement. Thus, the whole statement can be considered to be a separate block.

Due to the relatively late standardization of the language, there are still systems in which i is declared after the loop. This should be taken into account when implementing portable code.

4.3.7   Copy Constructors

In the sample program, the fraction x is initialized with a temporary fraction, which is the result of the w*w operation:

```
Fraction w(7,3);

...

Fraction x = w*w;        // declaration and initialization of x
```

This notation for the initialization of x is equivalent to

```
Fraction x(w*w);         // declaration and initialization of x
```

and means that x is created and initialized with a fraction (the temporary result from w*w). When x is created, a constructor is called that uses a fraction as its parameter.

This kind of constructor, which creates an object with an existing object of the same type, is called a *copy constructor*, because, in principle, it creates a copy of an existing object. Like the assignment operator, this is also a function that does not have to be declared, as it is defined automatically for every class. The *default copy constructor* copies member-wise. Every member of the object to be created is initialized with the corresponding member of the object it is initialized with. If a member is an object of a class itself, then its copy constructor is called. In our example, the numerator and denominator of x are therefore initialized with the numerator and denominator of w*w.

However, member-wise copying for creating copies may not be suitable. This is typically the case when pointers are used as members. The copy constructor must therefore sometimes be defined for specific tasks. This will be discussed in Section 6.1.3 on page 360.

Copy Constructors and Assignments

In C++, there is a difference between a declaration with simultaneous initialization, and a declaration without initialization but with a later assignment.

The initializations

```
CPPBook::Fraction tmp;

...

CPPBook::Fraction x = tmp;     // copy constructor
```

and

```
CPPBook::Fraction tmp;

...

CPPBook::Fraction x(tmp);      // copy constructor
```

are different from the assignment

```
CPPBook::Fraction tmp;
...
CPPBook::Fraction x;            // default constructor
x = tmp;                        // assignment
```

In the first case, the copy constructor is called, while in the second case the default constructor is called, followed by the assignment operator.

In principle, x should have the same state after both ways of creation and initialization. However, as usual, this is up to the programmer to ensure this equivalence. Because constructors and assignment operators are implemented independently, their implementation can lead to different results. However, this should not usually be the case.

4.3.8 Summary

- *Default arguments* can be defined for the parameters of functions. These are used if the corresponding parameters in a function call are not passed.
- Functions and operator functions can be declared *inline*. This enables the compiler to replace a function call with the statements of the respective function. This has no effect on the semantics of a program, and is only used to reduce the running time.
- *Declarations* do not necessarily have to be made at the beginning of a block. In cases where a declaration is made in the middle of code, the scope starts from the declaration and lasts until the end of the block.
- A constructor that creates a new object using an existing object of the same type is called a *copy constructor*.
- There is a *default copy constructor* that copies member-wise.
- By using *using declarations* and *using directives*, the qualification of symbols with a namespace can be omitted.
- Using directives should *not* be used in header files.
- A function is also automatically searched for in the namespaces of any arguments passed.

4.4 References and Constants

This section discusses a new language feature of C++: *references*.

It must be made clear that references in C++ are not pointers (which are introduced in Section 3.7.1 on page 104). Both mechanisms enable variables to 'refer' to something. For this reason, th term *reference* is sometimes also used for pointers (especially in C because there was no language feature for references). Thus, in C++ we have to distinguish between a *pointer* and a *reference* (although both can *refer* to something).

References are an essential language feature, whose use can greatly improve running time. But there are also other reasons why their introduction into C++ was necessary.

4.4.1 Copy Constructors and Argument Passing

In C++, in general (if nothing else is indicated), a parameter is always a copy of the argument passed (the so-called *call-by-value* mechanism). This means that with every function call in which a fraction is passed, the copy constructor is automatically called. The same applies when passing a return value.

The call of the *= operator is an example of this. By using the expression

```
x *= w
```

which means the same as

```
x.operator *= (w)
```

a copy of w will be made, which is used as a parameter by the operator function. Consider the following implementation of the operator:

```
Fraction Fraction::operator *= (Fraction f)
       // b is a local copy of the second operand
       // and could be manipulated
{

       *this = *this * f;      // 'x *= y' => 'x = x * y'

       return *this;
       // a copy of the first operand is returned
}
```

The parameter f in the implementation of the operator function becomes a copy of w that is created using the predefined copy constructor of Fraction. Inside the operator function, f could be manipulated without any effect on the passed w argument.

In the same way, a *copy* of *this is returned by the function. Because in our example the operator function is called for x as first operand, a copy of x is returned as a temporary object. Again, this copy is created using the copy constructor.

If performance is an issue, creating copies is acceptable when creating simple types such as ints, floats and pointers. With objects with several fairly complex members, this can lead to a considerable running-time disadvantage because a copy of the object must be made with every parameter passed.

The usual alternative in C would be to pass pointers. Thus, instead of passing an object, the address of an object is passed. As a consequence, in order to access the passed object, you must dereference the pointer. An additional consequence is that any modification of the passed object now also modifies the actual object. The implementation with pointers then emulates the counterpart to *call-by-value*, this being *call-by-reference*.

If the running-time disadvantages, resulting from copies being created when arguments are passed, can only be dealt with by using pointers, it would no longer be possible to use abstract types in the same way as fundamental types. A multiplication of fractions could then only be declared with a pointer as a second operand. In the application program, a call for multiplication would have the following form, then:

```
x * &a              // multiply x by a (without copy)
```

To avoid this ugly syntax, references were introduced into C++. These enable arguments to be passed without making copies or using pointers. Thus, call-by-reference is supported.

There are now only two problems:

- As an object passed as an argument might get modified, you can no longer pass constants. This affects temporary objects that are constant.
- There is a danger of objects passed by reference being accidentally modified in the function called.

However, here we can benefit from the fact that objects (including parameters) may be declared as being constant. By declaration a parameter to be constant, you can specify that a passed argument is not modified, which implies that you can pass constant and temporary values, then.

4.4.2   References

A variable declared as a reference is merely a *second name* assigned *to an existing object*. A reference is declared using an additional &. For example, the following statement declares r as a reference (second name) for a:

```
int& r = x;          // r is a reference (second name) for x
```

Although the notation suggests to C programmers that this is a pointer, this is not the case. A reference is *not* a pointer. In fact, it has the same type as the object that it references. Its application does not differ from that of the object for which it defines a second name. After the above declarations, it is irrelevant whether r or x is used (as long as both are valid).

The declaration of a reference does not create a new object. Rather, it defines an alternative description for an existing object. The object for which it stands for must be given by the declaration, and cannot be changed.

The following example should clarify this:

```
int  x = 7;          // normal variable initialized with 7
int  y = 13;         // normal variable initialized with 13
int& r = x;          // reference (second name) for x
```

When the reference r is declared, it is initialized with x:

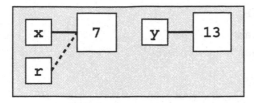

If r is now used, this has the same effect as if x is used:

    r = y;   // r *or* x *is assigned the value of* y

An assignment to r therefore corresponds to an assignment to x. In contrast to initialization, r is not assigned a new object, but a new value that also contains x:

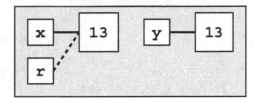

References as Parameters

If a reference is declared as a parameter, it will be initialized by a function call with the passed argument. Again, no new object is created, but a second name for the passed argument is defined. Every modification of the parameter inside the called function will therefore also be performed with the argument (the *call-by-reference* mechanism)[4].

For example, a function can be implemented that swaps two arguments:

```
// progs/swap.hpp

void swap (int& a, int& b)
{
    int tmp;

    tmp = a;
    a = b;
    b = tmp;
}
```

---

[4] Pascal programmers will already be familiar with references as parameters. Instead of &, they use the `var` keyword for the parameter declaration.

If you pass two integers to this function, their values are swapped:

```
// progs/swap.cpp

#include <iostream>
#include "swap.hpp"

int main()
{
    int x = 7;
    int y = 13;

    std::cout << "x: " << x                      // x: 7, y: 13
              << "  y: " << y << std::endl;

    swap (x, y);                                 // swaps values of x and y

    std::cout << "x: " << x                      // x: 13, y: 7
              << "  y: " << y << std::endl;
}
```

When swap() is called, a is defined as a second name for x, and b as a second name for y. An assignment to a therefore changes x, and an assignment to b changes y.

This kind of language feature has its advantages and disadvantages. For C programmers, who do not have this feature, this might be a pleasant dream or a nightmare, depending on their point of view:

- The advantage of references is that we are no longer forced to pass pointers as arguments if we want to modify objects or improve running time. For the function above, simply calling 'swap(x,y)' is sufficient for the values to be swapped. To achieve the same effect in C, 'swap(&x,&y)' has to be called, and the swap() function has to be implemented with pointers.

- The disadvantage of references is that, in C++, it is no longer clear at the point of the call whether the passed argument can be modified. In C, when 'swap(x,y)' is called, it is guaranteed that both arguments cannot be modified, as copies have been made in both cases. In C++, in order to know whether an argument can be manipulated within a function, you will have to look at the function declaration.

Note that it only depends on the parameter declaration whether or not copies are made. The statements inside the function use a and b as if they were defined as ordinary integers. In other words: references do not affect the type of variables and objects; they only affect whether copies are created.

Using References with Classes

In the Fraction class, for example, you should declare the *= operator function with references in order to prevent copies from being made:

```
Fraction& Fraction::operator *= (Fraction& f)
{
    // 'x *= y' => 'x = x * y'
    *this = *this * f;

    // object (first operand) is returned
    return *this;
}
```

By declaring f as a reference, f is no longer a copy of the second operand, but a second name for it.

The return value is now also a reference. Thus we return a second name instead of a copy of it. As we return the first operand, we therefore return the original first operand instead of a copy of it.

Note that the statements inside the function have not been changed. Anyone who initially has difficulties when reading the declaration should simply imagine that the characters for the reference declaration & were not written.

4.4.3 Constants

References as Constants

There is still one problem with the *= operator function: as the value of the submitted parameters can be modified inside the function, we must pass an object for which this is allowed. However, this rules out both constants and temporary objects. A call such as

```
x *= CPPBook::Fraction(2,3);
```

or

```
x *= w * w;
```

would not be possible. For this reason, a parameter passed as a reference should be declared as a constant if it is not to be changed.

This leads to the following definition of the *= operator:

```
Fraction& Fraction::operator *= (const Fraction& f)
{
    // 'x *= y' => 'x = x * y'
    *this = *this * f;

    // object (first operand) is returned
    return *this;
}
```

By doing so, a constant or a temporary object can also be used as a second operand.

The return value could also be declared as a constant reference:

```
const Fraction& Fraction::operator *= (const Fraction& f)
{
    // 'x *= y' => 'x = x * y'
    *this = *this * f;

    // object (first operand) is returned
    return *this;
}
```

This means that the first operand is returned as a read-only value. This has the consequence that you cannot assign anything to the returned value. Calling

```
if ((x *= 2) < 7)       // if x, after doubling, is smaller than 7
```

would be possible; however, calling

```
(x *= 2) *= x           // x is doubled and then squared
```

results in an error message, which would not have been raised if the return value was declared as not being constant.

In order to avoid misunderstandings, it should be noted that by returning the first operand x as const only restricts the access to x inside this statement. You could still modify x after the statement, as you could before:

```
x *= 2;
x *= x;                 // OK
```

In this respect, I prefer (and would recommend) declaring returned objects as constant references instead of variable references. However, this is not what is usually recommended in C++.

Please note that you still have to consider whether it is useful to return a value by reference. If it is a local value of the function being called, this would result in an error because a second name for an object is returned that no longer exists. Therefore, returning references only makes sense for objects that exist outside the scope of the function being called. Returning *this is the typical case.

Constants in General

Every object can be defined as a constant in C++. The const keyword simply has to be used during its declaration. Constness is part of the type. The type checking of the compiler verifies that no constants are accidentally modified.

For example:

```
const int MAX = 3;
const double pi = 3.141592654;
```

The const keyword replaces the historical practice in C of defining constant values using the preprocessor statement #define. The 'blind' replacement by the preprocessor is replaced by the declaration of a symbol, for which the usual type checking and scope rules apply. The only (but decisive) difference from variables is that their values cannot be modified. This means that their values have to be initialized at the time of their creation.

In the same way, a fraction can be declared as a constant:

```
const CPPBook::Fraction vat(16,100);
```

If a constant is authorized as a second operand for the *= operation, calling x *= vat is permitted.

4.4.4 Constant Member Functions

But what about the first operand? These are modified within the *= operation, and therefore no constants can be used as an operand. Nevertheless, with a pure multiplication (w * w), it is reasonable that the first operand for which the operator is called can be constant.

For this to be possible, a member function that can be called for constant objects must be labeled as such. This kind of *constant member function* is declared using the const keyword between the parameter list and the function body.

The multiplication must then be declared as follows:

```
Fraction Fraction::operator * (const Fraction& f) const
{
    return Fraction(numer*f.numer, denom*f.denom);
}
```

The const at the end of the declaration determines that the fraction for which this operation is called (therefore the first operand) is not modified. Every attempt to manipulate numer or denom will therefore cause a syntax error.

No reference is returned by the multiplication, as it is a return value of a local object. If this was not the case, a second name would be returned, which would no longer exist when the function was left. This is the temporary fraction created by the expression

```
Fraction(numer*f.numer, denom*f.denom)
```

Most compilers recognize this kind of error and output an appropriate warning.

As a copy is returned rather than a reference, the return value does not have to be declared with the const keyword. Temporary objects are basically constant.

4.4.5 The Fraction Class with References

We will now discuss the new version of the Fraction class with an appropriately changed application program.

Header File

The header file now declares the function with references and constants, provided that it makes sense, and has the following structure:

```
// classes/frac4.hpp

#ifndef FRACTION_HPP
#define FRACTION_HPP

// include standard header files
#include <iostream>

// **** BEGIN namespace CPPBook *****************************
namespace CPPBook {

class Fraction {

  private:
    int numer;
    int denom;

  public:
    /* default constructor, and one- and two-parameter constructor
     */
    Fraction(int = 0, int = 1);

    // output (defined inline)
    void print() const {
        std::cout << numer << '/' << denom << std::endl;
    }

    // multiplication
    Fraction operator * (const Fraction&) const;

    // multiplicative assignment
    const Fraction& operator *= (const Fraction&);

    // comparison
    bool operator < (const Fraction&) const;
};
```

```
/* operator *
 * - defined inline
 */
inline Fraction Fraction::operator * (const Fraction& f) const
{
    /* simply multiply numerator and denominator
     * - no reducing yet
     */
    return Fraction(numer * f.numer, denom * f.denom);
}


} // **** END namespace CPPBook ******************************


#endif   // FRACTION_HPP
```

The `print()`, `operator*()` and `operator<()` member functions do not modify the object for which they are called (the first operand), and are therefore declared as constant member functions. For all three operator functions, the parameter is declared as a reference. As it is also declared as a constant, it can be a constant or a temporary object.

In other words, to get the same semantics for the caller, you can always replace a parameter declared as passed by-value as being a constant reference. This will only be a problem if the parameter is modified inside the function. However, this will be noticed by the compiler and, due to the resulting error message, you could then switch back to passing an argument by-value.

Dot-C File

The declaration of the `Fraction` class is adjusted accordingly in the dot-C file. This only affects the declarations. The implementation of the functions do not have to be altered:

```
// classes/frac4.cpp

// include header file of the class
#include "frac.hpp"


// include standard header files
#include <cstdlib>


// **** BEGIN namespace CPPBook ******************************
namespace CPPBook {


/* default constructor, and one- and two-paramter constructor
 * - default for n: 0
 * - default for d: 1
 */
```

```
Fraction::Fraction(int n, int d)
{
    /* initialize numerator and denominator as passed
     * - 0 is not allowed as denominator
     * - move any negative sign for the denominator to the numerator
     */
    if (d == 0) {
        // exit program with error message
        std::cerr << "error: denominator is 0" << std::endl;
        std::exit(EXIT_FAILURE);
    }
    if (d < 0) {
        numer = -n;
        denom = -d;
    }
    else {
        numer = n;
        denom = d;
    }
}

/* operator *=
 */
const Fraction& Fraction::operator *= (const Fraction& f)
{
    // 'x *= y' => 'x = x * y'
    *this = *this * f;

    // object (first operand) is returned
    return *this;
}

/* operator <
 */
bool Fraction::operator < (const Fraction& f) const
{
    // since the numerator cannot be negative, the following is sufficient:
    return numer * f.denom < f.numer * denom;
}

} // **** END namespace CPPBook ******************************
```

Application

The declarations that have been changed do not have any influence on the application program at all. However, constant objects can also be used here, provided that they make sense:

```
// classes/ftest4.cpp

// include header files for the classes that are being used
#include "frac.hpp"

int main()
{
    using namespace CPPBook;    // all symbols of the namespace CPPBook
                                // are considered global in this scope

    // new: declare fraction w as a constant
    const Fraction w(7,3);

    w.print();                  // output fraction a

    // declare x and initialize with the square of w
    Fraction x = w * w;

    // as long as x is less than 1000
    while (x < Fraction(1000)) {
        // multiply x by w and output
        x *= w;
        x.print();
    }
}
```

Here, `print()` can only be called for the fraction constant a because the function is declared as a constant member function.

In addition, the comparison `x < Fraction(1000)` is only possible because the parameter passed to the operator function `<` as a second operand can be a constant. The expression `Fraction(1000)` returns a temporary object that is constant, like all temporary objects.

4.4.6   Pointers to Constants versus Pointer Constants

This section concludes with some remarks about working with constants. Pointers can also refer to constants. However, constancy is part of the type. Therefore, in the declaration, you have to specify that they refer to objects that cannot be modified. These kinds of pointers can also refer to variables (but not vice versa).

For example:

```
int i;                 // int variable
const int c = 77;      // int constant

const int* ip;         // pointer to int constant

ip = &c;               // OK: ip refers to constant c

ip = &i;               // OK: ip now refers to variable i

*ip = 33;              // ERROR: i may not be changed via ip
```

In this case, whatever ip refers to is considered as being constant (regardless of whether the object it refers to really is). Any attempt to manipulate whatever ip refers to therefore causes an error message.

In contrast, a *pointer constant*, which always points to the same object, is declared as follows:

```
int i;                 // int variable
const int c = 77;      // int constant

int* const ip = &i;    // pointer constant to i

ip = 33;               // OK: i is assigned 33

ip = &c;               // ERROR: ip cannot refer to something else
```

In this case, the ip pointer constant refers to the object that was passed at initialization. Any attempt to make it refer to something else is acknowledged by the compiler with an appropriate error message. However, whatever it refers to may be manipulated.

A combination of both constants is also possible. In the following example, s refers to a character string whose content is also constant:

```
const char* const s = "hello";
```

Positioning const

The const keyword can be placed both before and after the type:

```
const int i2 = 13;          // OK
int const i1 = 12;          // OK
```

However, it is normally put at the front.

Constant references can also be declared differently:

```
void f1 (const int &);      // OK
void f2 (int const &);      // OK
```

However, they cannot be placed behind the reference character:

```
void f2 (int & const);        // ERROR
```

If the `const` keyword stands between the type and the asterisk, it belongs to the type to which it refers. The declaration

```
int const * ip;               // defines a pointer to constant int
```

is therefore equivalent to the following declaration:

```
const int * ip;               // defines a pointer to constant int
```

Nevertheless, putting `const` in front of the type may be a source of trouble. Consider the following two type definitions:

```
typedef char* CHARS;
typedef CHARS const CPTR;   // constant pointer to chars
```

The meaning of the second declaration is preserved when you textually replace CHARS with what it stands for:

```
typedef char* const CPTR;   // constant pointer to chars
```

However, if you write `const` *before* the type it qualifies, this principle no longer applies. Indeed, consider the alternative to our first two `typedef`s above:

```
typedef char* CHARS;
typedef const CHARS CPTR;   // constant pointer to chars
```

Textually replacing CHARS results in a type with a different meaning:

```
typedef const char* CPTR;   // pointer to constant chars
```

In addition, putting `const` after the type provides an easier answer to the question 'what is constant?': it is always what is in front of the `const` qualifier. Indeed, while

```
const int N = 100;
```

is equivalent to

```
int const N = 100;
```

there is no equivalent for

```
int* const bookmark = ... ;   // constant pointer
```

that would place the `const` qualifier before the pointer operator '*'. In this example, it is the pointer itself that is constant, not the `int` that is pointed to.

I was really not sure how to handle this topic in this book. Putting `const` in front is very usual in the C++ community. Thus, programmers are familiar with this style. However, as discussed, it might introduce some problems that would not occur otherwise. Nevertheless, I decided to follow the style that is used in general.

Constants Becoming Variables

There follows a warning concerning constants: constants do not offer total security from modifications, as, in principle, it is possible to convert constants into variables using explicit type conversions. This will work, provided that the constant is not in the read-only area of a program.

There are even examples in which the act of converting a constant into a variable may make sense, or may even be necessary. Section 6.2.4 on page 381 discusses this in more detail, and introduces the mutable keyword, which is related to this issue. In Section 3.4.4 on page 68, the const_cast keyword is introduced, which is provided for type conversions that remove constness.

It should be noted at this point that not all compilers report the use of constants as variables as an error. Other compilers only issue a warning in such cases (for example, the GCC). However, these kinds of warnings should always be regarded as an error.

4.4.7   Summary

- A *reference* is declared using the statement & in the type of a declaration. A reference is a (temporary) 'second name' for an existing object.
- The reference symbol does not affect the type of an object.
- By using references in the declaration of parameters and return values, the creation of copies is prevented (*call-by-reference* instead of *call-by-value*).
- References must be initialized when they get defined and cannot change the object or value to which they refer.
- *Constants* can be declared using the const keyword.
- A const placed after the parameter list in a member function defines a *constant member function*. This means that the object for which it is called may not be modified. This object can therefore also be a constant, then.
- const should always be used if something cannot, or should not, be modified. This guarantees that temporary objects can be used as arguments.
- You can place the const keyword before or after the type being declared to be constant.

4.5   Input and Output Using Streams

We have already used objects and symbols from the C++ standard library, such as `std::cout`, `std::cerr`, and `std::endl`, for input and output. The objects and classes do not belong to the core language of C++. They are provided as a standardized application of the language, using language features already discussed, plus some extensions that will be introduced in the following sections.

In this section, we will discuss in more detail the fundamental abilities of the classes and objects used for I/O. This includes the facility to extend I/O techniques to user-defined types. However, in order to fully understand the stream library, language features must be used that have not yet been introduced (especially inheritance). Therefore, Chapter 8 will discuss the standard I/O library later in detail. This discussion will include techniques for formatted I/O, as well as file access.

4.5.1   Streams

I/O in C++ is provided using streams. A stream is a 'data stream', in which the characters are read and written in a formatted way. As stream objects are an application of the object-oriented concept, their properties are defined in classes. Various global objects are predefined for the standard channel for I/O.

Stream Classes

As there are different kinds of I/O (input, output, data access, etc.), there are also different classes to handle them. The two most important classes are the following:

- **istream**
  The `istream` class is an 'input stream' from which data can be read.
- **ostream**
  The `ostream` class is an 'output stream' on which data can be output.

Like all elements of the standard library, both classes are defined in the `std` namespace. Thus, their declaration may look as follows:

```
namespace std {
    class istream {
        ...
    };
    class ostream {
        ...
    };
    ...
}
```

However, this is highly simplified. In reality, there are numerous classes, and the classes are also defined in a fairly complicated way. In Section 8.1 on page 472, additional classes and examples of their use are introduced in more detail.

Global Stream Objects

Three global objects belong to the `istream` and `ostream` classes. These play a central role in I/O, and are defined by the stream library:

- **cin**
  `cin` (`istream` class) is the standard input channel from which a program normally reads the input. It corresponds to the C variable `stdin` and is typically assigned by the run-time systems to the keyboard.

- **cout**
  `cout` (`ostream` class) is the standard output channel to which a program normally writes the output. It corresponds to the C variable `stdout` and is typically assigned by the run-time system to the screen.

- **cerr**
  `cerr` (`ostream` class) is the standard error output channel to which a program normally writes error messages. It corresponds to the C variable `stderr` and is typically assigned by the run-time system to the screen. The output to `cerr` is not buffered.

By separating output into 'normal' outputs and error messages, the two can be treated differently in the operating system environment called by the program. This is the result of the Unix concept of I/O redirection, for which C was originally written. While the normal output of a program could be redirected to a file, the error message could still be displayed on the screen.

These three stream objects are also defined in the `std` namespace, which can be simplified as follows:

```
std::istream cin;
std::ostream cout;
std::ostream cerr;
```

There is also a fourth globally predefined object, `clog`, but this does not play such a significant role. It is provided for protocol output, and sends its buffered output to the standard error output channel.

4.5.2   Using Streams

We have already used the standard I/O stream classes a bit (see, for example, Section 3.1.4 on page 27 and Section 3.4.2 on page 64). However, let us introduce and clarify some further aspects by another simple program. This program reads two integer numbers, divides the first by the second, and outputs the result:

```cpp
// io/ioprog.cpp

// header file for I/O with streams
#include <iostream>

// general header file for EXIT_FAILURE
#include <cstdlib>

int main()
{
    int x, y;

    // output start string
    std::cout << "Integral division (x/y)\n\n";

    // read x
    std::cout << "x: ";
    if (! (std::cin >> x)) {
        /* error when reading
         * => exit program with error message and error status
         */
        std::cerr << "Error when reading an integer"
                  << std::endl;
        return EXIT_FAILURE;
    }

    // read y
    std::cout << "y: ";
    if (! (std::cin >> y)) {
        /* error when reading
         * => exit program with error message and error status
         */
        std::cerr << "Error when reading an integer"
                  << std::endl;
        return EXIT_FAILURE;
    }

    // error if y is zero
    if (y == 0) {
        /* division by zero
         * => exit program with error message and error status
         */
```

```
        std::cerr << "Error: division by 0" << std::endl;
        return EXIT_FAILURE;
    }

    // output operands and result
    std::cout << x << " divided by " << y << " gives "
            << x / y << std::endl;
}
```

First, the header file for the stream classes and global stream objects, `<iostream>`, is included:

```
// header file for I/O with streams
#include <iostream>
```

In the line

```
std::cout << "Integral division (x/y):\n\n";
```

a string literal is written to the standard output channel. This is done by calling the `<<` operator for the `std::cout` object, with a string literal as a second operand. The `<<` operator is the output operator for streams, and is defined so that whatever is passed as the second operand is written to the stream (the data are sent in the direction of the arrow).

The special feature of this operator is that it is not only overloaded for all fundamental types, but can also be overloaded for any user-defined type. Therefore, the second operand can be of any type. Depending on the type, the appropriate operator function will be called automatically, which outputs the second operand (converted into a sequence of characters). For example:

```
int i = 7;
std::cout << i;              // outputs '7'

float f = 4.5;
std::cout << f;              // outputs '4.5'

CPPBook::Fraction x(3,7);
std::cout << x;              // outputs '3/7' (provided it is defined this way)
```

This is a fundamental improvement in comparison to the I/O techniques of C using `printf()`:

- The format of the output objects do not have to be specified but are automatically derived from their type.
- The mechanism is not restricted to fundamental types and is therefore universally applicable.

More than one object can be written using the operator `<<`. The output operator returns the first operand (the stream) for further use. This enables a concatenated call of output operators, as shown in the last line of the example:

```
std::cout << x << " divided by " << y << " gives "
        << x / y << std::endl;
```

Because the operator << is evaluated from left to right,

```
std::cout << x
```

is executed first. As this expression returns std::cout,

```
std::cout << " divided by "
```

is then executed. Similarly, the integer y follows, followed by the string literal " gives ", and finally followed by the result of the expression x / y (the division operator has a higher priority).

For example, if x and y have the values 91 and 7, the following is output:

```
91 divided by 7 gives 13
```

With the knowledge acquired so far, we can introduce the implementation of the ostream class necessary to provide this interface. For objects of this type, the << operator is overloaded with all fundamental types as the second operand:

```
namespace std {
    class ostream {
      public:
        ostream& operator<< (char);          // output character
        ostream& operator<< (int);           // output integer
        ostream& operator<< (long);          // output long integer
        ostream& operator<< (double);        // output floating-point value
        ostream& operator<< (const char*);   // output C-string
        ...
    };
}
```

The first operand (therefore the stream itself) is returned when calling these operators. For example:

```
namespace std {
    ostream& ostream::operator<< (char) {
        ...                     // low-level function to output the character
        return *this;           // return stream for chaining output
    }
    ...
}
```

Manipulators

A *manipulator* is included at the end of most output assignments:

```
std::cout << std::endl
```

As the name suggests, manipulators are special objects whose 'output' manipulates the stream. For example, output formats can be defined or buffers can be emptied. Thus, although the manipulator is 'sent as output' to the stream, it does not necessarily mean that something is written to the underlying channel.

The `endl` manipulator stands for 'endline' and does two things:

- It outputs a newline (the character '\n').
- It flushes the output buffer (i.e. empties the output buffer by sending all characters to the underlying output channel).

The most important predefined manipulators are listed in Table 4.1.

Manipulator	Class	Meaning
`std::flush`	`std::ostream`	flush output buffer
`std::endl`	`std::ostream`	write '\n' and flush output buffer
`std::ends`	`std::ostream`	write '\0' and flush output buffer
`std::ws`	`std::istream`	skip whitespace

Table 4.1. Most important predefined manipulators

Section 8.1.5 explains exactly what manipulators are, which ones exist, and how they can be implemented.

The Input Operator >>

In the line

```
if (! (cin >> x)) {
    ...
}
```

a new value is read into the integer x. This is done using the counterpart to the output operator, the input operator >>:

```
cin >> x
```

The >> operator is defined for streams so that whatever is submitted as the second operand is read in (again, the data are sent in the direction of the arrow).

In principle, the input operator can also be overloaded for any type and called in a chain:

```
double d;
CPPBook::Fraction f;

std::cin >> f >> d;      // read a fraction and a floating-point value
```

By default, any leading whitespace is skipped.

With an input operator, the second operand is a parameter whose value is modified. In principle, the implementation of these operators is therefore done in the same way as with the output operator, with the difference that references are used:

```
namespace std {
    class istream {
      public:
        istream& operator>> (char&);      // read in characters
        istream& operator>> (int&);       // read in integers
        istream& operator>> (long&);      // read in long integers
        istream& operator>> (double&);    // read in floating-point values
        ...
    };
}
```

Streams and Boolean Conditions

In the above example, the input operator is not called in a chained fashion for multiple values. This is because, for each reading, an immediate check is performed to see whether the reading process has been successful (reading could always go wrong). The check is done by calling the ! operator. For streams, the ! operator is defined so that it yields whether the stream is (still) in good shape. If this is not the case, our program outputs an error message and exits:

```
if (! (std::cin >> x)) {
    std::cerr << "Error when reading an integer"
              << std::endl;
    return EXIT_FAILURE;
}
```

What actually happens here is quite tricky. The expression

```
std::cin >> x
```

returns *no* Boolean value. Instead, std::cin is returned, so that a chained call is possible. By applying the ! operator to the stream object std::cin, a Boolean value is returned, which indicates whether this object has an error status.

The statement

```
if (! (std::cin >> x)) {
    ...
}
```

therefore corresponds to

```
std::cin >> x;
if (! std::cin) {
    ...
}
```

For stream objects, the ! operator is defined so that a Boolean value is returned, which states whether the stream has an error status:

```
namespace std {
   class istream {
     public:
        // returns true if there is something wrong with the stream
        bool operator ! ();
        ...
   };
}
```

Using a similar trick, the corresponding positive test is also possible. Boolean statements in `if` or `while` statements either require an integral type (all forms of `int` or `char`) or a type conversion of an object of a class in an arithmetic or a pointer type.

Because there is such a conversion function defined for streams, we can write

```
if (std::cin >> x) {
    // reading was successful
    ...
}
```

Again, this has the same semantics as the following:

```
std::cin >> x;
if (std::cin) {
    ...
}
```

Such a usage of the stream object is possible because there is a corresponding implicit type conversion defined. What occurs here exactly will be explained in the section on conversion functions (see Section 4.6.4 on page 227) and the use of dynamic members with classes (see Section 6.2.3 on page 378).

A typical example of the ability to query the status of a stream by its use in a condition is a loop that reads in and processes objects:

```
// as long as obj can be read in
while (std::cin >> obj) {
    // process obj (in this case, output)
    std::cout << obj << std::endl;
}
```

This is the classical filter framework of C for C++ objects. However, note that the `>>` operator skips leading whitespace. Therefore the version with `char` as `obj` must be implemented in another way to process all characters (see Section 8.1.4 on page 480).

However nice the use of these special operators in conditions may be, one thing should be taken into account: the 'double negation' does *not* neutralize the call, here:

- 'std::cin' is a stream object of the std::istream class.
- '!!std::cin' is a Boolean value, describing the state of std::cin.

This example shows that the mechanism must be used with caution (and can also be considered dubious). The expression in the `if` statement is not what is normally expected, namely a Boolean value. An implicit type conversion, whose existence and meaning has to be known in order to understand the code, makes the expression comprehensible.

As in C, one can argue whether the current programming style is better or not. However, there is no doubt that using the `good()` member function (which returns whether or not a stream has an error-free status) would make the program (even) more readable:

```
std::cin >> x;
if (! std::cin.good()) {
    ...
}
```

4.5.3   Status of Streams

Using the `!` operator shows that a stream can exist in several states. To represent the principle conditions of a stream, different bit constants are defined as flags, managed in an internal stream member (see Table 4.2).

Bit Constants	Meaning
goodbit	everything is OK
eofbit	end-of-file
failbit	failure: error, but stream usable
badbit	fatal error: stream not usable anymore

Table 4.2. Bit constants for the stream state

The difference between `failbit` and `badbit` is basically that `badbit` signals a fatal error:

- `failbit` is set if an event could not be carried out correctly; the stream, however, can still be used, in principle.
- `badbit` is set if the stream is, in principle, no longer OK, or data has been lost.

The status of the flags can be determined using the `good()`, `eof()`, `fail()`, and `bad()` member functions. They return a Boolean value, indicating whether one or several flags are set. In addition, there are two more general member functions for setting and querying these flags: `rdstate()` and `clear()` (see Table 4.3).

By calling `clear()` without parameters, all error flags (including `ios::eofbit`) are deleted:

```
// unset all error flags (including eofbit)
strm.clear();
```

However, if a parameter is passed, the corresponding flags are set and all others are unset. The following example tests whether the `failbit` flag is set in the `strm` stream, and deletes it if necessary:

Member Function	Meaning
good()	everything is OK (ios::goodbit is set)
eof()	end-of-file (ios::eofbit is set)
fail()	error (ios::failbit or ios::badbit are set)
bad()	fatal error (ios::badbit is set)
rdstate()	returns the currently set flags
clear()	deletes or sets individual flags

Table 4.3. Functions for setting and querying stream status flags

```
if (strm.rdstate() & std::ios::failbit) {
    std::cout << "failbit was set" << std::endl;

    // set all of them again apart from ios::failbit
    strm.clear (strm.rdstate() & ~std::ios::failbit);
}
```

The & and ~ bit-operators are used here:

- The & operator links the bits via the AND function. Only the bits that are set by both operands remain. As only the failbit is set in the second operand of the if condition, the expression is not 0 (and therefore true) if the failbit is also set in the first operand.

- The ~ operator provides the bit complement. The expression ~ios::failbit therefore returns a result in which all the flags except the failbit are set. By using the AND operation with all the flags that are currently set (rdstate()), all flags except the failbit will remain as they are.

As well as the status flags and the member functions for setting and querying, there are numerous other members and functions for streams. For example, characters can be read one at a time using the get() member function, without the leading whitespace characters being skipped. The output format can be influenced by using other functions. This is discussed in detail in Section 8.1 on page 472.

4.5.4   I/O Operators for User-Defined Types

As previously mentioned, a significant advantage of streams is that the I/O mechanism can be extended to user-defined types. The << and >> operators just have to be overloaded for these types. There is only one problem with this: the additional versions of the << and >> operators cannot be declared inside the class structure of the stream classes because these stream classes are part of a closed library.

A special feature of C++ for the interpretation of the call of binary operators helps at this point. When a compiler meets an expression of the form

```
a * b
```

it can evaluate this in two different ways:

- It can be interpreted in a strictly object-oriented fashion (taking the first operand as the receiving object and the second operand as the argument of the message):

  ```
  a.operator*(b)
  ```

- It can also be viewed as a global combination of just two operands (both passed as arguments, with no receiving object):

  ```
  operator*(a,b)
  ```

In the first case, an appropriate operator in the class of the first operand, a, must be defined. In the second case, an operator outside any class must be defined that handles both operands. In this case, the first operand is also a parameter.

The same applies to a call such as

```
std::cout << x
```

Here, x must either have a type for which the operator << is defined within std::ostream:

```
namespace std {
    class ostream {
      public:
        ostream& operator << (type);      // parameter is second operand
        ...
    };
}
```

or an operator that combines both operands with << must be defined outside any class:

```
// both operands are parameters:
std::ostream& operator << (std::ostream&, type);
```

The former applies to all fundamental types. The second possibility is used to extend this mechanism to custom types. If access to the internal data of the custom type is required, a member function of the appropriate class of the second parameter is called.

How this actually looks is now clarified with the following updated version of the Fraction class.

Header File of the Fraction Class Using I/O Streams

The header file of the Fraction class now has the following structure:

```
// classes/frac5.hpp

#ifndef FRACTION_HPP
#define FRACTION_HPP

// include standard header files
#include <iostream>
```

```
// **** BEGIN namespace CPPBook ********************************
namespace CPPBook {

class Fraction {

  private:
     int numer;
     int denom;

  public:
     /* default constructor, and one- and two-parameter constructor
      */
     Fraction(int = 0, int = 1);
     // multiplication
     Fraction operator * (const Fraction&) const;

     // multiplicative assignment
     const Fraction& operator *= (const Fraction&);

     // comparison
     bool operator < (const Fraction&) const;

     // new: output to a stream
     void printOn(std::ostream&) const;

     // new: input from a stream
     void scanFrom(std::istream&);
};

/* operator *
 * - defined inline
 */
inline Fraction Fraction::operator * (const Fraction& f) const
{
     /* simply multiply numerator and denominator
      * - no reducing yet
      */
     return Fraction (numer * f.numer, denom * f.denom);
}
```

```
/* new: standard output operator
 * - overload globally and define inline
 */
inline
std::ostream& operator << (std::ostream& strm, const Fraction& f)
{
    f.printOn(strm);      // call member function for output
    return strm;          // return stream for chaining
}
```

```
/* new: standard input operator
 * - overload globally and define inline
 */
inline
std::istream& operator >> (std::istream& strm, Fraction& f)
{
    f.scanFrom(strm);     // call member function for input
    return strm;          // return stream for chaining
}
```

```
} // **** END namespace CPPBook *******************************
```

```
#endif   // FRACTION_HPP
```

To enable fractions to be used with the standard stream mechanism, the I/O operators (<< or >>) are globally overloaded:

```
inline
std::ostream& operator << (std::ostream& strm, const Fraction & f)
{
    f.printOn(strm);      // call member function for output
    return strm;          // return stream for chaining
}
```

```
inline
std::istream& operator >> (std::istream& strm, Fraction& f)
{
    f.scanFrom(strm);     // call member function for input
    return strm;          // return stream for chaining
}
```

As we need access to the internal members of the fraction (numer and denom) to perform the input and output, both operator calls delegate the actual work to the corresponding member function of the Fraction class.

The member function for outputting is a modified form of print(). This is used to pass the additional parameter of the stream to which the fraction must be written:

```
class Fraction {
    ...
    // output to a stream
    void printOn(std::ostream&) const;
    ...
};
```

A member function is added to read in a fraction; its parameter is an input stream:

```
class Fraction {
    ...
    // input from a stream
    void scanFrom(std::istream&);
    ...
};
```

When implementing global operator functions, you must ensure that *no* copies of the manipulated streams are made. This not only takes time, but also leads to errors: the stream is manipulated via the operation (the buffer changes, the status can change to an error status, etc.). However, these manipulations would be lost if they are done in a copy, which could then lead to inconsistencies. If the original stream is used again in a later expression, its condition is not changed and therefore does not correspond to the actual situation. For this reason, stream parameters and return values must *always* be declared as references.

Dot-C File of the Fraction Class Using I/O Streams

Appropriate changes are made in the dot-C file of the Fraction class.

First, the previous output function print() must be replaced with the printOn() member function. This outputs numerator and denominator to the passed output stream (strm) in the form '*numerator/denominator*':

```
void Fraction::printOn(std::ostream& strm) const
{
    strm << numer << '/' << denom;
}
```

Second, the scanFrom() member function is added, which reads the fraction of the passed input stream (strm) by reading the numerator and denominator as integers in sequence:

```cpp
// classes/frac5scan.cpp

// **** BEGIN namespace CPPBook *******************************
namespace CPPBook {
...


/* new: scanFrom()
 * - read fraction from stream strm
 */
void Fraction::scanFrom(std::istream& strm)
{
    int n, d;

    // read numerator
    strm >> n;

    // read optional separator '/' and denominator
    if (strm.peek() == '/') {
        strm.get();
        strm >> d;
    }
    else {
        d = 1;
    }

    // read error?
    if (! strm) {
        return;
    }

    // denominator equals zero?
    if (d == 0) {
        // set failbit
        strm.clear (strm.rdstate() | std::ios::failbit);
        return;
    }

    /* OK, assign read values
     * - move negative sign of the denominator to the numerator
     */
    if (d < 0) {
        numer = -n;
```

```
            denom = -d;
    }
    else {
        numer = n;
        denom = d;
    }
}
```

```
} // **** END namespace CPPBook *******************************
```

For the input format to correspond to the output format, the '/' character must appear between the numerator and denominator. However, the operator is implemented in a way that both the '/' character and the denominator are optional. Thus you could read an integral number as fraction. The peek() stream function is used to decide whether an integral number or a complete fraction is read. It returns the next character without reading it. If there is a '/' character, the get() stream function then reads this character (compare with page 478).

The integer values to be read are first stored in auxiliary variables. The intention behind this is that an object should only be changed after a successful reading (a common C++ convention). However, several errors may occur:

- It may happen that an integer cannot be read because the format of the input buffer does not match (for example, the next character is a letter). In this case, the stream switches to an error condition that will be checked in the following if query:

  ```
  // read error?
  if (! strm) {
      return;
  }
  ```

The subsequent reaction really depends on the situation. For example, you could exit the program with an error message, or try to read the value again after the output of an error message. Depending on the situation, one or the other, or even both of, these cases may not make sense. The stream might, for example, represent a file or another process. The error should therefore *always* be dealt with by the calling environment. As the stream changes into an error status, these can also be recognized and evaluated by the calling environment.

This is exactly what happens in this case. The behavior is the same whether reading in a fraction or an integer. The advantage of this is that the application program knows the circumstances under which the function can be called, and can react accordingly. The disadvantage is that if the application program does not carry out this test, the reading errors will remain unnoticed.

Utilizing the concept of exception handling, a better mechanism for handling errors can be established. This will be looked at in Section 4.7 on page 234, where a modified version of this reading-in function will be presented.

- An error can also appear when the format does match, e.g. the denominator can be 0. This case will also be treated as a format error. To do this, the error flag of the streams is set[5]:

```
// denominator == 0?
if (d == 0) {
    // set Failbit
    strm.clear (strm.rdstate() | std::ios::failbit);
    return;
}
```

The complete dot-C file for the `Fraction` class is shown below:

```
// classes/frac5.cpp

// include header file of the class
#include "frac.hpp"

// include standard header files
#include <cstdlib>

// **** BEGIN namespace CPPBook ********************************
namespace CPPBook {

/* default constructor, and one- and two-paramter constructor
 * - default for n: 0
 * - default for d: 1
 */
Fraction::Fraction(int n, int d)
{
    /* initialize numerator and denominator as passed
     * - 0 is not allowed as denominator
     * - move negative sign of the denominator to the numerator
     */
    if (d == 0) {
        // exit program with error message
        std::cerr << "error: denominator is 0" << std::endl;
        std::exit(EXIT_FAILURE);
    }
    if (d < 0) {
        numer = -n;
        denom = -d;
```

---

[5] The bit operator | links the bits together with the OR function and returns all bits that are set in both operands.

```
        }
        else {
            numer = n;
            denom = d;
        }
}


/* operator *=
 */
const Fraction& Fraction::operator *= (const Fraction& f)
{
    // 'x *= y' => 'x = x * y'
    *this = *this * f;

    // object (first operand) is returned
    return *this;
}


/* operator <
 */
bool Fraction::operator < (const Fraction& f) const
{
    // since the numerator cannot be negative, the following is sufficient:
    return numer * f.denom < f.numer * denom;
}


/* new: printOn()
 * - output fraction on stream strm
 */
void Fraction::printOn(std::ostream& strm) const
{
    strm << numer << '/' << denom;
}


/* new: scanFrom()
 * - read fraction from stream strm
 */
void Fraction::scanFrom(std::istream& strm)
{
    int n, d;
```

```cpp
    // read numerator
    strm >> n;

    // read optional separator '/' and denominator
    if (strm.peek() == '/') {
        strm.get();
        strm >> d;
    }
    else {
        d = 1;
    }

    // read error?
    if (! strm) {
        return;
    }

    // denominator equals zero?
    if (d == 0) {
        // set failbit
        strm.clear (strm.rdstate() | std::ios::failbit);
        return;
    }

    /* OK, assign read values
     * - move negative sign of the denominator to the numerator
     */
    if (d < 0) {
        numer = -n;
        denom = -d;
    }
    else {
        numer = n;
        denom = d;
    }
}

} // **** END namespace CPPBook ******************************
```

Application of the Fraction Class Using I/O Streams

The test program now implements its output using stream mechanisms:

```cpp
// classes/ftest5.cpp

// include standard header files
#include <iostream>
#include <cstdlib>

// include header files for the classes that are being used
#include "frac.hpp"

int main()
{
    const CPPBook::Fraction a(7,3);        // declare fraction constant a
    CPPBook::Fraction x;                   // declare fraction variable x

    // new: output fraction a with stream operator
    std::cout << a << std::endl;

    // new: read fraction x
    std::cout << "enter fraction (numer/denom): ";
    if (! (std::cin >> x)) {
        // input error: exit program with error status
        std::cerr << "Error during input of fraction" << std::endl;
        return EXIT_FAILURE;
    }
    std::cout << "Input was: " << x << std::endl;

    // as long as x is less than 1000
    while (x < CPPBook::Fraction(1000)) {
        // multiply x by a
        x = x * a;
        // new: output with stream operator
        std::cout << x << std::endl;
    }
}
```

The call

```
std::cout << a << std::endl;
```

first calls the global overloaded output operator << for cout and a, defined in the Fraction class. This operator then calls the printOn() member function for a, which finally outputs the value of the fraction.

In addition, the program now checks to see whether the reading in of fractions was successful. If the stream does not have an error-free status after the reading, the program exists with an appropriate error message:

```
if (! (std::cin >> x)) {
    // input error: exit program with error status
    std::cerr << "Error during input of fraction" << std::endl;
    std::exit(EXIT_FAILURE);
}
```

At this point, the manner of the error could be examined and reacted to accordingly:

```
// classes/ftest5b.cpp

while (! (std::cin >> x)) {
    char c;

    if (std::cin.bad()) {
        // fatal input error: exit program
        std::cerr << "fatal error during intput of fraction"
                << std::endl;
        std::exit(EXIT_FAILURE);
    }
    if (std::cin.eof()) {
        // end of file: exit program
        std::cerr << "EOF with input of fraction" << std::endl;
        std::exit(EXIT_FAILURE);
    }
    /* non-fatal error:
     * - reset failbit
     * - read everything up to the end of the line and try again (loops!)
     */
    std::cin.clear();
    while (std::cin.get(c) && c != '\n') {
    }
    std::cerr << "Error during input of fraction, try again: "
            << std::endl;
}
```

If, when reading, an error occurs that is not fatal, we use

```
cin.clear();
```

to clear the error flag and

```
while (cin.get(c) && c != '\n') {
}
```

to read the rest of the line. The get() member function reads in a character and assigns it to the passed parameter c.

As the example shows, handling errors when reading can be very complicated for an error-tolerant application. It may be worth writing a helper function that reads in the particular types with the corresponding error handling.

4.5.5 Summary

- I/O is not part of the C++ language, but is provided by a standard class library.
- There are various stream classes. The most important of these are istream for objects that can be read from and ostream for objects that can be written to.
- The global objects cin, cout and cerr are predefined as standard I/O channels.
- Streams have a status, which is altered by I/O operations, and which can be queried.
- The >> and << operators are typically used for I/O. These can be called in a chained fashion.
- Manipulators allow streams to be manipulated in an input or output operation.
- By globally overloading the I/O operators, the I/O concept can also apply to custom types.
- Streams should always be passed as references.

4.6   Friends and Other Types

This chapter covers the topic of (automatic) type conversions. It discusses how they are defined, when they take place and under what circumstances they should be avoided.

In this context, one of the most controversial language features of C++ is introduced, namely the friend keyword.

4.6.1   Automatic Type Conversions

The previous version of the application program can be made more readable without any changes to the Fraction class:

```
// classes/ftest6.cpp

// include standard header files
#include <iostream>
#include <cstdlib>

// include header file for the classes that are being used
#include "frac.hpp"

int main()
{
    const CPPBook::Fraction a(7,3);      // declare fraction constant a
    CPPBook::Fraction x;                 // declare fraction variable x

    std::cout << a << std::endl;         // output fraction a

    // read fraction x
    std::cout << "enter fraction (numer/denom): ";
    if (! (std::cin >> x)) {
        // input error: exit program with error status
        std::cerr << "Error during input of fraction" << std::endl;
        return EXIT_FAILURE;
    }
    std::cout << "Input was: " << x << std::endl;

    // as long as x is less than 1000
    // new: instead of while (x < CPPBook::Fraction(1000))
    while (x < 1000) {
        // multiply x by a and output result
        x = x * a;
```

```
          std::cout << x << std::endl;
      }
  }
```

The subtle difference is the direct comparison of a fraction with the number 1000:

```
// new: instead of while (x < CPPBook::Fraction(1000))
while (x < 1000) {
    ...
}
```

This is possible because every constructor that can be called with one argument automatically defines an *automatic type conversion (implicit type conversion)*. This also includes constructors with more than one parameter if there are default values for the other parameters.

The one-parameter constructor of the Fraction class therefore enables an automatic type conversion of an int into a fraction:

```
namespace CPPBook {
    class Fraction {
        ...
        // one-parameter constructor defines an automatic type conversion
        Fraction(int = 0, int = 1);
        ...
    };
}

int main()
{
    CPPBook::Fraction x;
    ...
    // automatic type conversion: 1000 => CPPBook::Fraction(1000)
    while (x < 1000) {
        ...
    }
}
```

This means that when a fraction is used as a parameter, an integer can always be used instead. To make this possible for other types as well, respective constructors have to be defined. It would, for example, be feasible to define an automatic type conversion for floating-point values:

```
namespace CPPBook {
    class Fraction {
        // constructor for automatic type conversion
        // from double into CPPBook::Fraction
        Fraction(double);
```

```
        ...
    };
}

int main()
{
    CPPBook::Fraction x;
    ...
    // automatic type conversion: 3.7 => CPPBook::Fraction(3.7)
    if (x < 3.7) {
        ...
    }
    ...
}
```

An automatic type conversion can be avoided by directly implementing the operation with the correct types. An overloaded function, in which the parameter type fits exactly, has a higher priority than a version for which a type conversion is necessary. By doing this, you can avoid any possible run-time disadvantages caused by the type conversion:

```
namespace CPPBook {
    // comparison with an int
    bool Fraction::operator < (int i) const
    {
        // because the denominator cannot be negative, the following is sufficient:
        return numer < i * denom;
    }
}
```

At this point, there has to be a balance between the effort of implementation and any corresponding run-time advantages.

4.6.2 The explicit Keyword

The definition of an automatic type conversion via a constructor can be prevented. In order to do this, the constructor needs to be declared using the explicit keyword:

```
namespace CPPBook {
    class Fraction {
        ...
        // constructor only for explicit type conversion
        // from double to CPPBook::Fraction
        explicit Fraction(double);
    };
}
```

```
int main()
{
    CPPBook::Fraction x;
    ...
    if (x < 3.7) {      // ERROR: no automatic type conversion possible
        ...
    }
    if (x < CPPBook::Fraction(3.7)) {    // OK
        ...
    }
    ...
}
```

In this case, the two different forms of object initialization during definition are noticeable. An initialization of the form

```
X x;
Y y(x);      // explicit type conversion
```

is done using an explicit type conversion. On the other hand, an initialization of the form

```
X x;
Y y = x;     // implicit type conversion
```

is done using an implicit type conversion.

If the constructor is declared as being `explicit`, the second form is therefore not possible.

4.6.3   Friend Functions

There is a problem with automatic type conversion for member functions: The comparison `x < 1000` is possible, but the `1000 < x` comparison is not:

```
namespace CPPBook {
    class Fraction {
        ...
        bool operator < (const Fraction&) const;
        ...
    };
}

int main()
{
    CPPBook::Fraction x;
    ...
```

```
        if (x < 1000)        // OK
        ...
        if (1000 < x)        // ERROR
        ...
    }
```

The comparison

```
    x < 1000
```

is interpreted as

```
    x.operator< (1000)
```

Because 1000 is a parameter and there is an unambiguous type conversion, the following is automatically produced:

```
    x.operator< (CPPBook::Fraction(1000))
```

For the comparison

```
    1000 < x
```

there is no appropriate interpretation. The interpretation as

```
    1000.operator< (x)      // ERROR
```

is an error, because a fundamental type such as int can have no member function.

The problem is that automatic type conversions are only possible for parameters. Because the first operand in an implementation of a operation as a member function is not a parameter, an automatic type conversion is not legal. An explicit type conversion is still possible. For example:

```
    CPPBook::Fraction(1000) < x          // OK
```

However, the expression

```
    1000 < x
```

could be interpreted in another way (as discussed already on page 204, in the definition of the output operator for this class). Here, the expression could be seen as a global combination of two operands that are both passed as parameters:

```
    operator< (1000, x)
```

Such an operation must be declared as a global, rather than a member, function:

```
    bool operator < (const CPPBook::Fraction&, const CPPBook::Fraction&)
```

However, this operation is not a member function of Fraction anymore; therefore, there is no access to private members of the CPPBook::Fraction class. Provided that such an access is required, auxiliary member functions of the class can also be called that carry out the actual comparison:

```
namespace CPPBook {
    class Fraction {
        ...
        bool compareWith(const Fraction&) const;
        ...
    };
}

bool operator < (const CPPBook::Fraction& op1,
                 const CPPBook::Fraction& op2)
{
    return op1.compareWith(op2);
}
```

There is another option. Using the friend keyword, the class can declare the global operation as a 'friend' of the class. All 'friends' of a class have access to its private members ('there are no secrets among friends').

When declaring a global friend function, an automatic type conversion is therefore possible for both the first and second parameters:

```
namespace CPPBook {
    class Fraction {
        ...
        friend bool operator < (const Fraction&, const Fraction&);
        ...
    };
}

int main()
{
    CPPBook::Fraction x;
    ...
    if (x < 1000)        // OK
    ...
    if (1000 < x)        // also OK!
    ...
}
```

The Fraction Class Using Friend Functions for Automatic Type Conversions

To enable global automatic type conversions, the declaration of the Fraction class should be changed as follows:

```cpp
// classes/frac6.hpp

#ifndef FRACTION_HPP
#define FRACTION_HPP

// include standard header files
#include <iostream>

// **** BEGIN namespace CPPBook ********************************
namespace CPPBook {

class Fraction {

  private:
    int numer;
    int denom;

  public:
    /* default constructor, and one- and two-paramter constructor
     */
    Fraction(int = 0, int = 1);

    /* multiplication
     * - new: global friend function, so that an automatic
     * type conversion of the first operand is possible
     */
    friend Fraction operator * (const Fraction&, const Fraction&);

    // multiplicative assignment
    const Fraction& operator *= (const Fraction&);

    /* comparison
     * - new: global friend function, so that an automatic
     * type conversion of the first operands is possible
     */
    friend bool operator < (const Fraction&, const Fraction&);

    // output to a stream
    void printOn(std::ostream&) const;

    // input from a stream
    void scanFrom(std::istream&);
};
```

```
/* operator *
 * - new: global friend function
 * - defined inline
 */
inline Fraction operator * (const Fraction& a, const Fraction& b)
{
    /* simply multiply numerator and denominator
     * - no reducing yet
     */
    return Fraction(a.numer * b.numer, a.denom * b.denom);
}


/* standard output operator
 * - overload globally and define inline
 */
inline
std::ostream& operator << (std::ostream& strm, const Fraction& f)
{
    f.printOn(strm);      // call member function for output
    return strm;          // return stream for chaining
}


/* standard input operator
 * - overload globally and define inline
 */
inline
std::istream& operator >> (std::istream& strm, Fraction& f)
{
    f.scanFrom(strm);     // call member function for input
    return strm;          // return stream for chaining
}

} // **** END namespace CPPBook *******************************

#endif   // FRACTION_HPP
```

In this version, both the < and * operators are declared as global friend functions. This is based on the premise that if x * 1000 is possible by using an automatic type conversion for the second operand, the expression 1000 * x should also be possible.

This does not mean that all operators should be defined as global friend functions. Candidates for friend functions tend to be binary operators, in which the first operand is not modified:

- Being a global friend function does not make sense for unary operators, because it involves a function of the Fraction class, so at least one fraction should be involved in the original call.
- For binary operators that modify the first operand (for example, assignment operators), it makes no sense to have the first operand as a temporary object created by a type conversion.

Implementing Friend Functions for Classes

The modified version of the header file shows that the friend functions will have to be implemented differently. There are no longer implicit submitted objects (i.e. the first operand) whose members can be accessed directly. The inline-defined multiplication in the header file therefore has a different implementation. Instead of

```
/* fraction multiplication as a member function
 */
inline Fraction Fraction::operator * (const Fraction& f) const
{
    return Fraction(numer * f.numer, denom * f.denom);
}
```

the implementation now looks like

```
/* fraction multiplication as a global friend function
 */
inline Fraction operator * (const Fraction& a, const Fraction& b)
{
    return Fraction(a.numer * b.numer, a.denom * b.denom);
}
```

There are now two parameters, a and b, from which the numerator and denominator are accessed. Access to these private data is permitted, because this is a friend function of the Fraction class. As there are no objects from which the function can be called, this does not exist, and neither numer nor denom can be accessed.

The implementation of the class must also be modified in the dot-C file because the definition of the comparison operator has now become a definition of a global function:

```
// classes/frac6.cpp

// include header file of the class
#include "frac.hpp"
...
/* operator <
 * - new: global friend function
 */
```

```
bool operator < (const Fraction& a, const Fraction& b)
{
    // since the numerator can not be negative, the following is sufficient:
    return a.numer * b.denom < b.numer * a.denom;
}
...
```

Here, both operands are passed as parameters, whose members can only be accessed directly, via a and b.

Note that you cannot see in the implementation of a function whether or not it is a friend of a class. The declaration in the class structure is the decisive factor.

'Normal' Member Functions as Friend Functions

The solution presented here—of defining operators globally to enable an automatic type conversion for the first operator—is used fairly often in commercial classes because, for most binary operators, the first operand is not modified. However, a global definition can also be useful for 'normal' member functions that do not define any operators. However, unlike for operator functions, you can see the difference when calling 'normal' member functions.

Consider as an example a function that outputs the reciprocal value of a fraction. It is used as follows when declared as a member function:

```
namespace CPPBook {
    class Fraction {
        ...
        Fraction reciprocal() const;        // return reciprocal value
        ...
    };
}

int main()
{
    CPPBook::Fraction x, y;
    ...
    y = x.reciprocal();        // called as a member function
                               // (no type conversion is possible)
}
```

By being declared as a global friend, the function is no longer called for a particular object, but is called globally, and an automatic type conversion is possible:

```
namespace CPPBook {
    class Fraction {
        ...
```

```
            // return reciprocal value
            friend Fraction reciprocal(const Fraction&);

            ...

        };

    }


    int main()
    {

        CPPBook::Fraction x, y;

        ...

        y = reciprocal(x);          // call as a global function


        y = reciprocal(7);          // automatic type conversion over
                                    // int constructor possible (returns 1/7)

    }
```

However, note that an automatic type conversion from an object-oriented programming point of view can be seen as questionable. By doing so, objects receive abilities that lie outside the actual class structure. If you do not ensure that these functions belong to the class and are compiled with it, this can lead to unintended behavior. Even worse, friend functions cause problems with inheritance. This is discussed in more detail in Sections 4.6.5 and 4.6.7.

The declaration of a friend function can always be omitted. As with the I/O functions, it is possible to define global functions that call public auxiliary functions. For example, you could implement multiplication as a global operation in which you delegate the multiplication to a call of the *= operation:

```
    CPPBook::Fraction operator * (const CPPBook::Fraction& a,
                                  const CPPBook::Fraction& b)
    {
        CPPBook::Fraction result(a);
        return a *= b;
    }
```

The globally declared function no longer uses internal data, but calls public member functions (a copy constructor and the *= operator). Any possible run-time disadvantages can be avoided by implementing this as an inline function.

4.6.4   Conversion Functions

One-parameter constructors define how an object of the class can be produced *from* an object of a remote type. There is also the possibility of a reversed conversion, that is, the conversion of the object *into* a remote type. This can be done using *conversion functions*.

The conversion function is declared using the operator keyword, followed by the conversion type.

For example, in the Fraction class, it is possible to define a type conversion to floating-point values. We define a function as operator double(). It returns a temporary value, to which the fraction is converted. For example[6]:

```
namespace CPPBook {
    class Fraction {
        ...
        // automatic type conversion to double
        operator double() const;
    };
}


inline Fraction::operator double() const
{
    // return quotient from numerator and denominator
    return double(numer)/double(denom);
}
```

Like a constructor, a conversion function is declared without any return type (not even void). However, the function returns a value, which is the object representing the value of the performed conversion. In this respect, the type of the return value is implicitly defined by the name of the conversion function.

The type into which the function converts can be a type of another class. However, neither constructors nor conversion functions can be friend functions, which is why there cannot be any direct access to private members of the remote class in those functions (however, there may be auxiliary functions provided for this).

By using the conversion function of the Fraction class, a fraction can always be used if an object of the double type is used as an argument. For example, the square-root function of the mathematical C library can be called:

```
// classes/sqrt1.cpp

#include <iostream>
#include <cmath>
#include "frac.hpp"

int main()
{
    CPPBook::Fraction x(1,4);
    ...
    std::cout << std::sqrt(x) << std::endl;  // output root of x as a double
}
```

---

[6] Note that without the conversion of numer or denom to double, both operands of the division would be ints. As a consequence, the result would be rounded. Hence the explicit type conversion to double.

4.6.5   Problems with Automatic Type Conversions

You might think that better use could be made of the Fraction class if it converted integers into fractions and fractions into floating-point values. However, this is not (necessarily) the case. The present working example highlights some of the disadvantages of using automatic type conversions. In fact, the application program introduced at the beginning of this section can no longer be compiled[7]:

```cpp
// classes/ftest6.cpp

// include standard header files
#include <iostream>
#include <cstdlib>

// include header file for the classes that are being used
#include "frac.hpp"

int main()
{
    const CPPBook::Fraction a(7,3);      // declare fraction constant a
    CPPBook::Fraction x;                 // declare fraction variable x

    std::cout << a << std::endl;         // output fraction a

    // read fraction x
    std::cout << "enter fraction (numer/denom): ";
    if (! (std::cin >> x)) {
        // input error: exit program with error status
        std::cerr << "Error during input of fraction" << std::endl;
        return EXIT_FAILURE;
    }
    std::cout << "Input was: " << x << std::endl;

    // as long as x is less than 1000
    // new: instead of while (x < CPPBook::Fraction(1000))
    while (x < 1000) {
        // multiply x by a and output result
        x = x * a;
        std::cout << x << std::endl;
    }
}
```

---

[7] In practice, the program is compilable on occasions. However, this indicates a fault with the compiler, rather than bug-free code.

The problem is the expression

```
x < 1000
```

It has now become ambiguous with the current class declaration:

- On the one hand, it can be interpreted in the following way:

```
x < Fraction(1000)
```

- However, the fact that a conversion function to `double` now exists enables another interpretation:

```
double(x) < double(1000)
```

Both interpretations are possible and equally valid. This is because every kind of user-defined automatic type conversion has the same priority (which is lower than predefined type conversions such as from `int` to `double`. If there are two different equally valid interpretations, the expression is always ambiguous.

The rules for automatic type conversion are one of the most difficult topics in C++ and are covered in Section 10.3 on page 573.

'Avoid Automatic Type Conversions!'

This example shows that functions for automatic type conversion should be avoided. Cyclic type conversions should especially never be possible automatically.

Primarily, this means that there should exist no conversion function that carries out the reversed conversion of a (non-`explicit`) one-parameter constructor. This ensures that if a class defines a constructor for objects of another class, this class does not define the reversed constructor (which, in addition, would introduce a cyclic dependency and would be even worse).

Avoiding functions that offer automatic type conversion not only minimizes the danger of ambiguity. It also means that the object-oriented concept is adhered to more strongly. Custom types are created so that there is a fixed set of permitted operations. Automatic type conversions go against this concept.

This does not mean that type conversions should never be used. The point is that they should only ever be performed by explicit function calls.

Common practice is to define member functions such as 'as*Type*()' or 'to*Type*()'. In the `Fraction` class, instead of the conversion function `operator double()`, the member function `toDouble()` should be defined:

```
namespace CPPBook {
    class Fraction {

        ...

        // explicit type conversion to double
        double toDouble() const;
    };
}
```

The application of this kind of conversion now becomes clearer:

```
// classes/sqrt2.cpp

#include <iostream>
#include <cmath>
#include "frac.hpp"

int main()
{
    CPPBook::Fraction x(1,4);
    ...
    std::cout << std::sqrt(x.toDouble())   // output root of x as a double
              << std::endl;
}
```

4.6.6   Other Uses of the `friend` Keyword

With the `friend` keyword, in principle, every function can be given access to the internal data of a class. Only the =, (), [ ] and -> operators constitute an exception (the table on page 572 provides a detailed overview of what functions may be friend functions).

It is also possible to declare an entire class as a friend. The declaration

```
class X {
    friend class Y;
    ...
};
```

means that all functions of the Y class have access to the X class. However, this does not apply to friend functions of Y ('my friend's friend is not automatically my friend'). Therefore, a friend relation is not transitive.

Declaring a class to be a `friend` is occasionally used for more effective implementation of two classes that belong together (a typical example is a `Matrix` and a mathematical `Vector` class). However, they should be part of the same file or distribution.

4.6.7   `friend` versus Object-Oriented Programming

One of the most common disputes about C++ is the question of whether using the `friend` keyword is consistent with the concept of object-oriented programming. The following is worth noting.

C++ is a language that does not force object-oriented programming, but supports it. This support can be handled in various ways. The question of whether the `friend` keyword is consistent with object-oriented programming—as with the question of whether C++ is object-oriented—therefore cannot be answered with a simple yes or no. It depends on how C++ is used.

The `friend` keyword can be used to extend the abilities of automatic type conversions by replacing a member function with a global operation, which is declared as a `friend` function. The examples discussed in this section demonstrated this with the multiplication and reciprocal functions. The use of `friend` in these cases was non-critical, as they were only different implementations of the operations for a class. As these functions were defined in the same file as the class itself, it is still a 'closed' system, and no additional access to internal data is introduced in any way.

In this case, using the `friend` keyword is a concession to the fact that a few things in C++ are programmed using loopholes (for reasons of efficiency or compatibility with C). It is a matter of taste as to whether you make function calls using the global syntax or the syntax for member functions.

However, problems with friend functions could be attributed to inheritance and polymorphism. This will be covered in Section 6.3.3 on page 399. In this respect, friend functions can be a hindrance to the concepts of the object-oriented ideal.

Another consequence of using friend declarations is the transfer of access to the private data of one class to another. The principle of strict data encapsulation is softened by doing so, as functions other than those declared as member functions of global friend functions can access the private data of a class.

However, it has been proved that, under some circumstances, a considerable run-time advantage can be achieved. If, for example, we need to compute the product of a vector and a matrix, the internal data of both classes have to be accessed. Without direct access, every access to a member in the vector or the matrix must be executed via a member function. (However, it should be noted that by using inline functions, you could also get this performance without making use of the `friend` keyword.)

Such a use of `friend` therefore softens the concept of strict data encapsulation in favour of run-time advantages. Because performance is always an important criteria for programs, in practice, this is often seen as acceptable.

It should be made clear that using a friend function can make the checking and maintenance of a class considerably more difficult, as access is transferred to external functions. It is always best to use a friend declaration with a guilty conscience, so that the `friend` keyword is not merely used for convenience.

In any case, it is not disputed that the `friend` keyword can produce nonsense. However, everybody is likely to have had the experience of making friends with the wrong person. For this reason, a declaration of friend classes should always be clearly indicated.

To prevent misunderstandings, it should be noted that it is not possible to use `friend` to gain access to the private members of a class from the outside. The class decides whom it has befriended in its declaration. Nobody can declare himself a friend of another.

4.6.8   Summary

- A one-parameter constructor defines the possibility of an automatic or explicit *type conversion* from the type of the parameter to an object of the class.

- Using the `explicit` keyword, an automatic type conversion by a constructor can be prevented.

- *Conversion functions* provide a facility for converting an object in a class, implicitly or explicitly, into another type. They are declared with '`operator` *type*`()`' and have a return statement, but are declared without a return type.

- Ambiguities threaten functions for automatic type conversion. Conversion functions should therefore be avoided, and one-parameter constructors should be used carefully.

- Using the `friend` keyword, single operations or entire classes can be granted access to the private members of a class.

- Automatic type conversions for the first operand of operator functions implemented as a member function have to be declared globally. Nevertheless, by using the `friend` keyword, the implementation can access private members.

- `friend` is not transitive (i.e. 'my friend's friend is not necessarily my friend').

4.7   Exception Handling for Classes

The concept of exception handling was introduced in Section 3.6 on page 93. In this chapter, we show how to integrate exceptions in classes and how to design suitable exception classes. We also give some additional details for working with exceptions.

4.7.1   Motivation for Exception Handling in the Fraction Class

One of the typical problems of conventional error handling can be seen in the first implementation of the Fraction class (see Section 4.1.7 on page 140). Here, when 0 was passed to the constructor as the initialization for the denominator, although the error could be recognized, it was not handled in a meaningful way. This is due to the fact that when classes are implemented, no assumptions can usually be made about the circumstances in which they are applied. In particular, it was not known in what situation 0 could be given as the initialization for the denominator. In practice, there may even be many different reasons for a faulty call, so no meaningful uniform reaction is possible. In the original implementation, the program was simply exited with an appropriate error message:

```
Fraction::Fraction(int n, int d)
{
    /* initialize numerator and denominator as submitted
     * - 0 as denominator is not allowed
     */
    if (d == 0) {
        // exit program with error message
        std::cerr << "Error: denominator is 0" << std::endl;
        std::exit(EXIT_FAILURE);
    }
    ...
}
```

This problem is not only restricted to constructors. For example, a similar problem exists for a string class or a collection class if a character or element is accessed with the [] operator. We can see in the function whether an incorrect index has been passed. However, there is no possibility for handling the problems meaningfully, because the calling circumstances are not known and there are no suitable possibilities for error handling: the only way to inform the caller is via the return value, which, however, is expected to be the value that was accessed with the index operator. Thus, when calling the statement

```
s[i] = 'q';            // hopefully the index i is not too large
```

how can we write application code so that we test whether the i index is too large for s?

The basic problem is the same in both cases: error situations occur, which are found, but cannot be resolved because the context from which the error originates is unknown. Furthermore, the error cannot be reported back to the caller, because return values are either not defined at all, or are used for other things.

Here, the concept of exception handling helps. At any given place in the code, errors can be detected and reported to the caller as exceptions. The error can then be intercepted and dealt with meaningfully. If the error cannot be handled, it is not just simply ignored, but instead leads to a controlled program exit, rather than an undefined behavior or an unexpected program abortion.

4.7.2 Exception Handling for the `Fraction` Class

There has to be a class or type for every kind of exception or error. Therefore, when declaring a class that uses exception handling, classes for corresponding exceptions have to be provided. If exception classes are not used for multiple classes, this can be done by the error classes being declared as so-called *nested class* within the scope of the class to which the errors belong. Although *nested classes* are presented in Section 6.5.4 on page 424, we will use this ability here.

The following version of `Fraction` defines the error class for the exception `DenomIsZero`:

```
// classes/frac8.hpp

#ifndef FRACTION_HPP
#define FRACTION_HPP

// include standard header files
#include <iostream>

// **** BEGIN namespace CPPBook ********************************
namespace CPPBook {

class Fraction {

  private:
    int numer;
    int denom;

  public:
    /* new: error class
     */
    class DenomIsZero {
    };

    /* default constructor, and one- and two-paramter constructor
     */
    Fraction(int = 0, int = 1);
```

```cpp
      /* multiplication
       * - global friend function, so that an automatic
       *   type conversion of the first operand is possible
       */
      friend Fraction operator * (const Fraction&, const Fraction&);

      // multiplicative assignment
      const Fraction& operator *= (const Fraction&);

      /* comparison
       * - global friend function, so that an automatic
       *   type conversion of the first operand is possible
       */
      friend bool operator < (const Fraction&, const Fraction&);

      // output to and input from a stream
      void printOn(std::ostream&) const;
      void scanFrom(std::istream&);

      // explicit type conversion to double
      double toDouble() const;
};

/* operator *
 * - global friend function
 * - defined inline
 */
inline Fraction operator * (const Fraction& a, const Fraction& b)
{
      /* simply multiply denomiator and numerator
       * - no reducing yet
       */
      return Fraction(a.numer * b.numer, a.denom * b.denom);
}

/* standard output operator
 * - overload globally and define inline
 */
inline
std::ostream& operator << (std::ostream& strm, const Fraction& f)
{
```

```
        f.printOn(strm);        // call member function for output
        return strm;            // return stream for chaining
}
```

```
/* standard input operator
 * - overload globally and defined inline
 */
inline
std::istream& operator >> (std::istream& strm, Fraction& f)
{
        f.scanFrom(strm);       // call member function for input
        return strm;            // return stream for chaining
}
```

```
} // **** END namespace CPPBook ******************************
```

```
#endif  // FRACTION_HPP
```

The DenomIsZero error class is declared inside the Fraction class:

```
class Fraction {
  ...
  public:
    class DenomIsZero {
    };
  ...
};
```

We are dealing here with the shortest declaration possible for classes: an empty class. The only role of an object of this class is to exist. No data or operations are required.

In the implementation, if the denominator is zero, a corresponding error object is now created:

```
// classes/frac8.cpp
```

```
// include header file of the classn
#include "frac.hpp"
```

```
// **** BEGIN namespace CPPBook ******************************
namespace CPPBook {
```

```
/* default constructor, and one- and two-paramter constructor
 * - default for n: 0
 * - default for d: 1
 */
```

```
Fraction::Fraction(int n, int d)
{
    /* initialize numerator and denominator as passed
     * - 0 is not allowed as a denominator
     * - move negative sign from the denominator to the numerator
     */
    if (d == 0) {
        // new: throw exception with error object for 0 as denominator
        throw DenomIsZero();
    }
    if (d < 0) {
        numer = -n;
        denom = -d;
    }
    else {
        numer = n;
        denom = d;
    }
}


/* operator *=
 */
const Fraction& Fraction::operator *= (const Fraction& f)
{
    // 'x *= y' => 'x = x * y'
    *this = *this * f;

    // object (first operand) is returned
    return *this;
}


/* operator <
 * - global friend function
 */
bool operator < (const Fraction& a, const Fraction& b)
{
    // since the numerator cannot be negative, the following is sufficient:
    return a.numer * b.denom < b.numer * a.denom;
}
```

```
/* printOn
 * - output fraction on stream strm
 */
void Fraction::printOn(std::ostream& strm) const
{
    strm << numer << '/' << denom;
}


/* scanFrom
 * - read fraction from stream strm
 */
void Fraction::scanFrom(std::istream& strm)
{
    int n, d;

    // read numerator
    strm >> n;

    // read optional separator '/' and denominator
    if (strm.peek() == '/') {
        strm.get();
        strm >> d;
    }
    else {
        d = 1;
    }

    // read error?
    if (! strm) {
        return;
    }

    // denominator equals zero?
    if (d == 0) {
        // new: throw exception with error object for 0 as denominator
        throw DenomIsZero();
    }

    /* OK, assign read values
     * - move negative sign from the denominator to the numerator
     */
```

```
        if (d < 0) {
            numer = -n;
            denom = -d;
        }
        else {
            numer = n;
            denom = d;
        }
    }
```

```
    // type conversion to double
    double Fraction::toDouble() const
    {
        // return quotient form numerator and denominator
        return double(numer)/double(denom);
    }
```

```
    } // **** END namespace CPPBook *******************************
```

The code for the constructor is modified here accordingly. If the error occurs, an error object is created and is thrown into the environment of the program:

```
    Fraction::Fraction(int n, int d)
    {
        /* initialize numerator and denominator as passed
         * - 0 is not allowed as a denominator
         * - move negative sign from the denominator to the numerator
         */
        if (d == 0) {
            // new: throw exception with an error object for 0 as denominator
            throw DenomIsZero();
        }
        ...
    }
```

At run time, the `throw` statement becomes equivalent to a sequence of return statements that are called in all nested blocks and functions in which the program is situated at that time. All scopes of the program are terminated immediately and the error propagated up until it is either caught and handled or the program quits.

Note that this is not a jump to the next superior `catch` that deals with the error, but rather an 'ordered retreat'. Destructors are called for the local objects created within all blocks. Objects explicitly created with `new`, however, remain valid and, if necessary, must be removed by the catch area. This process is also known as *stack unwinding*. The program stack is unwound until an appropriate exception is defined.

Even if the exception is not handled and leads to a program exit, the program is not just simply aborted, but is left in an orderly manner. In contrast to `exit()`, all destructors of local objects are called (`exit()` only calls destructors of static objects). As a local object can represent an opened file or a running database query (which might be flushed and closed by the destructor), this is an important distinction.

Exception Handling

The handling of the exception occurs in the application program that directly or indirectly caused the error. The following program shows how this may look like:

```cpp
// classes/ftest8.cpp

// include standard header files
#include <iostream>
#include <cstdlib>

// include header files for the classes that are being used
#include "frac.hpp"

int main()
{
    CPPBook::Fraction x;        // fraction variable

    /* try to read the fraction x, and handle
     * exceptions of the type DenomIsZero
     */
    try {
        int n, d;
        std::cout << "numerator: ";
        if (! (std::cin >> n)) {
            // input error: exit program with error status
            std::cerr << "error during input of numerator"
                    << std::endl;
            return EXIT_FAILURE;
        }
        std::cout << "denominator: ";
        if (! (std::cin >> d)) {
            // input error: exit program with error status
            std::cerr << "error during input of denominator"
                    << std::endl;
```

```
            return EXIT_FAILURE;
        }
        x = CPPBook::Fraction(n,d);
        std::cout << "input was: " << x << std::endl;
    }
    catch (const CPPBook::Fraction::DenomIsZero&) {
        /* exit program with an appropriate error message
         */
        std::cerr << "input error: numerator can not be zero"
                  << std::endl;
        return EXIT_FAILURE;
    }


    // this point is only reached if x was read successfully
    ...

}
```

For the area enclosed by `try`, special error handling is installed, defined by the following catch statement:

```
try {
    int n, d;
    std::cout << "numerator: ";
    ...
    x = CPPBook::Fraction(n,d);
    std::cout << "input was: " << x << std::endl;
}
catch (const CPPBook::Fraction::DenomIsZero&) {

    ...

}
```

If any given exception occurs in the `try` block, the block is exited immediately. If this is an exception of the `Fraction::DenomIsZero` type, then the statements in the necessary `catch` block are executed. After the statements in the `catch` block are processed, the program continues at the next statement after the `catch` block (thus the `try` block, where the exception was thrown, in not re-entered).

If, in the constructor, zero is given as the denominator d, then the statement

```
x = CPPBook::Fraction(n,d);
```

causes an exception to be thrown. As a consequence, both the constructor and the `try` block are left immediately. The following output statement inside the `try` block

```
std::cout << "input was: " << x << std::endl;
```

is therefore *not* executed.

With every other exception, due to lack of an appropriate `catch` clause, even the `main()` function is exited.

The exception in the catch block is passed as a constant reference, for the same reason as references are used for function parameters. By not using references, copies of the passed (exception) object are made. By using a reference, the unnecessary copying of the exception object is avoided.

Exception or I/O Error?

An interesting question is whether we should throw an exception inside the `Fraction` class, if we get zero as the denominator when reading a fraction from a stream:

```
if (d == 0) {
    // throw exception with an error object for 0 as denominator
    throw DenomIsZero();
}
```

Instead of setting an I/O flag, exception handling would also be used in this case. However, I/O is a good example of the difference between exceptions and errors. Input errors are very common and therefore, by definition, are not exceptions. It is therefore normal to set appropriate status flags when incorrectly formatted streams are encountered (see also the implementation on page 208ff.). In this way, we can distinguish other input errors from the specific error of inputting a zero as the denominator. However, this complicates the interface. The boundaries between exceptions and errors are fuzzy, and, in this respect, this kind of decision is always a question of design.

4.7.3 Exception Classes

Exception classes are classes just like any other. This means that they can have members and member functions. In principle, any type (classes and fundamental types) can be used as a type for exceptions. The particular significance of these classes is that they *are used* with the `throw` and `catch` keywords. For example, we can use strings for exception objects. The statement

```
throw "exception: something went wrong here";
```

throws an exception of the `const char*` type, which we then can process as follows:

```
// catch string exceptions
catch (const char* s) {
    // print string as error message
    std::cerr << s << std::endl;
}
```

If exception classes have members, these are the attributes of the exception. In this way, exceptions and errors can be parametrized. Constructors may be provided to initialize these members. If dynamic members are used, a destructor can also be defined. It is called after an exception handling, when the exception object gets destroyed.

The use of an invalid index in an array is a classic example of the use of parameters in exception objects. If a string is accessed with an invalid index, the value of the index is usually of interest and should be passed to the caller. An example of this is presented and explained in Section 6.2.7 on page 387.

4.7.4   Rethrowing Exceptions

It is possible to rethrow an error that is being dealt with in a catch area, in order to achieve an exception handling in the outer scope for it. This is useful if some reaction is needed without being able to handle the exception.

A typical example of this is the closing of opened files or the freeing of allocated memory, provided that this is not undertaken by the destructor. In the event of an exception, the following example frees explicitly allocated memory:

```
std::string* createNewString()
{
    std::string* newString = NULL;       // pointer to (created) string

    try {
        newString = new std::string("cup");   // explicitly create string
        ...                                    // and modify
    }
    catch (...) {
        /* for any exception, release the explicitly created string
         * and rethrow the exception  to the caller of this function
         * for additional handling
         */
        delete newString;
        throw;
    }

    // return pointer to created string (if no exception was thrown)
    return newString;

}
```

The naked `throw` statement (i.e. 'throw;', without the detail of a class) is responsible for throwing the error back into the program, so that it is handled from the caller (or outer block).

This sort of 'rethrow' is also required to implement an auxiliary function for the general handling of various exceptions. This is discussed in Section 3.6.6 on page 101.

4.7.5 Exceptions in Destructors

Nesting two exceptions is not possible. If an exception is thrown in a destructor that is called because of a previous exception, the normal exception handling is aborted, and `std::terminate()` is called (which usually calls `std::abort()`, see Section 3.6.5 on page 100). To avoid exceptions during stack unwinding, you should make sure that, in general, destructors throw no exceptions.

4.7.6 Exceptions in Interface Declarations

The exceptions that may be thrown by a function are part of its interface (such as parameters and return value). In fact, for any function, we can declare what exceptions can be thrown. To do this, after the parameter list of a function, you can specify an *exception specification* (or *exception list* or *throw specification*) with the `throw` keyword. Thus, the exceptions are part of the signature, as shown below:

```
void doSomething() throw (Fraction::DenomIsZero, String::RangeError);
```

The declaration determines that only the given exceptions can be thrown by the function. If no exception specification is declared, any exception can be thrown. An empty list indicates that no exceptions can be thrown:

```
void doSomething() throw ();
```

Unexpected Exceptions

The exception specification only describes what exceptions can occur from the caller's point of view. Internally, other exceptions can occur and be dealt with. However, if an exception occurs inside the function that is neither handled nor contained in the exception specification, the `std::unexpected()` function is called. This function is predefined so that it calls `std::terminate()` (which usually calls `std::abort()`, see Section 3.6.5 on page 100).

An alternative function for handling unexpected exceptions can be defined using `std::set_unexpected()`. The function cannot have any parameters or a return value. The currently defined function for unexpected exceptions is returned when calling `std::set_unexpected()`

Class `std::bad_exception`

If `std::bad_exception` is part of an exception specification, the function `std::unexpected()` automatically throws an exception of this type if an unexpected exception occurs:

```
void doSomething() throw (Fraction::DenomIsZero, std::bad_exception)
{
    ...
    throw String::RangeError();   // calls unexpected(),
    ...                           // which throws std::bad_exception
}
```

If an exception specification therefore covers the class std::bad_exception, every exception that does not belong to any of the listed types is replaced within the function by an exception of the type std::bad_exception.

4.7.7 Hierarchies of Exception Classes

Exception classes can be organized in hierarchies. In this way, general error types can be specialized or different error types can be summarized with a common term. An application program then has the simple option, depending on the situation, to either handle different exceptions by using the general error type or to treat special errors individually.

When forming exception class hierarchies, the concept of inheritance is used (this will be introduced in Chapter 5). As this feature has not yet been introduced, the following is a preview of topics that are dealt with later on.

Example of an Error Class Hierarchy

Again, the Fraction class can be used as an example of an exception class hierarchy. Various errors can occur when using fractions. In order to be able to deal with each, a corresponding hierarchy is defined (see Figure 4.5).

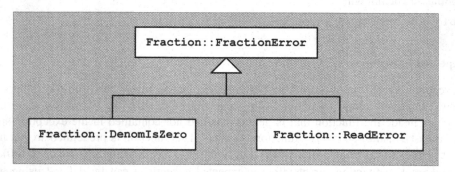

Figure 4.5. Simple hierarchy of exception classes

Among the common types of FractionError, we have the special cases DenomIsZero and ReadError. Thus three classes are declared in which the two special cases are derived from the common one.

In order to do this, the declaration of the Fraction class has the following structure:

```
// classes/frac10.hpp

class Fraction {
  private:
    int numer;
    int denom;
```

```
public:
    /* error classes:
     * - new: common-case class with two derived classes
     */
    class FractionError {
    };
    class DenomIsZero: public FractionError {
    };
    class ReadError : public FractionError {
    };

    /* default constructor, and one- and two-parameter constructor
     */
    Fraction(int = 0, int = 1);

    /* output to and input from a stream
     */
    void printOn(std::ostream&) const;
    void scanFrom(std::istream&);
    ...
};
```

In the case of an error, the corresponding special exception objects are thrown in the dot-C file:

```
// classes/frac10.cpp

/* default constructor, and one- and two-parameter constructor
 * - default for n: 0
 * - default for d: 1
 */
Fraction::Fraction(int n, int d)
{
    /* initialize nomiator and denominator as passed
     * - 0 is not allowed as a denominator
     * - move negative sign from the denominator to the numerator
     */
    if (d == 0) {
        // throw exception with error object for 0 as denominator
        throw DenomIsZero();
    }
    if (d < 0) {
        numer = -n;
```

```
            denom = -d;
        }
        else {
            numer = n;
            denom = d;
        }
    }

    /* scanFrom
     * - read fraction from stream strm
     */
    void Fraction::scanFrom(std::istream& strm)
    {
        int n, d;

        // read numerator
        strm >> n;

        // read optional separator '/' and denominator
        if (strm.peek() == '/') {
            strm.get();
            strm >> d;
        }
        else {
            d = 1;
        }

        // read error?
        if (! strm) {
            // throw exception with error object for read error
            throw ReadError();
        }

        // denominator equals zero?
        if (d == 0) {
            // throw exception with error object for 0 as denominator
            throw DenomIsZero();
        }

        /* OK, assign read numbers
         * - move negative sign from the denominator to the numerator
         */
```

```
        if (d < 0) {
            numer = -n;
            denom = -d;
        }
        else {
            numer = n;
            denom = d;
        }
    }
```

To handle any kind of error of the `Fraction` class within the application program in `main()`, we use a catch clause that refers to the common base class:

```
// classes/ftest10.cpp

int main()
{
    try {
        CPPBook::Fraction x;
        ...
        x = readFraction();
        ...
    }
    catch (const CPPBook::Fraction::FractionError&) {
        // exit main() with error message and error status
        std::cerr << "Exception through error in class fraction"
                  << std::endl;
        return EXIT_FAILURE;
    }
}
```

In the special event of reading a fraction, an input error caused by `scanFrom()` can be treated individually, so that a new read attempt is forced:

```
// classes/ftest10read.cpp

CPPBook::Fraction readFraction()
{
    CPPBook::Fraction x;           // fraction variable
    bool              error;       // error occurred?

    do {
        error = false;     // no error yet

        /* try to read the fraction x and catch
```

```
    * errors of the type DenomIsZero
    */
try {
    std::cout << "enter fraction (numer/denom): ";
    std::cin >> x;
    std::cout << "input was: " << x << std::endl;
}
catch (const CPPBook::Fraction::DenomIsZero&) {
    /* output error message and continue the loop
     */
    std::cout << "input error: numerator can not be zero"
            << std::endl;
    error = true;
}
} while (error);

return x;                      // return read fraction
}
```

4.7.8   Design of Exception Classes

According to the same pattern, a general exception class should be declared as the basic class for related error types, from which all special exception classes are derived (see Figure 4.6).

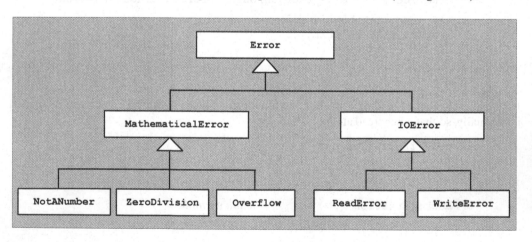

Figure 4.6. Example of an exception class hierarchy

This has the advantage that different errors can be handled with a single catch statement. Furthermore, not all exceptions need be declared in the exception specification of a function that can return different exceptions. So, instead of

```
void doSomething() throw (NotANumber, ZeroDivision, Overflow);
```

the statement of the common base class is sufficient:

```
void doSomething() throw (MathematicalError);
```

Error Messages

A common basic class for all exception classes should define a member for an error message, which then belongs to all error objects and can be processed if the error is not handled in another, more individual, way:

```
namespace CPPBook {
    class Error {
      public:
        std::string message;      // default error message

        // constructor: initialize error message
        Error (const std::string& s) : message(s) {
        }
        ...
    };
}
```

The error message could, for example, then be written to the standard error channel in main():

```
int main()
{
    try {
        ...
    }
    ...
    // catch all Errors not handled yet
    catch (const CPPBook::Error& error) {
        std::cerr << "ERROR: " << error.message << std::endl;
        return EXIT_FAILURE;
    }
    // catch all other exceptions not handled yet
    catch (...) {
        std::cerr << "ERROR: unknown exception" << std::endl;
        return EXIT_FAILURE;
    }
}
```

In the standard exceptions, what() takes on this role (see Section 3.6.4 on page 99).

4.7.9   Throwing Standard Exceptions

We can also throw standard exceptions (see Section 3.6.3 on page 95) ourselves. This has the advantage that application programmers can handle these exceptions in the same way as other standard exceptions. The disadvantage is that we cannot recognize whether an exception is thrown by the standard library or by a user-defined class.

In order to trigger a standard exception, we must simply throw an object of the standard exception class (see Section 3.6.3 on page 95), initialized by a `string`. The passed string is then returned by `what()` during the processing of the exception. For example:

```
std::string s;
...
throw std::out_of_range(s);
```

Because there is a constant type conversion from `const char*` to `string`, we can also use string literals for the initialization:

```
throw std::out_of_range("index is too large");
```

The standard exception classes that support this capability are the classes `logic_error` and `runtime_error`, as well all the classes derived from these. All other standard exceptions are not intended for this.

4.7.10   Exception Safety

For classes and libraries, the way they deal with exceptions is an issue. In principle, the following behavior regarding exceptions is possible:

- An exception may bring a class in an undefined behavior.
- There may be a guarantee that an exception will not leak resources or violate invariants of a class.
- There may be a guarantee that an operation has no effect if an exception is thrown.

While the first behavior means that an object of the class is useless after an exception, the two other approaches give you a level of *exception safety*:

- The approach that guarantees that an exception will not leak resources or violate invariants is sometimes called the *basic guarantee for exception safety*. It allows to continue to use objects after an exception altough they might have a special state.
- The approach that guarantees that an operation has no effect if an exception is thrown means that an operation either succeeds or has no effect. Such operations can be considered to be *atomic* with respect to exceptions. Or, to use terms from database programming, you could say that these operations support *commit-or-rollback* behavior or are *transaction safe*.

Of course, it is always the goal to provide as much safety as possible. However, exception safety may have a serios impact on performance. For example, to guarantee that a complicated operation either succeeds or has no effect usually means that you create a copy of the modified operands at the beginning of the operation, which you can use to restore the initial state in case of an exception. Thus, if good performance is a design goal you can't provide perfect exception handling in all cases.

The atomic guarantee is sometimes even impossible to give. For example, if you want to provide a function that removes an element from a collection and returns this element, it might happen that the copying of the return element throws an exception. Thus, the operation fails but the number of elements was decremented. For this reason vectors and other standard containers provide no operation that removes and returns an element (see also Section 7.3.1 on page 438).

Note that all these guarantees are based on the requirement that destructors never throw. When destructors throw you can't guarantee anything.

4.7.11 Summary

- Classes should throw exceptions when errors are encountered.
- The type of the exception might be an auxiliary inner class.
- Destructors should never throw exceptions.
- With the help of *exception specifications*, you can declare what exceptions a function can trigger.
- Error classes for exception handling can be organized hierarchically in order to refine general error types or to summarize different error types with a single generic type.
- Classes can also throw standard exceptions.
- Classes can provide different levels of exception safety. They should at least give the guarantee that an exception will not leak resources or violate invariants.

5

Inheritance and Polymorphism

After looking at programming with classes and data encapsulation, this chapter introduces two other essential features of object-oriented programming: *inheritance* and *polymorphism*.

Inheritance allows properties of a class to be derived from another class. This means that new classes need only implement supplementary aspects. Properties that have been implemented in another class can be *derived*, and do not need to be implemented again. As well as reducing the size of the code, this also helps to ensure consistency because identical properties do not appear in several places, and therefore only need to be checked or modified once.

Polymorphism makes it possible to work with *common terms* (a way of abstraction used in everyday life)[1]. Various objects can be combined and managed under a common term, without their different properties being lost.

Inheritance is the typical way polymorphism is implemented is C++. A class has to be defined for the common term, from which other classes are derived. If an object is used as its common term, it can be accessed with the type of the class that has been defined for the common term. However, the fact that the object has a special type is not lost. At run time, a function call automatically determines the actual class of an object and the corresponding function for this class is called automatically.

Terminology for Inheritance

There are various terms used for inheritance, partly because every object-oriented programming language introduces its own vocabulary. In the following, we will only use C++ terms, but will also briefly introduce other terms.

If a class takes on the properties of another class, this process is called *inheritance*. A new class *inherits* or *derives* the properties from an existing class.

---

[1] *Generic term* is probably a better phrase than *common term*. However, as *generic* has a special meaning in C++, I decided to use *common term* here.

The class from which properties are inherited is called the *base class* (also *superclass*, *parent class*). The class that inherits is called the *derived class* (also *subclass*, *child class*).

Because a derived class can also be a base class itself, this may create a whole *class hierarchy*, as shown in Figure 5.1.

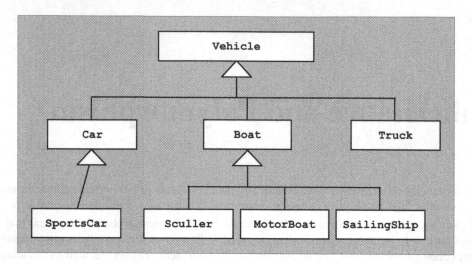

Figure 5.1. Example of a class hierarchy

The class `Vehicle` describes the properties of vehicles. The class `Car` inherits these properties and extends them. The class `SportsCar` inherits the properties from `Car` (therefore the extended properties of `Vehicle`) and extends them further still. Other branches can be introduced accordingly. The result is a class hierarchy for vehicles, in which `Vehicle` is the common term.

Inheritance is indicated with the so-called *is-a* relationship: A sports car *is a* car. A car *is a* vehicle.

As shown in the figure, UML uses an isosceles triangle to denote inheritance, with the top pointing to the base class.

Single and Multiple Inheritance

There are different kinds of inheritance:

- *Single inheritance.*
- *Multiple inheritance.*

With single inheritance, a derived class can only have one base class, while multiple inheritance allows several base classes. This means that, with single inheritance, only tree-like hierarchies can occur; with multiple inheritance, these can be graphs. C++ supports both single and multiple inheritance.

Multiple inheritance is very useful, but can lead to complications. For this reason, we will start with single inheritance and will delay looking at the special features of multiple inheritance until Section 5.4 on page 329.

5.1   Single Inheritance

As an example of single inheritance, we will derive the class Fraction, introduced in the previous chapter. To do this, we will extend the version introduced in Section 4.7 on page 234.

By using inheritance, the Fraction class is to be extended with the addition of an extra property: it will be able to be reduced. This property can, of course, be implemented directly in the Fraction class, but we operate under the assumption that we should not change the Fraction class, either because it makes sense to manage fractions that cannot be reduced, or because the previous version of the Fraction class is part of a closed class library.

The basic concept of inheritance is introduced in this section. The initial version of the derived class described here can, however, lead to problems when implemented. These problems, and suggestions as to how to avoid them, are discussed in Section 5.2 on page 276.

5.1.1   The Fraction Class as a Base Class

Before the Fraction class can be derived as a base class, the implementation introduced in Chapter 4 must be slightly modified. Previous versions of the class Fraction did not support inheritance, and therefore, without these changes, derivation would not be possible.

We need to make two remarks at this point:

- If the previous versions of the Fraction class were part of a closed class library, they should, of course, already contain the modifications if this class is provided for inheritance.

- Because of the problems mentioned above, further modifications have to be carried out. In this respect, this version is not yet an effective and suitable implementation of the Fraction class.

A version of the Fraction class that could also be used as a base class for other classes requires the following modified class declaration:

```
// inherit/frac91.hpp

#ifndef FRACTION_HPP
#define FRACTION_HPP

// include standard header files
#include <iostream>

// **** BEGIN namespace CPPBook ********************************
namespace CPPBook {

class Fraction {
  protected:
    int numer;
    int denom;
```

```
  public:
      /* error class
       */
      class DenomIsZero {
      };

      /* default constructor, and one- and two-parameter constructor
       */
      Fraction(int = 0, int = 1);

      /* multiplication
       * - global friend function so that an automatic
       *   type conversion of the first operand is possible
       */
      friend Fraction operator * (const Fraction&, const Fraction&);

      // multiplicative assignment
      const Fraction& operator *= (const Fraction&);

      /* comparison
       * - global friend function so that an automatic
       *   type conversion of the first operand is possible
       */
      friend bool operator < (const Fraction&, const Fraction&);

      // output to and input from a stream
      void printOn(std::ostream&) const;
      void scanFrom(std::istream&);

      // type conversion to double
      double toDouble() const;
};

/* operator *
 * - global friend function
 * - inline defined
 */
inline Fraction operator * (const Fraction& a, const Fraction& b)
{
      /* simply multiply numerator and denominator
       * - this saves time
```

```cpp
    */
    return Fraction(a.numer * b.numer, a.denom * b.denom);
}


/* standard output operator
 * - overloaded globally and inline defined
 */
inline
std::ostream& operator << (std::ostream& strm, const Fraction& f)
{
    f.printOn(strm);      // call member function for output
    return strm;          // return stream for chaining
}


/* standard input operator
 * - overloaded globally and inline defined
 */
inline
std::istream& operator >> (std::istream& strm, Fraction& f)
{
    f.scanFrom(strm);     // call member function for input
    return strm;          // return stream for chaining
}


} // **** END namespace CPPBook ********************************

#endif    // FRACTION_HPP
```

The `protected` Access Keyword

The decisive difference from the previous declaration of the Fraction class is that now the protected access keyword, instead of `private`, precedes the members numer and denom:

```cpp
namespace CPPBook {
  class Fraction {
    protected:
      int numer;
      int denom;
    ...
  };
  ...
}
```

Using `protected`, access to members by the user of the class is prevented in the same way as with `private`. However, derived classes are granted access. With `private`, even derived classes would be refused access.

Because inheritance is a basic concept of C++, the class designer should support this by using `protected`, instead of `private`, for access of members. Because we need access to these members in order to reduce them, a derivation with the semantics we'd like to have would otherwise not be possible. Without having access to the internal values of the fraction, we would only be able to add new properties that can be implemented using the public interface of the base class.

5.1.2 The Derived Class `RFraction`

Now that the `Fraction` class has been prepared for its role as a base class, we can derive the `RFraction` class (see Figure 5.2). The name 'RFraction' stands for 'reducible fraction'. This means that the objects of this class are fractions that, in principle at least, can be reduced.

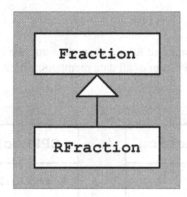

Figure 5.2. `RFraction` as a derived class of `Fraction`

New Operations

We introduce three new functions:

- The function `isReducible()` tells us whether the fraction can be reduced.
- The function `gcd()` returns the greatest common divisor (GCD) (of the numerator and denominator) with which the fraction can be reduced.
- The function `reduce()` reduces the fraction (as long as it has not already been reduced).

Reimplemented Operations

In addition to the new operations, some of the existing operations must be redefined for use with the RFraction class:

- The constructors must be redefined, because, in principle, they are not inherited.
- The operator *= and the input function scanFrom() must be redefined, because their implementation cannot be derived from the class Fraction and must be *overridden* (the reasons for this will be explained later).

New Members

In addition to the members numer and denom, which are inherited from the base class Fraction, the new Boolean member reducible is introduced. This determines whether the fraction is reducible, or whether it has already been reduced. Of course, this could be recalculated whenever needed, but having the information available in a member saves time because the property is only calculated when there is a change in the value of the fraction.

UML Notation

Figure 5.3 shows the UML notation of RFraction class and the relevant parts of the base class Fraction. Note the hash sign in front of all data members, which signifies protected member access.

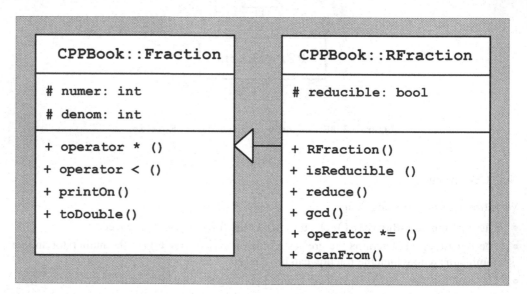

Figure 5.3. Derived and new members of the RFraction class

5.1.3   Declaration of the Derived Class RFraction

As usual, the class declaration is found in a separate header file, which has the following structure:

```
// inherit/rfrac1.hpp

#ifndef RFRACTION_HPP
#define RFRACTION_HPP
```

// header file of the base class
```
#include "frac.hpp"
```

*// **** BEGIN namespace CPPBook *******************************
```
namespace CPPBook {
```

```
/* class RFraction
 * - derived from Fraction
 * - access to inherited members limited (public remains public)
 */
class RFraction : public Fraction {
  protected:
    bool reducible;          // true: fraction is reducible

    // auxiliary function: returns the GCD of the numerator and denominator
    unsigned gcd() const;

  public:
    /* default constructor, and one- and two-parameter constructor
     * - parameters are passed to the Fraction constructor
     */
    RFraction(int n = 0, int d = 1) : Fraction(n,d) {
        reducible = (gcd() > 1);
    }

    // multiplicative assignement (reimplemented)
    const RFraction& operator*= (const RFraction&);

    // input from a stream (reimplemented)
    void scanFrom(std::istream&);

    // reduce fraction
    void reduce();
```

```
    // test reducililty
    bool isReducible() const {
        return reducible;
    }
};


} // **** END namespace CPPBook *******************************

#endif     // RFRACTION_HPP
```

First, the header file of the base class must be included because the declaration of the derived class uses it:

```
#include "frac.hpp"
```

The class declaration actually makes it explicit that it is a derived class:

```
class RFraction : public Fraction {
    ...
};
```

A derived class is declared with a colon, followed by an optional access keyword and the name of the base class. It does not matter whether or not the base class itself is a derived class.

The syntax for the declaration of a derived class reads as follows[2]:

```
class derivedclass :  [access] baseclass {
        declarations
};
```

The optional access keyword indicates whether and to what extent access to inherited members is restricted:

- With `public`, there are no additional limitations. Public members of the base class are also public in the derived class, `protected` members remain `protected` and `private` members remain `private`.

- With `protected`, restrictions apply. All public members of the base class become members that can no longer be accessed by the user; however, derived classes do have access. Therefore, `public` becomes `protected`, `protected` remains `protected` and `private` remains `private`.

- With `private`, all members of the base class become private members. Neither the user nor derived classes have access to these members.

In other words, the access keyword for base classes specifies the minimum encapsulation derived members get from the perspective of the derived class.

---

[2] As we will see in Section 5.4.1 on page 332, multiple base classes can also be specified.

The default value for the optional access keyword is `private`, but you should always explicitly specify it in order to improve readability (many compilers will output a warning message if no access keyword is entered for the base class).

The `RFraction` class does not limit access to derived members of the `Fraction` class any further. This means that the inherited public member functions such as `printOn()`, and the multiplication and comparison operators, can also be called from `RFraction`:

```
namespace CPPBook {
  class Fraction {
    ...
    public:
      void printOn(std::ostream&) const;
    ...
  };

  class RFraction : public Fraction {
    ...
  };
}

void foo()
{
    CPPBook::RFraction rf;
    ...
    rf.printOn(std::cout);   // OK: printOn() is also public for RFraction
}
```

5.1.4 Inheritance and Constructors

Constructors play a special role in inheritance. In effect, they cannot be inherited. All constructors for objects of a derived class must be redefined. As for any class, if no constructors are defined, only the default constructor and the copy constructor are provided.

Although constructors of base classes are not inherited, they do play a part in the initialization of an object. Constructors are called in a top-down fashion. When an object of a derived class is created, the constructor of the base class is called, which only initializes the part of the object that is derived from the base class. Afterwards, the constructor of the derived class is called, which initializes any newly added members. It can also be used to modify initializations of the constructor of the base class, which might no longer be useful from the point of view of the derived class. In our example, during the creation of an object of the `RFraction` class, a `Fraction` constructor is called first, followed by an `RFraction` constructor.

Note that the arguments for the construction of the object are *not* automatically passed to the constructor of the base class. Provided that nothing else is specified, the default constructor of the base class is called instead. This is because the parameters for the constructor of the derived class may have very different semantics from those of the base class. There could also be a different number of parameters, or different types.

Initialization lists also play a role here. They offer the possibility of passing arguments to the constructor of the base class. These arguments might be the parameters of the constructor of the derived class, or any other data.

The following demonstrates the declaration of the first constructor of the RFraction class:

```
class RFraction : public Fraction {
  public:
    RFraction(int n = 0, int d = 1) : Fraction(n,d) {
        reducible = (gcd() > 1);
    }
    ...
};
```

The constructor is declared with the same parameters and default arguments that are used in the Fraction class. Therefore, a numerator and a denominator can be passed as an integer. If this is not the case, 0 and 1 are used as default values. These parameters are then passed on to the constructor of the base class Fraction, where they are used for the initialization of numer and denom.

The statements of the RFraction constructor are executed after the call to the Fraction constructor. Thus numer and denom are already initialized when the statements of the RFraction constructor are executed. In this case, we use the values of numer and denom to process the initial value of reducible.

Example of the Initialization of an Object of the RFraction Class

The exact procedure of initialization will be explained in the following example.

With the declaration

```
CPPBook::RFraction x(91,39);
```

an object x of the RFraction class is created and initialized with $\frac{91}{39}$. This happens in the following steps:

- First, memory is allocated for the object, whose value is undefined:

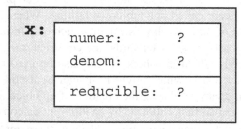

- The initializer list of the constructor of RFraction defines that the int/int constructor of the Fraction class has to be called with the parameters (or default values) passed to it:

```
class RFraction : public Fraction {
    ...
    RFraction(int n = 0, int d = 1) : Fraction(n,d) {
        reducible = (gcd() > 1);
    }
    ...
};
```

- Therefore, the int/int constructor of the Fraction class is called with the values 91 and 39, which initializes the part of the object inherited from Fraction:

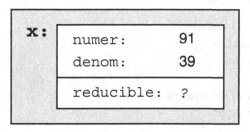

- Finally, the statements of the RFraction constructor are executed, which initialize the member reducible by a call of gcd():

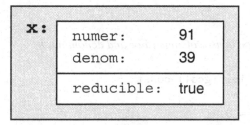

The fact that the statements in the base constructor are called before those in the constructor of the derived class is important. Only this way, the derived class can evaluate the initialized members of the base class. This also gives the opportunity to modify the initializations of the base class. However, note that you should never use this ability to change the semantic meaning of inherited members (see Section 5.5 on page 344 for some design pitfalls regarding this).

The whole mechanism is recursive. If a base class is a derived class itself, the constructor of its base class is called first. Again, the initializer list of the base class indicates what parameters are passed to the constructor of its base class. Thus, an initializer list can only submit arguments to its direct base class.

If constructors have to be called for base classes as well as for members, then the constructors of the base classes are called first.

Inheritance and Destructors

Destructors (the counterpart to the constructors), on the other hand, are called bottom-up. The statements of the destructor of a derived class are executed first, and then those of the base class.

If destructors have to be called for base classes and also for data members, then the destructors for the members are called first.

Thus destructors are always called in the opposite order to that of constructors.

5.1.5   Implementation of Derived Classes

The implementation of a derived class looks the same as with every other class. The dot-C file of the RFraction class looks as follows:

```cpp
// inherit/rfrac1.cpp

// header file for min() and abs()
#include <algorithm>
#include <cstdlib>

// include header file of the separate class
#include "rfrac.hpp"

// **** BEGIN namespace CPPBook *****************************
namespace CPPBook {

/* gcd()
 * - greatest common divisor of numerator and denominator
 */
unsigned RFraction::gcd() const
{
    if (numer == 0) {
        return denom;
    }

    /* determine the greatest number that divides, without remainder,
     * the denominator and the numerator
     */
    unsigned divisor = std::min(std::abs(numer),denom);
    while (numer % divisor != 0  ||  denom % divisor != 0) {
        --divisor;
    }
    return divisor;
}

/* reduce()
 */
```

```
void RFraction::reduce()
{
    // if reducible, divide numerator and denominator by CGD
    if (reducible) {
        int divisor = gcd();

        numer /= divisor;
        denom /= divisor;

        reducible = false;          // no longer reducible
    }
}

/* operator *=
 * - reimplemented
 */
const RFraction& RFraction::operator*= (const RFraction& f)
{
    // as with the base class:
    numer *= f.numer;
    denom *= f.denom;

    // still reduced?
    if (!reducible) {
        reducible = (gcd() > 1);
    }

    return  *this;
}

/* scanFrom()
 */
void RFraction::scanFrom(std::istream& strm)
{
    Fraction::scanFrom(strm);     // call scanFrom() of the base class

    reducible = (gcd() > 1);      // test reducibility
}

} // **** END namespace CPPBook *******************************
```

First, the newly introduced member function for the calculation of the GCD is implemented. If the numerator is 0, the GCD is the denominator (the fraction $\frac{0}{7}$ therefore has the GCD 7). Otherwise, the first number that divides the numerator and the denominator without remainder is searched in a loop (the modulo operator % returns the remainder after the division). If no other divisor is found, the loop will end with 1 as the GCD. For the initial value of the loop, the standard function `std::min()`, defined in `<algorithm>`, which returns the minimum of the two values, and the standard function `std::abs()`, defined in `<cstdlib>`, which returns the absolute value of an integer, are used[3].

The other new function, `reduce()`, divides the numerator and denominator by the calculated GCD, as long as the fraction is reducible.

Reimplementation of Derived Functions

Derived member functions and operators may have to be reimplemented if their implementation in the base class is no longer valid. In this example, this is the case for the `*=` operator and the input function `scanFrom()`. The process of replacing an implementation of a base class by another in a derived class is called *overriding*.

In both cases, without a reimplementation, the RFraction may get an inconsistent status after these operations. This is because the two functions manipulate `numer` and `denom`. Their values, however, determine the value of `reducible`. Because their implementation in the base class does not change `reducible` (`reducible` is not yet known there), this member may not have a valid value.

In fact, using the `*=` operator, the RFraction for which this operation is called may change from a non-reducible to a reducible status. This is, for example, the case if the non-reducible object $\frac{7}{3}$ is multiplied by $\frac{3}{7}$. Without a reimplementation, `reducible` would remain `false`, even though the value has changed to $\frac{21}{21}$.

With `scanFrom()`, the value of the RFraction is modified so that it gets an arbitrary new value. Without overriding the implementation, no adjustment of the `reducible` member would be carried out. This could also lead to `reducible` not being set correctly. The information about whether the RFraction is reducible, therefore, has to be redetermined every time a new value is read.

With a reimplementation, there are two options:

- A complete reimplementation.
- A call of the implementation of the base class, with corrections.

As usual, a decision has to be made between consistency and possible run-time advantages. A complete reimplementation, as has been done with the `*=` operator, saves running time, but may need to be altered if there are changes in the base class. With the second option, as used with `scanFrom()`, additional procedural steps need only be reimplemented for the derived classes.

---

[3] There are, undoubtedly, better algorithms for the calculation of a GCD.

5.1.6 Application of Derived Classes

A derived class is used in the same way as any other class. Objects are created by constructors and are manipulated using derived, new or overridden operations.

The following sample program clarifies this:

```cpp
// inherit/rftest1.cpp

// header files
#include <iostream>
#include "rfrac.hpp"

int main()
{
    // declare reducible fraction
    CPPBook::RFraction x(91,39);

    // output x
    std::cout << x;
    std::cout << (x.isReducible() ? " (reducible)"
                                  : " (non reducible)") << std::endl;

    // reduce x
    x.reduce();

    // output x
    std::cout << x;
    std::cout << (x.isReducible() ? " (reducible)"
                                  : " (non reducible)") << std::endl;

    // multiply x by 3
    x *= 3;

    // output x
    std::cout << x;
    std::cout << (x.isReducible() ? " (reducible)"
                                  : " (non reducible)") << std::endl;
}
```

It has the following output:

```
91/39 (reducible)
7/3 (non reducible)
21/3 (reducible)
```

First, the object x of the RFraction class is created using the declaration

```
CPPBook::RFraction x(91,39);
```

and is initialized with $\frac{91}{39}$. This happens as explained on page 266.

Next, x is written:

```
std::cout << x;
```

It is also written whether x is reducible. The expression

```
x.isReducible() ? " (reducible)" : " (non-reducible)"
```

processes whether '(reducible)' or '(non-reducible)' is written. Because the ternary operator ?: (introduced in Section 3.2.3 on page 40) has a lower priority than the output operator <<, the expression must be placed in parentheses.

After the call to reduce(), x's status is output again. Finally, x is multiplied by 3 and is output once more. The multiplication by an integer is made possible by the RFraction constructor. Because it can also only be called using a single-integer argument, it defines an automatic type conversion from integers to RFractions (see Section 4.6.1 on page 217). Thus, 3 is converted into the RFraction $\frac{3}{1}$ and passed as a parameter to the *= operator.

The output operator of the RFraction class has not been overridden, so the operation that was declared in the Fraction class is used automatically:

```
std::ostream& operator << (std::ostream& strm, const Fraction& f);
```

Using the Is-A Relationship

When outputting an RFraction with

```
std::cout << x;
```

we need to note the following: although the operator function is only defined for a Fraction as its second operand, an RFraction can also be passed. This example shows that an object of type RFraction can be used in place of a Fraction object.

This is a direct consequence of the *is-a* relationship. Because the RFraction class is derived from Fraction, an RFraction *is a* Fraction, and can be used as such at any time. By means of inheritance, in principle, an automatic type conversion of an object of a derived class to an object of its base class is defined. With the conversion, the object is only processed with the properties that objects of the base class possess. In particular, it only has the data members of the base class. The members that were added due to inheritance are simply left out, or are ignored.

In this case, this is not a problem, as only numerators and denominators are used in the output of an RFraction. There are, however, cases in which this automatic type conversion can be problematic. We will look at relevant pitfalls in Section 5.5 on page 344.

5.1.7 Constructors for Base-Class Objects

Multiplication for the RFraction class was inherited from Fraction. However, it cannot be used as expected. This is because although two objects of type RFraction can be multiplied, the result cannot be assigned to an RFraction:

```
CPPBook::RFraction rf;
...
std::cout << rf * rf;      // OK: outputs the square of rf
...
rf = rf * rf;              // ERROR: assignment to RFraction not allowed
```

The multiplication inherited from the Fraction class still returns a Fraction. However, a Fraction is not an RFraction (the *is-a* relationship only applies the other way around). Therefore, a Fraction cannot be assigned to an RFraction.

One way to eliminate this problem is to reimplement the multiplication operator. The problem can, however, also be solved by defining a type conversion from a Fraction to an RFraction, which is made possible by implementing another constructor:

```
class RFraction : public Fraction {
  public:
      /* constructor for the type conversion of Fraction to RFraction
       * - parameter is passed to the copy constructor of Fraction
       */
      RFraction (const Fraction& f) : Fraction(f) {
          reducible = (gcd() > 1);
      }
      ...
};
```

As usual, when creating an RFraction, a constructor of the Fraction class is called first, followed by the statements of the constructor of the RFraction class. Because the Fraction constructor is called for the Fraction that was passed to the RFraction constructor, the copy constructor of the Fraction base class is called.

Because the constructor has only one parameter, it defines an automatic type conversion of Fraction to RFraction. As a consequence, a Fraction, which is the result of a multiplication, can be assigned to an RFraction:

```
CPPBook::RFraction rf;
...
rf = rf * rf;          // OK: using type conversion of Fraction to RFraction
```

In the same way, a Fraction can also be used as a parameter for multiplicative assignment:

```
CPPBook::RFraction rf;
CPPBook::Fraction f;
...
rf *= f;               // OK: using type conversion of f to RFraction
```

Without this implicit type conversion, the parameter of the *= operator must be declared as Fraction:

```
class RFraction : public Fraction {
    ...
    const RFraction& RFraction::operator*= (const Fraction&);
    ...
};
```

Limitations of Constructors for Base-Class Objects

It is rarely useful to have a constructor that can convert an object of the base class into an object of a derived class. This should only be available if there is a reasonable implicit initialization for all additional attributes. Regarding this, this is a special example because whether or not the fraction is reducible depends directly on the members that are already available to Fractions (i.e. numerator and denominator)[4].

Often, attributes are added whose values are independent of previous attributes. If we had introduced, for example, a class ColoredFraction, where a fraction is assigned a certain color as an additional attribute, a type conversion from a Fraction would not be very useful. The color of a fraction is a property that has no relation to previous properties. One can actually adopt a default color. However, it is usually more useful to disallow conversions of a Fraction to a ColoredFraction, so that, in a program that uses colored fractions, uncolored fractions are not used as colored fractions by mistake or accident.

Note that each automatic type conversion increases the danger of an unintentional behavior, because the compiler can no longer recognize whether an object is incorrectly used as an object of another class or not. Again, a function for explicit type conversion can be useful here. A function might, for example, require a Fraction and a color as its arguments. Ultimately, it is a design decision, which you have to balance by taking into account the risk of an unintentional type conversion and the advantage of a simplified type conversion.

5.1.8 Summary

- Classes can be connected to one another by *inheritance*.
- A *derived class* takes on (*inherits* or *derives*) all properties of the *base class* and typically supplements these with new properties.
- Objects of derived classes include the members of the base class and all newly added members.
- The characteristic of inheritance is the *is-a* relationship: An object of a derived class *is an* object of the base class (with additional properties).

---

[4] Please excuse this rather untypical example. Nevertheless, it helps demonstrate several problems that you should be aware of.

- An object of a derived class can be used as an object of the base class at any time. It then reduces itself to the properties of the base class.
- Constructors are not inherited, but are called top-down. Destructors are called bottom-up.
- Using initializer lists, parameters can be passed to the constructors of a base class. Without an initializer list the default constructor of the base class is called.
- You can, and sometimes have to, *override* derived operations.

5.2 Virtual Functions

The first version of the RFraction ('reducible fraction') class, introduced in the previous section, has a potential problem: its use can lead to inconsistencies with objects of the class. This is due to the fact that some of the functions of the base class have been overridden (which, ironically enough, was done to avoid possible inconsistencies). Under certain circumstances, the overridden functions of the base class can still be called for objects of the derived class.

This section describes the various problems that can arise when overriding functions of a base class, and how they can be avoided. Doing this, a fundamental language feature is introduced for inheritance and polymorphism: virtual functions.

5.2.1 Problems with Overriding Functions

The RFraction class that was introduced in the previous section, overrides two functions of the base class Fraction, operator*=() and scanFrom(). This was necessary because the implementation of the derived functions was not suitable for RFractions (see Section 5.1.5 on page 268). In the base class Fraction, the declaration of these functions looks as follows:

```
class Fraction {
   ...
  public:
    // multiplicative assignment
    const Fraction& operator *= (const Fraction&);

    // input from a stream
    void scanFrom(std::istream&);
    ...
};
```

In the derived class RFraction, we have:

```
class RFraction : public Fraction {
   ...
  public:
    // multiplicative assignment (reimplemented)
    const RFraction& operator*= (const RFraction&);

    // input from a stream (reimplemented)
    void scanFrom(std::istream&);
    ...
};
```

However, this reimplementation can cause problems, which should be identified and, if possible, eliminated.

The following application program uncovers these problems:

```
// inherit/rftest2.cpp

// header files
#include <iostream>
#include "rfrac.hpp"
#include "frac.hpp"

int main()
{
    // declare RFraction
    CPPBook::RFraction x(7,3);

    // pointer to fraction refers to x
    CPPBook::Fraction* xp = &x;

    // declare fraction with reciprocal value of x
    CPPBook::Fraction f(3,7);

    *xp *= f;               // PROBLEM: calls Fraction::operator*=()

    // output x
    std::cout << x;
    std::cout << (x.isReducible() ? " (reducible)"
                                  : " (non reducible)") << std::endl;

    std::cout << "enter fraction (numer/denom): ";

    std::cin >> x;          // PROBLEM: indirectly calls Fraction::scanFrom()

    // output x
    std::cout << x;
    std::cout << (x.isReducible() ? " (reducible)"
                                  : " (non reducible)") << std::endl;
}
```

Two statements of the program are problematic. In both cases, we have that objects of a derived class can also be used as objects of the base class.

Manipulations via Pointers to the Base Class

In the first case, the problem arises from the manipulation of the RFraction x being carried out via a pointer that is declared as a pointer to objects of the base class:

```
CPPBook::RFraction x(7,3);
CPPBook::Fraction* xp = &x;

CPPBook::Fraction  f(3,7);

*xp *= f;              // PROBLEM: calls Fraction::operator*=()
```

The fact that a pointer of the type Fraction* points to an RFraction is absolutely fine. It is a consequence of the is-a relationship, which signifies inheritance:

- An RFraction *is a* Fraction.
- An RFraction can therefore be used as a Fraction at any time.

In this case, the RFraction x is used as a Fraction, to which xp points.

If, however, the x is now manipulated via the fraction pointer xp, the member function of the class Fraction, instead of the class RFraction, is called. This is because, during compilation, the compiler binds this call as call of the *= operation for Fractions, because it is a pointer to a Fraction. This implementation of *=, however, only knows the members numer and denom and does not adapt reducible.

We are therefore faced with an inconsistency in the existing program. The fraction 7/3 is multiplied by 3/7, but the reducible member keeps its old value, even though it is incorrect. This becomes clear with the following output statement:

```
21/21 (non reducible)
```

Manipulations via References to the Base Class

A similar problem, although not so easy to detect, is the input of the RFraction x:

```
CPPBook::RFraction x(7,3);
...
std::cin >> x;    // PROBLEM: indirectly calls Fraction::scanFrom()
```

The input function of the base class is used incorrectly here. This is due to the fact that the RFraction x is used by a reference of the Fraction class. The input function that has already been defined in the base class Fraction is then called:

```
inline std::istream& operator >> (std::istream& strm, Fraction& f)
{
    f.scanFrom(strm);      // call member function for input
    return strm;           // return stream for chaining
}
```

This is also an application of the is-a relationship. The RFraction x is a fraction and can therefore be used for the initialization of the fraction reference f. Because f is a second name for a Fraction, the member function scanFrom() of the class Fraction is called to read the new value of f. This reads numer and denom, but does not set the member reducible, because it is not known to Fractions. The RFraction thus maintains the old status in the member reducible, despite the fact that a new (possibly reducible) value has been input.

Due to the usage of the type Fraction, the reimplemented function for reading objects of the class RFraction is not called when using the >> operator. Only a direct call of scanFrom() would work.

5.2.2 Static and Dynamic Binding of Functions

Static Binding of Functions

There same basic problem also occurs with these examples:

- An object of a derived class may be used as an object of the base class anytime, due to the is-a relationship.
- This is also valid if it is manipulated via pointers or references to objects of the base class.
- Because the compiler assumes that it is an object of the base class, the faulty member function of the base class is called, even if it was reimplemented for objects of the derived class.

The compiler makes sure that the member function of the base class is called, because it usually binds function calls statically. This means that it determines the type of an object for which a function is called, and generates code that calls the function that belongs to this type. This also usually applies to pointers and references.

In general, static binding means that, at run time, if a pointer points to an object of a derived class, the incorrect member function of the base class is called, instead of the reimplemented version of the derived class. This applies to references as well. Because of the static binding, any additional information that objects of a derived class contain is therefore lost during function calls.

Dynamic Binding by Means of Virtual Functions

To keep the information of the original type of objects when they are being manipulated with function calls, the calls must not be bound statically. Instead, code has to get generated that, at run time, the correct function is called, depending on the actual type of the object. This behavior is described as *dynamic binding* or *late binding*[5].

Dynamic binding is possible in C++. To do this, the virtual keyword is used. If a member function is declared as a virtual function, then, with the use of pointers and references, at run time it is decided what function is actually called. In this way, the appropriate function is called.

---

[5] Rather confusingly, the term *dynamic binding* is also used to describe the mechanism of *shared libraries*. However, the two concepts are not related.

Thus the functions that we reimplemented in the derived class RFraction need to be declared in the base class Fraction as virtual. As a base class usually does not which functions are reimplemented by derived classes, in general all functions of the base class that can be overridden by derived classes should be declared as virtual. Only by doing this is a class properly prepared for inheritance.

If the functions of the base class are not declared as virtual, the problems that were described earlier arise. For this reason, with inheritance, one should stick to the following rules:

- Non-virtual functions should not be overridden.
- If this is necessary for the implementation of a derived class, it should not be derived.

The declaration of the base class Fraction therefore reads as follows:

```cpp
// inherit/frac92.hpp

#ifndef FRACTION_HPP
#define FRACTION_HPP

// include standard header files
#include <iostream>

// **** BEGIN namespace CPPBook ********************************
namespace CPPBook {

class Fraction {

  protected:
    int numer;
    int denom;

  public:
    /* error class
     */
    class DenomIsZero {
    };

    /* default constructor, one-, and two-parameter constructor
     */
    Fraction(int = 0, int = 1);

    /* multiplication
     * - global friend function, so that an automatic
     *   type conversion of the first operand is possible
     */
```

```
        friend Fraction operator * (const Fraction&, const Fraction&);

        /* multiplicative assignment
         * - new: virtual
         */
        virtual const Fraction& operator *= (const Fraction&);

        /* comparison
         * - global friend function, so that an automatic
         *   type conversion of the first operand is possible
         */
        friend bool operator < (const Fraction&, const Fraction&);

        /* output to and input from a stream
         * - new: virtual
         */
        virtual void printOn(std::ostream&) const;
        virtual void scanFrom(std::istream&);

        /* type conversion to double
         * - new: virtual
         */
        virtual double toDouble() const;
};

/* operator *
 * - global friend function
 * - inline defined
 */
inline Fraction operator * (const Fraction& a, const Fraction& b)
{
        /* simply multiply numerator and denominator
         * - this saves time
         */
        return Fraction(a.numer * b.numer, a.denom * b.denom);
}

/* standard output operator
 * - overloaded globally and inline defined
 */
inline
```

```
std::ostream& operator << (std::ostream& strm, const Fraction& f)
{
    f.printOn(strm);        // call member function for output
    return strm;            // return stream for chaining
}


/* standard input operator
 * - overloaded globally and inline defined
 */
inline
std::istream& operator >> (std::istream& strm, Fraction& f)
{
    f.scanFrom(strm);       // call member function for input
    return strm;            // return stream for chaining
}


} // **** END namespace CPPBook *******************************

#endif    // FRACTION_HPP
```

All functions that can be reimplemented in derived classes, for any reason, can be declared as virtual. Only constructors and friend functions, which, in principle, cannot be virtual, are excluded from this rule.

Reading an RFraction Using Virtual Functions

Now when reading a reducible fraction, everything works as expected. The scanFrom() implementation of the derived class RFraction is used, because the operator>>() function knows that an RFraction is actually being read:

```
namespace CPPBook {
  class Fraction {
    ...
    public:
      virtual void scanFrom(std::istream&);
      ...
  };


  inline
  std::istream& operator >> (std::istream& strm, Fraction& f)
  {
      f.scanFrom(strm);   // because of virtual: correct scanFrom() is called
      return strm;        // return stream for chaining
```

```
    }

    class RFraction : public Fraction {
      ...
      public:
        virtual void scanFrom(std::istream&);
        ...
    };
}

int main()
{
    CPPBook::RFraction x (7,3);
    ...
    std::cin >> x;          // OK: indirectly calls RFraction::scanFrom()
    ...
}
```

If the overloaded operator function >> for fractions calls the member function scanFrom() for its parameter f, as f is a reference and scanFrom() is declared as being virtual, at run time, it is decided what class f actually belongs to. If it is an object of a derived class, the implementation of scanFrom() of this class is automatically called, as long as it has one.

The function scanFrom() does not necessarily need to be declared as being virtual in the derived class. Because the function in the base class is virtual, it is automatically virtual in the derived class as well.

Running-Time Disadvantages of virtual

Note that, by declaring a function as being virtual, a call to it can last considerably longer. For pointers and references, instead of a direct function call, code has to be generated to determine what function has to be called at run time.

Particularly striking is the difference with inline functions. Because, in the case of pointers and references, the function that is called is decided at run time, the function call cannot be replaced by the statement in the function body during compilation. Thus the run-time advantage of inline functions does not apply to pointers and references if virtual functions are used.

For this reason, in practice, it can be useful to equip classes with just a few, or even no, virtual functions. The classes are then not very suitable for inheritance. However, the performance is significantly better. This is, again, a design decision.

5.2.3   Overloading versus Overriding

Assuming that everything works with virtual functions, one can restart the application program from page 277 and surprisingly find that one problem is solved, but the other still stands: the multiplicative assignment using the pointer xp does not work with virtual functions either.

This is due to the fact that the virtual operator function of the base class was not overridden, but overloaded. The parameters are not equal:

```
namespace CPPBook {
  class Fraction {
    ...
    public:
      virtual const Fraction& operator *= (const Fraction&);
      ...
  };

  class RFraction : public Fraction {
    ...
    public:
      virtual const RFraction& operator*= (const RFraction&);
      ...
  };
}

int main()
{
    CPPBook::RFraction x(7,3);
    CPPBook::Fraction  f(3,7);
    CPPBook::Fraction* xp = &x;
    ...
    *xp *= f;              // PROBLEM: still calls Fraction::operator*=()
    ...
}
```

In the base class, the parameter of the operator *= has the class Fraction, but in the derived class it has the class RFraction. Because of this, the implementation of the derived class is not a true substitution for the implementation of the base class, but just an addition.

The new implementation is called for objects of the derived class. For pointers and references of the Fraction class, however, it is still the case that only the implementation of the base class exists. It is not overridden in the derived class. Although the functions to be called are decided at run time, the implementation of the base class Fraction is also used for RFractions, because there is no reimplementation of the operation defined in the base class.

When overriding inherited functions, you should therefore adhere to the following rule:

- A virtual function of a base class is only really overridden in a derived class if the number and type of the parameters are identical.

In order to deal with the problem, the *= operator in the derived class needs to be declared with the same parameters and the same return type as those of the base class:

```
namespace CPPBook {
  class RFraction : public Fraction {
    ...
  public:
    virtual const Fraction& operator*= (const Fraction&);
    ...
  };
}
```

As with the overloading of functions in general, a differentiation of the return type only is not allowed.

There is, however, one exception to this rule. If a virtual function of a base class returns a pointer or reference of this base class, with a new implementation in a derived class, a pointer or reference of this derived class may be returned instead. However, a pointer must remain a pointer and a reference must remain a reference.

Thus the following reimplementation is also possible:

```
namespace CPPBook {
  class RFraction : public Fraction {
    ...
  public:
    virtual const RFraction& operator*= (const Fraction&);
    ...
  };
}
```

5.2.4 Access to Parameters of the Base Class

Using the solution introduced here (that the parameter of a member function is an object of the base class) immediately creates another problem: with the implementation of the operator, it is no longer possible to access the non-public members of the parameter:

```
const Fraction& RFraction::operator*= (const Fraction& f)
{
    numer *= f.numer;        // ERROR: no access to f.numer
    denom *= f.denom;        // ERROR: no access to f.denom
    ...
}
```

The operator is implemented for the class RFraction, but uses an object of a different class as a parameter. It does not matter whether the class is a base class and whether there is private or protected access to its members. From the RFraction class's point of view, Fractions are objects of a different type, for which only public access is granted. Thus we have another rule:

- For objects of the base class that are submitted as parameters, there is only access to public members in derived classes.

For this reason, access to the members of the parameter can only be achieved via a public interface. Because no member functions for the querying of numerators and denominators exist (commercial classes would, of course, provide these), in this case, the implementation of the base class has to be called, which multiplies the RFraction with the submitted parameter. Possible inconsistencies that may occur can then be removed:

```
const Fraction& RFraction::operator*= (const Fraction& f)
{
    /* new: calling the implementation of the base class
     * - no access to non-public members of f exists
     */
    Fraction::operator*= (f);

    // still reduced?
    if (!reducible) {
        reducible = (gcd() > 1);
    }

    return  *this;
}
```

5.2.5   Virtual Destructors

There is another problem that can arise with inheritance. It concerns explicit memory management.

If an object of a derived class is created using new, its type is clear:

```
// create object of the class RFraction
CPPBook::RFraction* kbp = new CPPBook::RFraction;
```

However, when deleting the object using the delete keyword, this clarity may not exist. Because an object of a derived class can be used as an object of a base class, it can also be released as such:

```
CPPBook::Fraction* bp;

bp = new CPPBook::RFraction;      // create RFraction
...
delete bp;                        // release RFraction using Fraction pointer
```

The same problem that appears with reimplemented functions in derived classes also appears here: the `delete` operator leads to the call of all destructors that may be available. As long as no dynamic binding takes place, the fact that an object of a derived class is actually being released is lost, and only the destructor of the class `Fraction` is called. Therefore, even if a destructor is implemented for `RFractions`, this is not called. This means that if the destructor of a derived class, for example, releases memory allocated for additional members, this would not be released.

For this not to arise, a *virtual destructor* has to be declared *in the base class*. This applies even if the base class does not actually need a destructor (the default destructor is not virtual).

We therefore have yet another rule for inheritance:

- A class is only generally suitable for inheritance if a virtual destructor is declared.

In our example, this means that the base class `Fraction` must have a (albeit empty) virtual destructor:

```
namespace CPPBook {
  class Fraction {
    ...
    public:
      virtual ~Fraction() {
      }
      ...
  };
}
```

5.2.6 Using Inheritance Correctly

To summarize, we will go through the example of the `Fraction` and `RFraction` classes again, highlighting all possible problems and their solutions.

Declaration of the Base Class `Fraction`

The base class `Fraction` must meet the requirements that makes it suitable for inheritance:

- All functions that can be overridden must be declared as virtual.
- A virtual destructor must be defined.

This therefore produces the following header file for the base class `Fraction`:

```
// inherit/frac93.hpp

#ifndef FRACTION_HPP
#define FRACTION_HPP

// include standard header files
#include <iostream>
```

```
// **** BEGIN namespace CPPBook *********************************
namespace CPPBook {

class Fraction {
  protected:
    int numer;
    int denom;

  public:
    /* error class
     */
    class DenomIsZero {
    };

    /* default constructor, one-, and two-parameter constructor
     */
    Fraction(int = 0, int = 1);

    /* multiplication
     * - global friend function, so that an automatic
     *   type conversion of the first operand is possible
     */
    friend Fraction operator * (const Fraction&, const Fraction&);

    /* multiplicative assignment
     * - new: virtual
     */
    virtual const Fraction& operator *= (const Fraction&);

    /* comparison
     * - global friend function, so that an automatic
     *   type conversion of the first operand is possible
     */
    friend bool operator < (const Fraction&, const Fraction&);

    /* output to and input from a stream
     * - new: virtual
     */
    virtual void printOn(std::ostream&) const;
    virtual void scanFrom(std::istream&);
```

```
    /* type conversion to double
     * - new: virtual
     */
    virtual double toDouble() const;

    // new: virtual destructor (without instructions)
    virtual ~Fraction() {
    }
};

/* operator *
 * - global friend function
 * - inline defined
 */
inline Fraction operator * (const Fraction& a, const Fraction& b)
{
    /* simply multiply numerator and denominator
     * - this saves time
     */
    return Fraction(a.numer * b.numer, a.denom * b.denom);
}

/* standard output operator
 * - overloaded globally and inline defined
 */
inline
std::ostream& operator << (std::ostream& strm, const Fraction& f)
{
    f.printOn(strm);      // call member function for output
    return strm;          // return stream for chaining
}

/* standard input operator
 * - overloaded globally and inline defined
 */
inline
std::istream& operator >> (std::istream& strm, Fraction& f)
{
    f.scanFrom(strm);     // call member function for input
    return strm;          // return stream for chaining
}
```

```
} // **** END namespace CPPBook ********************************

#endif   // FRACTION_HPP
```

The corresponding implementation corresponds to the version on page 237.

Declaration of the Derived Class `RFraction`

In the derived class, the following points need to be taken into account:

- The derived class may only override functions that were defined in the base class as being virtual. While doing this, the parameters and the return type must match.
- If the derived class is to be suitable for further inheritance, every additional function that can be overridden must also be declared as being virtual.

This produces the following header file for the derived class RFraction:

```
// inherit/rfrac3.hpp

#ifndef RFRACTION_HPP
#define RFRACTION_HPP


// header file of the base class
#include "frac.hpp"

// **** BEGIN namespace CPPBook ********************************
namespace CPPBook {

/* class RFraction
 * - derived from Fraction
 * - new no access to inherited members
 *   (public remains public)
 * - suitable for further inheritance
 */
class RFraction : public Fraction {
  protected:
    bool reducible;          // true: fraction is reducible

    // auxiliary function: returns the GCD of the numerator and denominator
    unsigned gcd() const;

  public:
    /* default constructor, and one- and two-parameter constructor
     * - parameters are passed to the Fraction constructor
```

```
    */
    RFraction (int n = 0, int d = 1) : Fraction(n,d) {
        reducible = (gcd() > 1);
    }

    // multiplicative assignment (reimplemented)
    virtual const RFraction& operator*= (const Fraction&);

    // input from a stream (reimplemented)
    virtual void scanFrom(std::istream&);

    // reduce fraction
    virtual void reduce();

    // test reducibility
    virtual bool isReducible() const {
        return reducible;
    }
};

} // **** END namespace CPPBook *****************************

#endif      // RFRACTION_HPP
```

Implementation of the Derived Class `RFraction`

In the dot-C file of the derived class, the new and overridden functions are implemented. One must make sure that only public access is granted to parameters that have the type of the base class:

```
// inherit/rfrac3.cpp

// header file for min() and abs()
#include <algorithm>
#include <cstdlib>

// include header file for seperate class
#include "rfrac.hpp"

// **** BEGIN namespace CPPBook *****************************
namespace CPPBook {
```

```
/* gcd()
 * - greatest common divisor of numerator and denominator
 */
unsigned RFraction::gcd() const
{
    if (numer == 0) {
        return denom;
    }

    /* determine the greatest number that divides, without remainder,
     * the denominator and the numerator
     */
    unsigned divisor = std::min(std::abs(numer),denom);
    while (numer % divisor != 0  ||  denom % divisor != 0) {
        divisor--;
    }
    return divisor;
}


/* reduce()
 */
void RFraction::reduce()
{
    // if reducible, divide numerator and denominator by CGD
    if (reducible) {
        int divisor = gcd();

        numer /= divisor;
        denom /= divisor;

        reducible = false;          // no longer reducible
    }
}


/* operator *=
 * - reimplemented for overwriting with types of the base class
 */
const RFraction& RFraction::operator*= (const Fraction& f)
{
    /* call implementation of the case class
     * - no access to non-public members of f exists
```

```
    */
    Fraction::operator*= (f);


    // still reduced ?
    if (!reducible) {
        reducible = (gcd() > 1);
    }


    return  *this;
}


/* scanFrom()
 */
void RFraction::scanFrom(std::istream& strm)
{
    Fraction::scanFrom (strm);      // call scanFrom() of the base class

    reducible= (gcd() > 1);      // test for reducible
}

} // **** END namespace CPPBook ******************************
```

5.2.7   Additional Pitfalls when Overriding Functions

When overriding member functions of the base class, there are some further issues that one has
to watch out for. We discuss these in the following paragraphs.

Differing Default Arguments

The default arguments of functions are used during compilation. They are therefore always static.

If virtual functions in the base class have a different default value than in the implementation
of the derived class, the correct function is called, but the incorrect default value is submitted.

Let us assume, for example, that a function init() is defined for Fractions and has 0 as
a default argument. The derived class RFraction overrides the function, but assigns 1 as the
default argument:

```
class Fraction {
    ...
    virtual void init(int = 0);
};
```

```
class RFraction : public Fraction {
    ...
    virtual void init(int = 1);
};
```

A call of the function init() can then lead to the different default values being used, although the implementation of the derived class is called:

```
CPPBook::RFraction x;
x.init();              // for x, calls RFraction::init(1)

CPPBook::Fraction* xp = &x;
xp->init();            // for x, calls RFraction::init(0)
```

In order to avoid this, we should heed the following rule:

- Overridden functions should have the same default argument as their base class.

Overloading means Overlapping

We have already seen that, when overriding an inherited function, the parameter types should be the same, because otherwise an overloading occurs instead of a true overriding. However, overloading a function in a derived class may be intentional. An inherited function can be supplemented with a function of the same name, but with additional parameters. In this case, it is important to know that although the function of the base class is not overridden, it can no longer be called by objects of the derived class. The overloaded implementation hides the derived one.

Let us look at the following example. The base class Fraction defines the member function init(), with an int as a parameter. The derived class RFraction also defines a function init(), but has a Fraction as its parameter:

```
class Fraction {
    ...
    void init(int = 0);
};

class RFraction : public Fraction {
    ...
    void init(const Fraction&);
};
```

For objects of the derived class, init() can only be called with a Fraction as a parameter:

```
CPPBook::RFraction x;
CPPBook::Fraction a;
...
x.init(a);          // OK
...
x.init(7);              // ERROR: Fraction::init(int) was overlapped
```

In derived classes, overloading therefore always means overlapping. This property was introduced in C++ for safety, so that an inadvertently incorrect parameter type could be recognized as an error more easily.

If the function of the base class is still to be usable, it must be redefined:

```cpp
class Fraction {
    ...
    void init(int);
};


class RFraction : public Fraction {
    ...
    void init(const Fraction&);
    void init(int i = 0) {
        Fraction::init (i);
    }
};
```

5.2.8   Private Inheritance and Pure Access Declarations

The implementation of the class RFraction may still cause problems. It is still the case still that, for RFractions, the inherited implementations of the base class may be called, instead of the reimplemented versions. However, this requires explicit type conversions and cannot happen by accident.

By using the scope operator, it can be explicitly required that, for all objects of the derived class, implementations of the base class are called:

```cpp
// inherit/rftest4.cpp

// header files
#include <iostream>
#include "rfrac.hpp"

int main()
{
    // declare RFraction
    CPPBook::RFraction x(7,3);

    /* multiply x by 3
     * BUT: use operator of the base class fraction
     */
    x.CPPBook::Fraction::operator *= (3);
```

```
// output x
std::cout << x;
std::cout << (x.isReducible() ? " (reducible)"
                              : " (non reducible)") << std::endl;
}
```

As the output of this program demonstrates, this can lead to inconsistencies (the fraction x is reducible after the multiplication, but returns that it is not):

```
21/3 (non reducible)
```

This kind of call is possible because, according to the declaration of the class RFraction, it was specified that public functions of the base class remain public. This still applies, even if they are overridden and virtual is used.

We can now argue as to whether this presents a problem or not. Because it must be explicitly indicated that the implementation of the base class is to be used, this kind of inconsistency cannot occur by mistake. Therefore, if this is what is required, one should be aware of the consequences. On the other hand, classes were introduced to provide a well-defined interface so that inconsistencies cannot be produced.

This problem can be avoided by using the access keywords private or protected for the base class when declaring the derived class:

```
class RFraction : protected Fraction {
    ...
};
```

The outcome of this is that all member functions of the base class are no longer public. They cannot be called by the user of the class unless they are reimplemented.

In the example of the RFraction class, this would, for example, mean that the I/O operations have to be declared (and implemented) as public functions once more. However, because we now need to reimplement each derived function again, it would seem that there is no benefit from using inheritance anymore. The same functionality could be provided by a separate RFraction class, which only *uses* an object of type Fraction internally.

However, members can be inherited with different scope limitations. To do this, a class has to be derived as protected or private. The scope limitation can then be suspended for individual members. This happens via so-called *pure access declarations*.

Using pure access declarations, the declaration of the RFraction class looks as follows:

```
// inherit/rfrac5.hpp

#ifndef RFRACTION_HPP
#define RFRACTION_HPP

// header file of the base class
#include "frac.hpp"

// **** BEGIN namespace CPPBook ********************************
```

```
namespace CPPBook {

/* class RFraction
 * - derived from Fraction
 * - new: no access to inherited members (public becomes protected)
 * - therefore, the is-a relationship is not longer valid
 */
class RFraction : protected Fraction {
  protected:
    bool reducible;              // true: fraction is reducible

    // auxiliary function: returns the GCD of the numerator and denominator
    unsigned gcd() const;

  public:
    /* default constructor, and one- and two-parameter constructor
     * - parameters are passed to the Fraction constructor
     */
    RFraction(int n = 0, int d = 1) : Fraction(n,d) {
        reducible = (gcd() > 1);
    }

    // new: pure access declaration for operations that remain public
    Fraction::printOn;
    Fraction::toDouble;

    // multiplicative assignment
    virtual const RFraction& operator*= (const Fraction&);

    // input from a stream
    virtual void scanFrom (std::istream&);

    // reduce fraction
    virtual void reduce();

    // test reducibility
    virtual bool isReducible() const {
        return reducible;
    }
};
```

```
    } // **** END namespace CPPBook *********************************

    #endif      // RFRACTION_HPP
```

Using this implementation, the multiplicative assignment of the base class can no longer be called for objects of the derived class. I/O operations and conversions to a floating-point value are still able to be called by means of a pure access declaration:

```
namespace CPPBook {
  class RFraction : protected Fraction {
    public:
        // new: pure access declaration for operations that remain public
        Fraction::printOn;
        Fraction::asDouble;
        ...
  };
}
```

The pure access declaration ensures that printOn() and asDouble() stay public, although, in general, derived public members become protected. Note that there are no parentheses after the derived members in a pure access declaration.

Private Inheritance versus Is-A Relationships

Non-public inheritance reduces the general concepts of inheritance to that of a pure reuse of code. In particular, the is-a relationship does **not** apply anymore. Thus you can no longer use an object of a derived class as an object of the base class:

```
CPPBook::RFraction x(91,39);
...
CPPBook::Fraction* xp = &x;  // ERROR: no is-a relationship with private inheritance
```

For the same reason, neither the friend functions nor the standard I/O operations of the class Fraction can be used anymore. They all have to be redefined for the class RFraction. Without the reimplementation of the output operator for RFractions, you cannot write their value to the standard output channel:

```
CPPBook::RFraction x(91,39);
...
std::cout << x;           // ERROR: no operator<<(ostream,RFraction) defined
```

Semantically speaking, this form of inheritance is not actually inheritance, but another form of *composition*. Using this type of inheritance, code for members and member functions can easily be reused by other classes. A conceptual inheritance, which, for example, is used when working with common terms and plays a part in the design of a program (see Section 5.3 on page 300), can only be implemented by means of public inheritance.

5.2.9 Summary

- Function calls are automatically bound statically. For objects, pointers, and references, the member function is called that is defined for the class with which the object, pointer, or reference was declared.
- The `virtual` keyword changes the static binding for pointers and references into a *dynamic or late binding*. At run time, code is generated that calls the function that corresponds to the actual class of the object.
- Using virtual functions, it is possible to override functions of base classes, without problems arising from the use of pointers or references of the base class.
- A class that is suitable for inheritance should fulfil the following requirements:
  - All functions that can be overridden by derived classes must be declared as virtual functions.
  - A virtual destructor must be defined.
- When implementing a derived class, attention should be paid to the following points:
  - Overriding non-virtual functions in the base class can cause many problems and should normally be avoided.
  - Functions of the base class are only overridden if the parameters and the return type match. As an exception for return types, a pointer or reference of the base class may become a pointer or reference of the derived class, respectively.
  - Overridden functions should have the same default arguments.
  - Using the scope operator, overridden virtual functions can still be called.
  - Only public access is granted to objects of a base class that are submitted as a parameter.
- Using non-public inheritance, the is-a relationship can be avoided. In this case, the only consequence of the inheritance is the reuse of code.

5.3   Polymorphism

This section introduces the concept of polymorphism and its application in C++.

5.3.1   What is Polymorphism?

Polymorphism describes the ability of one operation to be called for various objects, which, in turn, may react differently. The call of an operation for an object is treated as a message to that object, which is interpreted by the object itself. Because an operation can have different definitions for different objects, this means that the same operation can cause different reactions.

In the context of C++, this means that objects that have different classes can react differently to the same function call. The facts that the same function name can be used in different classes and that functions can be overloaded are polymorphic language features of C++, which we have already discussed. However, there is more.

Abstraction Using Common Terms

A special polymorphic quality of C++, which is discussed in this section, is the fact that the class-specific differences of objects can be lost at times. This reinforces the basic notion that object-oriented languages are superior to conventional languages, as they support the means of the abstraction of *common terms*[6]: different objects can be seen under the same common term at times, and can also be manipulated. However, during this manipulation, the differences are not lost.

There is a wealth of examples of the uses of common terms:

- Cars, buses, lorries and bikes are all grouped under the common term 'vehicle'. As a vehicle, they can be situated at a particular position and can drive to a different position.
- Integers, floating-point values, fractions and complex numbers are all regarded as 'numeric values', which can be added and multiplied.
- Circles, rectangles, lines, etc., are 'geometric objects', which are found in a figure, have a color and can be drawn.
- Customers, employees, managers, heads of departments, etc., are different types of 'people', who have a name and various other properties.

This means that in programs in which different kind of objects are grouped together under one common term, no consideration has to be given to their actual class:

- A function for vehicles thus need only use the type `Vehicle`. With this, it can automatically manage cars, buses, lorries, etc.
- A graphics editor, only using the type `GeometricObject`, can automatically manage, output and manipulate circles, rectangles, lines, etc.

---

[6] *Generic term* is probably a better phrase for *common term*. However, as *generic* has a special meaning in C++, I decided to use *common term* here.

Due to polymorphism, the differences still play a part, because the operations of the objects that are managed are interpreted differently:

- If a vehicle drives (i.e. the member function `drive()` is called), the appropriate function is automatically called, depending on the actual type of the object. Thus, if the vehicle is a lorry, the 'drive' defined for lorries is executed (i.e. `drive()` of the class `Lorry`); if it is a car, the 'drive' defined for cars is automatically executed.
- If a graphical object is output, the appropriate operation is automatically called, depending on what kind of object it is. If it is a circle, the operation for laying out a circle is called; if it is a rectangle, the layout operation defined for rectangles is used.

With the implementation of the application code for the use of common terms, we do not even have to know what types are combined under the common term:

- If boats are introduced as a new kind of vehicle, the function for vehicles can automatically let boats drive as well.
- If triangles or text elements are introduced as a new kind of geometric object, the graphics editor can manage these automatically.

Polymorphism therefore makes it possible for different objects to be processed under a common term in non-homogeneous collections. Then, depending on the actual type of the object, the correct function is automatically called.

5.3.2 Polymorphism in C++

Polymorphism has different implementations in different languages. For example, in Smalltalk, the 'mother' of all object-oriented languages, polymorphism is realized as a language feature by having no type binding for variables. In principle, variables can manage any object of any type (or class). If an operation is called for an object, the appropriate function is called by evaluating the actual type of the object at run time. If there is no appropriate function, an error message is output[7]. Thus Smalltalk is an interpretative language.

Polymorphism with Type Checking

In C++, on the other hand, we have type binding. At compile time, the compiler checks whether a function call is allowed. This concept is preserved with polymorphism. A class that represents a common term, has to determine what functions can be called for objects under the common term. However, these functions do not have to be implemented yet.

If an object of a class is created that can be managed under the common term, it is verified that, for all operations that are declared under the common term, an implementation exists. This implementation may be provided by the base class for the common term or the derived class. The compiler thus ensures that every function call is possible at run time. In contrast to Smalltalk,

---

[7] To be precise, in object-oriented terminology, this means that objects in Smalltalk are sent a 'message', which is dealt with by an appropriately defined 'method'.

the C++ run-time system does not produce a message when a function call cannot be performed due to the fact that it is called for an object that does not have an appropriate member function.

This kind of polymorphism can be implemented in C++ with two different language features: inheritance and templates. The usual form of polymorphism with inheritance is introduced later on in this section. The implementation of polymorphism with templates is dealt with in Section 7.5.3 on page 457.

Language Features of Polymorphism

The general language features of polymorphism are already known:

- For the general properties of different classes, simply common base classes are used. The attributes and operations defined in these classes apply to the appropriate common term. The different kind of objects that can be grouped under the common term are derived from the classes for the common term. Thus the operations defined in the base class can be implemented differently in the derived classes.
- Because of the is-a relationship, the objects of the different derived classes are temporarily regarded as objects of the base class and can therefore be used under their common term. In order that the correct function is called at run time, the functions are declared as virtual.

As an additional language feature, functions can be declared in the base class for a common term without them being implemented. This specifies that the operation can be called for all objects that fall under the common term. What really happens during the call must then be implemented in the respective derived classes.

Abstract and Concrete Classes

Base classes for common terms are typically so-called *abstract classes*. Abstract classes are classes in which the very act of creating a concrete object is nonsensical.

C++ supports abstract classes in that it ensures that objects of an abstract class cannot be created (not all object-oriented languages provide this ability).

The counterpart to an abstract class (i.e. a class in which it makes sense, and is possible, to create concrete objects) is called a *concrete class*.

5.3.3   An Example of Polymorphism in C++

The management of different geometric objects can be used as an example of the uses of polymorphism. First, we define two types of geometric object:

- A Line.
- A Circle.

These can be regarded as being geometric objects under the common term GeoObj, which can be manipulated and used together.

In this example, all geometric objects have a reference point, can be moved with move() and drawn with draw(). For move(), there is a default implementation that simply moves the reference point accordingly. A `Circle` additionally has a radius and implements a function for laying out. The function for moving is inherited. A `Line` has a second point (the first point is used as the reference point) and reimplements the function for moving, as well as the function for drawing.

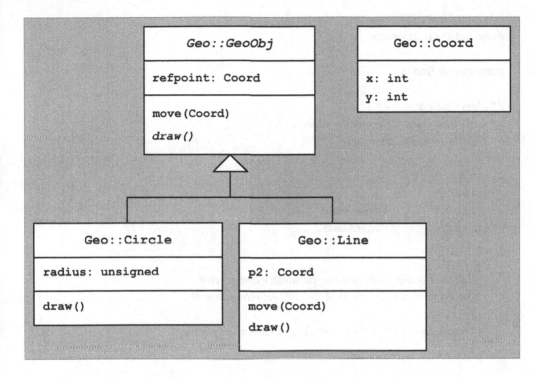

Figure 5.4. Class hierarchy for the polymorphism example

Figure 5.4 clarifies the resulting class hierarchy, using the UML notation. The italic font of the base class `GeoObj` denotes that it is an abstract class. The operation `draw()` is also italicized in the base class: this means that it is an *abstract operation*, and must therefore be implemented by concrete classes.

The Auxiliary Class `Coord`

We now introduce the auxiliary class `Coord`. It is simply provided to manage two X and Y coordinates as a common object. It is not a geometric object (the corresponding geometric object would be the point), but a pair of values that can be used absolutely (as a position) or relatively (as an offset).

The construction and the operations are so simple that the class can be implemented entirely in a header file:

```cpp
// inherit/coord.hpp

#ifndef COORD_HPP
#define COORD_HPP

// header file for I/O
#include <iostream>

namespace Geo {

/* class Coord
 * - auxiliary class for geometric objects
 * - not suitable for inheritance
 */
class Coord {
  private:
    int x;        // X coordinate
    int y;        // Y coordinate

  public:
    // default constructor, and two-parameter constructor
    Coord() : x(0), y(0) {        // default values: 0
    }
    Coord(int newx, int newy) : x(newx), y(newy) {
    }

    Coord operator + (const Coord&) const;      // addition
    Coord operator - () const;                  // negation
    void  operator += (const Coord&);           // +=
    void  printOn(std::ostream& strm) const;    // output
};

/* operator +
 * - add X and Y coordinates
 */
inline Coord Coord::operator + (const Coord& p) const
{
    return Coord(x+p.x,y+p.y);
}

/* unary operator -
 * - negate X and Y coordinates
```

```
    */
inline Coord Coord::operator - () const
{
    return Coord(-x,-y);
}


/* operator +=
 * - add offset to X and Y coordinates
 */
inline void Coord::operator += (const Coord& p)
{
    x += p.x;
    y += p.y;
}


/* printOn()
 * - output coordinates as a pair of values
 */
inline void Coord::printOn(std::ostream& strm) const
{
    strm << '(' << x << ',' << y << ')';
}


/* operator <<
 * - conversion for standard output operator
 */
inline std::ostream& operator<< (std::ostream& strm, const Coord& p)
{
    p.printOn(strm);
    return strm;
}


} // namespace Geo

#endif // COORD_HPP
```

The class should be self-explanatory. However, it is worth mentioning that only no parameters or two parameters can be passed to the constructor. If no parameters are passed, both the X and Y coordinates are initialized with 0.

5.3.4 The Abstract Base Class `GeoObj`

The class `GeoObj` is the base class for the common term. It determines what properties all geometric objects have. These include common attributes and operations that can be called for all objects of type `GeoObj`.

As a common data member is defined:

- a reference point

As operations are defined:

- moving the object by a relative offset
- drawing the object

For simplicity, this class is also defined entirely in a header file:

```cpp
// inherit/geoobj.hpp

#ifndef GEOOBJ_HPP
#define GEOOBJ_HPP

// header file for coordinates
#include "coord.hpp"

namespace Geo {

/* abstract base class GeoObj
 * - common base class for geometric objects
 * - provided for inheritance
 */
class GeoObj {
  protected:
    // every GeoObj has a reference point
    Coord refpoint;

    /* constructor for an initial reference point
     * - not public
     * - there is no default constructor available
     */
    GeoObj(const Coord& p) : refpoint(p) {
    }

  public:
    // move geometric object according to passed relative offset
    virtual void move(const Coord& offset) {
        refpoint += offset;
    }
```

```
        /* draw geometric object
         * - pure virtual function
         */
        virtual void draw() const = 0;

        // virtual destructor
        virtual ~GeoObj() {
        }
    };


    } // namespace Geo


#endif   // GEOOBJ_HPP
```

First, the members for the reference point and the constructor of the class are defined as non-public:

```
class GeoObj {
  protected:
    Coord refpoint;

    GeoObj(const Coord& p) : refpoint(p) {
    }
    ...
};
```

The fact that the constructor is non-public makes it clear that GeoObj is an abstract class. As a result, no concrete objects of the class can be created. Because the constructor has a parameter with which the reference point is initialized, there is no default constructor. The outcome of this is that, in their constructors, directly derived classes always have to submit a coordinate (by means of initializer lists) for the initialization of the reference point.

Next, the public functions that are defined for all geometric objects are declared. These include the virtual destructor, which makes the class suitable for inheritance.

In addition to this, the movement of an object is both declared and implemented:

```
class GeoObj {
    ...
  public:
    virtual void move(const Coord& offset) {
        refpoint += offset;
    }
    ...
};
```

The implementation simply moves the reference point by adding the passed offset. This is sufficient for objects whose absolute position is only defined via the reference point. Objects that use multiple coordinates to define their position must override this implementation.

Pure Virtual Functions

Finally, the function for drawing is declared:

```
class GeoObj {
  ...
  public:
    virtual void draw() const = 0;
    ...
};
```

At this point, something unusual happens: instead of an implementation, the function is assigned the value 0. This means that the function for the class is declared, but is not implemented. The implementation therefore has to be carried out by the classes derived from it.

This kind of function is known as a *pure virtual function*. Pure virtual functions fulfil an important purpose: they declare that a particular function can be called for a class that is used as a common term, without actually defining it. In object-oriented modeling, this kind of operation is described as an `abstract operation`.

As long as a class contains a pure virtual function, it is defined incompletely. No objects of the class can be created. Because of this, the class automatically becomes an abstract class. This is also true for derived classes. The compiler makes sure that pure virtual functions are implemented in derived classes. (An exception to this is if the derived class is itself an abstract class.) The creation of an object of a derived class is only allowed if all pure virtual functions have an implementation.

Pure virtual functions can nevertheless have a default implementation in base classes. This is discussed in Section 5.3.7 on page 326.

Abstract classes can also be defined if there are no pure virtual functions available. In order to do so, the constructors must simply be declared as `private` or `protected`, as we have done here.

The Derived Class `Circle`

Now `Circle` is defined as a derived class of `GeoObj`. It makes sense to create concrete objects (instances) of this class. It is therefore a concrete class.

A circle consists of a center point, which is the reference point, and a radius, which is an additional member (see Figure 5.5).

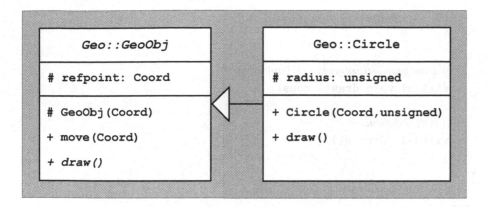

Figure 5.5. Members of the class `Circle`

The `Circle` class is also fully implemented in a header file:

```
// inherit/circle.hpp

#ifndef CIRCLE_HPP
#define CIRCLE_HPP

// header file for I/O
#include <iostream>

// header file of the base class
#include "geoobj.hpp"

namespace Geo {

/* class Circle
 * - derived from GeoObj
 * - a circle consists of:
 *    - a center point (reference point, inherited)
 *    - a radius (new)
 */
class Circle : public GeoObj {
  protected:
    unsigned radius;      // radius

  public:
    // constructor for center point and radius
    Circle(const Coord& m, unsigned r)
```

```
                : GeoObj(m), radius(r) {
        }


        // draw geometric object (now implemented)
        virtual void draw() const;


        // virtual destructor
        virtual ~Circle() {
        }
    };


    /* drawing
     * - defined inline
     */
    inline void Circle::draw() const
    {
        std::cout << "Circle around center point " << refpoint
                  << " with radius " << radius << std::endl;
    }


    }  // namespace Geo

#endif // CIRCLE_HPP
```

The constructor requires a center point and a radius as parameters for the initialization. The center point is submitted to the constructor of the base class GeoObj via the initializer list, where it is used for the initialization of the reference point. Using the radius as the second parameter, the corresponding member is initialized.

The class implements the drawing function draw(). Because of this, the class no longer contains a pure virtual function and can therefore be used as a concrete class for the creation of objects. The function itself simulates the drawing by outputting a corresponding text.

The function move() is derived from the base class, because only the center point defines the position of the circle and therefore a movement of this point is sufficient.

The Derived Class Line

In principle, the class Line has the same contents as the class Circle. However, a line consists of two absolute coordinates: the start point and the end point. In addition to the reference point, which is taken as the start point, a second point is therefore needed (see Figure 5.6).

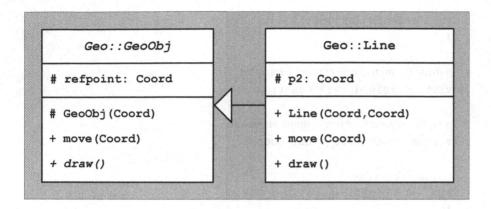

Figure 5.6. Members of the class Line

The class Line is also entirely defined in a header file:

```
// inherit/line.hpp

#ifndef LINE_HPP
#define LINE_HPP

// header file for I/O
#include <iostream>

// header file of the base class
#include "geoobj.hpp"

namespace Geo {

/* class Line
 * - derived from GeoObj
 * - a line consists of:
 *      - a start point (refernce point, inherited)
 *      - an end point (new)
 */
class Line : public GeoObj {
  protected:
     Coord p2;       // second point, end point

  public:
     // constructor for start and end points
     Line(const Coord& a, const Coord& b)
```

```cpp
        : GeoObj(a), p2(b) {
    }

    // draw geometric object (now implemented)
    virtual void draw() const;

    // move geometric object (reimplemented)
    virtual void move(const Coord&);

    // virtual destructor
    virtual ~Line() {
    }
};

/* output
 * - defined inline
 */
inline void Line::draw() const
{
    std::cout << "Line from " << refpoint
              << " to " << p2 << std::endl;
}

/* move
 * - reimplemented, inline
 */
inline void Line::move(const Coord& offset)
{
    refpoint += offset;     // represents GeoObj::move(offset);
    p2 += offset;
}

}   // namespace Geo

#endif  // LINE_HPP
```

In this case, the constructor requires two coordinates as parameters for the initialization. The first coordinate is passed to the constructor of the base class `GeoObj` via the initializer list, where it is used for the initialization of the reference point. The second coordinate is used to initialize the additional member for the end point of the line.

The drawing function `draw()`, which outputs a descriptive text, is implemented in a similar way to that of the `Circle` class.

The function `move()` is reimplemented, because the start point and the end point both have absolute coordinates. Thus the implementation of the base class, which only moves the single reference point, is not enough. One could also have implemented the second point as an offset to the first point, in which case `move()` could be derived from the base class. However, then appropriate transformations between a relative offset and the absolute coordinates would have to be implemented in other functions, such as, for example, `draw()`.

Application Example

A small sample program will now clarify the use of polymorphism. In the example, circles and lines are seen and manipulated as common geometric objects. However, when moving and drawing the objects, the implementation of the actual class is used:

```
// inherit/geotest1.cpp

// header files for used classes
#include "line.hpp"
#include "circle.hpp"
#include "geoobj.hpp"

// forward declaration
void printGeoObj(const Geo::GeoObj&);

int main()
{
    Geo::Line l1(Geo::Coord(1,2), Geo::Coord(3,4));
    Geo::Line l2(Geo::Coord(7,7), Geo::Coord(0,0));
    Geo::Circle c(Geo::Coord(3,3), 11);

    // array as an inhomogenous collection of geometric objects:
    Geo::GeoObj* coll[10];

    coll[0] = &l1;        // collection contains: - line l1
    coll[1] = &c;         //                       - circle c
    coll[2] = &l2;        //                       - line l2

    /* move and draw elements in the collection
     * - the correct function is called automatically
     */
    for (int i=0; i<3; i++) {
        coll[i]->draw();
```

```
            coll[i]->move(Geo::Coord(3,-3));
    }

    // output individual objects via auxiliary function
    printGeoObj(l1);
    printGeoObj(c);
    printGeoObj(l2);
}

void printGeoObj(const Geo::GeoObj& obj)
{
    /* the correct function is called automatically
     */
    obj.draw();
}
```

After the creation of two `Lines` and a `Circle`, these are used as geometric objects in an array of pointers to the type `GeoObj`. The variable `coll` therefore represents an *inhomogeneous collection* of geometric objects.

Every element that is in the collection is then drawn and moved in a loop. Because virtual functions are used, at run time, the real class of the geometric object is evaluated and the corresponding function is called.

In the same way, the correct function is called when a reference is used, as occurs with the function `printGeoObj()`.

The output of the program is as follows:

```
Line from (1,2) to (3,4)
Circle around center point (3,3) with radius 11
Line from (7,7) to (0,0)
Line from (4,-1) to (6,1)
Circle around center point (6,0) with radius 11
Line from (10,4) to (3,-3)
```

Polymorphism is only possible if the identity of an object is not lost. This means that an object can only be seen as an object of the class `GeoObj` by means of pointers and references. A variable of the type `GeoObj` is, and remains, of the `GeoObj` type, even if a `Circle` or a `Line` is assigned.

In this case, no variable of the `GeoObj` type can be declared, because it is an abstract class (i.e. it has a pure virtual function and no public constructor). However, we can also conceive base classes, from which it also makes sense to create objects. In this case, an object loses its identity if, for example, it becomes an object of the base class through assignment or a type conversion. Polymorphism can then no longer take place, as it only works with pointers and references.

In order for this not to happen by mistake, when using polymorphism, one should make sure that the base classes are always abstract. This is always possible simply by declaring all constructors as non-public.

5.3.5 Application of Polymorphism Inside Classes

The previous example demonstrates the technique of polymorphism, although, in this case at least, it may be difficult to spot any advantages in its use.

Another application, which better shows the advantages of polymorphism, is the use of polymorphism inside classes. This is demonstrated now by introducing a class that is able to combine multiple geometric objects together to form a group of geometric objects. This class is called `GeoGroup`. Because a group of geometric objects can also be seen as a geometric object, the class itself is derived from `GeoObj`. The class `GeoGroup` therefore describes a geometric object that is a collection of geometric objects. The resulting class hierarchy is shown in Figure 5.7.

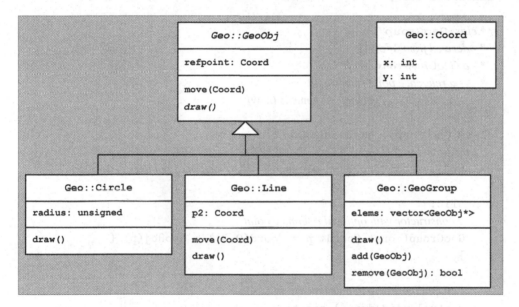

Figure 5.7. Polymorphism example with polymorphic class `GeoGroup`

The class `GeoGroup` also implements the function `draw()` and inherits the function `move()`. A vector (see Section 3.5.1 on page 70) is added as a new data member to manage the elements of the group (i.e. the geometric objects). Additional member functions provide the ability to insert and remove an element. Of course, in practice, other functions would be provided, but this is enough to demonstrate the principle.

Header File of the Class `GeoGroup`

As usual, the header file of the class `GeoGroup` contains the class declaration:

```
// inherit/geogroup.hpp

#ifndef GEOGROUP_HPP
#define GEOGROUP_HPP

// include header file of the base class
#include "geoobj.hpp"

// header file for the internal management of the elements
#include <vector>

namespace Geo {

/* class GeoGroup
 * - derived from GeoObj
 * - a GeoGroup consists of:
 *    - a reference point (inherited)
 *    - a collection of geometric elements (new)
 */
class GeoGroup : public GeoObj {
  protected:
    std::vector<GeoObj*> elems;       // collection of pointers to GeoObjs

  public:
    // constructor with optional reference point
    GeoGroup(const Coord& p = Coord(0,0)) : GeoObj(p) {
    }

    // output (now also implemented)
    virtual void draw() const;

    // insert element
    virtual void add(GeoObj&);

    // remove element
    virtual bool remove(GeoObj&);

    // virtual destructor
    virtual ~GeoGroup() {
```

```
        }
    };


    }   // namespace Geo


    #endif   // GEOGROUP_HPP
```

A vector is used internally for the management of the elements:

```
class GeoGroup : public GeoObj {
    protected:
        std::vector<GeoObj*> elems;        // collection of pointers to GeoObjs
    ...
};
```

The vector manages pointers to the geometric objects that comprise the group. The use of pointers is necessary in order to maintain the actual type of the element. It would not be possible to use GeoObj as an element type, because it is an abstract class. The use of references is also not possible, as, for references, the objects they represent must be established at initialization time. In this case, elements are inserted and removed at run time.

The constructor is passed a parameter, which is used by the constructor of the base class to initialize the reference point:

```
class GeoGroup : public GeoObj {
    public:
        // constructor with optional reference point
        GeoGroup(const Coord& p = Coord(0,0)) : GeoObj(p) {
        }
    ...
};
```

As a default argument, it contains the origin (the coordinate (0,0)). The reference point is used by the GeoGroup as an offset to the elements of the group. The coordinates of the elements are relative and refer to the reference point of the GeoGroup.

Dot-C File of the Class GeoGroup

In the dot-C file of the class GeoGroup, the functions for inserting and removing elements, as well as the function for drawing all elements, are defined:

```
// inherit/geogroup.cpp

#include "geogroup.hpp"
#include <algorithm>

namespace Geo {
```

```cpp
/* add
 * - insert element
 */
void GeoGroup::add(GeoObj& obj)
{
    // keep address of the passed geometric object
    elems.push_back(&obj);
}


/* draw
 * - draw all elements, taking the reference points into account
 */
void GeoGroup::draw() const
{
    for (unsigned i=0; i<elems.size(); ++i) {
        elems[i]->move(refpoint);      // add offset for the reference point
        elems[i]->draw();              // draw element
        elems[i]->move(-refpoint);     // subtract offset
    }
}


/* remove
 * - delete element
 */
bool GeoGroup::remove(GeoObj& obj)
{
    // find first element with this address and remove it
    // return whether an object was found and removed
    std::vector<GeoObj*>::iterator pos;
    pos = std::find(elems.begin(),elems.end(),&obj);
    if (pos != elems.end()) {
        elems.erase(pos);
        return true;
    }
    else {
        return false;
    }
}


}   // namespace Geo
```

The function for inserting an element simply stores the address of the added element in an internal collection:

```
void GeoGroup::add(GeoObj& obj)
{
    // keep address of the passed geometric object
    elems.push_back(&obj);
}
```

Because only references and pointers are used for the submitted geometric object, the real class of this object is still known.

Use of this information is then made when drawing the elements:

```
void GeoGroup::draw() const
{
    for (unsigned i=0; i<elems.size(); ++i) {
        elems[i]->move(refpoint);     // add offset for the reference point
        elems[i]->draw();             // draw element
        elems[i]->move(-refpoint);    // substract offset
    }
}
```

Using a for loop, all elements of the GeoGroup are drawn by calling the draw() function for each one. As virtual functions are used, the correct function is automatically called: if the element is a Circle, Circle::draw() is called; if the element is a Line, Line::draw() is called; if the element is a group of geometric objects (which can also be a geometric object in a group), GeoGroup::draw() is called, which, in turn, calls the correct draw() function for all the elements that it contains.

Before and after drawing, the object is manipulated in order to process the offset of the whole geometric group. The offset is then added to the coordinates before drawing, and subtracted after drawing, so that the position of the element remains stable. In practice, one would definitely provide the draw() function with the offset as a parameter instead. However, this example shows how, by depending on the actual type of the element, the suitable move() implementation is automatically called.

The class is finished off with the function for removing an element:

```
bool GeoGroup::remove(GeoObj& obj)
{
    // find first element with this address and remove it
    // return whether an object was found and removed
    std::vector<GeoObj*>::iterator pos;
    pos = std::find(elems.begin(),elems.end(),&obj);
    if (pos != elems.end()) {
        elems.erase(pos);
        return true;
    }
```

```
    else {
        return false;
    }
}
```

In this case, the position of the passed geometric object is searched for with the help of the find() algorithm. Note that the addresses are compared, which means that only identical objects are found. If the object is found, it is removed from the collection using erase, and true is returned. If the object is not found, the function returns false.

Application Example

The first application program for geometric objects (see page 313) can now be rewritten to include the use of groups of geometric objects:

```
// inherit/geotest2.cpp

// header file for I/O
#include <iostream>

// header files for used classes
#include "line.hpp"
#include "circle.hpp"
#include "geogroup.hpp"

int main()
{
    Geo::Line l1(Geo::Coord(1,2), Geo::Coord(3,4));
    Geo::Line l2(Geo::Coord(7,7), Geo::Coord(0,0));
    Geo::Circle c(Geo::Coord(3,3), 11);

    Geo::GeoGroup g;

    g.add(l1);          // GeoGroup contains: - line l1
    g.add(c);           //                    - circle c
    g.add(l2);          //                    - line l2

    g.draw();           // draw GeoGroup
    std::cout << std::endl;

    g.move(Geo::Coord(3,-3));  // move offset of GeoGroup
    g.draw();                  // draw GeoGroup again
    std::cout << std::endl;
```

```
        g.remove(l1);          // GeoGroup now only contains c and l2
        g.draw();              // draw GeoGroup again
}
```

First, geometric objects of different kinds are added to the group:

```
    g.add(l1);          // GeoGroup contains: - line l1
    g.add(k);           //                    - circle k
    g.add(l2);          //                    - line l2
```

The call

```
    g.draw();
```

calls the `draw()` function of the class `GeoGroup`, which loops through calls of the correct `draw()` functions for the elements contained within.

The program has the following output:

```
Line from (1,2) to (3,4)
Circle around center point (3,3) with radius 11
Line from (7,7) to (0,0)

Line from (4,-1) to (6,1)
Circle around center point (6,0) with radius 11
Line from (10,4) to (3,-3)

Circle around center point (6,0) with radius 11
Line from (10,4) to (3,-3)
```

Note that the interface of the GeoGroup hides the internal use of pointers. Thus the application programmer need only pass the objects that need to get inserted or removed.

Because a GeoGroup is itself a geometric object, it can also be inserted into a GeoGroup:

```
GeoGroup g2;

g2.add(g);          // GeoGroup g2 contains GeoGroup g
```

However, this ability may cause some problems. For example, if you try to insert a GeoGroup in itself, infinite run-time loops may occur. There are ways to solve these problems (for example, marking the object while it gets processed); however, they go beyond the scope of this book.

5.3.6   Polymorphism is not a Selection

An important aspect of the `GeoGroup` class should be made clear: as can be seen, the `GeoGroup` object basically works as a non-homogeneous collection of geometric objects. The `GeoGroup` class contains no code that refers to any concrete type of the geometric objects it contains. It only uses the `GeoObj` class for the managed geometric objects, which is used as the common term for all geometric objects. By doing so, the class can also manage objects of any other class, as long as it is derived from GeoObj.

Therefore, if new geometric objects, such as triangles or text, are introduced, we only need to make sure that the corresponding classes are derived from GeoObj. The GeoGroup class remains unchanged and does not need to be recompiled. This is a very important advantage. As long as the requirements on the common term do not change, the system can be extended without altering the existing implementations for the common term. Complex processes such as moving, outputting and grouping geometric objects need only be implemented once.

5.3.7   Reconversion of an Object into its Actual Class

When using polymorphism, from time to time there is the following problem. Because of the strict binding, the actual class of the object that is seen under its common term is lost syntactically. If, for example, a GeoGroup is used as a GeoObj, no special function that is defined for GeoGroups can be called:

```
Geo::GeoGroup g;           // group of geometric objects

g.add(l1);                 // OK: group contains line l1
...

Geo::GeoObj& geoobj = g;   // group is seen as a geometric object

geoobj.add(l1);            // ERROR: add() not defined for GeoObj
```

If different kinds of objects are temporarily seen under the same common term, there is the problem that it is not immediately obvious what they actually are. Thus, you cannot simply use a GeoObj as a GeoGroup, even if this is the actual type of the object. There are good reasons for this restriction. The fact of whether or not a GeoObj is a GeoGroup is only clear at run time. Because C++ is a language that checks at compile time whether a function call is valid, the compiler cannot allow to use a GeoObj as a GeoGroup and just call, for example, add() for it.

In C++, for polymorphic types, it is, however, possible to request and process so-called *run-time type information* (RTTI). We can make use of these in two different ways:

- We can try to convert an object into its actual type using a so-called *downcast*.
- We can actually query the class of an object.

It should be noted that both are only possible with polymorphic types, i.e. types that have at least one virtual member function.

Downcasting with the dynamic_cast Operator

Using the dynamic_cast operator, we can convert an object back into its actual type:

```
void insertInGroup(Geo::GeoObj& obj, const Geo::GeoObj& elem)
{
    dynamic_cast<GeoGroup&>(obj).add(elem);
        // exception if obj is not a GeoGroup
}
```

The `dynamic_cast` operator gets as its first argument (inside the angled brackets) the type into which the object is to be converted. This needs to be a reference. The second argument (in parentheses) is the actual object that is to be converted:

```
dynamic_cast<GeoGroup&>(obj)
```

The fact that the destination type must be a reference ensures that no new object, but just a temporary second 'view' of the existing object, is returned. This view is only valid if the submitted object is actually an object of the submitted class or a class derived from it. If this is not the case, an exception of the type `std::bad_cast` is thrown, which can be dealt with as described in Section 3.6 on page 93.

We can also convert pointers to polymorphic objects back to the original type using the `dynamic_cast` operator. In this case, 0 or NULL is returned if there is an error:

```
void specialTreatment(Geo::GeoObj* objptr)
{
    Geo::GeoGroup* p = dynamic_cast<GeoGroup*>(objptr);
    if (p != NULL) {
        // OK: *objptr is a GeoGroup
        p->add(... );
    }
    else {
        // *objptr is not a GeoGroup
    }
}
```

This can also be used to evaluate the actual type of objects that are not pointers at run time:

```
void specialTreatment(const Geo::GeoObj& obj)
{
    Geo::GeoGroup* p = dynamic_cast<GeoGroup*>(&obj);
    if (p != NULL) {
        // OK: obj is a GeoGroup
        Geo::GeoGroup& group = *p;
        ...
    }
    else {
        // obj is not a GeoGroup
    }
}
```

If we only want to find out if an object is of a certain type, the following is enough:

```
void typequery(const Geo::GeoObj& obj)
{
    if (dynamic_cast<GeoGroup*>(&obj) != NULL) {
        // obj is a GeoGroup
        ...
    }
    else {
        // obj is not a GeoGroup
        ...
    }
}
```

Concrete Type Queries Using the `typeid` Operator

By using the `typeid` operator, we can even determine the type at run time. The following example shows how this can be done:

```
#include <typeinfo>

void foo(const Geo::GeoObj& obj)
{
    // output type
    std::cout << typeid(obj).name() << std::endl;

    // compare type
    if (typeid(t) == typeid(Geo::GeoGroup)) {
        ...
    }
}
```

For an object or a class, `typeid` returns a description object that has the type `std::type_info` (defined in `<typeinfo>`), on which the following operations can be called:

- The `name()` function returns the name of the class as a C-string. The way this string looks is implementation specific.
- The `==` and `!=` operators return whether two types are the same. Because an object or a class can be passed to the `typeid` operator as an argument, we can find out whether the type of two objects is the same, and can also determine whether an object has a particular type.
- Using `before()`, a type can also be compared to another for the purpose of sorting.

If an argument for `typeid` is a pointer, and if this pointer has the value 0 or NULL, then an exception of the type `std::bad_typeid` is thrown. This can be dealt with as described in Section 3.6 on page 93.

RTTI and Design

RTTI must be used with care because, particularly when using `typeid`, code becomes dependent on concrete types. The following code segment is an example of very poor design:

```
int area(const Geo::GeoObj& obj)   // very bad example
{
    if (typeid(obj) == typeid(Geo::Circle) ||
        typeid(obj) == typeid(Geo::Rectangle)) {
            // calculate area
            ...
    }
    else {
        return 0;
    }
}
```

With this kind of coding, the whole advantage of programming with common terms is nullified, because the `area()` function must be verified and adapted with the introduction of every new kind of geometric object.

It would be better to have a design that introduces another abstract class `GeoArea`, under the class `GeoObj`, from which all concrete area objects are derived. In this case, the code does not need to be rewritten:

```
int area(const Geo::GeoObj& obj) // somewhat better example
{
    GeoArea* fp = dynamic_cast<GeoArea*>(&obj)
    if (fp != NULL) {
        // calculate area
        return fp->calcArea();
    }
    else {
        return 0;
    }
}
```

However, care has to be taken that geometric objects do not exist for which it makes sense to calculate an area, but that are not derived from `GeoArea`.

A design that allows the area of all objects to be calculated is best:

```
int area(const Geo::GeoObj& obj)   // OK
{
    return obj.calcArea(); // inquire about the area of every object
}
```

For this, a default implementation can be provided in `Geo::GeoObj` that returns 0 for all objects that do not have an area:

```
class GeoObj {
  public:
    virtual int calcArea() const {
        return 0;
    }
    ...
};
```

To make sure that this default implementation is not derived without further thinking, a default implementation can be provided even when the function is declared as being pure virtual:

```
class GeoObj {
  public:
    virtual int calcArea() const  = 0;      // pure virtual
    ...
};
...

int GeoObj::calcArea() const                // but available
{
    return 0;
}
```

Although derived classes must then implement this function, they can simply call the implementation of the base class:

```
class Line : public GeoObj {
  public:
    virtual int calcArea() const {
        // derive default implementation from base class
        return GeoObj::calcArea();
    }
    ...
};
```

5.3.8   Design by Contract

Abstract base classes are the most important means of separating modules and components from each other in large programs. As an *interface*, they define a *contract* between an object that provides a particular service and the objects that use this service. If the agreement is defined as an abstract base class, both sides can be developed and modified independently of each other [8].

This kind of interface can, for example, be used as follows:

```
class Printable {
  public:
    virtual void print() = 0;
};
```

On the one hand, we can now implement any class that implements this interface:

```
class XYZ : public Printable {
  ...
  public:
    virtual void print() {
      ...
    }
};
```

On the other hand, we can write functions that call appropriate member functions for all objects that satisfy this agreement (and are therefore derived from `Printable`):

```
void foo(const Printable& obj)
{
  ...
  obj.print();
  ...
}
```

These *abstract base classes* are also simply known as *ABC*s. In principle, it is a good guideline to only implement base classes as abstract base classes.

5.3.9 Summary

- *Polymorphism* describes the ability of identical operation calls leading to different operations or behavior for different object.
- C++ supports polymorphism through
  - members of different classes having the same name,
  - the overloading of functions, and
  - virtual functions.
- Using polymorphism, the means of abstraction with a common term can be implemented.

---

[8] Java programmers are familiar with this concept, which is offered to them via the keywords `interface` and `implements`. In C++, however, there are no special keywords: You simply implement an abstract base class with only pure virtual functions.

- *Abstract classes* are classes that cannot be instantiated. They can be used to combine common properties of different classes in order to be able to work with common terms. The counterpart to this, a class from which objects can be created, is a *concrete class*.
- *Pure virtual functions* are functions that are declared but not implemented. Instead, they are implemented in derived classes. They are defined through an assignment of 0.
- Default implementations are possible for pure virtual functions.
- The operators `typeid` and `dynamic_cast` are provided for the query of types at run time and for the downcast from a common term to the actual class respectively. As a rule of thumb, you should try to avoid using them, because they often result in poorly designed code (closed hard-coded selections instead of open polymorphism).

5.4 Multiple Inheritance

In this section, we discuss the possibility of a class having two or more base classes. This is known as *multiple inheritance*. Like single inheritance, multiple inheritance is characterized as an *is-a* relationship. An object of a doubly derived class assumes the type of both.

Multiple inheritance can lead to a few problems, which must be taken into account (e.g. naming conflicts). We will explain these problems and provide possible solutions. Generally, it can be said that multiple inheritance should only be used with caution and after careful design considerations.

5.4.1 An Example of Multiple Inheritance

A simple example of multiple inheritance is a class for amphibious vehicles that are derived from the classes Car and Boat (see Figure 5.8). The *is-a* relationship applies here twice:

- An amphibious vehicle *is a* Car.
- An amphibious vehicle *is a* Boat.

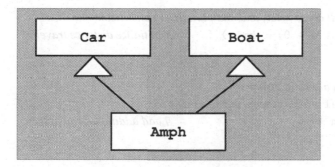

Figure 5.8. Example of multiple inheritance

Using this example, we will look at the problems that can arise with multiple inheritance. These are usually name conflicts due to the fact that members of different base classes can have the same names.

The Base Classes Car and Boat

First we look at the base classes. They have deliberately been kept simple for this example.

For the purposes of this example, a Car contains just one member, which stores the distance (in kilometers) it has traveled. This can be initialized during the creation of an object of the Car class; if not, it is initialized with the default value 0. A Car can travel a certain distance, and the number of kilometers a Car traveled can be output:

```cpp
// inherit/car.hpp

#ifndef CAR_HPP
#define CAR_HPP

// include header file for I/O
#include <iostream>

namespace CPPBook {

/* Car class
 * - suitable for inheritance
 */
class Car {
  protected:
    int km;                            // kilometers traveled

  public:
    // default constructor, and one-parameter constructor
    Car(int d = 0) : km(d) {           // initialize distance traveled
    }

    // travel a certain distance
    virtual void travel(int d) {
        km += d;                       // add additional kilometers
    }

    // output distance traveled
    virtual void printTraveled() {
        std::cout << "The car has traveled "
                  << km << " km " << std::endl;
    }

    // virtual destructor
    virtual ~Car() {
    }
};

} // namespace CPPBook

#endif    // CAR_HPP
```

In principle, the same applies to the Boat class, although distances are measured in sea miles rather than kilometers:

```cpp
// inherit/boat.hpp

#ifndef BOAT_HPP
#define BOAT_HPP

// include header file for I/O
#include <iostream>

namespace CPPBook {

/* Boat class
 * - suitable for inheritance
 */
class Boat {
  protected:
    int sm;                          // sea miles traveled

  public:
    // default constructor, and one-parameter constructor
    Boat(int d = 0) : sm(d) {        // initialize distance traveled
    }

    // travel a certain distance
    virtual void travel(int d) {
        sm += d;                     // add additional sea miles
    }

    // output distance traveled
    virtual void printTraveled() {
        std::cout << "The boat has traveled "
                << sm << " sm " << std::endl;
    }

    virtual ~Boat() {                // virtal destructor
    }
};

}   // namespace CPPBook

#endif      // BOAT_HPP
```

Declaration of the Derived Class `Amph`

The class for amphibious vehicles, `Amph`, is derived from the classes `Car` and `Boat` as follows:

```cpp
// inherit/amph.hpp

#ifndef AMPH_HPP
#define AMPH_HPP

// include header files of the base classes
#include "car.hpp"
#include "boat.hpp"

namespace CPPBook {

/* Amph class
 * - derived from Car and Boat
 * - suitable for further derivation
 */
class Amph : public Car, public Boat {
  public:
    /* default constructor, and one- and two-parameter constructor
     * - Car constructor is called with first parameter
     * - Boat constructor is called with second parameter
     */
    Amph(int k = 0, int s = 0) : Car(k), Boat(s) {
        // thus there is nothing more to do
    }

    // output distance traveled
    virtual void printTraveled() {
        std::cout << "The amphibious vehicle has traveled "
                  << km << " km and " << sm << " sm " << std::endl;
    }

    // virtual destructor
    virtual ~Amph() {
    }
};

} // namespace CPPBook

#endif    // AMPH_HPP
```

As can be seen, the names of the base classes are given after the Amph class declaration, separated by a colon:

```
class Amph : public Car, public Boat {
    ...
};
```

For each base class, it is indicated to what extent access to the inherited members is limited (see Section 5.1.3 on page 262).

Application of the Derived Class Amph

Because the Amph class is derived from the two base classes Car and Boat, the properties of the class Car, as well as the properties of the class Boat, are inherited. An amphibious vehicle therefore has the members km *and* sm. These can be output using, for example, the newly implemented member function printTraveled(), as shown in the following program:

```
// inherit/amphtest.cpp

// header file for the class Amph
#include "amph.hpp"

int main()
{
    /* create amphibious vehicle and initialize
     * with 7 kilometers and 42 sea miles
     */
    CPPBook::Amph a(7,42);

    // output distance traveled
    a.printTraveled();
}
```

The declaration

```
CPPBook::Amph a(7,42);
```

creates an object of type Amph. The constructors of the base classes are called in the order that they are declared; the order given in the initializer list is immaterial. In fact, the creation is done in the following steps:

- First of all, the memory for the object is allocated:

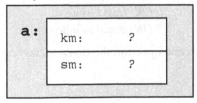

- Then the one-parameter constructor of the class Car is called, which initializes the part of the object that is inherited from Car:

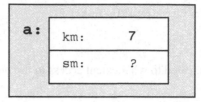

- Afterwards, the one-parameter constructor of the class Boat is called, which initializes the part of the object that is inherited from Boat:

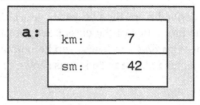

- Because the constructor of the class Amph has no statements in the body, and no new members have been added either, the object is fully initialized.

If constructors have to be called for base classes as well as for members, the constructors of the base classes and called first, and then the constructors of the new members.

The statement

```
a.printTraveled();
```

calls the member function printTraveled(), which is newly implemented in the Amph class and outputs the total distance traveled.

Ambiguities

Notice that a call to travel() is not possible for amphibious vehicles. Because this member function is inherited from both the Car class and the Boat class, it is not clear what one should be called:

```
CPPBook::Amph a(7,42);
...
a.travel(77);              // ERROR: ambiguous
```

The scope operator can be used to solve this ambiguity:

```
CPPBook::Amph a(7,42);
...
a.Car::travel (77);    // OK: travel as a Car
a.Boat::travel(23);    // OK: travel as a Boat
```

In order to avoid using the scope operator, the derived class can also offer the functions under another name:

```
class Amph : public Car, public Boat {
    ...
    virtual void travelAsCar(int d) {
        // renaming of Car::travel()
        Car::travel(d);
    }
    virtual void travelAsBoat(int d) {
        // renaming of Boat::travel()
        Boat::travel(d);
    }
};
```

Of course, it is also possible to implement the functions directly. However, the necessary modifications of implementation of the base class may generate inconsistencies. Here, as so often, the advantage of maintaining consistency has to be weighed up against the disadvantage of increasing running time.

If the amphibious vehicle is seen as a Car or a Boat, then it is obvious which travel() is meant and the call is therefore possible without a qualification:

```
CPPBook::Amph a(7,42);
...
CPPBook::Boat& b(a);        // amphibious vehicle is seen as a Boat
b.travel(23);               // OK: travel as a Boat
```

5.4.2 Virtual Base Classes

If a class has several base classes, these can be directly or indirectly derived from the same base class. If this happens, there is the question of whether the multiply inherited members of the base class are available once or more than once.

Let us assume, for example, that the classes Car and Boat are both derived from the class Vehicle (see Figure 5.9). If the Vehicle class defines a member yearOfManufacture, both a Car and a Boat also have a year of manufacture. In this case, an amphibious vehicle should only have one year of manufacture, even though it derives from both Car and Boat. On the other hand, if the Vehicle class defines another member maxspeed (for the maximum speed), it may well be useful to have two copies of this member for amphibious vehicles—one for the maximum speed as a Car and once for the maximum speed as a Boat.

C++ provides for both possibilities: multiply inherited members can be used as one, or as distinct members.

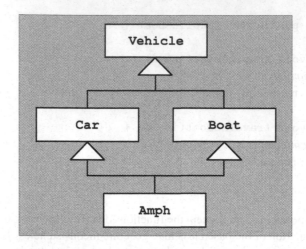

Figure 5.9. Multiply deriving from the same base class

Non-Virtual Base Classes

By default, members from the same base classes inherited via different classes are distinct members in C++. In the following definition, an amphibious vehicle has two copies of `maxspeed`:

```
// inherit/vehiclehier.hpp

namespace CPPBook {

class Vehicle {
  protected:
    int maxspeed;        // maximum speed
  ...
};

class Car : public Vehicle {
  ...
};

class Boat : public Vehicle {
  ...
};

class Amph : public Car, public Boat {
  ...
};

}  // namespace CPPBook
```

Because maxspeed is inherited from Car as well as from Boat, it can only be accessed for amphibious vehicles using the scope operator:

```
void Amph::f()
{
    maxspeed = 100;              // ERROR: ambiguous
    Car::maxspeed = 100;         // OK: maxspeed of Car
    Boat::maxspeed = 70;         // OK: maxspeed of Boat
    Vehicle::maxspeed = 100;     // ERROR: ambiguous
}
```

Virtual Base Classes

In order to make a member that is inherited from a base class via different classes unique, the classes that derive directly from the common base class have to define this base class as a *virtual base class*. This is done using the virtual keyword in the specification of the base class:

```
class Vehicle {
  protected:
    int yearOfManufacture;       // year of manufacture
    ...
};

class Car : virtual public Vehicle {
    ...
};

class Boat : virtual public Vehicle {
    ...
};

class Amph : public Car, public Boat {
    ...
};
```

By using the virtual keyword for the base class Vehicle, if the derived classes come together again later in a common derived class, the members of the class Vehicle are only available once. Note that the virtual keyword can be placed before or after the access keyword.

Because yearOfManufacture is inherited virtually from Car as well as from Boat, the member is only available once in Amph. Access without a scope operator is now clear and therefore possible:

```
void Amph::f()
{
    yearOfManufacture = 1983;               // OK
```

```
        Car::yearOfManufacture = 1983;        // OK
        Boat::yearOfManufacture = 1983;        // OK
        Vehicle::yearOfManufacture = 1983;     // OK
}
```

It is decisive for the common use of the members of the class that the directly derived classes declare their base class as virtual. The keyword `virtual` must therefore be given for `Car` and `Boat`, as has happened here. Whether `Amph` is derived virtually from `Boat` and `Car` is irrelevant.

Virtual and Non-Virtual Base Classes

But what happens if an amphibious vehicle's `yearOfManufacture` should be available just once, but `maxspeed` available twice? Here, we need an auxiliary class in order to separate the members that are to be used as one unique member from the ones that are to be used multiple times.

This is depicted in Figure 5.10. Because all the classes that derived directly from class `VehicleVirtual` (here, this is just the class `VehicleNonVirtual`) use virtual inheritance, the members of `VehicleVirtual` are available only once. Because the classes derived directly from `VehicleNonVirtual` are non-virtual, its members are available twice.

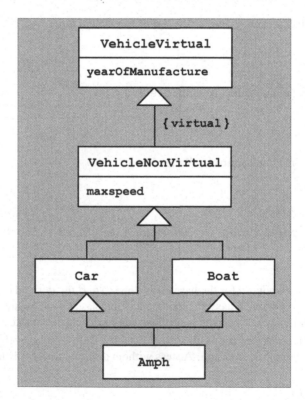

Figure 5.10. `Vehicle` class as a virtual and non-virtual base class

5.4.3 Identity and Addresses

Until now, it has always been assumed that objects are identical if their addresses are the same. Because of this, with the implementation of a separate assignment operator, an assignment to itself is identified by means of a comparison of addresses (see Section 6.1.5 on page 362):

```
// assignment to itself?
if (this == &obj) {
    return *this;        // return object unchanged
}
```

However, with multiple inheritance objects can be identical even though their addresses are *not* the same. This is due to the way that objects are typically managed at run time.

The layout of an object is usually put together from the members of the classes that were involved in its creation. Typically, the members are managed in the order they were declared (see Figure 5.11). An object of a derived class can, however, in principle at least, be used as an object of its base class. In this case, the object is reduced so that it only contains the members that are already known in the base class.

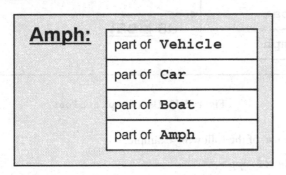

Figure 5.11. Typical layout of an object of the class Amph

With simple inheritance, the members of the derived class, which reside at the end of the storage of the object, are just ignored. The address of the objects is the same. This also happens with multiple inheritance, as long as only the partial objects that reside at the end of the storage are left out. This typically happens, for example, with our amphibious vehicle if it is seen as a car (see Figure 5.12).

However, if the amphibious vehicle is seen as a boat, just ignoring the car part of the object does not work because this part resides between the parts for Vehicle and Boat.

For this reason, a 'shadow object' is created, which has the correct layout for Boats. The parts of the object are actually only internal references to the original object (see Figure 5.13). As a result, the object gets a different address.

The addresses even remain different if the Car and the Boat are seen as a Vehicle. The data of the Vehicle is then once a part of the original object and once a part of the shadow object. As a result, the view of the same object with the same type can result in different addresses.

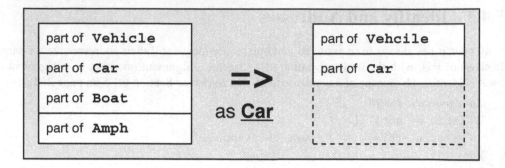

Figure 5.12. Use of Amph as a Car

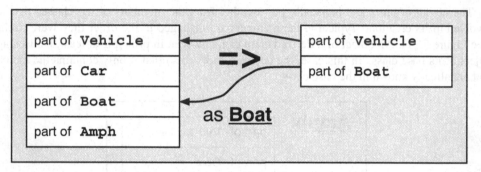

Figure 5.13. Use of Amph as a Boat

To test this, we make use of the following example:

```
// inherit/ident1.cpp

#include "vehiclehier.hpp"
#include <iostream>

void fVehicle(const CPPBook::Vehicle& a)
{
    std::cout << "    as vehicle: "
              << static_cast<const void*>(&a) << std::endl;
}

void fCar(const CPPBook::Car& a)
{
    std::cout << "&a    as car: "
              << static_cast<const void*>(&a) << std::endl;
    fVehicle(a);
}
```

```
void fBoat(const CPPBook::Boat& a)
{
    std::cout << "&a   as boat: "
              << static_cast<const void*>(&a) << std::endl;
    fVehicle(a);
}


int main()
{
    CPPBook::Amph a;

    fCar(a);
    fBoat(a);
}
```

The function fVehicle(), which is called in two different ways, will (with almost all compilers) output two different addresses for the same object a.

Instead of using references, we can also carry out the test with pointers:

// inherit/ident2.cpp

```
#include "vehiclehier.hpp"
#include <iostream>

int main()
{
    using std::cout;
    using std::endl;

    CPPBook::Amph a;

    // address of a
    cout << "&a: " << (void*)&a << "\n" << endl;

    // adress of a => as Car and as Boat
    cout << "(CPPBook::Car*) &a: "
         << (void*)(CPPBook::Car*)&a << "\n";
    cout << "(CPPBook::Boat*) &a: "
         << (void*)(CPPBook::Boat*)&a << "\n\n";

    // address of a => as Car => as Vehicle
    cout << "(CPPBook::Vehicle*) (CPPBook::Car*) &a: "
```

```
          << (void*)(CPPBook::Vehicle*)(CPPBook::Car*)&a << endl;

     // address of a => as Boat => as Vehicle
     cout << "(CPPBook::Vehicle*) (CPPBook::Boat*) &a: "
          << (void*)(CPPBook::Vehicle*)(CPPBook::Boat*)&a << endl;
}
```

It is not even guaranteed that just two different addresses are output. The fact that an object always has the same address is not a language specification of C++, but is instead based on the fact that compilers, for as long as possible, usually manage objects using the same address.

In order to recognize identical objects in any case, there is only one possibility: appropriate mechanisms have to be self-implemented. Each object needs to have both a unique ID as a member and a member function for comparing this ID. Section 6.5.1 on page 414 demonstrates how this can be implemented.

5.4.4   Multiple Derivation of the Same Base Class

It is not possible to directly derive one and the same class multiple times (see Figure 5.14). If this were the case, non-resolvable name conflicts would arise. When using initializer lists, for example, it would not be clear what base class is meant.

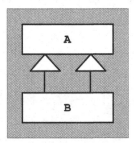

Figure 5.14. Directly deriving the same base class twice

It could be argued that this ability might be useful, although I have yet to see any conclusive evidence of this. Such a situation would mean that an object of type B is, on the one hand, an object of type A, but, on the other hand, is also an object of the same type A.

In practice, if you experience this kind of problem with inheritance, you should check whether your design is sound, and that it does not mean that an object of type B *contains* two objects of type A, i.e. has two objects of type A as members.

If you ever happen upon a case where it is useful to directly derive the same base class twice, you should do two things:

- Write to me so that I can use your example in the next edition of the book[9].
- Introduce dummy classes so that the path to the same base class is unique (see Figure 5.15).

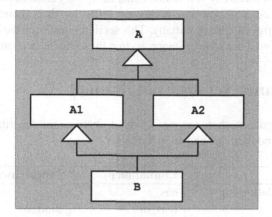

Figure 5.15. Indirectly deriving the same base class twice

5.4.5 Summary

- C++ allows *multiple inheritance*: derived classes can have multiple base classes.
- If name conflicts for the access to members arises from this, the scope operator should be used.
- Base classes can be used multiple times by means of multiple inheritance. Using *virtual base classes*, the members defined in the common base class are then only available once.
- With multiple inheritance, the same object can have different addresses. This is possible even though it is seen as having the same type. In order to remove any doubt as to the identity of an object, members that allow the definition and querying of a unique ID must be introduced.

---

[9] The only meaningful example that I can think of is the class `SplitPersonality`, derived twice from the class `Person`.

5.5   Design Pitfalls of Inheritance

The structure of a class hierarchy is a fundamental design decision in the development of software, which can only be corrected later with great difficulty. It is therefore important that the minimum number of errors are made initially. This section introduces the different kinds of error that exist in the conceptual use of inheritance, so that these can be recognized and avoided.

5.5.1   Inheritance versus Containment

In object-oriented languages, there are two kinds of abstraction: inheritance and containment. The relationships behind these are shown in Table 5.1.

	Containment	Inheritance
relationship	has_a	is_a
	part_of	kind_of
	containment	inheritance
	composition	generalization
language feature	member, reference	derived class

Table 5.1. Containment versus inheritance

We will look at this fundamental difference using the example of a car:

- A car *is a* vehicle.
- A car *has an* engine, bodywork and can be driven.

For a car, the difference between *inheritance* and *containment* might be obvious. However, this is not always the case. In this chapter, we will introduce various examples where it is not always clear whether inheritance or composition is the correct design decision.

5.5.2   Design Error: Limiting Inheritance

What would your answer be to the following question: *What is the relationship between the classes* Rectangle *and* Square?

If you assume that it is an inheritance relationship you are wrong. Inheritance is characterized by the *is-a* relationship, but the English language uses this relationship in a different way.

What is meant semantically by the is-a relationship is that everything that can be done with an object of a base class is also possible and useful for an object of the derived class. If I now claim, in the object-oriented sense, that 'a square is a rectangle', I am saying that I can do everything with a square that I can do with a rectangle. But this is not correct! I can change the height and width of a rectangle by different values. This is not possible with a square, otherwise the square would no longer be a square.

The design error is that a specialized condition is established for the inherited members, which means that the height and width must always be the same.

The following rule for inheritance therefore holds:

- An object of a derived class must be able to represent every value an object of a base class can represent.

Unfortunately, the inheritance relationship is often described as *specialization* (i.e. 'a rectangle is a special kind of a geometric object'). However, this is not meant in a limiting sense, but in a sense to become more concrete. I therefore prefer to describe the inheritance relationship as a *concretion*.

Dealing with Limiting Inheritance

There are three possibilities when dealing with limiting inheritance:

- *Ignoring possible effects.* Although we know that this can be problematic, a Square can be derived from a Rectangle, and, according to the saying 'whoever tries to change the width and height of squares by different values is a misled soul', the application programmer is left holding the baby.

  This kind of design is, of course, quite poor because an undetected error can arise, which can lead to an inconsistency.

- *Eliminating possible effects.* Another possibility is to derive Square from Rectangle and to reimplement the functions that could lead to inconsistencies in the class Square. These new implementations could

  - output an error message;
  - throw an exception;
  - ignore the call (do nothing);
  - try to interpret the call in the special case (for example, scale the square with the average value for the width and height).

  This possibility is not as worrying as the first because at least the error does not lead to inconsistencies. But it is still far from ideal, as the error can still occur.

  At this point, polymorphism must always be taken into account. One can sometimes use a square as a rectangle, or even manage a collection of different rectangles. If it is possible to scale the width and height differently, this should apply to each object that is used as a rectangle. Otherwise, due to the clumsy inheritance, the application programmer needs to worry about what special cases can occur. Finally, note that classes can also be derived without the knowledge of the programmers and users of the base class.

- *Eliminating potential sources of errors by better design.* The correct use of limiting inheritance is to avoid all possible occurrences of an error by not actually making the inheritance error in the first place.

  Because a square is not a rectangle and a rectangle is not a square, there is no inheritance relationship at all. Anyone who only wants to implement the common properties that undoubtedly exist can implement a common abstract base class such as Quadrilateral.

5.5.3   Design Error: Value-Changing Inheritance

What would your answer be to following the question: *What is the relationship between the classes* Fraction *and* FractionWithWholeNumber (e.g. $3\frac{1}{4}$)?

You may now have become careful and, to be on the safe side, answer that you do not know, which is a not a bad response because there is no correct answer.

The implementation could, in principle, look as follows:

```
class Fraction {
  private:
    int numer;
    int denom;
  ...
};

class FractionWithWholeNumber : public Fraction {
  private:
    int number;
  ...
};
```

The decisive point is that the class FractionWithWholeNumber adds a new member that gives a new meaning to the existing members of the class Fraction. If the object is initialized with $\frac{13}{4}$, the numer and denom members have a different internal state for Fractions and FractionWithWholeNumbers. In FractionWithWholeNumber, the Fraction $\frac{13}{4}$ would be represented as $3\frac{1}{4}$ (see Figure 5.16).

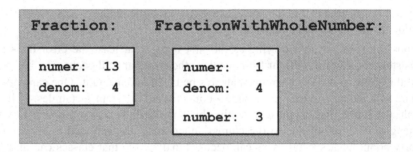

Figure 5.16. Fraction versus FractionWithWholeNumber

Note that the inheritance relationship means that a derived object can always be used as an object of the base class. In this case, the object is reduced to the members that already exist in the base class. Therefore, $3\frac{1}{4}$ would be implemented as $\frac{1}{4}$, which could lead to misleading results[10]. The design error is that the inherited members are supplemented with new members, through which their semantics change.

Therefore, another rule for inheritance is the following:

- The status that the members of a base class have to represent a certain value, must not be different for a derived class to represent the same value.

Again, a class should not be derived in this case, so that this kind of error can be avoided.

This is clearly a *has-a* relationship. The name of the class, FractionWithWholeNumber, expresses that two objects, a fraction and a whole number, are combined to make one object. The class would therefore be better declared as follows:

```
class FractionWithWholeNumber {
  private:
    Fraction  fraction;
    int       number;
    ...
};
```

However, in this example, there is another possible implementation. Inheritance can be used, without giving inherited members different values for the same status represented by the object. In order to do so, the implementation must be changed so that, when passed the value $\frac{13}{4}$, the class FractionWithWholeNumber initializes the member numer with the value 13 and the member denom with the value 4. The only difference would then be that the object is output in a different form (i.e. in two parts: a whole number and a fraction). Therefore, only the output operation is rewritten. This way, inheritance causes no problems.

5.5.4 Design Error: Value-Interpreting Inheritance

Let us assume that the class Fraction need only be defined for positive fractions:

```
class Fraction {
  private:
    unsigned int numer;
    unsigned int denom;
    ...
};
```

In this case, a derivation with the class SignedFraction would be incorrect:

```
class SignedFraction : public Fraction {
  private:
    bool isNegative;
    ...
};
```

---

[10] Do not assume that this could be a useful type conversion. Automatic type conversion should always be obvious.

The information content of a fraction is supplemented with the information that can change the meaning of the inherited members. This is because the potential value range is doubled (all positive and negative fraction values).

If, however, a negative fraction is assigned to a Fraction, $-\frac{13}{4}$ suddenly becomes $\frac{13}{4}$, which is problematic. I can hear some readers claiming that this would be a nice 'feature'. The only question is whether this kind of behavior is so intuitive that it can take place without an explicit call. It would be somewhat critical if, by mistake, you make a positive balance of half a million euros out of a negative balance of half a million euros.

The design error is that the inherited members are supplemented by new members that cause their values to change meaning.

Yet another rule for inheritance is therefore the following:

* The semantics of the members of a base class must not change for a derived class.

This design problem is also detected because an assignment to an object of a base class is not always useful for every value of an object of a derived class, which exposes this kind of inheritance as limiting inheritance.

The only meaningful solution here is to implement an independent class with Fraction and sign as members:

```
class SignedFraction {
  private:
    Fraction fraction;
    bool     isNegative;
    ...
};
```

The problem could also be solved by using a more descriptive naming convention: if the class Fraction was called UnsignedFraction, it would be obvious that a SignedFraction was not an UnsignedFraction.

5.5.5 'Avoid Inheritance!'

Most newcomers to object-oriented programming tend to use inheritance too often. This is always problematic because inheritance is a closer binding between types than composition or containment. If just classes are only *used*, nothing happens as long as the public interface is not changed. Because derived classes also have access to protected members, modifications in the base class are more critical and can easily lead to inconsistencies. In particular, a derivation of third-party classes is always critical.

Therefore, I tend to recommend avoiding inheritance, making use of it only if something cannot be implemented in another way. One should always question whether there is no containment implied.

If derivation *is* done, the semantics of inherited operations and members should never be limited or modified. Objects of derived classes should be able to be used as objects of the base class, at any time, without limitations. This principle is known as the *Liskov substitution principle*[11].

Sometimes, it may be useful to implement a containment relationship by means of private inheritance (see Section 5.2.8 on page 295). This kind of inheritance is occasionally called *implementation inheritance* and clarifies the fact that it is not a matter of a conceptional inheritance in the sense of the *is-a* relationship, but a simple way of implementing a class that reuses code of another class. This should also be avoided. In the long term, a robust design with as few dependencies as possible is well worthwhile.

5.5.6 Summary

- Not every *is-a* relationship you can formulate using your native English language is necessarily a characteristic of inheritance. In particular, (public) inheritance should be avoided
  - if not all inherited operations are still useful;
  - if inherited operations get a different meaning;
  - if inherited get a different meaning; or
  - if the properties of members of the base class are limited.
- It must make sense to assign all possible objects of a derived class to an object of the base class, simply by ignoring the members supplemented in the derived class.
- Avoid inheritance.

---

[11] Due to Barbara Liskov, who formally introduced this principle for the first time in 1988.

6

Dynamic and Static Members

In the previous chapters, classes were introduced that had 'simple' members. This means that they had members such as `int`, `string` or `vector`, which could be copied and assigned without any problems. However, this is not the case with all types. Especially when using pointers, these members are particularly difficult to copy or assign to each other. For this reason, one has to interfere in operations such as copying, assignment and clean-ups. This chapter addresses this topic under the heading 'dynamic members'.

Static members are also explained in this chapter. These are members that are only contained once in the program and are used by all objects/instances of a class.

A custom implementation of a string class and a simple class for representing information about people are used as sample classes.

6.1 Dynamic Members

This section introduces the management and use of classes. The special features that have to be taken into account when using dynamic members are introduced using a simple custom implementation of a class for strings.

6.1.1 Implementing a `String` Class

An implementation of the `CPPBook::String` class is introduced below, which enables simple operations, similar to the standard class `std::string`. Thus, in most cases, a simple type definition could be used to switch between the standard class and this custom class.

The implementation transfers all operations of this string class to functions for strings and arrays adopted from C (this is briefly introduced in Table 3.12 on page 112). For example, assignment is implemented using the function `memcpy()`. The operators `new` and `delete` are used for internal memory management (see Section 3.8 on page 114).

Header File of the `CPPBook::String` Class

The header file of the `CPPBook::String` is as follows:

```cpp
// dyna/string1.hpp

#ifndef STRING_HPP
#define STRING_HPP

// header file for I/O
#include <iostream>

// **** BEGIN namespace CPPBook ******************************
namespace CPPBook {

class String {

  private:
    char*    buffer;      // character sequence as dynamic array
    unsigned len;         // current number of characters
    unsigned size;        // size of buffer

  public:
    // default and C-string constructor
    String(const char* = "");

    // due to dynamic members:
```

```cpp
        String(const String&);              // copy constructor
        String& operator= (const String&);  // assignment
        ~String();                          // destructor

        // comparison of strings
        friend bool operator== (const String&, const String&);
        friend bool operator!= (const String&, const String&);

        // concatenating strings
        friend String operator+ (const String&, const String&);

        // output to a stream
        void printOn(std::ostream&) const;

        // input from a stream
        void scanFrom(std::istream&);

        // number of characters
        unsigned length() const {
            return len;
        }

    private:
        /* constructor from length and buffer
         * - internal for operator +
         */
        String(unsigned, char*);
};

// standard output operator
inline std::ostream& operator << (std::ostream& strm, const String& s)
{
    s.printOn(strm);      // output string to stream
    return strm;          // return stream
}

// standard input operator
inline std::istream& operator >> (std::istream& strm, String& s)
{
    s.scanFrom(strm);     // read string from stream
    return strm;          // return stream
}
```

```
/* operator !=
 * - implemented as inline conversion to operator ==
 */
inline bool operator!= (const String& s1, const String& s2)
{
    return !(s1==s2);
}


} // **** END namespace CPPBook *******************************


#endif    // STRING_HPP
```

Let us first look at the members that describe the internal layout of a string:

```
class String {
  private:
    char*    buffer;      // character sequence as a dynamic array
    unsigned len;         // actual number of characters
    unsigned size;        // size of buffer
    ...
}
```

A String object comprises a dynamic pointer buffer, which manages the actual characters of the string as an array of chars, as well as two members that manage the actual number of characters in the string and the amount of memory that belongs to it.

The character sequence itself does not directly belong to the object, but is instead managed as dynamic memory. Figure 6.1 clarifies this. The string s, in its current status, contains the character string hello, with five characters. These characters are stored in a separate memory segment for eight characters, to which buffer points.

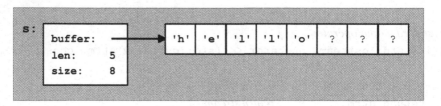

Figure 6.1. Internal layout of CPPBook::Strings

Alternatively, an array with a fixed size could be declared. However, this has the disadvantage that the number of characters in the string is noticeably limited and/or a lot of memory is wasted for small strings.

The dynamic memory managed via buffer does not automatically belong to the object, but must be explicitly created when the object itself is formed. The memory has to be allocated where necessary if manipulations are carried out, and freed again when the object is destroyed. This is possible because the implementation of all operations is left entirely under the control of the class programmer.

Each constructor must therefore allocate memory explicitly, in order to be able to use this for character strings. This includes the copy constructor (copy constructors are introduced in Section 4.3.7 on page 179), which has to be implemented for this reason. The default copy constructor just copies member-wise, which means that it would just copy the pointer, instead of creating a new array and actually copying the character sequence of the source string.

For the same reason, the assignment operator must also be implemented. The default assignment operator, which assigns member-wise, would only assign the pointer and not the character sequence to which the pointer refers.

Finally, the memory that is explicitly created for every object has to be freed when the object is destroyed. For this reason, the destructors (the counterpart to the constructors) are defined. A destructor is called when an object is destroyed, and enables it to be 'cleaned up'. The function name of the destructor is the class name, with a ~ character preceding it:

```
class String {
  public:
    ...
    ~String();       // destructor
};
```

Dot-C File of the `CPPBook::String` Class

The CPPBook::String class is implemented using the operators introduced in Section 3.8 on page 114 for dynamic memory management, new[] and delete[]. Apart from the function that reads a string from a stream, the dot-C file has the following contents (the input function is discussed in Section 6.1.7 on page 366):

```
// dyna/string1a.cpp

// header file of the separate class
#include "string.hpp"

// C header files for string functions
#include <cstring>
#include <cctype>

// **** BEGIN namespace CPPBook *****************************
namespace CPPBook {

/* constructor from C-string (const char*)
 * - default for s: empty string
 */
```

```
String::String(const char* s)
{
    len = std::strlen(s);          // number of characters
    size = len;                    // number of characters determines size of memory
    buffer = new char[size];       // allocate memory
    std::memcpy(buffer,s,len);     // copy characters into memory
}


/* copy constructor
 */
String::String(const String& s)
{
    len = s.len;                   // copy number of characters
    size = len;                    // number of characters
                                   // determines size of memory
    buffer = new char[size];       // allocate memory
    std::memcpy(buffer,s.buffer,len);  // copy characters
}


/* destructor
 */
String::~String()
{
    // release memory allocated with new[]
    delete [] buffer;
}


/* operator =
 * - assignment
 */
String& String::operator= (const String& s)
{
    // assignment of a string to itself has no effect
    if (this == &s) {
        return *this;              // return string
    }

    len = s.len;                   // copy number of characters

    // if there is not enough space, enlarge
    if (size < len) {
```

```cpp
        delete [] buffer;          // release old memory
        size = len;                // number of characters determines new size
        buffer = new char[size];   // allocate memory
    }

    std::memcpy(buffer,s.buffer,len);   // copy characters

    return *this;                  // return modified string
}
```

```cpp
/* operator ==
 * - compares two strings
 * - global friend function, so that an automatic
 *   type conversion of the first operand is possible
 */
bool operator== (const String& s1, const String& s2)
{
    return s1.len == s2.len &&
           std::memcmp(s1.buffer,s2.buffer,s1.len) == 0;
}
```

```cpp
/* operator +
 * - appends two strings
 * - global friend function, so that an automatic
 *   type conversion of the first operand is possible
 */
String operator+ (const String& s1, const String& s2)
{
    // allocate buffer for the concatenated string
    char* buffer = new char[s1.len+s2.len];

    // copy characters into the buffer
    std::memcpy (buffer,          s1.buffer, s1.len);
    std::memcpy (buffer+s1.len, s2.buffer, s2.len);

    // create concatenated string from these data and return it
    return String(s1.len+s2.len, buffer);
}
```

```cpp
/* constructor for uninitialized string of a certain length
 * - internally for operator +
```

```
  */
String::String(unsigned l, char* buf)
{
    len = l;          // copy number of characters
    size = len;       // number of characters determines size of memory
    buffer = buf;     // copy memory
}


/* output to stream
 */
void String::printOn(std::ostream& strm) const
{
    // simply output character string
    strm.write(buffer,len);
}


}  // **** END namespace CPPBook ********************************
```

As previously mentioned, a dynamic memory management is implemented internally, which ensures that the strings always have enough memory for their respective character sequences. For this reason, much care has to be taken when dealing with functions that allocate or manipulate the memory.

6.1.2   Constructors and Dynamic Members

We will now consider the constructor that has a C-string as an argument (type const char*):

```
String::String(const char* s)
{
    len = std::strlen(s);        // number of characters
    size = len;                  // number of characters determines memory size
    buffer = new char[size];     // allocate memory
    std::memcpy(buffer,s,len);   // copy character into memory
}
```

This constructor is called if a new String object is created. For example:

```
CPPBook::String s = "hello";
```

The C++ run-time system only allocates memory for each member, that is, the len and size integers and the buffer pointer. As always with fundamental types, the values are initially not defined:

Next, `len` and `size` are initialized. The length of the passed C-string is determined using `strlen()`:

```
len = std::strlen(s);
size = len;
```

Then, by using the statement

```
buffer = new char[size];
```

memory is allocated that is large enough for the character sequence, and its address is assigned to the `buffer` of the `String` object. The content of this memory is not defined initially either:

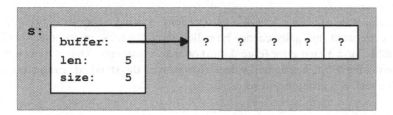

Using the statement

```
std::memcpy(buffer,s,len);
```

the individual characters of the character string are copied. The standard `memcpy()` function adopted from C copies the number passed to characters of an array of `char` (or bytes). All `len`'s characters are copied from s into the memory, to which `buffer` points:

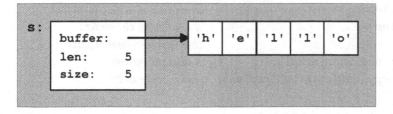

The `String` object is now initialized as an independent object.

Use as a Default Constructor

The C-string constructor can be called as a default constructor using the default argument (an empty string). This creates a `String` object, where `buffer` points to a character string without elements:

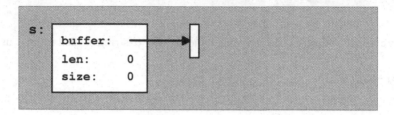

Here, we take advantage of the fact that an array with no elements can be created using `new`. In commercial implementations, however, a special treatment of the empty string would be better, as the allocation of memory takes some time. In this case, `buffer` would be initialized with NULL internally. However, this special case must be handled with each access to the characters of the string.

Note that NULL cannot be used as a default argument for the string constructor, because the string functions that are used internally cannot be called with NULL as an argument (calling `strlen(NULL)` would cause a fatal error (core dump) on many systems). Thus a special treatment is needed when using NULL as a default value. However, as the standard string classes do not implement such a test, it is also omitted here.

6.1.3 Implementing a Copy Constructor

In principle, the copy constructor works in the same way as the other constructor. The only difference is that the character sequence, with which the created `String` object is to be initialized, is not a parameter itself, but is passed as part of a parameter:

```
String::String(const String& s)
{
    len = s.len;                    // copy number of characters
    size = len;                     // number of characters
                                    // determines memory size
    buffer = new char[size];        // allocate memory
    std::memcpy(buffer,s.buffer,len); // copy characters
}
```

It should be noted at this point that the default copy constructor cannot be used, as this only copies member-wise. The `buffer` pointer of the created string would then not point to independent memory, but to the same memory that `buffer` points to in the string that was copied.

6.1.4 Destructors

With the `String` class, the destructor is used to free the explicitly allocated memory when the `String` is destroyed. As it is an array of characters, the array syntax of the delete operator has to be used:

```
String::~String()
{
    // release memory allocated with new[]
    delete [] buffer;
}
```

The destructor is called immediately before the memory for the actual object is freed. For example, this is the case if the scope of a locally created object is left:

```
void f()
{
    CPPBook::String s = "hello";          // constructor for s
    ...
} // end of block: destructor for s called
```

The destructor is called for every object created. This also applies to statically, temporarily and explicitly created objects:

```
static CPPBook::String s;    // default constructor when program starts
                             // destructor when program ends


void f()
{
    CPPBook::String names[10];    // ten calls of the default constructor

    names[0] = newString("hello");
            // first assignment of the temporary return value to names[0],
            // then destructor for temporary return value

} // end of block: ten calls of the destructor


CPPBook::String newString(const char* s)
{
    CPPBook::String ret = s;      // const char* constructor

    return ret;
        // copy constructor for temporary return value
} // end of block: destructor for ret called
```

6.1.5   Implementing the Assignment Operator

In principle, the assignment operator is a combination of a destructor and a copy constructor. An existing string is replaced by a copy of another one. However, it can often be optimized. For example, releasing the existing memory and allocating new memory is only necessary if the memory is no longer sufficient:

```cpp
String& String::operator= (const String& s)
{
    // assigning a string to itself has no effect
    if (this == &s) {
        return *this;           // return string
    }

    len = s.len;                // copy number of characters

    // if there is not enough space, enlarge
    if (size < len) {
        delete [] buffer;       // release old memory
        size = len;             // number of characters determines new size
        buffer = new char[size]; // allocate memory
    }

    std::memcpy(buffer,s.buffer,len);   // copy characters

    return *this;               // return modified string
}
```

When implementing a custom assignment operator, the following should be taken into account:

- An assignment should always return the object for which it was called as a reference. This enables chained assignments or tests after assignments:

```cpp
CPPBook::String a, b, c;
...
a = b = c;
...
if ((a = b) != CPPBook::String("")) {
    ...
}
```

Generally, the typical head of the function of an assignment operator is therefore:

> *class*& *class*::operator = (const *class*& obj)

- As it usually makes no sense to carry out other manipulations with the temporary return value inside the same expression, the return value can also be declared as being constant. The head of the function of an assignment operator can therefore also look as follows:

```
const class& class::operator = (const class& obj)
```
However, this is rarely used in practice.

- A test should first be carried out in the assignment operator to see whether an object is assigned to itself. Assigning an object to itself can always take place in an application program that uses pointers or references. For example:

```
CPPBook::String   s;        // string
CPPBook::String* sp;        // pointer to a string

...

sp = &s;                    // sp points to s

...

*sp = s;                    // s is assigned to itself using sp
```

If the test it not carried out, computing time is wasted. Furthermore, the program could continue running with errors. For example, if you implemented the assignment operator so that it always releases existing memory, allocates new memory and then copies the characters, you would have released the memory of the source string while releasing the destination string. Therefore, you would copy characters from memory that is not valid anymore.

All implementations of assignment operators should therefore begin with the following statement:

```
// assignment to itself?
if (this == &obj) {
    return *this;        // return object unmodified
}
```

Note that two objects are not compared to see whether they are equal, but to see whether they are *identical*. Therefore, it is the addresses that are compared.

6.1.6 Other Operators

The other operators and functions of the `String` class are simply transformations to the corresponding C functions.

Test for Equality

Two strings are the same if the character strings are the same. The `memcmp()` function can be used for the comparison (it returns 0 if two character sequences are equal). However, it is checked in advance whether the number of characters is the same:

```
bool operator== (const String& s1, const String& s2)
{
    return s1.len == s2.len &&
           std::memcmp(s1.buffer,s2.buffer,s1.len) == 0;
}
```

The AND operator && evaluates the left and right side only until the first subexpression evaluates to `false`. Thus, if the number of characters is different, the call of `memcmp()` is not performed.

The function is declared as a global friend function in order to enable an automatic type conversion for the first operand (see also Section 4.6.3 on page 220):

```
CPPBook::String s;
...
if ("hello" == s)        // i.e. if (CPPBook::String("hello") == s)
```

The test for inequality is carried out in the same way as the test for equality:

```
class String {
  public:
    ...
    friend bool operator== (const String&, const String&);
    friend bool operator!= (const String&, const String&);
};
...
inline bool operator!= (const String& s1, const String& s2) {
    return !(s1==s2);
}
```


Concatenating with the + Operator

The + operator is used for concatenating two strings. It is also defined as a global friend function in order to enable an automatic type conversion for the first operand:

```
class String {
  public:
    ...
    friend String operator+ (const String&, const String&);
};
```

In the implementation, a new object for the concatenated string has to be created. A naive implementation can do this in the following way:

```
String operator+ (const String& s1, const String& s2)
{
    // create concatenated string
    String sum;

    // allocate sufficient memory
    // - but don't forget that sum has already allocated memory
    delete [] sum.buffer;
    sum.buffer = new char[s1.len+s2.len];
```

```
// copy characters
std::memcpy(sum.buffer,s1.buffer,s1.len);
std::memcpy(sum.buffer+s1.len,s2.buffer,s2.len);

// return concatenated string
return sum;
}
```

However, this implementation contains several run-time disadvantages. First, a local string is created with initial memory, which is freed immediately in order to enlarge it (releasing the initial memory could easily be forgotten, resulting in a memory leak). Finally, the actual return value is created as a copy of sum, using the return statement, and then destroyed again. As a result, new is called three times and delete is called twice.

It would be better if new was only called once, because both new and delete are 'expensive' operations. For this purpose, a special constructor is defined that creates a string, to which the initial size, as well as the completely initialized buffer, is passed, along with the character string of the concatenated string:

```
String::String(unsigned l, char* buf)
{
    len = l;        // copy number of characters
    size = len;     // number of characters determines size of memory
    buffer = buf;   // copy memory
}
```

This constructor is a special optimization, which would be dangerous as a public interface. It cannot be guaranteed that memory of len length, created with new[], and then initialized, is always passed as a second parameter. For this reason, the constructor cannot be called from the outside:

```
class String {
    ...
    private:
        String(unsigned, char*);
};
```

Now the + operator can be implemented so that the buffer of the concatenated string can be created with the correct size, and be initialized at the same time:

```
String operator+ (const String& s1, const String& s2)
{
    // allocate buffer for the concatenated string
    char* buffer = new char[s1.len+s2.len];

    // copy characters into the buffer
    std::memcpy(buffer,        s1.buffer, s1.len);
```

```
        std::memcpy(buffer+s1.len, s2.buffer, s2.len);

        // create concatenated string from these data and return it
        return String (s1.len+s2.len, buffer);
}
```

As the special constructor is part of the return statement, the operation is typically optimized so that this concatenated string is created directly as the return value. The function `new` is therefore only called once.

This example shows the optimization potential that exists if all operations of a type can be accessed. This optimization has no influence on the interface of the user. The user can concatenate strings with both implementations. However, this happens noticeably faster using the optimized implementation.

6.1.7   Reading a `String`

Reading an object with dynamic members is not usually easy. One problem is that it is not initially clear how large the memory required by the object will be. It must also be defined when the read of the `String` begins, and how it is ended.

Bearing these concerns in mind, the input function of the CPPBook::String class is as follows:

```
// dyna/string1b.cpp

// **** BEGIN namespace CPPBook ********************************
namespace CPPBook {

void String::scanFrom(std::istream& strm)
{
    char c;

    len = 0;                 // initially, the string is empty

    strm >> std::ws;         // skip leading whitespace

    /* as long as the input stream strm, after the read
     * of a character c, is fine
     */
    while (strm.get(c)) {              // >> would skip whitespace

        /* if there is a whitespace at the end of the string input,
         * RETURN
         */
```

```
        if (std::isspace(c)) {
            return;
        }

        /* if there is not enough memory, enlarge it
         */
        if (len >= size) {
            char* tmp = buffer;              // pointer to old memory
            size = size*2 + 32;              // increase size of memory
            buffer = new char[size];         // allocate new memory
            std::memcpy(buffer,tmp,len);     // copy characters
            delete [] tmp;                   // release old memory
        }

        // enter new characters
        buffer[len] = c;
        ++len;
    }

    // end of read because of error or EOF
}


} // **** END namespace CPPBook *******************************
```

In principle, the input function is implemented so that it reads a string as a word, skipping leading whitespaces. The input is completed with a whitespace or the end of the input (i.e. end of file, EOF).

After the length of the string to be read has been set to 0, leading whitespace is skipped:

```
std::strm >> std::ws;
```

The std::ws manipulator takes on this work. The name stands for 'whitespace', such as newlines, tabs and spaces.

Finally, a loop is run that reads and processes a character:

```
while (strm.get(c)) {   // while character c is successfully read
    // process c
    ...
}
```

The get() member function is used to read the next character. The >> operator cannot be used here, as it skips leading whitespace; thus we could never read a whitespace with it. However, we need to know whether a whitespace was read, as this would terminate the string input.

The get() function returns the stream that was read from. This is then used as a condition for whether the loop should carry on running. As explained in Section 4.5.2 on page 201, the condition is only met if the stream is fine (has neither EOF nor an error state). The loop therefore runs for as long as an individual character can be successfully read.

A test is carried out in the loop to find out whether a whitespace was read. If this is the case, it is seen as the end of the input, and the function is exited[1]:

```
if (std::isspace(c)) {
    return;
}
```

If no whitespace is encountered, the new character needs to be inserted into the internal character array. To do this, we must ensure that there is enough space available for it. It is a common error to assume that an input can only be 80 characters long. The fact is that an input can have any length (for example, a data stream only has a separator after 10 000 characters). If the memory space is no longer sufficient, new memory of more than double the previous size is allocated, and the characters read so far are copied to it:

```
if (len >= size) {
    char* tmp = buffer;              // pointer to old memory
    size = size*2i + 32;             // increase size of memory
    buffer = new char[size];         // allocate new memory
    std::memcpy(buffer,tmp,len);     // copy characters
    delete [] tmp;                   // release old memory
}
```

The new character can now be appended, and the number of characters is incremented accordingly:

```
buffer[len] = c;
++len;
```

6.1.8   Commercial Implementations of String Classes

The implementation of CPPBook::String only represents a rudimentary extract from an implementation of a standard-conforming string class. However, one of the most important operations is missing, namely a facility for accessing the characters using the index operator. This is discussed in Section 6.2.1 on page 373.

The class can also be optimized further. We have already optimized a little already. However, as the class is a fundamental type, each optimization that improves run-time behavior is worthwhile.

---

[1] Note that, on some systems, isspace() is defined incorrectly in <cctype>, without being in the namespace std. If you get an error here, remove the leading (std::) qualification.

A consequence of the usual optimization with commercial string classes is that most functions are implemented inline. As header files are readable (they must be, in order to be included), I recommend that you take a look at one.

Reference Counting

One optimization possibility, which also demonstrates the powerful abilities of programming classes in C++, is the use of a technique called *reference counting*. This is based on the premise that copying and assigning strings is expensive, occurs very frequently and that strings are hardly ever manipulated (that is, individual characters are only very rarely changed).

The trick is that a string object itself is only a simple *handle* that refers to the actual string object (the so-called *body*). The actual data of a string, with the actual character string, is therefore moved into an auxiliary class:

```
class StringBody {
  private:
    char*    buffer;      // character sequence as a dynamic array
    unsigned len;         // current number to characters
    unsigned size;        // size of buffer
    unsigned refs;        // number of strings that use this body
    ...
};
```

The objects of the StringBody auxiliary class manage the actual character string, and can be used by several strings that all have the same value. The refs members determines how many strings share this body.

With every initialization, a body object is created with the actual data and a handle. In the body, it is initialized that there is exactly one owner (refs is set to 1). The handle itself is a fairly simple object that only refers to the body:

```
class String {
  private:
    StringBody* body;   // pointer to the actual string
    ...
};
```

If a string is now copied, only the handle is copied, and the number of strings that use this body gets incremented. Two strings then use the same character string. Conversely, if a string is destroyed, the number of strings that refers to it is decremented appropriately in its body. If this number is 0, the body object itself is destroyed.

Every read access to a string (for example, a query of its length) is simply passed on to the body. Only if a string is changed, whose body is shared by more than one string, is a true copy of the body created and assigned to the string that gets modified.

Because passing of strings (copying and assigning) typically happens more often than changes to individual characters, we avoid many explicit memory management operations, and thus save a lot of time.

Another typical optimization is the inclusion of special functions for substring processing, which is also carried out using internal auxiliary classes.

Reference counting can also be implemented using special *smart pointers*. This is discussed in Section 9.2.1 on page 536.

No Reference Counting

According to the explanation of the optimization facility with reference counting, we could now expect every implementation of the `std::string` class to be optimized in this way. However, this is incorrect.

Recently, it turned out that, in multi-threading programs, this kind of optimization with string classes can be counterproductive. The price of increased complexity, when added to the overhead of managing locks to handle the shares, is often higher than the benefit gained from avoiding copying. For this reason, all string implementations have removed this kind of optimization. Reference counting would only make sense if it was guaranteed that strings were not modified during their lifetime[2].

Instead, other kinds of optimizations have evolved, which are mostly based on the observation that most strings consist only of a very few characters. The good thing with C++ is that one can automatically benefit from this kind of knowledge and improvement, because the interface remains the same.

6.1.9   Other Uses of Dynamic Members

The term *dynamic member* can mean a lot more than members managed with `new` and `delete`. One of the most fascinating properties of C++ is that any complicated statements can be called in order to return an object to its starting position.

For example, a file management can be completely hidden in an abstract type. The constructor opens the file passed as an argument, and the destructor closes it again:

```
class File {
  private:
    FILE* fp;              // pointer to current file

  public:
    File(const char*);     // const char* constructor for the filename
    ~File();               // destructor
    ...
};
```

---

[2] The Java approach for handling strings turns out to be better here, as Java defines two types of string: one where you cannot manipulate characters and one where you can. However, in Java, strings cannot easily be compared with the `==` operator. (I think that I still have to write my own string class or programming language.)

```
File::File(const char* filename)
{
    // open file
    fp = fopen(filename,...);
    ...
}

File::~File()
{
    // close file
    fclose(fp);
}
```

In the application program, the file is automatically opened using the declaration of an object, then closed again when the block is exited:

```
void f()
{
    File d("testprog.cc");   // constructor opens the file
    ...

} // destructor at the end of the block automatically closes the file
```

The stream classes defined in the standard I/O library for accessing files work according to this principle (however, they call internal low-level functions for opening and closing files instead of fopen() and fclose(), which are provided by C). These classes are introduced in Section 8.2 on page 498.

Database connections, pipes, processes and other complex objects can be abstracted in such a way that their use is considerably simplified. In contrast to Java, there is also the advantage that the destructors are called at the moment when the scope of an object is left, instead of some undefined period of time later when garbage collection is performed. Thus concluding processes can also be programmed as objects. A typical example would be a class that represents ongoing transactions. Such a class could be used in C++ as follows:

```
void foo()
{
    Transaction t;
    ...                  // exception calls destructor, which calls t.cancel()
    t.commit();
}
```

The whole point of this use is that the application programmer does not have to program explicitly that at the end of the lifetime of the transaction t the transaction is canceled if it was not committed before. The destructor can ensure that an exception thrown before the commitment will cancel the transaction when the scope of t is left.

However, a great deal of care has to be taken with the implementation of these kinds of classes. Much thought and consideration must go into the implementation of the copy constructor and the assignment operator. (For example, what would happen during the copying of a file or a transaction?) In any case, the default implementation usually does not work.

The following can be used as a guideline (often referred to as *the rule of three*):

- A class needs a copy constructor, an assignment operator and a destructor, or none of these.

This means that if a custom implementation is necessary for either a copy constructor, or the assignment operator, or the destructor, then a custom implementation is usually required for *all* of these operations.

If it is not clear whether a copy constructor or an assignment operator is needed, one can simply prevent copying and assignment. To do this, the copy constructor or the assignment operator simply have to be declared as being non-public. This is discussed in Section 6.2.5 on page 383.

6.1.10   Summary

- Classes can have dynamic members. These are members that cannot simply be copied by assignment (typically pointers).
- Classes with dynamic members need a separate implementation of the copy constructor, the assignment operator and the destructor.
- A destructor is a function called automatically with the destruction of the object.
- An assignment operator should begin with a test that checks whether an object is being assigned to itself.
- An assignment operator should return the object to which something was assigned (that is, it should return *this).
- Using dynamic members, complex processes can be abstracted so that, when using an object, they are easy to handle.
- The ability to copy and assign objects of a class can be prevented.
- A class usually needs a copy constructor, an assignment operator and a destructor, or none of these.

6.2   Other Aspects of Dynamic Members

Classes with dynamic members display a fundamental strength of the concept of object-oriented programming: Complicated dynamic processes can be wrapped by a class so that the application program can just concentrate on the essentials. During the implementation of these kinds of classes, however, there are potential pitfalls. For example, you could unintentionally compromise the data encapsulation of a class. These aspects of the implementation of classes are discussed in this section.

6.2.1   Dynamic Members with Constant Objects

In this section, the class CPPBook::String introduced in the previous section is extended, with the inclusion of some useful operations. This will focus on a problem that is very important for the implementation of classes with dynamic members: the handling of constant objects that have dynamic members. Particular care has to be taken in order not to compromise the constancy of the objects.

Strings with the Operator [ ]

As strings can be seen as an array of characters, it is natural to provide access to individual characters using the index operator. However, one point is worth noting: With non-constant strings, the operator grants access to a character in the objects, which enables it to be modified. After calling

```
CPPBook::String s = "gray";
```

```
s[2] = 'e';
```

the string s should now have the value 'grey' (rather than 'gray'). In order to do this, the [ ] operator, which is called in the expression s[2], needs to return an *internal* part of the string (or access to an internal part of it), so that the string can be manipulated.

This is only possible if the [ ] operator grants access to the original characters of the string, rather than returning a copy, so that it can then be manipulated. This is easily done by returning a reference.

The operator must therefore be declared as follows:

```
namespace CPPBook {
  class String {
    private:
      char*    buffer;      // character sequence as a dynamic array
      unsigned len;         // current number to characters
      unsigned size;        // size of buffer

      ...
    public:
      char& operator [] (unsigned);   // access to a character
```

```
        ...
    };
}
```

The implementation can then look as follows:

```
// dyna/stridxvar.cpp

/* [] operator for variables
 */
char& String::operator [] (unsigned idx)
{
    // index not in permitted range?
    if (idx >= len) {
        throw std::out_of_range("string index out of range");
    }

    return buffer[idx];
}
```

After the test to see whether the passed index is valid, the character at index idx of the internal member buffer is returned as a reference. The returned character of the function is therefore not a copy, but the original character of the string, and can also be manipulated.

The [ ] Operator for Constant Strings

However, the implementation of the [ ] operator for strings as introduced above is not suitable for constant strings, as the operator would enable manipulation of the string. An obvious solution might be to declare it as a constant member function:

```
namespace CPPBook {
  class String {
    ...
    public:
      char& operator [] (unsigned) const;
    ...
  };
}
```

However, this results in the same problem:

```
const String s = "gray";

s[2] = 'e';      // this is not recognized as an error
```

You might expect that the compiler could actually recognize that a constant object is being accessed, and thus complain that manipulation using the [ ] operator is not possible in this case.

This is wrong! The problem here is that the actual object is not being changed. Its `buffer` member is only a pointer to the character string, and this pointer remains constant. However, what the pointer refers to is not constant (which is fine, because internally we have to change the characters of the string).

However, the operator should be defined for constant objects. It would be quite unreasonable if it were possible to access a character in a variable string only using the `[]` operator. The following should therefore also be possible:

```
const CPPBook::String s = "gray";
...
char c = s[0];
```

The solution is to provide two implementations of the `[]` operator: one for constants and one for variable strings. This kind of differentiation is possible. A function can be overloaded for both variables and constant objects (the function for constant objects is only used for variable objects if there is no separate function for variable objects).

For this reason, the `CPPBook::String` class should contain a second declaration for the `[]` operator:

```
namespace CPPBook {
  class String {
    private:
      char*    buffer;      // character sequence as a dynamic array
      unsigned len;         // current number to characters
      unsigned size;        // size of buffer
      ...
    public:
      // operator [] for variables
      char& operator [] (unsigned);

      // operator [] for constants
      char operator [] (unsigned) const;
      ...
  };
}
```

The statements for constant strings in the body of the function are no different from the version for variable strings:

```
// dyna/stridxconst.cpp

/* operator [] for constants
 */
char String::operator [] (unsigned idx) const
{
    // index not in permitted range?
```

```
        if (idx >= len) {
            throw std::out_of_range("string index out of range");
        }

        return buffer[idx];
    }
```

The only difference is that the character is no longer returned as a reference, but as a copy. For performance reasons, if the return value is a larger object, a constant reference should be used instead:

```
namespace CPPBook {
  class String {
    ...
    public:
      const char& operator [] (unsigned) const;
      ...
  };
}
```

6.2.2   Conversion Functions for Dynamic Members

Similar care is required when implementing conversion functions. It does not matter whether this relates to a function for automatic or explicit type conversion.

The String class is a good example. It is useful if a C-string can be created from an object of the String class, as numerous functions require a C-string as an argument.

On the basis of the considerations from Section 4.6.5 on page 229 (that functions for automatic type conversions should be avoided), the problem is demonstrated using a function for explicit type conversion.

In this case, access to the internal data of an object is granted very rarely (and very carefully), if ever. This should apply to constants as well as to variables, as otherwise manipulation of the string object would be possible. If you provide too much access to internal data, you open a hole, which breaks encapsulation, and that could lead to inconsistencies and unexpected behavior. Only very carefully should you give up control.

Accessing the internal element of the string can be avoided in two ways:

- A copy can be used.
- A constant can be used.

Copies as Return Values

If a copy is returned, the declaration and implementation look as follows:

```cpp
class String {
  private:
    char*    buffer;      // character sequence as a dynamic array
    unsigned len;         // current number to characters
    unsigned size;        // size of buffer
    ...
  public:
    char* toCharPtr() const;
};

char* String::toCharPtr() const
{
    // allocate memory for copy
    char* p = new char[len+1];

    // copy characters
    std::memcpy(p, buffer, len);

    // append end-of-string character
    p[len] = '\0';

    // and return
    return p;
}
```

However, This solution has several disadvantages:

- On one hand, the explicit creation of memory takes time.
- One the other hand, because extra memory is created, the application program must ensure that it is also freed: a requirement that will sooner or later lead to a memory leak.

     If this kind of implementation is used for a type conversion, at the very least, the function name should indicate that memory is created explicitly, which then needs to be freed at a later date (for example, the name asNewCharPtr()).

Constants as Return Values

It is usually better to return the internal character string and declare the return value so that the data cannot be changed:

```cpp
class String {
  private:
    char*    buffer;      // character sequence as a dynamic array
    unsigned len;         // current number to characters
    unsigned size;        // size of buffer
    ...
```

```
    public:
      const char* toCharPtr() const;
};


const char* String::toCharPtr() const
{
      // return character string
      return buffer;
}
```

In this case, the character string of the string is simply returned as a constant character string. This can also lead to problems:

- On one hand, an invalid address may be returned. As the string object may alter the internal memory used, there is always the danger that returned characters may no longer be valid (a problem that does not arise when a copy is made).
- An end-of-string character cannot easily be appended.

The standard `std::string` string class has two functions:

- `c_str()` returns the actual character string as a C-string (with appended end-of-string character '\0', see page 68).
- `data()` returns the internal character string as it is.

Implementations of the class typically use the following trick. Internally, an end-of-string character is always appended automatically. For this purpose, memory is always allocated for at least one more character. Both `c_str()` and `data()` then simply return this internal buffer[3]. This return value is then only valid up to the next operation that can manipulate the string or make it invalid. A copy should therefore always be made immediately before the `string` gets modified.

6.2.3   Conversion Functions for Conditions

With classes that contain dynamic members, the automatic type conversion is often used for testing conditions. Following the traditional C code of

```
    FILE* fp;              // pointer to the opened file


    fp = fopen ("hello", "r");


    if (fp) {
        // read data
        ...
```

---

[3] Caution: this does not mean that it is safe to assume that `data()` also ends with the end-of-string character. This is only the case with *most* implementations. Anyone who needs an end-of-string character should therefore always use `c_str()`.

```
}
else {
    // error: fp is NULL
    ...
}
```

with a class for opened files, the following is made possible:

```
CPPBook::File f("hello");      // constructor opens the file (hopefully)

if (f) {
    // read data
    ...
}
else {
    // error: f is not OK
    ...
}
```

In C, this technique is based on the fact that NULL often shows an error status with pointers. NULL is, however, simply the value 0, which, in turn, denotes `false`. The test

```
if (fp)
```

is therefore an abbreviation for

```
if (fp != NULL)
```

(It could be argued at this point whether or not this improves the readability of the program.)

Conversion to C++ can now be seen from the same point of view. Conditions in control constructs can be objects as long as an automatic type conversion into an integral or a pointer type is defined. If the integral or the pointer type has the value 0, the condition is not met.

Therefore, in order to enable the above if-query, a type conversion into a pointer type has to be implemented. For a class for opened files, this may look as follows:

```
namespace CPPBook {
  class File {
    private:
      FILE* fp;            // pointer to the opened file

    public:
      ...
      operator FILE* () {  // automatic conversion into FILE*
          return fp;
      }
  };
}
```

According to the declaration

```
CPPBook::File f("hello");
```

the call

```
if (f)
```

is evaluated as follows:

```
if ((f.operator FILE*()) != NULL)
```

However, providing such an automatic type conversion conceals the danger of losing the whole advantage of a secure interface. With a type conversion defined in this way, there is now a facility for accessing a private member and then modifying it. For example, the following would be possible, without an error message:

```
CPPBook::File f;
FILE* fp;
...
fp = f;
```

The first improvement would therefore be the conversion of the pointer into the void* type:

```
namespace CPPBook {
  class File {
    private:
      FILE* fp;                // pointer to the opened file

    public:
      ...
      operator void* () {
          return (void*)fp;
      }
  };
}
```

However, an internal member is still exported to the caller. It is even better to make sure that no internal address is exported:

```
namespace CPPBook {
  class File {
    private:
      FILE* fp;                // pointer to the opened file

    public:
      ...
      operator void* () {
          return  fp != NULL ? reinterpret_cast<void*>(32)
                             : static_cast<void*>(0);
      }
```

```
    };
}
```

In this case, the values 32 and 0 are converted into addresses using the operators for type conversion. While the use of 0 as an address is possible, and is therefore sufficient for the conversion of `static_cast`, 1 has to be converted using the 'most dramatic' of all type conversion operators, the operator `reinterpret_cast`.

The best thing to do is to avoid functions for automatic type conversion. A member function for explicit type conversion such as `isOK()` also works and leads to more-readable user code:

```
if (f.isOK())
```

The standard classes for I/O use the technique that has just been introduced. In the process, the operator ! is also overloaded in order to enable something like

```
if (! f)
```

This is discussed in more detail in Section 4.5.2 on page 201.

6.2.4   Constants Become Variables

With complex classes, it may be worthwhile, on the initialization of objects, to refrain from calculating every member that could be of interest. An appropriate calculation could be postponed to the moment when the information is needed for the first time. This kind of programming technique is described as *lazy evaluation*.

An example uses the class for opened files. In order to determine how many lines a file has, the whole file has to be run through, and the number of newlines counted. This takes quite some time with large files. For this reason, the number of lines is better kept in an internal member and only determined when the number is requested:

```
namespace CPPBook {
  class File {
    private:
      FILE* fp;          // pointer to the opened file
      int   lines;       // number of lines (a value of -1 denotes 'not yet known')

    public:
      // constructor
      File(... ) : lines(-1) {   // number of lines not yet known
          ...
      }

      int numberOfLines();              // returns the number of lines
      ...
  };
}
...
```

```
int File::numberOfLines()
{
    // determine the number of lines with the first query
    if (lines == -1) {
        lines = getNumberOfLines();
    }
    return lines;
}
```

However, this causes a problem. The number of lines cannot be determined for constant objects of the class[4]:

```
const CPPBook::File f("prog.dat");


std::cout << f.numberOfLines();        // error: no constant member functions
```

The problem is that `numberOfLines()` cannot be a constant member function, because the object is manipulated internally via the call. However, from the point of view of the application programmer, the file does not change when querying its number of lines; that is, logically, it is constant. Thus we have logical constness, but no technical constness.

For this purpose, the `mutable` keyword was introduced. If a member exists that plays no part in the logical constancy of an object, you can use `mutable` to declare that this member can even be changed by constant member functions.

With this, the `File` class is declared as follows:

```
namespace CPPBook {
  class File {
    private:
      FILE* fp;                // pointer to the opened file
      mutable int lines;       // number of lines (-1 denotes 'not yet known')
                               // - new: also modifiable for constants


    public:
      // constructor
      File(... ) : lines (-1) {  // number of lines not known at first
          ...
      }


      // member function for constants
      int numberOfLines() const;
```

---

[4] This example assumes that the constancy of a file determines whether write access is possible. The standard types for file access uses a different approach, namely it provides different types for read and write access.

```
      ...
   };
}
...

int File::numberOfLines() const
{
    // determine number of lines with first request
    if (lines == -1) {
        // OK: lines even modifiable for constant objects
        lines = getNumberOfLines();
    }
    return lines;
}
```

The number of lines can now be defined for files declared as constant:

```
const CPPBook::File f("prog.dat");

std::cout << f.numberOfLines();      // OK
```

There are also other possibilities for removing the constancy of variables, such as an explicit type conversion (see Section 3.4.4 on page 68). However, this solution is much clearer and more appropriate.

The `mutable` keyword is not only used to enable lazy evaluation: whenever there is a need to manipulate internal data, even though the object logically stays constant, `mutable` is appropriate. Another example of this would be a flag that is set inside an object while an operation is performed to detect any recursion during the operation. This could, for example, be used to output recursive data structures without running into endless loops.

6.2.5   Preventing Predefined Functions

The class for opened files is a good example of another important aspect that should always be taken into account when dealing with classes that contain dynamic members.

As explained in Section 6.1, the default operations provided for each class are unsuitable for classes with dynamic members. A custom copy constructor and a custom assignment operator must usually be implemented.

However, a copy or assignment could just be not useful. In this case, you should actually prohibit calls to them instead of just hoping that nobody calls them (never underestimate the fantasy of programmers). This can be done fairly easily by declaring them as non-public.

Thus, for the class of opened files, copying and assignment can be made impossible in the following way:

```
namespace CPPBook {
  class File {
    private:
      FILE* fp;                          // pointer to the opened file

      ...

    public:
      ...

    private:
      File(const File&);
      File& operator= (const File&);
  };
}
```

The declaration of this standard operation as `private` is enough; no implementation is necessary. Passing a parameter is then only possible by means of references:

```
void withCopy(CPPBook::File);
void withoutCopy(const CPPBook::File&);
...
void f()
{
    CPPBook::File f("prog.dat");
    CPPBook::File g("prog.old");

    withoutCopy(f);   // OK
    withCopy(f);      // ERROR: copies not allowed
    g = f;            // ERROR: assignments not allowed
}
```

6.2.6 Proxy Classes

Most of the problems discussed in this section have to do with the fact that control over the operations that are called for an object is lost. If a pointer to internal data is provided, this can be misused because you do not have control over what is done with pointers. If a reference to a character is returned via an index operator, you no longer have control over what happens with the character reference outside the class. For example, characters can also be manipulated in a string as follows:

```
CPPBook::String s("hello");

++s[2];     // increment third character
```

The best solution is to never give up control. This is also possible when you return or gain access to parts of an object. The trick is to maintain control of the return value. Of course, this should not lead to more complicated or less intuitive interfaces. Instead, we use so-called *proxy classes*.

A proxy can be described as a wrapper that, without changing the interface, gives control over
something that one normally has no control.

For example, in the string class, the index operator can be implemented so that a special type
is returned that *behaves* like a char, but does not permit all operations chars provide:

```cpp
class String {
  public:
    /* proxy class for access to individual characters
     */
    class reference {
      friend class String;        // String has access to private members
      private:
        char& ch;                 // internal reference to a character in the string


        // constructor (can only be called from the String class)
        reference(char& c) : ch(c) {        // create reference
        }

        reference(const reference&);        // copying forbidden
      public:

        // assignments of char and other references are OK
        reference& operator= (char c) {
            ch = c;
            return *this;
        }
        reference& operator= (const reference& r) {
            ch = r.ch;
            return *this;
        }

        // use as char creates a copy
        operator char() {
            return ch;
        }
    };

  public:
    // access to a character in the string
    reference operator [] (unsigned);
    char      operator [] (unsigned) const;
    ...
};
```

In the String class, the nested class reference is defined. This class represents references to characters in a String.

This kind of object is returned by the index operator for variables:

```cpp
String::reference String::operator [] (unsigned idx)
{
    // index not in permitted range?
    if (idx >= len) {
        throw std::out_of_range("string index out of range");
    }

    return reference(buffer[idx]);
}
```

The return value is initialized with the corresponding character inside the string, to which we grant access. Thus the reference member ch will be initialized with this character. In this way, we maintain control of the operations that are carried out with the return value of the index operator because we can program what is possible with a string::reference and what is not.

The use of this reference is shown in the following example:

```cpp
// dyna/stringtest2.cpp

#include <iostream>     // C++ header file for I/O
#include "string.hpp"   // C++ header file for strings

int main()
{
    typedef CPPBook::String string;

    // create two strings
    string firstname = "Jicolai";
    string lastname = "Nosuttis";
    string name;

    // mix up the first characters of the string
    char c = firstname[0];
    firstname[0] = lastname[0];
    lastname[0] = c;

    std::cout << firstname << ' ' << lastname << std::endl;
}
```

In the statement

```cpp
char c = firstname[0];
```

the expression `firstname[0]` yields a `string::reference`, which, by means of the conversion function `operator char()` (see Section 4.6.4 on page 227), can automatically be converted into, and thus assigned to, a `char`.

With

```
firstname[0] = lastname[0];
```

both sides of the assignment provide a `string::reference`. The assignment operator then allows an appropriate assignment.

With

```
lastname[0] = c;
```

the second form of the assignment operator is used, which allows a string reference to be assigned a `char`.

Copying, and every other operation using the return value of the index operator, is not allowed:

```
++firstname[0];      // error: ++ not defined for string::references
```

According to this pattern, control can always be maintained over nested expressions. You only have to make sure that you return one of your types to the applications programmer. However, the automatic type conversion from the proxy to the type it wraps makes sure that any read-only operation of the returned value is still possible.

6.2.7 Exception Handling Using Parameters

If an exception is thrown within a class, it is often useful to pass data about the error to the error object. For example, in the case of the index operator of strings, it might be useful to pass the invalid index and even the string for which the index was invalid. This makes it far easier to process an exception meaningfully (such as writing an error message with both the string and the invalid index).

Passing the Invalid Index as a Parameter

The `String` class (as introduced in Section 6.1 on page 352 and extended in Section 6.2.1 and Section 6.2.6) could define a special error class in which the error objects have the invalid index as a member:

```
// dyna/string3.hpp

namespace CPPBook {
  class String {
    public:
      class reference {
          ...
      };
```

```
// new: error class
class RangeError {
  public:
    int index;                          // invalid index
    RangeError(int i) : index(i) {    // constructor (initializes index)
    }
};

public:
  ...
  // operator [] for variables and constants
  reference operator [] (unsigned);
  char      operator [] (unsigned) const;
};
}
```

By using an initializer list[5], the constructor of the CPPBook::String::RangeError class makes sure that, during the creation of an error object, the index member is initialized with the invalid index passed as parameter i.

In the implementation of the operator [ ] for variables, an appropriate object has to be created as an exception when an invalid index is found. The index is then passed to this exception:

```
// dyna/string3.cpp

/* operator [] for variables
 */
String::reference String::operator [] (unsigned i)
{
    // index not in permitted range?
    if (i >= len) {
        // throw exception with invalid index
        throw RangeError(i);
    }

    return reference(buffer[i]);
}

/* operator [] for constants
 */
char String::operator [] (unsigned i) const
```

---

[5] Initialization lists are introduced in sections 4.1.7 and 6.4.2.

```
{
    // index not in permitted range?
    if (i >= len) {
        // throw exception with invalid index
        throw RangeError(i);
    }

    return buffer[i];
}
```

If the error now appears, the application program can not only recognize that the error has occurred, but can also retrieve the invalid index. For example, it would be possible to output the invalid index in an error message:

```
// dyna/stringtest3.cpp

int main()
{
    try {
        ...
    }
    catch (const CPPBook::String::RangeError& error) {
        // exit main() with error message and error status
        std::cerr << "ERROR: invalid index " << error.index
                  << " when accessing a string" << std::endl;
        return EXIT_FAILURE;
    }
}
```

A name must be declared for the object in the catch block, in the same way as with functions, in order to be able to access the members. In the catch block, the index member in the error object is accessed directly. For this reason, it is declared as public. It is not necessary to define the member as private, and define a member function for access, because data encapsulation is not so important here. The error object is not used to represent a state over some period of time. Instead, it is used to signal the error and pass the corresponding data. Its life cycle ends with the end of the error handling.

Information About the Error-Producing Object

If you want to pass the string that produced the error as a parameter of the exception object, you have to consider the following: This string has to get be copied, because it may be a local object that no longer exists when, during the processing of the exception (stack unwinding), its scope is left. The string therefore must not be declared as a pointer or a reference, but must be declared as a normal member, of type `String`, in the exception class. However, the following is not possible:

```cpp
namespace CPPBook {
  class String {
    public:
      // error class:
      class RangeError {
        public:
          String value;        // ERROR: type String incomplete
          ...
      };
      ...
  };
}
```

This is an error because `String` is used as a plain type meanwhile it is declared. Therefore, `String` is incomplete when the member `value` of the nested class is declared. Instead, you have to forward declare the nested class and define it afterwards:

```cpp
// dyna/string4.hpp

namespace CPPBook {
  class String {
    public:
      class reference {
          ...
      };


      // error class:
      // - forward declared because it contains a String
      class RangeError;

    public:
      ...
      // operator [] for variables and constants
      reference operator [] (unsigned);
      char      operator [] (unsigned) const;
  };

  class String::RangeError {
    public:
      int    index;        // invalid index
      String value;        // string for this purpose
```

```
    // constructor (initializes index and value)
    RangeError (const String& s, int i) : index(i), value(s) {
    }
  };
}
```

Now when an invalid index is found, both the string and the invalid index are passed for the initialization of the exception object:

```
// dyna/string4.cpp

/* operator [] for variables
 */
String::reference String::operator [] (unsigned i)
{
    // index not in permitted range?
    if (i >= len) {
        /* throw exception:
         * - new: pass string itself and invalid index
         */
        throw RangeError(*this,i);
    }

    return reference(buffer[i]);
}


/* operator [] for constants
 */
char String::operator [] (unsigned i) const
{
    // index not in permitted range?
    if (i >= len) {
        /* throw exception:
         * - new: pass string itself and invalid index
         */
        throw RangeError(*this,i);
    }

    return buffer[i];
}
```

An application can access both members:

```
// dyna/stringtest4.cpp

int main()
{
    try {
        ...
    }
    catch (const CPPBook::String::RangeError& error) {
        // exit main() with error message and error status
        std::cerr << "ERROR: invalid index " << error.index
                  << " when accessing string \"" << error.value
                  << "\"" << std::endl;
        return EXIT_FAILURE;
    }
}
```

As the object that threw an exception cannot be passed as a parameter to the exception without being copied, the identity of the object can no longer be determined. If this information is required, either object IDs (see Section 6.5.1 on page 414) or the address of the object as a pointer of the const void* type need to be passed. This ID/address can then be compared with the ID/address of the known object when dealing with the exception.

6.2.8   Summary

- Functions can be overloaded differently for variable and constant objects.
- If a member function provides write access to internal members, it must be ensured that the function cannot be called for constants.
- Functions that convert dynamic members into other types can return a copy or a constant, with different advantages and disadvantages.
- Automatic type conversions can be defined for conditions in control constructs that allow an object to be used directly as a condition. This should be used with care. By doing this, no access to internal members should be possible.
- The mutable keyword allows the modification of a member, even for constant member functions. Semantically, this means that, from an application programmer's point of view, the member has no relevance to the state of an object (thus, even when modifying it, the object logically stays constant).
- If copying and assigning is not useful, calling the copy constructor and assignment operator, respectively, should be forbidden. To do so, it is sufficient to declare them as private.
- In nested operations, proxy classes allow control to be maintained.
- Exception objects can have members. If the error-producing object is passed, a copy of it must be created.

6.3   Inheritance of Classes with Dynamic Members

This section deals with some additional issues that must be taken into account when deriving classes. This includes the aspects that play a part in classes with dynamic members. Problems with overriding friend functions will also be considered.

These aspects are demonstrated using an example of a derivation of the CPPBook::String class. This is extended by the introducing the concept 'to have a color'. The CPPBook::String class is also used as a type for the color. In this way, the derived class is also an application of the base class.

6.3.1   The CPPBook::String Class as a Base Class

For the CPPBook::String class to be derived, it must be implemented so that it is suitable for inheritance (the standard string class, std::string, is not suitable for inheritance). The declaration of the CPPBook::String class, introduced in Section 6.1 and extended in Section 6.2, has to be changed as follows:

- The private members are given the keyword protected (but the private constructor used for concatenation and the private members of the nested reference class remain private).
- The functions for I/O are declared as virtual.
- The destructor is declared as virtual.

The result is the following header file for the base class CPPBook::String:

```
// dyna/string5.hpp

#ifndef STRING_HPP
#define STRING_HPP

// header file for I/O
#include <iostream>

// **** BEGIN namespace CPPBook ********************************
namespace CPPBook {

class String {
  public:
    class reference {
        friend class String;   // String has access to private members
        private:
          char& ch;                    // internal reference to a character in the string
          reference(char& c) : ch(c) {      // constructor
          }
          reference(const reference&);      // copying forbidden
```

```
    public:
      reference& operator= (char c) {   // assignments
          ch = c;
          return *this;
      }
      reference& operator= (const reference& r) {
          ch = r.ch;
          return *this;
      }
      operator char() {                          // use as char creates a copy
          return ch;
      }
  };
```

```
  // error class:
  // - forward declared because it contains a String
  class RangeError;
```

```
protected:
  char*    buffer;      // character string as dynamic array
  unsigned len;         // current number of characters
  unsigned size;        // size of memory of buffer
```

```
public:
  // default and char* constructor
  String(const char* = "");
```

```
  // due to dynamic members:
  String(const String&);              // copy constructor
  String& operator= (const String&);  // assignment
  virtual ~String();                  // destructor (new: virtual)
```

```
  // comparison of strings
  friend bool operator== (const String&, const String&);
  friend bool operator!= (const String&, const String&);
```

```
  // appending strings one after the other
  friend String operator+ (const String&, const String&);
```

```
  // output to a stream
  virtual void printOn(std::ostream&) const;
```

```cpp
    // input from a stream
    virtual void scanFrom(std::istream&);

    // number of characters
    // note: cannot be overlooked during derivation
    unsigned length() const {
        return len;
    }

    // operator [] for variables and constants
    reference operator [] (unsigned);
    char      operator [] (unsigned) const;

  private:
    /* constructor from length and buffer
     * - internally for operator +
     */
    String(unsigned, char*);
};

class String::RangeError {
  public:
    int    index;      // invalid index
    String value;      // string for this purpose

    // constructor (initializes index and value)
    RangeError (const String& s, int i) : index(i), value(s) {
    }
};

// standard output operator
inline std::ostream& operator << (std::ostream& strm, const String& s)
{
    s.printOn(strm);      // output string to stream
    return strm;          // return stream
}

// standard input operator
inline std::istream& operator >> (std::istream& strm, String& s)
{
    s.scanFrom(strm);     // read string from stream
```

```
        return strm;        // return stream
}

/* operator !=
 * - implemented inline as conversion to operator ==
 */
inline bool operator!= (const String& s1, const String& s2) {
    return !(s1==s2);
}

} // **** END namespace CPPBook ******************************

#endif    // STRING_HPP
```

Virtual or Not Virtual?

It is worth noting that the member function `length()` is *not* declared as virtual. This is a design decision in favour of an improved running time (being virtual, inline processing is not possible for references and pointers; see Section 5.2.2 on page 283). The consequence of this decision is that there are problems if a derived class overrides this function and an object of the derived class is then used in the base class. Or, in other words, this member function is not provided for overriding. As the query of the number of characters cannot be implemented differently, this limitation is probably acceptable. (You might argue that the meaning of the `buffer` member can be changed; however, this would violate the basic rule that members in derived classes should keep their meaning; see Section 5.5.3 on page 347.)

6.3.2   The Derived `ColString` Class

The string class is derived as a string that has a specific color. The derived class is appropriately called `ColString`. It has the color of the string as additional member.

As previously mentioned, the color itself is an object of the `CPPBook::string` class. A list type could also have been used, although this variant makes it possible to clarify the use of the string class as a base class and as an applied class at the same time.

Header File of the `ColString` Class

The header file of the class `ColString` derived from `String` is as follows:

```
// dyna/colstring1.hpp

#ifndef COLSTRING_HPP
#define COLSTRING_HPP

// header file of the base class
#include "string.hpp"

// **** BEGIN namespace CPPBook *******************************
namespace CPPBook {

/* class ColString
 * - derived from String
 */
class ColString : public String {
  protected:
    String col;      // colour of the string

  public:
    // default, String and String/String constructor
    ColString(const String& s = "", const String& c = "black")
        : String(s), col(c) {
    }

    // query and set colour
    const String& color() {
        return col;
    }
    void color(const String& newColor) {
        col = newColor;
    }

    // output to and input from a stream
    virtual void printOn(std::ostream&) const;
    virtual void scanFrom(std::istream&);

    // comparison of ColStrings
    friend bool operator== (const ColString& s1,
                            const ColString& s2) {
        return static_cast<const String&>(s1)
               == static_cast<const String&>(s2)
            && s1.col == s2.col;
    }
```

```
       friend bool operator!= (const ColString& s1,
                               const ColString& s2) {
          return !(s1==s2);
       }
};


} // **** END namespace CPPBook *******************************

#endif // COLSTRING_HPP
```

First, the new member for color is defined. As the `color` symbol is used for the member functions that set and query the color, the member has the name `col` (meaningful names in interfaces are more important)[6]:

```
class ColString : public String {
  protected:
    String col;     // color of the string
    ...
};
```

The constructor is defined next. Up to two strings can be passed as parameters. The first string is the initial character sequence (default: empty string) and the second string is the initial color (default: 'black'):

```
class ColString : public String {
  ...
  public:
    // default, String and String/String constructor
    ColString(const String& s = "", const String& c = "black")
      : String(s), col(c) {
    }
  ...
};
```

In the initializer list, the first string `s` is passed as the initial character sequence of the `String` base class. The second parameter is used to initialize the `col` member.

The `color()` member function is overloaded, so that it can be used for setting as well as querying the color. This is a common technique in C++. If no parameter is passed, it provides the current color; if a parameter is passed, this is the new color:

---

[6] There is no general solution for the dilemma of name conflicts between a simple member and the member functions that set and query it. An underscore may be placed in front of the member name, it may be abbreviated, and often the member functions begin with prefixes such as `get` and `set` (that is why these functions are also called *getters* and *setters*).

```
class ColString : public String {
  ...
  public:
    const String& color() {                    // query color
        return col;
    }
    void color(const String& newColor) {   // set color
        col = newColor;
    }
    ...
};
```

Virtual or Not Virtual?

The member functions for setting and querying the color are not defined as virtual in this case. This means that they are not suitable for overriding during derivation. Once again, this is a design decision in favour of an improved running time. As setting and querying the color cannot be implemented differently, and the semantics of members should never change in derived classes, this limitation is acceptable once more. However, when the color is modified, this means that it is no longer possible to carry out other actions in the derived classes (unless no pointers or references to base classes are used, which is almost impossible to ensure).

Functions for I/O are, as in the base class, defined as virtual, so that the correct I/O function is called:

```
class ColString : public String {
  ...
  public:
    virtual void printOn(std::ostream&) const;
    virtual void scanFrom(std::istream&);
    ...
};
```

6.3.3   Deriving Friend Functions

In order to enable an automatic type conversion for the first operator, the operators for testing for equality and inequality are defined in the base class String as global friend functions. However, they must be overridden in the derived class, because, in addition to the character sequences, the colors of two ColStrings must also be the same.

In order to implement the test for equality as easily as possible, we use the implementation of the base class, supplemented with the test for equality for the new members. However, as it is a global function, this cannot be implemented with the scope operator, but must instead use an explicit type conversion:

```
class ColString : public String {
  ...

  public:
    friend bool operator== (const ColString& s1,
                            const ColString& s2) {
        return static_cast<const String&>(s1)
                == static_cast<const String&>(s2)
               && s1.col == s2.col;
    }
    ...
};
```

Using the `static_cast<>` operator, the parameters `s1` and `s2` are explicitly converted into the `const String&` type. By doing so, it is guaranteed that the equality operator is called for the type of the `String` base class. The additional test for equality is added for color, which leads to a further call of the equality operator of the `String` class, because the `col` member has this type.

There is now an equality operation for two `String`s and two `ColString`s. But what happens if a `String` is compared with a `ColString`? In this case, there are two possibilities:

- The `ColString` is implicitly converted into a `String`. This is possible because each object of a derived class can, in principle, be used as an object of the base class, and therefore an automatic type conversion of `ColString` into `String` is defined.

- The `String` is converted into a `ColString`. This is possible because there is a constructor for the `ColString` class to which a `String` can be passed as a parameter. This constructor automatically defines an appropriate type conversion.

The expression may appear ambiguous, which you might would cause problems when compiling the program. However, in C++, an automatic type conversion predefined by the language has a higher priority than user-defined functions, such as constructors and conversion functions (see also Section 10.3 on page 573). Therefore, the comparison operator for two strings is called.

friend and virtual

Friend functions are, in principle, not virtual. Calls of a friend function are always bound to the type the parameter has at compile time (even for pointers and references). This means that the comparison operator for the `String` type is called if two `ColString`s are compared using pointers or references to `String`s.

Anyone who wants the correct function to be called for the function at run time should define the operator as an member function. An additional global operation can then be defined, which compares an object of the `const char*` type with a `String` or with a `ColString`. Another possibility would be to implement the operator as a global function, which is not a friend function, but calls an internal auxiliary function instead (another example demonstrating this follows).

As friend functions cannot be virtual, the test for inequality must also be reimplemented, although it is implemented just as in the base class. It simply yields the negated result of the test for equality:

```
class ColString : public String {
   ...
   public:
     friend bool operator!= (const ColString& s1,
                             const ColString& s2) {
          return !(s1==s2);
     }
   ...
};
```

Because the implementation of the base class is not a virtual function, its test for inequality always calls the test for equality for objects of type String. This would then also be valid for use with ColStrings. Color would therefore no longer play a role. For this reason, the operator must be reimplemented.

Avoiding Friend Functions

It is worth noting that friend functions are a problem when used with inheritance. They are not inherited, but can be called for objects of the derived class. The objects then become objects of the base class, which, during the call of auxiliary functions in the friend functions, can lead to the wrong functions being called.

It is also not permitted for an operation to be defined as an member function as well as a friend function:

```
class String {
   ...
   public:
     bool operator== (const String& s2);
     friend bool operator== (const String& s1,
                             const String& s2);   // ERROR
   ...
};
```

Therefore, as long as a class is being used with inheritance, friend functions should, in principle, be omitted. The automatic type conversion for the first operands can be made possible by using additional global auxiliary functions instead.

Another possibility is the technique used with I/O operators. These are defined as global functions, whose only purpose is to call corresponding virtual function that do the actual work. In the base class, this would look as follows:

```
class String {
   ...
   public:
     virtual bool equals(const String& s2);   // compare Strings
   ...
};
```

```
inline bool operator== (const String& s1, const String& s2) {
    return s1.equals(s2);
} inline bool operator!= (const String& s1, const String& s2) {
    return !s1.equals(s2);
}
```

A derived class only has to implement the new version of `equals()`:

```
class ColString : public String {
  ...
  public:
    virtual bool equals(const ColString& s2) {
        return String::equals(s2) && col == s2.col;
    }
    ...
};
```

6.3.4   Dot-C File of the Derived ColString Class

The dot-C file of the derived ColString class only consists of relatively simple reimplementations of the functions for I/O:

```
// dyna/colstring1.cpp

// header file of this class
#include "colstring.hpp"

// **** BEGIN namespace CPPBook ****************************
namespace CPPBook {

/* output to stream
 */
void ColString::printOn(std::ostream& strm) const
{
    // output character sequence with colour in brackets
    String::printOn(strm);
    strm << " (in " << col << ')';
}


/* reading of a ColString from an input stream
 */
void ColString::scanFrom(std::istream& strm)
{
```

```
        // read character sequence and colour, one after the other
        String::scanFrom(strm);
        col.scanFrom(strm);
    }


    } // **** END namespace CPPBook ********************************
```

The function for input reads two strings: one for the content and one for the color. A more complicated implementation could interpret the color as an optional input by evaluating whether the opening and closing parentheses exist.

6.3.5 Application of the `ColString` Class

The `ColString` class is used in the same way as any other class, as the following example shows:

```
// dyna/cstest1.cpp

// header file for I/O
#include <iostream>

// header file for the class ColString
#include "colstring.hpp"

int main()
{
    CPPBook::ColString c("hello");          // ColString with default colour
    CPPBook::ColString r("red","red");      // ColString with colour red

    std::cout << c << " " << r << std::endl; // output ColStrings

    c.color("green");                        // set colour of f to green

    std::cout << c << " " << r << std::endl; // output ColStrings

    std::cout << "concatenated string: " << c + r << std::endl;

    c[0] = 'H';
    std::cout << "modified string:     " << c << std::endl;
}
```

The program has the following output:

```
hello (in black) red (in red)
hello (in green) red (in red)
concatenated string: hellored
modified string:     Hello (in green)
```

The + operator was not reimplemented for ColStrings. What color should the concatenated string have? Because ColStrings can be used as Strings, a concatenation is possible, which calls the implementation of the base class. The return value therefore is a String and not a ColString, as the output of the program shows.

6.3.6   Deriving the Special Functions for Dynamic Members

One may ask why the special functions for dynamic members were not also reimplemented in the ColString class (in the base class, the default implementations were replaced with a custom implementation and these members were inherited). However, the default implementations are defined in such a way that custom implementations are not necessary for derived classes:

- The copy constructors are called, like all constructors, top-down. The default copy constructor of a derived class automatically calls the valid copy constructor of the base class. The copy constructor of the base class therefore handles the inherited dynamic members.

    Newly added members are, by default, copied member-wise. Therefore, in this case, the col string member get copied automatically. As it is a type with a self-defined copy constructor, this copy constructor is called automatically.

- The same applies to the assignment operator. The generated default assignment operator assigns the inherited members by calling the self-defined assignment operator of the base class. Finally, all the new members are assigned member-wise. Thus the self-implemented assignment operator of the base class is called once for the inherited members and once for col.

- The destructors are called bottom-up. Thus all clean-up work of the base class is carried out automatically. As the destructor of the base class is virtual, the destructors of all derived classes are automatically virtual.

As you can see, the generated default operations deal with inherited dynamic members in a way, that no special handling in the derived classes is necessary if the base class is implemented correctly. This is important, because it means that dynamic members can be introduced in a base class, without all derived classes having to be changed.

If a copy constructor has to be implemented in a derived class, the following example shows how this would have to look for the ColString class. Using an initializer list, the copy constructor of the base class is called, and then every new member is copied:

```
class ColString : public String {
  ...
  public:
    ColString(const ColString& s)          // copy constructor
      : String(s), col(s.col) {
    }
  ...
};
```

The implementation of a custom assignment operator is similar. First, the assignment operator of the base class is called, and then all new members are assigned:

```
ColString& ColString::operator= (const ColString& s) {
    // assignment of a ColString to itself has no effect
    if (this == &s) {
        return *this;        // return ColString
    }

    // call assignment operator of the base class
    String::operator = (s);

    // assign new members
    col = s.col;

    return *this;            // return modified ColString
}
```

6.3.7 Summary

- Friend functions can never be virtual.
- For this reason, friend functions are problematic when used with inheritance and should be avoided.
- If a destructor in the base class is virtual, it will have virtual destructors in all derived classes.
- If a copy constructor, destructor or assignment operator are necessary in a base class, this does not mean that they are also necessary in a class derived from it. The default implementations of these operations in derived classes automatically call the self-defined implementations of the base class.

6.4   Classes Containing Classes

In this section, we introduce a class that represents people, in order to demonstrate some further properties of classes. First, we demonstrate in detail what happens if objects contain other objects. Then, the advantages of initializer lists are explained.

6.4.1   Objects as Members of Other Classes

In the previous examples, the members of a class were mostly fundamental types, such as `int` and `char`. However, in some classes, we have also used strings as members. In these cases, when a string-containing object is initialized, its sub-objects (i.e. the strings) are also initialized. This means that several constructors are called. The details of this are discussed in more detail below.

Constructors Calling Constructors

If objects of a class contain objects of another class, on initialization, several constructors are called. In addition to the constructor of the parent object, the objects that are members also have to be initialized.

The following applies:

- Before the statements in the body of a constructor are processed, constructors for the members of the object are called.

This order makes sense because only the constructor of the whole object knows the meaning of the sub-objects, and must therefore have a facility for evaluating or correcting the initial status of the sub-objects whenever necessary.

Furthermore, it is specified that the order of the calls of the constructors for the members corresponds to the order in which these members are declared inside the class structure. The order is *not* defined by the initializer list. However, this order should not matter, as otherwise we would end up with totally unreadable programs. It would mean that the behavior of a class, or even a program, would change because the order of the declarations was modified. The order is only defined to ensure that the destructors are always called in reverse order, which may be important in implementing custom memory management, for example.

6.4.2   Implementing the `Person` Class

Using objects of other classes as members is demonstrated with the example of a `Person` class. For the purpose of this example, a `Person` has just a first name and last name, which are both objects of a string class. The standard `std::string` string class is used here. However, when we describe the internal behavior of strings, we refer to the internal layout of objects of the `CPPBook::String` class, introduced in Section 6.1.1 on page 352.

The header file of the `Person` class is as follows:

```cpp
// dyna/person1.hpp

#ifndef PERSON_HPP
#define PERSON_HPP

// header files for auxiliary classes
#include <string>

// **** BEGIN namespace CPPBook ******************************
namespace CPPBook {

class Person {
  private:
    std::string fname;          // first name of the Person
    std::string lname;          // last name of the Person

  public:
    // constructor for last name and optional first name
    Person(const std::string&, const std::string& = "");

    // query of properties
    const std::string& firstname() const {     // return first name
        return fname;
    }
    const std::string& lastname() const {      // return last name
        return lname;
    }

    // comparison
    bool operator == (const Person& p) const {
        return fname == p.fname && lname == p.lname;
    }
    bool operator != (const Person& p) const {
        return fname != p.fname || lname != p.lname;
    }
    ...
};

} // **** END namespace CPPBook ******************************

#endif   // PERSON_HPP
```

Note that the Person class is *not* a class with dynamic members, even though it contains sub-objects that have dynamic members. The various problems of dynamic members are successfully solved and hidden by the sub-objects. It is ensured that the compiler-generated assignment operator, copy constructor and destructor work correctly there. The string class can now be used like the type int. If a Person is assigned to another Person, the default implementation of the assignment operator, which assigns member-wise, can be used. The same applies when creating copies. Also, when an object of the Person class is destroyed, the destructors or the sub-object are automatically called.

The constructor is defined in the dot-C file, and initializes the person using the parameters passed:

```
// dyna/person1.cpp

/* constructor for last name and first name
 * - default for first name: empty string
 */
Person::Person(const std::string& ln, const std::string& fn)
  : lname(ln), fname(fn)     // initialize first and last names with passed parameters
{
    // nothing else to do
}
```

Creating a `Person` Step by Step

If a Person is now created using

```
CPPBook::Person nico("Josuttis", "Nicolai");
```

the following steps happen (it is assumed that the std::string class is implemented in the same way as the CPPBook::String class from Section 6.1.1 on page 352):

- First of all, memory is created for the object:

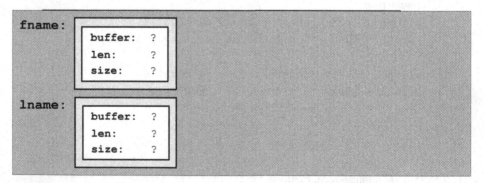

- Then, according to the initializer list, the last name and the first name are initialized with the arguments passed to the constructor. First the parameter fn is used to initialize fname. Because both are strings, the copy constructor of the string class is used to initialize the fname member with fn (see also Section 6.1.3 on page 360):

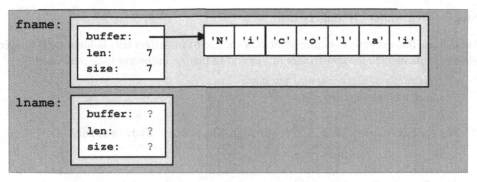

The fact that fname is initialized first is due to the fact that the fname member is declared in the Person class before the lname member. The order of initializations in the initializer list does not matter.

- Then, the copy constructor of the string class is called for the lname member, as the ln string is passed for initialization:

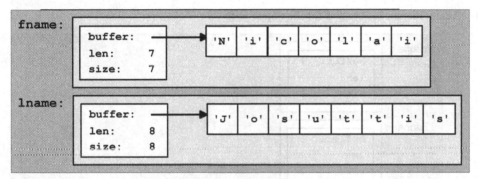

- Finally, the statements of the constructor of the Person class are processed. As the members are already completely initialized, there is nothing more to do (which is not untypical, by any means).

Note that an initializer list is not part of the declaration, but part of the implementation of a function.

Because no more statements have to be processed after the initialization, in practice, the constructor is usually defined in the header file as an inline function:

```
namespace CPPBook {
  class Person {
    ...
  public:
    Person(const std::string& ln, const std::string& fn = "")
      : lname(ln), fname(fn) {
    }
    ...
  };
}
```

Step by Step without Initializer Lists

We can use this example to demonstrate why the use of initializer lists is important. Imagine that we had implemented the constructor of Person so that no initializer lists were used:

```
/* constructor of last name and first name
 * - bad: without initializer list
 */
Person::Person(const std::string& ln, const std::string& fn)
{
    lname = ln;
    fname = fn;
}
```

If, in this case, a person is created using

```
CPPBook::Person nico("Josuttis", "Nicolai");
```

the following happens:

- Again, memory is created for the object first:

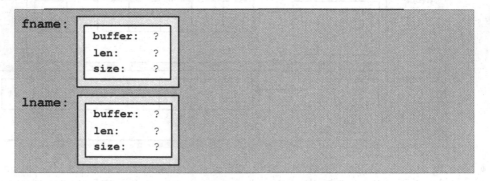

- Then the default constructor of the string class is called for the fname member (as no argument is submitted for the initialization). This initializes the first name with an empty string (see Section 6.1.2 on page 358):

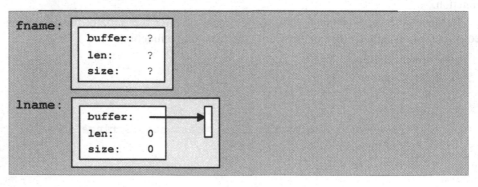

- After this, the `lname` member is initialized with an empty string, using the default constructor of the string class:

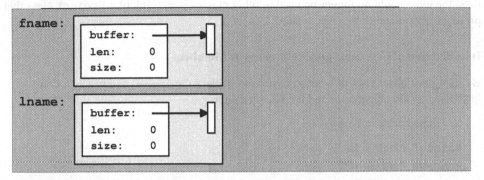

- Finally, the statements in the body of the constructor of the `Person` class are processed, which assign the correct values to the `fname` and `lname` members:

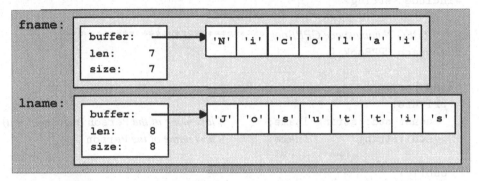

In order to do so, the assignment operator of the string class is called, which frees the memory for the recently initialized empty strings again, as well as allocating and initializing new memory (see Section 6.1.5 on page 362).

This example highlights some of the disadvantages of not using an initializer list. Both members are given a default value by the default constructor, which is incorrect, and has to be replaced immediately with an assignment. In our example, this means that memory is created unnecessarily and then freed immediately, because the initial memory is not large enough to initialize with the passed names. This means there is a considerable run-time disadvantage (memory management is time consuming). Such a disadvantage gets worse the more (complex) members you have in a class.

Furthermore, such a kind of faulty initialization not only takes a lot of time, but may also cause irreparable damage. For example, consider a class for opened files that opens an incorrect default file.

It may also happen that no default constructor exists for a class. This is always the case if at least one argument is needed for initialization. These kinds of object can then no longer be used as sub-objects in another class.

For example, the `Person` class has no default constructor, as, according to its specification, it makes no sense to create a `Person` without at least initializing the last name. Without initializer lists, the class could no longer be used in other classes (e.g. think of a `Project` class that has a project leader member as a `Person`).

Initialization of Constants and References as Members

By using initializer lists, it is also possible to declare the `lname` member as a constant, as it is initialized by the constructor and not changed later:

```
// dyna/person2.hpp

#ifndef PERSON_HPP
#define PERSON_HPP

// header files for auxiliary classes
#include <string>

// **** BEGIN namespace CPPBook ********************************
namespace CPPBook {

class Person {
  private:
    const std::string lname;        // last name of the Person (new: constant)
    std::string       fname;        // first name of the Person

  public:
    // constructor for last name and optional first name
    Person(const std::string& ln, const std::string& fn = "")
      : lname(ln), fname(fn) {
    }

    // query of properties
    const std::string& lastname() const {        // return last name
        return lname;
    }
    const std::string& firstname() const {       // return last name
        return fname;
    }
    ...
};

} // **** END namespace CPPBook ********************************

#endif   // PERSON_HPP
```

A word of caution: declaring members as constants means that they really cannot be modified as long as the object exists. This means, in particular, that no assignment is possible with the default assignment operator, which assigns new values to all members. In this respect, the declaration of the last name for the Person class might not be useful. A typical example of constant members are object IDs (see Section 6.5.1 on page 414).

In the same way, it is also possible that a class may have references as members. These must also be initialized using an initializer list. However, you must make sure that the object for which the reference stands does not exist for less time than the object that has the reference as a member. In this respect, members should actually be used as references, if the lifetime of the referenced object is controlled by the object that has the reference as a member, or if the referenced object stays valid until the end of the program.

6.4.3 Summary

- Members of a class can have any type. For the implementation of the class, it does not matter whether it is a type with dynamic members.
- By default, the default constructor is called for sub-objects of classes. If a default constructor is not defined or cannot be called for the base class, no object of the derived class can be created.
- Initialization lists make it possible for constructors to pass arguments to sub-objects, which means that, instead of the default constructor, another corresponding constructor is called.
- Initialization lists are preferred over assignments.
- Classes can have constants and references as members. These have to be initialized in the constructor, using an initializer list.

6.5   Static Members and Auxiliary Types

Using the sample `Person` class introduced in the previous section, we demonstrate that classes have a separate scope. This can be used to define class-specific variables that are not assigned to a particular object. In this section, we also show how types and auxiliary classes can be defined within classes. Semantically, the `Person` class is extended by an ID, which is implemented as a constant member, and a salutation, implemented as an enumeration type.

6.5.1   Static Class Members

The management of objects that represent people requires two properties of classes that are often needed:

- An explicit ID for the objects.
- Information about the number of existing objects.

Both properties can only be implemented using variables that do not belong to a concrete object, but to a class in general. These so-called *class variables*[7] are global variables that belong to the scope of the class.

In C++, class variables can be implemented by declaring static class members. Static class members are declared in the class structure using the keyword `static`. The variables belong to the scope of the class, and have to be accessed externally via the scope operator (which is, of course, only possible if they are declared as public members).

In contrast to non-static members, these are variables that are only created once for the whole life cycle of the program, and not for each individual object of the class. However, each object of the class has access to them.

The following specification adds two static class members to the `Person` class introduced in the previous section: `maxPID` as a counter to assign explicit person IDs; and `numPersons` as a variable that counts the number of existing `Persons`:

```
// dyna/person3.hpp

#ifndef PERSON_HPP
#define PERSON_HPP

// include header files
#include <string>

// **** BEGIN namespace CPPBook *******************************
namespace CPPBook {

class Person {
```

---

[7] The name *class variable* has its origins in the Smalltalk programming language.

```
/* new: static class members
 */
private:
  static long maxPID;           // highest ID of all Persons
  static long numPersons;       // current number of all Persons
public:
  // return current number of all Persons
  static long number() {
      return numPersons;
  }

// non-static class members
private:
  std::string lname;            // last name of the Person
  std::string fname;            // first name of the Person
  const long  pid;              // new: ID of the Person

public:
  // constructor from last name and optional first name
  Person(const std::string&, const std::string& = "");

  // new: copy constructor
  Person(const Person&);

  // new: destructor
  ~Person();

  // new: assignment
  Person& operator = (const Person&);

  // query of properties
  const std::string& lastname() const {     // return last name
      return lname;
  }
  const std::string& firstname() const {    // return first name
      return fname;
  }
  long id() const {                          // new: return ID
      return pid;
  }
```

```
    friend bool operator == (const Person& p1, const Person& p2) {
        return p1.fname == p1.fname && p2.lname == p2.lname;
    }
    friend bool operator != (const Person& p1, const Person& p2) {
        return !(p1==p2);
    }
    ...
};


} // **** END namespace CPPBook *****************************


#endif   // PERSON_HPP
```

Both `maxPID` and `numPersons` are declared as `static` members, so that they exist only once and are shared by all objects of the class:

```
class Person {
  private:
    static long maxPID;       // highest ID of all Persons
    static long numPersons;   // current number of all Persons
    ...
};
```

Static members can be accessed not only in 'ordinary' member functions, but also in special *static member functions* (also called *class methods* in object-oriented terminology):

```
namespace CPPBook {
  class Person {

    ...
    public:
      // return current number of all Persons
      static long number() {
          return numPersons;
      }
    ...
  };
}
```

In principle, this can be considered as a global function that belongs to the scope of the class `CPPBook::Person`. It has access to the private static members of the `Person` class and, in contrast to non-static member functions, it has the advantage of being able to be called independently, without any concrete objects of this class.

The following application program demonstrates this:

```
// dyna/ptest3.cpp

#include <iostream>
#include "person.hpp"

int main()
{
    std::cout << "number of people: " << CPPBook::Person::number()
              << std::endl;

    CPPBook::Person nico("Josuttis", "Nicolai");

    std::cout << "number of people: " << CPPBook::Person::number()
              << std::endl;
}
```

The number of Persons is determined here by calling th static number() function of the scope of CPPBook::Person. No concrete object of the class is used. The number can also be determined in this way without a Person existing at all.

In the object-oriented sense, static members mean that classes themselves have attributes and operations. A static member function might be regarded as a method of a class. The call of the static member function is then a message to this class, to which the class method reacts.

If a concrete object of the Person class exists, the call via this object is also possible:

```
CPPBook::Person nico("Josuttis","Nicolai");
...
std::cout << "number of persons: " << nico.number() << std::endl;
```

As this leads to the assumption that a certain property of a concrete Person has been requested, this kind of call is usually discouraged.

Initialization of Static Class Members

Inside a class structure, static class members are only ever declared. However, like any static variable, they also have to be defined (and initialized) once. The definition must happen *outside* of the class structure in a dot-C file (which is typically the dot-C file of the class). An initialization within the class structure is wrong.

Let us consider the implementation of the Person class:

```
// dyna/person3.cpp
```

```
// include header file of the class
#include "person.hpp"
```

```
// **** BEGIN namespace CPPBook *****************************
```

```
namespace CPPBook {

/* new: initialize static class members
 */
long Person::maxPID = 0;
long Person::numPersons = 0;

/* constructor for last name and first name
 * - default for first name: empty string
 * - first and last names are initialized with initialisation list
 * - new: the ID is initialized directly
 */
Person::Person(const std::string& ln, const std::string& fn)
  : lname(ln), fname(fn), pid(++maxPID)
{
    ++numPersons;   // increase number of existing Persons
}

/* new: copy constructor
 */
Person::Person(const Person& p)
  : lname(p.lname), fname(p.fname), pid(++maxPID)
{
    ++numPersons;   // increase number of existing Persons
}

/* new: destructor
 */
Person::~Person()
{
    --numPersons;   // reduce number of existing Persons
}

/* new: assignment
 */
Person& Person::operator = (const Person& p)
{
    if (this == &p) {
        return *this;
    }
```

```
    // assign everything apart from ID
    lname = p.lname;
    fname = p.fname;

    return *this;
}

} // **** END namespace CPPBook ******************************
```

The variable of the corresponding scope is accessed via the scope operator:

```
namespace CPPBook {
    long Person::maxPID = 0;
    long Person::numPersons = 0;
    ...
}
```

As usual, each static class member must be initialized only once in the program.

The constructor initializes the members of the Person class via the initializer list:

```
Person::Person(const std::string& ln, const std::string& fn)
    : lname(ln), fname(fn), pid(++maxPID)
{
    ++numPersons;   // increase number of existing Persons
}
```

The lname member is initialized with the first parameter, ln, and the fname member is initialized with the second parameter, fn. For the initialization of the newly added member pid, the incremented class member with the highest person ID, maxPID, is used. As the pid member is constant, this has to be initialized using an initializer list; a later assignment would not be possible. In the body of the function, the counter for the number of existing Persons is increased accordingly.

To keep the number of existing Persons correct, the counter must also be reduced when an object of the Person class is destroyed. For this reason, a corresponding destructor is defined:

```
Person::~Person()
{
    --numPersons;   // reduce number of existing Persons
}
```

The destructor is called for *every* object that exists and is subsequently destroyed. Thus the counter has to get incremented for each object created. In particular, we must not forget to define the copy constructor too, so that a new object ID is provided and the Person counter is increased if an object of the class is created as a copy of an existing object:

```
Person::Person(const Person& p)
  : lname(p.lname), fname(p.fname), pid(++maxPID)
{
    ++numPersons;    // increase number of existing Persons
}
```

If we neglected to implement a copy constructor, then, when an object was copied, the existing ID would be duplicated and the ID counter would not be increased (but would, however, be reduced when the object was destroyed).

In addition to this, the assignment operator must be implemented so that the ID is not assigned, but all other members are:

```
const Person& Person::operator = (const Person& p)
{
    if (this == &p) {
        return *this;
    }

    // assign everything apart from ID
    lname = p.lname;
    fname = p.fname;

    return *this;
}
```

As the ID was declared as a constant, an assignment would be impossible without providing this implementation. This is because the default assignment operator would also (try to) assign the ID, which would cause an error.

6.5.2   Type Declarations Within Classes

The facility introduced in the previous section for defining static members and functions in classes indicates that classes have a scope.

This can also be used to define class-specific types that are limited to the scope of the class. This has the advantage that global declarations are avoided. The global naming area is not unnecessarily 'polluted' with symbols, which reduces name conflicts.

For example, with a class for the management of people, this could be used to define a class-specific enumeration type (see Section 9.6.2 on page 566 for an introduction to enumeration types) for the salutation.

The Person class would then have the following specification:

```
// dyna/person4.hpp

#ifndef PERSON_HPP
#define PERSON_HPP
```

```
// include header files
#include <string>

// **** BEGIN namespace CPPBook ********************************
namespace CPPBook {

class Person {
    /* static class members
     */
  private:
    static long maxPID;        // highest ID of all Persons
    static long numPersons;    // current number of all Persons
  public:
    // current number of all Persons
    static long number() {
        return numPersons;
    }

  public:
    // new: special enumeration type for the salutation
    enum Salutation { Mr, Mrs, Ms, empty };

    /* non-static class members
     */
  private:
    Salutation  salut;    // new: salutation (can also be empty)
    std::string lname;    // last name of the Person
    std::string fname;    // first name of the Person
    const long  pid;      // ID of the Person

  public:
    // constructor for last name and optional first name
    Person(const std::string&, const std::string& = "");

    // copy constructor
    Person(const Person&);

    // destructor
    ~Person();

    // assignment
```

```
    Person& operator = (const Person&);

    // query of properties
    const std::string& lastname() const {      // return last name
        return lname;
    }
    const std::string& firstname() const {   // return first name
        return fname;
    }
    long id() const {                                    // return ID
        return pid;
    }
    const Salutation& salutation() const {   // new: return salutation
        return salut;
    }

    // compare
    friend bool operator == (const Person& p1, const Person& p2) {
        return p1.fname == p1.fname && p2.lname == p2.lname;
    }
    friend bool operator != (const Person& p1, const Person& p2) {
        return !(p1==p2);
    }
    ...
};

} // **** END namespace CPPBook ******************************

#endif   // PERSON_HPP
```

The `Salutation` enumeration type is simply defined and used in the class declaration. This has the advantage that, for the symbols that are used, `Salutation`, `Mr`, `Mrs`, `Ms` and `empty`, there is no danger of global name conflicts. However, the public declaration makes it possible to use these symbols outside the class. This happens with the scope operator, as shown in the following application example:

```
// dyna/ptest4.cpp

#include <iostream>
#include "person.hpp"

int main()
{
```

```
CPPBook::Person nico("Josuttis","Nicolai");

/* declare variable of the type Salutation of the class CPPBook::Person
 * and initialize it with the value empty of the class CPPBook::Person
 */
CPPBook::Person::Salutation noSalutation = CPPBook::Person::empty;
...
if (nico.salutation() == noSalutation) {
    std::cout << "salutation of Nico was not set" << std::endl;
}
}
```

As the declaration of noSalutation shows, the qualification with the scope operator is necessary when using the type as well as when using a value, as both the type and the value belong to the scope of the Person class.

In this way, separate types can also be created in classes using typedef.

6.5.3 Enumeration Types as Static Class Constants

A declared static member is occasionally required in the class structure. This is possible if it is an integer type or an enumeration type:

```
class MyClass {
  private:
    static const int MAXNUM = 100;   // OK (integer and constant)
    int elems[MAXNUM];               // OK
    ...
};
```

This facility was introduced fairly late in the standardization of C++. Until then, the trick of using an enumeration type was used. You may therefore occasionally see the following code:

```
class MyClass {
  private:
    enum { MAXNUM = 100 };   // OK
    int elems[MAXNUM];       // OK
    ...
};
```

The value for an enumeration type is not a constant object, but just a symbolic name for which a certain value can be set with a declaration.

6.5.4   Nested and Local Classes

The fact that classes have a separate scope also allows classes (or structures) to be limited to the scope of a class.

For example, such a *member class* or *nested class* can be defined as follows:

```
class MyClass {
  public:
    /* nested auxiliary class
     */
    class AuxiliaryClass {
      private:
        int x;
      public:
        void foo();
        ...
    };
    ...
};
```

The members of a nested class are accessed by means of a nested qualification using the scope operator. For example, the `foo()` function must be defined as follows:

```
void MyClass::AuxiliaryClass::foo()
{
    ...
}
```

Again, this is particularly useful with complex classes in order to avoid 'polluting' the global scope with auxiliary classes. This style avoids name conflicts and supports data encapsulation (the auxiliary classes can also be declared as `private`).

Typical examples of nested classes are error classes introduced with exception handling (see Section 4.7 on page 234).

It is even possible to declare classes locally, within the scope of a function. This is rarely used. However, it is clear that a structure in C++ is simply a class that has public members by default. This therefore means that local structures can be declared within functions, which makes more sense.

Forward Declaration of Nested Classes

The members of a nested class can also be declared outside of the surrounding class. Nested classes can even be defined in other modules.

The above example then looks as follows:

```
class MyClass {
  public:
    /* declare nested auxiliary class
     */
    class AuxiliaryClass;
  ...
};

class MyClass::AuxiliaryClass {
  private:
    int x;
  public:
    void foo();
    ...
};
```

Sometimes such a forward declaration is the only way to implement a nested class. This is, when the type of the outer class is used to declare a member in the nested class. See Section 6.2.7 on page 390 for an example.

6.5.5 Summary

- Classes can have *static members*. These are objects that only exist once per class, and are shared by all objects of the class. They represent global objects that are only visible in the scope of the class.
- Static class members must be defined (and initialized) once, *outside* of the class definition.
- *Static member functions* allow access to static members, without using an object of the class. They represent global functions that are limited to the namespace and scope of a class.
- Static class constants can be defined using enumeration types. They can also be used for declaring other members.
- Classes form a separate scope in which it is possible to define types, such as enumeration types or auxiliary classes (*nested classes*).
- For object IDs, all constructors (including the copy constructor) and the assignment operator of a class have to be defined. The member for the ID should be declared as a constant.
- For object counters, all constructors (including the copy constructor) and the destructor of a class have to be defined.

7

Templates

This chapter introduces the concept of templates. Templates can be used to parametrize source code for different types. A minimum function or a collection class can therefore be implemented before the type of the parameter or element has been determined. However, this code is not generated for arbitrary types; if the type of the parameter or element is defined, the usual type checking for all operations apply.

We first introduce function templates, followed by class templates. We concludes with notes on working with templates, including some special design techniques.

More information on templates can be found in Nicolai M. Josuttis and David Vandevoorde's book *C++ Templates – The Complete Guide*, published by Addison-Wesley, ISBN 0-201-73484-2 (see [*VandevoordeJosuttisTemplates*]). Inside this book you will find a similar introduction to templates, supplemented by a comprehensive reference, a wide range of coding techniques, and some advanced applications for templates.

7.1 Why Templates?

In programming languages with type-bound variables, it is often the case that functions that have the same purpose have to be defined repeatedly, as the types of the parameters are different. A typical example is a function that returns a maximum of two values, which must be reimplemented for every type for which the maximum of two values is needed. This requirement can be avoided in C by defining macros. However, as a macro is a simple text substitution, its implementation can lead to problems (no more type testing, side effects, etc.).

Much effort is required not only for the repeated implementation of functions, but also for special types, such as in the case of container classes. When the management of elements of a collection is implemented using different member functions, the type of these objects always plays a role. Without a special language feature, you would have to implement the member functions again and again for different types.

A typical example of a multiple implementation in the management of different objects is that of a stack. In a stack, elements of a particular type are stored and then removed. Using the language features known so far, this would have to be reimplemented for every individual type for which a stack is needed, as the type of the object that is managed has to be indicated during the declaration of the stack. For this reason, stacks must be implemented again and again, even though the algorithm is actually the same each time. This not only takes up unnecessary time, but is also a permanent source of errors.

C++ therefore offers the language feature of *templates*. Templates are functions and classes that are not implemented for a particular type, but for a type yet to be defined. To use these functions or classes the application programmer only has to specify the type for which the template should be realized. A maximum function for two objects of an arbitrary type therefore only needs to be implemented once. Container classes such as stacks, linked lists, etc., also have to be implemented and tested just once, and can then be used for each type that supports the operations that are performed.

The definition and use of templates is outlined below—first for functions, using the example of the maximum function, and then for classes, using the example of the stack class.

7.1.1 Terminology

The terms used to describe templates are not clearly defined. For example, a function for which a type is parametrized is sometimes called a *function template* and sometimes called a *template function*. However, as the latter term is a bit confusing (it might be a template of a function as well as a function out of a template), the term *function template* should be used. Similarly, a class for which types are parametrized should be called a *class template* instead of a *template class*.

The process of creating a regular class, function or member function from a template by substituting actual values for its arguments is called *template instantiation*. Unfortunately, the word *instantiate* is also used in object-oriented terminology for the creation of objects of a class. Therefore, in C++, the meaning of the word *instantiate* always depends on the exact context.

7.2 Function Templates

As mentioned in the previous section, function templates are used to define a group of functions that can be used for different types.

In contrast to macros, function templates are not 'blind' text substitutions, but functions that are checked semantically and compiled without undesirable side effects. For example, there is no danger (as with a macro) of repeatedly replacing an n++ parameter so that a single incrementation becomes multiple incrementations.

7.2.1 Defining Function Templates

Function templates are defined like normal functions, with the adopted type entered in front of the declaration. For example, a maximum template can be declared as follows:

```
template <typename T>
const T& max(const T&, const T&);
```

The first line defines T as a type parameter. The keyword typename is used, which establishes that the following symbol is a type. This keyword was introduced in C++ relatively late. Before this, the class keyword was used:

```
template <class T>
```

Semantically, there is no difference between these two words. Therefore, when using the keyword class here, the type does not necessarily have to be a class. In both cases, you can use any type (fundamental type, class, etc.), as long as it provides the operations that the template uses. In this case, type T has to support the < operator because a and b use this for comparison.

The use of the symbol T for a template type is not required, but is quite common. In the following declaration, T can be used as a type in a parameter declaration and denotes the parameter type passed during the call:

```
// tmpl/max1.hpp

template <typename T>
const T& max(const T& a, const T& b)
{
    return  a > b ? a : b;
}
```

The statements within the function are no different from those of other functions. In this case, the maximum of two values of type T is processed using the comparison operator and returned as a result. As has already been mentioned in Chapter 4.4, creating copies when passing the parameter and the return value is prevented through the use of constant references (const T&).

7.2.2   Calling Function Templates

A function template is used in the same way as any other function. The following sample program demonstrates this[1]:

```
// tmpl/max1.cpp

#include <iostream>
#include <string>
#include "max1.hpp"

int main()
{
    int           a, b;   // two variables of the datatype int
    std::string s, t;   // two variables of the type std::string
    ...
    std::cout << max(a,b) << std::endl;      // max() for two ints
    std::cout << ::max(s,t) << std::endl;   // max() for two strings
}
```

At the moment, as the max() function is called for two objects of one type, the template becomes real code. This means that the compiler uses the template definition and instantiates it by using int or std::string in place of T. This can be considered as the creation of the real code for int and std::string. A template is therefore not compiled as code that can deal with any type, but is only used to produce code for different types in different application cases. If max() is called for seven different types, seven function are compiled.

The process with which the code to be compiled is generated from the template code is called *instantiation* or more clearly (because this term is also used in object-oriented terminology for the creation of objects of a class) *template instantiation*.

Of course, a template instantiation is only possible if all of the operations that are used in the function template are also defined for the type of the parameter. Thus, in order to be able to call the maximum function for objects of the std::string class, the comparison operator < has to be defined for strings.

Note that, in contrast to macros, templates are not a straight text replacement. The call

```
max(x++, z *= 2);
```

is not very useful, but it works. The maximum of the two expressions that were passed as arguments is returned, and each expression is evaluated just once (i.e. x is only incremented once).

---

[1] The call of max() for strings is explicitly qualified for the global namespace, because a std::max() is also defined in the standard library. Because strings belong to std, this function is also found without qualification, which can cause ambiguity (see Koenig lookup on page 177).

7.2.3 Practical Hints for Working with Templates

Templates go beyond the ordinary compiler/linker model with separate translation units. One cannot simply define and compile templates in one module, compile the application of a template separately and then link them. Instead, it only becomes clear for which type a template has to be compiled when it actually used.

There are different ways of getting around this problem. The easiest and most portable way of doing this is to place the whole template code in header files. By including the header files in the application, the code is available for the compilation of the necessary types.

In this respect, it is no accident that the definition of the max() template in the previous example occurs in a header file. However, it should be noted that the word inline (see Section 4.3.3 on page 173) does not have to be used. For templates, it is fine to have multiple definitions in different translation units. Nevertheless, if you prefer inline substitution of the function template body at the point of call over the usual function call mechanism, you should still indicate this to the compiler by marking them as inline.

More aspects of working with templates are discussed in Section 7.6 on page 462.

7.2.4 Automatic Type Conversions with Templates

During the instantiation of a template, no automatic type conversion is considered. If multiple parameters of the type T are declared in a function template, the submitted argument must have the same type. Calling the maximum function with two objects of different types is therefore not possible:

```
template <typename T>
const T& max(const T&, const T&);   // both parameters have the type T

...

int i;
long l;

...

max(i,l)      // ERROR: i and l have different types
```

Explicit Qualification

An *explicit qualification* can be used when calling templates to determine for what type a template is to be used:

```
max<long>(i,l)      // OK, calls max() with T as long
```

In this case, the function template max<>() is instantiated for the long type as template parameter T. Now, as with ordinary functions, it is checked whether the passed arguments can be used as longs, which happens to be the case, as there is an implicit type conversion from int to long.

Templates with Multiple Parameters

Alternatively, the template can also be defined so that it allows parameters of different types:

```
template <typename T1, typename T2>
inline T1 max(const T1&, const T2&);   // parameter can have different types
{
    return  a < b ? b : a;
}
...
int i;
long l;
...
max(i,l)     // OK: returns maximum with type int
```

The problem here is that you have to decide on one of the parameter types to be the return type. This is bad in this example, as one cannot say which of the two argument types is the more powerful, and which therefore should be returned. In addition, if the second parameter is the maximum, a new local temporary object is created for the return value, because it has a different type. Such a local temporary cannot, however, be returned as a reference. Therefore, the return type now has to read as T instead of const T&.

In this respect, the ability of explicit qualification is definitely better in this case.

7.2.5   Overloading Templates

Templates can be overloaded for certain types. By doing this, a general template implementation can be replaced by another implementation for definite types. This has several advantages:

- Function templates can be provided for additional types and type combinations (for example, a function for the maximum of a float and a CPPBook::Fraction can be defined).
- Implementations can be optimized for a special type.
- Types for which the template implementation is unsuitable can be implemented correctly.

In the example of the max() function template, a call with C-strings (type const char*) would cause an error:

```
const char* s1;
const char* s2;
...
const char* maxstring = max(s1,s2);   // ERROR: compares addresses
```

In the template, the use of > compares the addresses, rather than the content of the strings (see Section 3.7.3 on page 110), which is definitely not useful with C-strings.

The problem is eliminated by overloading the template for C-strings:

```
inline const char* max (const char* a, const char* b)
{
    return  std::strcmp(a,b) > 0 ? a : b;
}
```

Overloading would also be possible for pointers in this case. In this way, you could ensure that, during the call of max() for pointers, instead of the pointers themselves (i.e. their addresses), the values of the objects to which they refer are compared. This might look as follows:

```
template <typename T>
T* const& max (T* const& a, T* const& b)
{
    return  *a > *b ? a : b;
}
```

Note that in order to submit the pointer as a constant reference, const must be entered after the asterisk. Otherwise, it would declare a pointer that refers to a constant (see also Section 4.4.6 on page 191).

In general, it is a good idea not to change more than necessary when overloading function templates. You should limit your changes to the number of parameters or to specifying template parameters explicitly. Otherwise, unexpected effects may happen. Thus, in our example for all overloaded implementations, you should pass all arguments by constant reference:

// tmpl/max2.hpp

```
#include <iostream>
#include <cstring>
```

// maximum of two values of any type
```
template <typename T>
inline const T& max (const T& a, const T& b)
{
    std::cout << "max<>() for T" << std::endl;
    return  a < b ? b : a;
}
```

// maximum of two pointers
```
template <typename T>
inline T* const& max (T* const& a, T* const& b)
{
    std::cout << "max<>() for T*" << std::endl;
    return  *a < *b ? b : a;
}
```

// maximum of two C-strings

```
inline const char* const& max (const char* const& a,
                               const char* const& b)
{
    std::cout << "max<>() for char*" << std::endl;
    return  std::strcmp(a,b) < 0  ?  b : a;
}
```

A suitable application program:

```
// tmpl/max2.cpp

#include <iostream>
#include <string>
#include "max2.hpp"

int main()
{
    int a=7;                                      // two variables of datatype int
    int b=11;
    std::cout << max(a,b) << std::endl;           // max() for two ints

    std::string s="hello";                        // two strings
    std::string t="holla";
    std::cout << ::max(s,t) << std::endl;         // max() for two strings

    int* p1 = &b;                                 // two pointers
    int* p2 = &a;
    std::cout << *max(p1,p2) << std::endl;        // max() for two pointers

    const char* s1 = "hello";                     // two C-strings
    const char* s2 = "otto";
    std::cout << max(s1,s2) << std::endl;         // max() for two C-strings
}
```

would produce the following output:

```
max<>() for T
11
max<>() for T
holla
max<>() for T*
11
max<>() for char*
otto
```

7.2.6 Local Variables

Function templates can have any internal variables of the template type. For example, a function template that mixes up the values of two parameters can be implemented as follows (compare with the implementation of the function swap() on page 183):

```
template <typename T>
void swap (T& a, T& b)
{
    T tmp(a);
    a = b;
    b = tmp;
}
```

The local variables can also be static. In this case, a static variable is created for every type for which the function is called.

7.2.7 Summary

- Templates are stencils for code that is compiled after the actual type has been set.
- The generation of compilable code from template code is called *(template) instantiation* in C++.
- Templates can have multiple template parameters.
- Function templates can be overloaded.

7.3   Class Templates

In the same way that types can be parametrized by functions, it is also possible to parametrize one or several types in classes. This is particularly useful with container classes, which are used to manage objects of a certain type. Class templates can be used to implement them, even though the type of the managed object is not yet clear. In object-oriented terminology, class templates are also called *parameterizable classes*.

The implementation of a class template is discussed below, using the example of a class for stacks. This uses a class template of the standard library internally, `vector<>` (see Section 3.5.1 on page 70 and Section 9.1.1 on page 518).

7.3.1   Implementation of the Class Template `Stack`

As for function templates, both the declaration and the definition of class templates is usually included in header files. The header file for the `Stack` class template looks as follows:

```cpp
// tmpl/stack1.hpp

#include <vector>
#include <stdexcept>

// **** BEGIN namespace CPPBook ******************************
namespace CPPBook {

template <typename T>
class Stack {
  private:
    std::vector<T> elems;   // elements

  public:
    Stack();                // constructor
    void push(const T&);    // store new top element
    void pop();             // remove top element
    T top() const;          // return top element
};

// constructor
template <typename T>
Stack<T>::Stack()
{
    // nothing more to do
}
```

```
template <typename T>
void Stack<T>::push(const T& elem)
{
    elems.push_back(elem);      // store copy as new top element
}

template<typename T>
void Stack<T>::pop()
{
    if (elems.empty()) {
        throw std::out_of_range("Stack<>::pop(): empty stack");
    }
    elems.pop_back();           // remove top element
}

template <typename T>
T Stack<T>::top() const
{
    if (elems.empty()) {
        throw std::out_of_range("Stack<>::top(): empty stack");
    }
    return elems.back();        // return top element as copy
}

} // **** END namespace CPPBook ******************************
```

Declaration of the Class Template

As with function templates, the template code is always preceded by an statement in which the T is manifested as the type parameter (of course, several type parameters can also be defined for class templates):

```
template <typename T>
class Stack {
    ...
};
```

Again, the class keyword can be used as an alternative to typename here:

```
template <class T>
class Stack {
    ...
};
```

Inside the class, the type T can then be used like any other type for the declaration of class members and member functions. In this example, the elements of the stack are managed internally using a vector for elements of type T (the template is therefore programmed using another template), the function push() uses a constant reference T as a parameter, and top() returns an object of type T.

The type of the class is Stack<T>, in which T is a template parameter. Therefore, this must be used whenever the type needs to be entered. Only for the entry of the class name

```
class Stack {
    ...
};
```

(and for the name of the constructors and destructor) is Stack used.

If parameters and return values need to be entered, this would look as follows (which shows an example of the declaration of copy constructor and assignment operator) [2]:

```
template <typename T>
class Stack {
    ...
    Stack (const Stack<T>&);              // copy constructor
    Stack<T>& operator= (const Stack<T>&);   // assignment operator
    ...
};
```

Implementing Member Functions

When defining the member functions for a class template, it also has to be specified that they are (part of) a template. As the example of push() shows, the entire type Stack<T> has to be used for the qualification:

```
template <typename T>
void Stack<T>::push(const T& elem)
{
    elems.push_back(elem);     // store copy
}
```

The functions delegate the work to the corresponding functions of the vector that is used internally to manage the elements. Doing this, the top element is always the element at the end of the vector.

Note that pop() removes the top element but doesn't return it. This behavior corresponds with pop_back() for vectors. The reason for this behavior is *exception safety* (see Section 4.7.10 on page 252). It is impossible to implement a version of pop() that returns the removed element and gives the optimal exception safety. Consider a version that returns the removed top element:

---

[2] In the standard, however, there are some rules that determine when an entry of Stack instead Stack<T> is sufficient inside a class declaration. However, as a rule of thumb, you should always use Stack<T> where the type of the class is required.

```
template<typename T>
T Stack<T>::pop()
{
    if (elems.empty()) {
        throw std::out_of_range("Stack<>::pop(): empty stack");
    }
    T elem = elems.back();      // keep copy of top element
    elems.pop_back();           // remove top element
    return elem;                // return copy of old top element
}
```

The problem is that the exception may be thrown by the copy constructor of the elements, when the element is returned. However, there is no chance to leave the stack in the original state because the number of elements is reduced already. Thus, you have to decide whether to give only the basic exception safety guarantee or not to return the element[3].

Note also that the member functions pop_back() and back() (the latter returns the last element) have an undefined behavior if the vector is empty (see pages 521 and 523). This is tested for both functions, and an exception of type std::out_of_range is thrown if necessary (see Section 4.7.9 on page 252):

```
template<typename T>
T Stack<T>::top() const
{
    if (elems.empty()) {
        throw std::out_of_range("Stack<>::top(): empty stack");
    }
    return elems.back();        // return top element as a copy
}
```

Of course, the functions can also be implemented within the class declaration:

```
template <typename T>
class Stack {
    ...
    void push(const T& elem) {
        elems.push_back(elem);      // store copy
    }
    ...
};
```

---

[3] This topic was first discussed by Tom Cargill in [CargillExceptionSafety] and is discussed as Item 10 in [SutterExceptional]).

7.3.2   Application of the Class Template `Stack`

If an object of the class template is declared or defined, it has to be explicitly specified what type should be used as a parameter:

```cpp
// tmpl/stest1.cpp

#include <iostream>
#include <string>
#include <cstdlib>
#include "stack1.hpp"

int main()
{
    try {
        CPPBook::Stack<int>         intStack;       // stack for integers
        CPPBook::Stack<std::string> stringStack;    // stack for strings

        // manipulate integer stack
        intStack.push(7);
        std::cout << intStack.top() << std::endl;
        intStack.pop();

        // manipulate string stack
        std::string s = "hello";
        stringStack.push(s);
        std::cout << stringStack.top() << std::endl;
        stringStack.pop();
        std::cout << stringStack.top() << std::endl;
        stringStack.pop();
    }
    catch (const char* msg) {
        std::cerr << "Exception: " << msg << std::endl;
        return EXIT_FAILURE;
    }
}
```

The class template gets instantiated with the corresponding type. By using `stringStack`, appropriate code for the type `std::string` is generated for the class and all member functions that are called.

Note that I wrote 'all member functions that are called'. For class templates, only those functions for which a call is made are instantiated. This feature not only has the advantage of saving time and space, but it also means that you could use a class template for types that do not provide operations for all member functions, as long as only those functions that are supported are called. An example of this would be a class in which some member functions are sorted with the operator <. As long as these member functions are not called, the type passed as a template parameter does not need to have the < operator defined.

In this case, code is generated for two classes, int and std::string. If a class template has static members, two different static members are created.

For every type used, a class template forms a separate type that can be used anywhere:

```
void foo(const CPPBook::Stack<int>& s)     // parameter s is int stack
{
    CPPBook::Stack<int> istack[10];      // istack is an array of ten int stacks
    ...
}
```

In practice, a typedef statement is frequently used in order to make the use of class templates more readable (and more flexible):

```
typedef CPPBook::Stack<int> IntStack;

void foo(const IntStack& s)     // parameter s is int stack
{
    IntStack istack[10];     // istack is an array of ten int stacks
    ...
}
```

The template arguments can be any type. For example, float pointers, or even a stack of stacks for ints:

```
CPPBook::Stack<float*>                 floatPtrStack;   // stack of float pointers
CPPBook::Stack<CPPBook::Stack<int> > intStackStack;   // stack of int stacks
```

The important thing is that all operations called for these types are provided.

Note that two consecutive closing template brackets need to be separated from each other by a space. Otherwise, it would denote the >> operator, which would produce a syntax error at this point:

```
// ERROR: >> not allowed
CPPBook::Stack<CPPBook::Stack<int>> intStackStack;
```

7.3.3   Specialization of Class Templates

Class templates can be *specialized*. This means that class templates can be implemented individually for special types. As with overloading function templates (see Section 7.2.5 on page 432), this is useful for optimizing implementations for certain types, or to avoid undesirable behavior caused by a template instantiation for a certain type. However, if you specialize a class template, you must also specialize all member functions. Although it is possible to specialize a single member function, once you have done so, you can no longer specialize the whole class.

For an explicit specialization, `template<>` has to be written in front of the class declaration, and the template type specified has to be entered after the class name:

```
template<>
class Stack<std::string> {
    ...
};
```

Every member function must begin with `template<>`, and T must be replaced by the specified template type:

```
template<>
void Stack<std::string>::push(const std::string& elem)
{
    elems.push_back(elem);      // store copy
}
```

The following is a complete example of a specialization of the Stack<> class template for the `std::string` type:

```
// tmpl/stack2.hpp

#include <deque>
#include <string>
#include <stdexcept>

// **** BEGIN namespace CPPBook *******************************
namespace CPPBook {

template<>
class Stack<std::string> {
  private:
    std::deque<std::string> elems;  // elements

  public:
    Stack() {                         // constructor
    }
    void push(const std::string&);  // store new top element
    void pop();                       // remove top element
    std::string top() const;          // return top element
};

void Stack<std::string>::push(const std::string& elem)
{
    elems.push_back(elem);                // remove top element
}
```

```
void Stack<std::string>::pop()
{
    if (elems.empty()) {
        throw std::out_of_range
                    ("Stack<std::string>::pop(): empty stack");
    }
    elems.pop_back();                    // remove top element
}

std::string Stack<std::string>::top() const
{
    if (elems.empty()) {
        throw std::out_of_range
                    ("Stack<std::string>::top(): empty stack");
    }
    return elems.back();                 // return top element as copy
}

} // **** END namespace CPPBook *******************************
```

In this case, for strings, the internal vector for the element is replaced by a deque. This has no decisive drawback, but it shows that the implementation of a class template for a special type can look completely different.

The numeric limits defined in the standard library are another example of the use of template specializations (see Section 9.1.4 on page 531).

Partial Specializations

Templates can only be partially specialized (*partial specialization*). For the class template

```
template <typename T1, typename T2>
class MyClass {
    ...
};
```

the following partial specialization can be given:

```
// partial specialization: both types are equal
template <typename T>
class MyClass<T,T> {
    ...
};

// partial specialization: the second type is an int
```

```
template <typename T>
class MyClass<T,int> {
  ...
};
```

```
// partial specialization: both types are pointers
template <typename T1, typename T2>
class MyClass<T1*,T2*> {
  ...
};
```

These templates are activated as follows:

```
MyClass<int,float> mif;      // MyClass<T1,T2>
MyClass<float,float> mff;     // MyClass<T,T>
MyClass<float,int> mfi;      // MyClass<T,int>
MyClass<int*,float*> mp;     // MyClass<T1*,T2*>
```

If several partial specializations are all equally suitable, the call is ambiguous:

```
MyClass<int,int> m;      // ERROR: matches MyClass<T,T>
                         //        and MyClass<T,int>
MyClass<int*,int*> m;    // ERROR: matches MyClass<T,T>
                         //        and MyClass<T1*,T2*>
```

The last ambiguity would be resolved if a partial specialization for pointers of the same type had been defined:

```
template <typename T>
class MyClass<T*,T*> {
  ...
};
```

7.3.4 Default Template Parameters

For class templates, default values can be defined for template parameters (this is not possible for function templates). The default values can refer to previous template parameters.

For example, we could parametrize the container that is used to manage the stack elements and define a vector as a default container:

```
// tmpl/stack3.hpp
```

```
#include <vector>
#include <stdexcept>
```

```
// **** BEGIN namespace CPPBook *******************************
```

```
namespace CPPBook {

template <typename T, typename CONT = std::vector<T> >
class Stack {
  private:
    CONT elems;        // elements

  public:
    Stack();                   // constructor
    void push(const T&);   // store new top element
    void pop();                // remove top element
    T top() const;             // return top element
};

// constructor
template <typename T, typename CONT>
Stack<T,CONT>::Stack()
{
    // nothing more to do
}

template <typename T, typename CONT>
void Stack<T,CONT>::push(const T& elem)
{
    elems.push_back(elem);     // store copy as new top element
}

template <typename T, typename CONT>
void Stack<T,CONT>::pop()
{
    if (elems.empty()) {
        throw std::out_of_range("Stack<>::pop(): empty stack");
    }
    elems.pop_back();          // remove top element
}

template <typename T, typename CONT>
T Stack<T,CONT>::top() const
{
    if (elems.empty()) {
        throw std::out_of_range("Stack<>::top(): empty stack");
```

```
        }
        return elems.back();              // return top element
    }


} // **** END namespace CPPBook *****************************
```

This stack can be used like the previous stacks. In addition, you could specify a different container for the elements:

```
// tmpl/stest3.cpp

#include <iostream>
#include <deque>
#include <cstdlib>
#include "stack3.hpp"

int main()
{
    try {
        // stack for integers
        CPPBook::Stack<int> intStack;
        // stack for floating-point values
        CPPBook::Stack<double,std::deque<double> > dblStack;

        // manipulate integer stack
        intStack.push(7);
        std::cout << intStack.top() << std::endl;
        intStack.pop();

        // manipulate floating-point value stack
        dblStack.push(42.42);
        std::cout << dblStack.top() << std::endl;
        dblStack.pop();
        std::cout << dblStack.top() << std::endl;
        dblStack.pop();
    }
    catch (const char* msg) {
        std::cerr << "Exception: " << msg << std::endl;
        return EXIT_FAILURE;
    }
}
```

Using

```
CPPBook::Stack<double,std::deque<double> >
```

a stack for floating-point values is declared that uses a deque internally as a container.

7.3.5 Summary

- Classes can also be implemented as templates for types that have not yet been defined.
- Using class templates, container classes that manage other objects can be parametrized for the type of the managed elements.
- For class templates, only the functions that are actually used are instantiated.
- Implementations of class templates can be specialized for certain types. Partial specialization is also possible.
- It is possible to define default values for template parameters of class templates.

7.4   Non-Type Template Parameters

Template parameters do not necessarily have to be types; they can also be ordinary values, as with function parameters. By doing this, you can define a group of functions or classes that are parametrized for a certain value.

7.4.1   Example of Using Non-Type Template Parameters

For example, a stack template could be defined in which the stack manages the elements in a fixed-sized array. This avoids the overhead of dynamic memory management in the stack.

The class declaration then looks as follows:

```
// tmpl/stack4.hpp

#include <stdexcept>

// **** BEGIN namespace CPPBook ********************************
namespace CPPBook {

template <typename T, int MAXSIZE>
class Stack {
  private:
    T elems[MAXSIZE];      // elements
    int numElems;          // current number of elements entered

  public:
    Stack();               // constructor
    void push(const T&);   // store new top element
    void pop();            // remove top element
    T top() const;         // return top element
};

// constructor
template <typename T, int MAXSIZE>
Stack<T,MAXSIZE>::Stack()
  : numElems(0)      // no elements
{
    // nothing more to do
}

template <typename T, int MAXSIZE>
void Stack<T,MAXSIZE>::push(const T& elem)
```

```
{
    if (numElems == MAXSIZE) {
        throw std::out_of_range("Stack<>::push(): stack is full");
    }
    elems[numElems] = elem;      // enter element
    ++numElems;                  // increase number of elements
}

template<typename T, int MAXSIZE>
void Stack<T,MAXSIZE>::pop()
{
    if (numElems <= 0) {
        throw std::out_of_range("Stack<>::pop(): empty stack");
    }
    --numElems;                  // reduce number of elements
}

template <typename T, int MAXSIZE>
T Stack<T,MAXSIZE>::top() const
{
    if (numElems <= 0) {
        throw std::out_of_range("Stack<>::top(): empty stack");
    }
    return elems[numElems-1];    // return top element
}

} // **** END namespace CPPBook ******************************
```

The second parameter of the stack template, MAXSIZE, is used to determine the size of the stack. This is not only used to declare the array, but also, in push(), to determine whether the stack is already full.

When using this stack template, both the type of the element being managed and the size of the stack have to be specified:

```
// tmpl/stest4.cpp

#include <iostream>
#include <string>
#include <cstdlib>
#include "stack4.hpp"
```

```
int main()
{
    try {
        CPPBook::Stack<int,20>          int20Stack;    // stack for 20 ints
        CPPBook::Stack<int,40>          int40Stack;    // stack for 40 ints
        CPPBook::Stack<std::string,40> stringStack;    // stack for 40 strings

        // manipulate integer stack
        int20Stack.push(7);
        std::cout << int20Stack.top() << std::endl;
        int20Stack.pop();

        // manipulate string stack
        std::string s = "hello";
        stringStack.push(s);
        std::cout << stringStack.top() << std::endl;
        stringStack.pop();
        std::cout << stringStack.top() << std::endl;
        stringStack.pop();
    }
    catch (const char* msg) {
        std::cerr << "Exception: " << msg << std::endl;
        return EXIT_FAILURE;
    }
}
```

It must be taken into account that, in this case, int20Stack and int40Stack have different types, and cannot be assigned to each other or used mutually.

Default values for the template parameters can also be defined:

```
template <typename T = int, int MAXSIZE = 100>
class Stack {
    ...
};
```

I consider this not to be useful in this case. Default values should intuitively be correct. Neither int as the element type nor a maximum size of 100 are intuitive. In this respect, it is better if the specification of both is left to the application programmer.

7.4.2 Limitations of Non-Type Template Parameters

There are limitations in using other template arguments. Template arguments, in addition to types, may be constant integral expressions, or addresses of objects or functions, which can be globally accessed in the program.

Floating-point numbers and class-type objects are not allowed as non-type template parameters:

```
template <double VAT>            // ERROR: floating-point values are not
double process(double v)         //            allowed as template parameters
{
    return v * VAT;
}


template <std::string name>      // ERROR: class-type objects are not
class MyClass {                  //            allowed as template parameters
    ...
};
```

The use of string literals also leads to problems:

```
template <typename T, const char* name>
class MyClass {
    ...
};


MyClass<int,"hello"> x;      // ERROR: string literal "hello" not allowed
```

String literals are not global objects that are available anywhere in the program. If 'hello' is defined in two different modules, these are then two different strings.

Using a global pointer is also of no help:

```
template <typename T, const char* name>
class MyClass {
    ...
};


const char* s = "hello";
MyClass<int,s> x;      // ERROR: "hello" is always static
```

The pointer s may be a global pointer, but what it points to is still not global.

The solution to the problem is as follows:

```
template <typename T, const char* name>
class MyClass {
    ...
};
```

```
extern const char s[] = "hello";

void foo() {
    MyClass<int,s> x;      // OK

    ...
}
```

The global array s is initialized with the character string 'hello', whereby s is the global character string 'hello'.

7.4.3 Summary

- Templates can have parameters that are values rather than types.
- These values cannot be floating-point values or objects, and cannot be local.
- The use of string literals as template arguments is only possible with restrictions.

7.5   Additional Aspects of Templates

This section introduces other relevant aspects of templates that have not yet been introduced but should be known. In it, we will discuss the typename keyword and the possibility of defining members as templates. Finally, we will look at the possibility of implementing polymorphism using templates.

7.5.1   The `typename` Keyword

The typename keyword was introduced during the standardization of C++ in order to be able to define for code that uses a class template that a symbol of the class template is a type. This is demonstrated by the following example:

```
template <typename T>
class MyClass {
    typename T::SubType * ptr;
    ...
};
```

In this case, typename is used in order to determine that SubType is a type that is defined in the class T. Therefore, ptr is declared as a pointer to this SubType.

Without typename, it would be assumed that SubType is a static value (variable or object) of the class T. Thus

```
T::SubType * ptr
```

would be the multiplication of this value by the value ptr.

A typical example of the use of typename is a function template, in which STL containers are accessed via iterators (see Section 3.5.4 on page 75):

```
// tmpl/printcoll.hpp

#include <iostream>

// output elements of an STL container
template <typename T>
void printcoll(const T& coll)
{
    // output number of elements
    std::cout << "number of elements: " << coll.size() << std::endl;

    // output element itself
    std::cout << "elements: ";
    typename T::const_iterator pos;
    for (pos=coll.begin(); pos!=coll.end(); ++pos) {
```

```
            std::cout << *pos << ' ';
        }
        std::cout << std::endl;
    }
```

In this function template, an STL container of the type T is expected as a parameter. The output of the elements of this container is achieved using a local iterator. This iterator has an auxiliary type that is defined by the container. Its declaration must be carried out using the typename keyword:

```
    typename T::const_iterator pos;    // const_iterator is an auxiliary type of T
```

7.5.2 Members as Templates

Members of classes can also be templates. This is also the case for inner auxiliary classes, as well as for member functions.

The use of this ability can be clarified using an example of the class Stack<>. Normally, stacks can only be assigned to stacks whose elements have the same type. An assignment of a stack with elements of other types is not possible, because the default assignment operator requires that both sides of the assignment have the same type. This is, however, not the case with stacks for different element types.

This facility can be achieved by defining an assignment operator as a template. To do this, the class Stack<> is declared as follows:

```
// tmpl/stack5decl.hpp

template <typename T>
class Stack {
  private:
    std::deque<T> elems;    // elements

  public:
    void push(const T&);    // store new top element
    void pop();             // remove top element
    T top() const;          // return top element
    bool empty() const {    // return whether the stack is empty
        return elems.empty();
    }

    // assign stack of elements of type T2
    template <typename T2>
    Stack<T>& operator= (Stack<T2> const&);
};
```

The following was changed:

- The declaration of an assignment of a stack of elements of a different type, T2.
- The stack uses a deque internally. This is also due to the implementation of the assignment operator.

The assignment operator for stacks of elements of a different type is implemented as follows:

```
// tmpl/stack5assign.hpp

template <typename T>
 template <typename T2>
Stack<T>& Stack<T>::operator= (const Stack<T2>& op2)
{
    if ((void*)this == (void*)&op2) {      // assignment to itself?
        return *this;
    }


    Stack<T2> tmp(op2);                    // create a copy of the assigned stack

    elems.clear();                         // remove existing elements
    while (!tmp.empty()) {                 // copy all elements
        elems.push_front(tmp.top());
        tmp.pop();
    }
    return *this;
}
```

First we look at the syntax for the definition of templates that are defined in class templates. A template with parameter T2 is defined in the template with parameter T:

```
template <typename T>
 template <typename T2>
  ...
```

With this implementation, one would think it sufficient simply to access all elements of the submitted stack op2 directly, and to copy them into the separate stack. However, note again that templates instantiated for different types are themselves different types. For this reason, Stack<T2> is a different type than that for which this function was implemented. Therefore, op2 can only be accessed using the public interface. The only chance of accessing the elements via the public interface is using the member function top(). However, each element has to become a top element, then. Thus, a copy of op2 must first be made, so that the elements are taken from that copy by calling pop(). Because pop() returns the last element pushed onto the stack, we have to use a container that supports the insertion of elements at the other end of the collection. For this reason, we use a deque, which provides push_front() to put an element on the other side of the collection.

Note that this function does not turn off type checking. Stacks still cannot be assigned to each other if their element types cannot be assigned to each other. If, for example, an attempt is made to assign a stack of strings to a stack of ints, an error message is produced for the line

```
elems.push_front(tmp.top());      // insert copy at front
```

because `tmp.top()` returns a string, which cannot be used as an `int`.

Note also that a template version of an assignment operator does not cover the default assignment operator. The default assignment operator is still generated, and is called with an assignment between two stacks with the same element type.

However, one can change the implementation so that a vector can also be used as a container for the elements. To do this, the declaration is changed as follows:

```
template <typename T, typename CONT = std::deque<T> >
class Stack {
  private:
    CONT elems;   // elements

  public:
    Stack();                      // constructor
    void push(const T&);          // store new top element
    void pop();                   // remove top element
    T top() const;                // return top element
    bool empty() const {          // return whether the stack is empty
        return elems.empty();
    }

    // assign stack for elements of the type T2
    template <typename T2, typename CONT2>
    Stack<T,CONT>& operator= (const Stack<T2,CONT2>&);
};
```

As only the functions that are actually used are instantiated and compiled in a class template, you can also create a stack that uses a vector for the elements:

```
// stack for ints, that uses a vector
CPPBook::Stack<int,std::vector<int> > vStack;
...
vStack.push(42);
vStack.push(7);
std::cout << vStack.top() << std::endl;
vStack.pop();
```

As long as an attempt is not made to assign a stack with elements of another type, this program is correct.

The complete example is in both `tmpl/stack6.hpp` and `tmpl/stest6.cpp`. Do not be discouraged if your compiler reports an error. As we make use of almost all of the important language features of templates, some (non-standard-conforming) C++ compilers will not be able to cope.

7.5.3   Static Polymorphism with Templates

Polymorphism is usually implemented in C++ via inheritance (see Section 5.3 on page 300). It is, however, also possible to implement polymorphism with templates. This will be discussed in this section.

Dynamic Polymorphism

If inheritance is used for the implementation of polymorphism, then an (abstract) base class defines the common interface (the *common term*) that is used by a number of concrete types (see Section 5.3 on page 300).

If one has, for example, a group of geometric classes, an abstract class `GeoObj` (as introduced in Section 5.3.3 on page 302) can be given, from which all possible concrete classes are derived (see Figure 7.1).

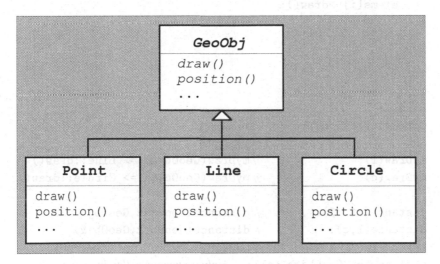

Figure 7.1. Dynamic polymorphism implemented with inheritance

In order to program with the common term, references or pointers to the objects of the base class are used. This may look as follows:

```
// tmpl/dynapoly.cpp

// draw any geometric object
void myDraw (const GeoObj& obj)
{
    obj.draw();
}


// process distance between two geometric objects
Coord distance (const GeoObj& x1, const GeoObj& x2)
{
    Coord a = x1.position() - x2.position();
    return a.abs();
}


// draw inhomogenous collection of geometric objects
void drawElems (const std::vector<GeoObj*>& elems)
{
    for (unsigned i=0; i<elems.size(); ++i) {
        elems[i]->draw();
    }
}


int main()
{
    Line l;
    Circle c, c1, c2;

    myDraw(l);               // myDraw(GeoObj&) => Line::draw()
    myDraw(c);               // myDraw(GeoObj&) => Circle::draw()

    distance(c1,c2);         // distance(GeoObj&,GeoObj&)
    distance(l,c);           // distance(GeoObj&,GeoObj&)

    std::vector<GeoObj*> coll;  // inhomogenous collection
    coll.push_back(&l);         // insert line
    coll.push_back(&c);         // insert circle
    drawElems(coll);            // draw collection
}
```

The functions are compiled for the GeoObj type. The functions that are called depends on what arguments are passed at run time. For example, in mydraw(), it is decided during run time what draw() must be called for the geometric object. If a circle is passed, Circle::draw() is called; if a line is passed, Line::draw() is called. Accordingly, in distance(), it is decided during run time what member function position() must be called for a geometric object. A non-homogeneous collection of geometric objects can also be declared using a pointer to the type GeoObj (alternatively, the use of a smart pointer is recommended, see Section 9.2.1 on page 536).

Static Polymorphism

Instead of inheritance, templates can also be used for polymorphism. In this case, there is no base class that the common interface explicitly defines. Instead, the necessary properties are implicitly defined as operations of a template parameter.

The previous sample program can then be rewritten as follows:

```
// tmpl/staticpoly.cpp

// draw any geometric object
template <typename GeoObj>
void myDraw (const GeoObj& obj)
{
    obj.draw();
}


// calculate distance between two geometric objects
template <typename GeoObj1, typename GeoObj2>
Coord distance (const GeoObj1& x1, const GeoObj2& x2)
{
    Coord a = x1.position() - x2.position();
    return a.abs();
}


// output homogenous set of geometric objects
template <typename GeoObj>
void drawElems (const std::vector<GeoObj>& elems)
{
    for (unsigned i=0; i<elems.size(); ++i) {
        elems[i].draw();
    }
}
```

```
int main()
{
    Line l;
    Circle c;
    Circle c1, c2;

    myDraw(l);            // myDraw<Line>(GeoObj&) => Line::draw()
    myDraw(c);            // myDraw<Circle>(GeoObj&) => Circle::draw()

    distance(c1,c2);      // distance<Circle,Circle>(GeoObj&,GeoObj&)
    distance(l,c);        // distance<Line,Circle>(GeoObj&,GeoObj&)

    // std::vector<GeoObj*> coll;   // ERROR: no inhomogenous collection possible
    std::vector<Line> coll;        // OK: homogenous collection
    coll.push_back(l);             // insert line
    drawElems(coll);               // draw collection
}
```

For the first two functions, `draw()` and `distance()`, the type `GeoObj` becomes a template parameter. By using two different template parameters, the transfer of two different kinds of geometric objects is made possible in `distance()`:

```
distance(l,c);     // distance<Line,Circle>(GeoObj1&,GeoObj2&)
```

A non-homogeneous collection is no longer possible with templates. However, the types of the elements in the collection no longer have to be declared as pointers:

```
std::vector<Line> coll;   // OK: homogenous collection
```

This can have significant advantages.

Dynamic versus Static Polymorphism

The two forms of polymorphism in C++ can be described as follows:

- Polymorphism implemented using inheritance is *bound* and *dynamic*:
  - *bound* means that the concrete types are dependent on another type (the base class);
  - *dynamic* means that the connection between function calls and the called functions is set at run time.
- Polymorphism implemented using templates is *unbound* and *static*:
  - *unbound* means that the concrete types are not dependent on other types;
  - *static* means that the connection between function calls and the called functions is set at compile time.

Dynamic polymorphism is an abbreviated name for *bound dynamic polymorphism*. *Static polymorphism* is therefore actually an abbreviated name for *unbound static polymorphism*. Other programming languages offer different combinations (for example, Smalltalk supports unbound dynamic polymorphism).

The advantages of dynamic polymorphism are as follows:

- It makes non-homogeneous collections possible.
- It requires less code (the functions are only compiled once for the type GeoObj).
- Polymorphic operations can be provided as object code (template code must be provided as source code).
- The error handling of the compiler is better (see Section 7.6.2 on page 468).

The advantages of static polymorphism are as follows:

- It leads to an improved run-time behavior (better optimizations are possible as there are no virtual functions). Experience shows that a factor of between 2 and 10 is possible.
- It is unbound (classes are not dependent on any other code). Because of this, the use of fundamental types is possible.
- It avoids the use of pointers.
- Concrete types do not need to provide the complete interface (templates only need the operations that are called).

With regards to type safety, both forms have their advantages and disadvantages. With dynamic polymorphism, the common term has to be given explicitly. With static polymorphism, objects of a class can be used as geometric objects, only because the class offers the corresponding operations. On the other hand, the type safety of homogeneous sets is not guaranteed with dynamic polymorphism. In order to ensure there are only lines in a collection of geometric objects, for example, appropriate queries have to be programmed, which take place during run time.

Taking these considerations into account, in practice, due to possibly improved run-time behavior, one should think about using static polymorphism, as long as the parameters are known at compile time and no non-homogeneous collections are required.

7.5.4 Summary

- If, during the use of a template parameter, an auxiliary type that has been defined for the template is accessed, this has to be qualified using the typename keyword.
- Inner classes and member functions can also be used as templates. In doing so, implicit type conversions can be made possible for operations of class templates. This does not disable type checking.
- Template versions of the assignment operators do not hide the default assignment operator.
- Polymorphism can be implemented using templates. This has its advantages and disadvantages.

7.6   Templates in Practice

A template is a new form of source code. It can be checked syntactically. However, it can only become object code if the types are defined. This new concept creates some problems, which are discussed in this section.

7.6.1   Compiling Template Code

Templates are actually checked twice: once syntactically during the compilation of the template code, and once during the compilation of the code generated for the actual types. As explained in Section 7.2.3 on page 431, this breaks the ordinary compiler/linker model.

It is therefore easiest to place templates in header files. However, this method has considerable disadvantages:

- On the one hand, the same code is compiled again and again. For example, each module that uses stacks for elements of the type int recompiles the code generated for this. This not only takes up compile time, but also makes the compiled code available in several object files. If these object files are combined to make an executable program, one would need a linker that removes the surplus code, otherwise an unnecessarily large executable program would be produced.

- On the other hand, template code can only be provided as source code. This is critical if the code represents a fundamental part of the 'knowhow' of a company, which is, of course, priceless because otherwise any competitive advantage is lost.

There are two other options for dealing with templates, which are now introduced. However, each of these has its disadvantages. There is therefore no perfect solution (yet).

There are also numerous proprietary solutions of individual manufacturers. For example, one can define special preprocessor statements for dealing with templates. Such solutions will not be looked at here.

Explicit Instantiation

One way of avoiding multiple compilations of the same template code is offered by the technique of explicit instantiation.

In this case, the templates are actually only declared in header files:

```
// tmpl/expl1.hpp

#ifndef EXPL_HPP
#define EXPL_HPP

// declaration of the function template max()
template <typename T>
const T& max(const T& a, const T& b);
```

```
// declaration of the class template Stack<>
#include <vector>

// **** BEGIN namespace CPPBook *********************************
namespace CPPBook {

template <typename T>
class Stack {
  private:
    std::vector<T> elems;    // elements
  public:
    Stack();                      // constructor
    void push(const T&);     // store new top element
    void pop();                   // remove top element
    T top() const;             // return top element
};

} // **** END namespace CPPBook *********************************

#endif // EXPL_HPP
```

The definition of templates is in a separate header file, which binds the header file with the declarations:

```
// tmpl/expldef1.hpp

#ifndef EXPLDEF_HPP
#define EXPLDEF_HPP

#include "expl.hpp"
#include <stdexcept>

// definition of the function template max()
template <typename T>
const T& max(const T& a, const T& b)
{
    return (a > b ? a : b);
}

// definition of the functions of the class template Stack<>
```

```cpp
// **** BEGIN namespace CPPBook ********************************
namespace CPPBook {

// constructor
template <typename T>
Stack<T>::Stack()
{
    // nothing more to do
}

template <typename T>
void Stack<T>::push(const T& elem)
{
    elems.push_back(elem);      // store copy as new top element
}

template<typename T>
void Stack<T>::pop()
{
    if (elems.empty()) {
        throw std::out_of_range("Stack<>::pop(): empty stack");
    }
    elems.pop_back();                // remove top element
}

template <typename T>
T Stack<T>::top() const
{
    if (elems.empty()) {
        throw std::out_of_range("Stack<>::top(): empty stack");
    }
    return elems.back();          // return top element as copy
}

} // **** END namespace CPPBook ********************************

#endif // EXPLDEF_HPP
```

Templates can now be used by only including the declarations:

```cpp
// tmpl/expltest1.cpp

#include <iostream>
#include <string>
#include <cstdlib>
#include "expl.hpp"

int main()
{
    try {
        CPPBook::Stack<int>         intStack;      // stack for integers
        CPPBook::Stack<std::string> stringStack;   // stack for strings

        // manipulate integer stack
        intStack.push(7);
        intStack.push(max(intStack.top(),42));   // max() for ints
        std::cout << intStack.top() << std::endl;
        intStack.pop();

        // manipulate string stack
        std::string s = "hello";
        stringStack.push(s);
        stringStack.pop();
        stringStack.pop();
    }
    catch (const char* msg) {
        std::cerr << "Exception: " << msg << std::endl;
        return EXIT_FAILURE;
    }
}
```

The necessary instantiation can be explicitly generated separately:

```cpp
// tmpl/expldef1.cpp

#include <string>
#include "expldef.hpp"

// explicitly instantiate necessary function template
template const int& max(const int&, const int&);

// explicitly instantiate necessary class templates
template CPPBook::Stack<int>;
template CPPBook::Stack<std::string>;
```

You can identify such a *explicit instantiation* by the fact that the opening brackets do not directly follow the `template` keyword. As can be seen, one can explicitly instantiate individual functions and whole classes. In the case of classes, all member functions are instantiated.

With classes, one can also explicitly instantiate individual functions. Our example application program could therefore also be called with the following explicit instantiations:

```
// tmpl/expldef2.cpp

#include <string>
#include "expldef.hpp"

// explicitly instantiate function template
template const int& max(const int&, const int&);

// explicitly instantiate necessary functions of Stack<> for int
template CPPBook::Stack<int>::Stack();
template void CPPBook::Stack<int>::push(const int&);
template int CPPBook::Stack<int>::top() const;
template void CPPBook::Stack<int>::pop();

// explicitly instantiate necessary functions of Stack<> for std::string
// - top() is not required
template CPPBook::Stack<std::string>::Stack();
template void CPPBook::Stack<std::string>::push(const std::string&);
template void CPPBook::Stack<std::string>::pop();
```

Figure 7.2 demonstrates the organization of the source code for the `max()` template.

Using the procedure of explicit instantiation, significant time can occasionally be saved. It is therefore worthwhile dividing template code between two separate header files (one for the declaration and one for the definition). If one does not want to explicitly instantiate, one simply has to include the header file with the definitions instead of the header file with the declarations. Thus this method creates considerably more flexibility without having to put up with significant disadvantages.

If one wants to retain the advantage of inline functions, these have to implemented in the header file with the declarations in the same way as with other classes.

The Template Compilation Model

Another option for dealing with templates is defined as the *template compilation model* in the standard. This establishes that a template can be qualified via the `export` keyword. By doing so, it is automatically exported into a template database or into a template repository.

```
max.hpp:

    #ifndef MAX_HPP
    #define MAX_HPP

    template <typename T>
    const T& max (const T&, const T&);

    #endif
```

```
maxdef.hpp:

    #ifndef MAXDEF_HPP
    #define MAXDEF_HPP

    #include "max.hpp"

    template <typename T>
    const T& max (const T& a, const T& b)
    {
        return  a > b ? a : b;
    }

    #endif
```

```
maxtest.cpp:

    #include "max.hpp"

    int foo (int x, int y)
    {
        ...
        z = max(x,y);
        ...
    }
```

```
maxdef.cpp:

    #include "maxdef.hpp"

    template const int& max (const int&, const int&);
```

Figure 7.2. Example of the code organization of templates

If this kind of template is implemented, the repository is used to clarify whether the template was already compiled for the types, or, if this is not the case, whether it is automatically compiled and bound to the running program.

This method is very much implementation specific. Until now, there were almost no compilers that supported this language feature. As a result, in practice, this cannot be used at the moment.

7.6.2   Error Handling

Templates also create problems when errors are made by the programmer. The main problem is
that the compiler recognizes type errors during the compilation of the template for certain types.
It then usually reports where the error was identified. This kind of error message makes it virtually impossible to do anything about it. In commercial code, the substitutions and additions
carried out using templates are so complicated that any error message is rendered incomprehen-
sible.

For example, the following code contains a deliberate error. It defines a search criteria, using
greater<>, and submits an int as a parameter instead of std::string:

```
std::list<std::string> coll;

...

// find first element larger than "A"
std::list<std::string>::iterator pos;
pos = find_if (coll.begin(), coll.end(),                    // range
               std::bind2nd(std::greater<int>(),"A")); // search criteria
```

This produces the following error message:

```
/local/include/stl/_algo.h: In function 'struct _STL::_List_iterator<_STL::basic
_string<char,_STL::char_traits<char>,_STL::allocator<char> >,_STL::_Nonconst_tra
its<_STL::basic_string<char,_STL::char_traits<char>,_STL::allocator<char> > > >
_STL::find_if<_STL::_List_iterator<_STL::basic_string<char,_STL::char_traits<cha
r>,_STL::allocator<char> >,_STL::_Nonconst_traits<_STL::basic_string<char,_STL::
char_traits<char>,_STL::allocator<char> > > >, _STL::binder2nd<_STL::greater<int
> > >(_STL::_List_iterator<_STL::basic_string<char,_STL::char_traits<char>,_STL:
:allocator<char> >,_STL::_Nonconst_traits<_STL::basic_string<char,_STL::char_tra
its<char>,_STL::allocator<char> > > >, _STL::_List_iterator<_STL::basic_string<c
har,_STL::char_traits<char>,_STL::allocator<char> >,_STL::_Nonconst_traits<_STL:
:basic_string<char,_STL::char_traits<char>,_STL::allocator<char> > > >, _STL::bi
nder2nd<_STL::greater<int> >, _STL::input_iterator_tag)':
/local/include/stl/_algo.h:115:   instantiated from '_STL::find_if<_STL::_List_i
terator<_STL::basic_string<char,_STL::char_traits<char>,_STL::allocator<char> >,
_STL::_Nonconst_traits<_STL::basic_string<char,_STL::char_traits<char>,_STL::all
ocator<char> > > >, _STL::binder2nd<_STL::greater<int> > >(_STL::_List_iterator<
_STL::basic_string<char,_STL::char_traits<char>,_STL::allocator<char> >,_STL::_N
onconst_traits<_STL::basic_string<char,_STL::char_traits<char>,_STL::allocator<c
har> > > >, _STL::_List_iterator<_STL::basic_string<char,_STL::char_traits<char>
,_STL::allocator<char> >,_STL::_Nonconst_traits<_STL::basic_string<char,_STL::ch
ar_traits<char>,_STL::allocator<char> > > >, _STL::binder2nd<_STL::greater<int>
>)'
testprog.cpp:18:   instantiated from here
/local/include/stl/_algo.h:78: no match for call to '(_STL::binder2nd<_STL::grea
ter<int> >) (_STL::basic_string<char,_STL::char_traits<char>,_STL::allocator<cha
r> > &)'
/local/include/stl/_function.h:261: candidates are: bool _STL::binder2nd<_STL::g
reater<int> >::operator ()(const int &) const
```

This is one single error message, which warns of the following:

- In a function in /local/include/stl/_algo.h
  - instantiated by line 115 of /local/include/stl/_algo.h
  - instantiated by line 18 of testprog.cpp
- in line 78 there is no suitable function for calling something,
- for which there is a candidate in line 261 of /local/include/stl/_function.h.

The good thing is that this compiler report the position in the application code that (may have) caused the error. This is the case in the following line of the above error message:

```
testprog.cpp:18:   instantiated from here
```

As can be seen, even finding the line that causes an error can be a problem [4].

Now, you only have to understand the problem. With a lot of practice and background knowledge, one may find that something with basic_string it searched for, but only something with int is available. If you cannot find this out, there is at least the possibility of seeing the place in the code that has triggered the error and hopefully coming to the conclusion that int in the line must simply be replaced by std::string.

The error message in the example also highlights another problem. Templates can themselves lead to warnings or errors. This is due to the fact that, because of the many replacements, very long internal symbol names are produced. Symbols with up to 10 000 characters are possible. Not all compilers and linkers can cope with such long symbols. Some of them simply output a warning, which can safely be ignored.

7.6.3 Summary

- Templates break the ordinary compiler/linker model.
- Templates can be explicitly instantiated.
- By separating templates into different header files for their declaration and definition, they can be dealt with more flexibly.
- There exists a compilation model for templates, which, in practice, unfortunately cannot yet be used.
- Template error messages are a problem. It is important to find the place that triggered the error and to recognize the problem.
- Templates can lead to very long symbols.

---

[4] Unfortunately, there are C++ compilers that do not even provide information about which line led to the error. You should complain about this! However, there are also exemplary compilers that only output an error message for the affected line in the code.

8

The Standard I/O Library in Detail

Now that the standard techniques for inputting and outputting with stream classes have been introduced (see Sections 3.1.4 and 4.5), this chapter will look at the details of the standard I/O library. From this, one should get an impression of the full extent of the possibilities that this library offers.

Formatted access to files and strings is also part of this chapter.

However, note that this book is unable to deal with all the features of the I/O library. I will concentrate instead on the details that are important for daily I/O use. For other aspects, I suggest that you refer to texts devoted to the standard library or the I/O library; for example, my book *The C++ Standard Library* (see [*JosuttisStdLib*]) or the book *Standard C++ IOStreams and Locales* from Langer and Kreft (see [*LangerKreftIO*]).

8.1   The Standard Stream Classes

In this section, the common classes for I/O (istream, ostream and iostream) are discussed in detail.

8.1.1   Stream Classes and Stream Objects

Classes and Class Hierarchy

The class hierarchy for the I/O classes is shown in Figure 8.1. For all classes that are provided as templates, the top line of the box shows the template type, while the bottom line shows the type for the instantiations for types char and wchar_t.

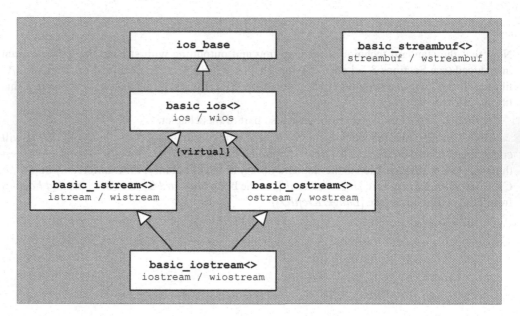

Figure 8.1. Hierarchy of the fundamental stream classes

The classes of this hierarchy have the following structure:

- The base class **ios_base** defines the properties of all stream classes that are not dependent on the character type. In principle, these are members and functions for status flags and format flags.
- The class template **basic_ios<>** is derived from ios_base and defines the general properties of all stream classes that are dependent on the character type. This also includes the definition of the buffer that is used by the streams. The buffer is an object of a class derived from **basic_streambuf<>**. It is used for the actual reading and writing of individual

characters. The other stream classes look after the formatting of the data (for example, the conversion of the number 42 into the character sequence '4' and '2').

- The class templates **basic_istream<>** and **basic_ostream<>** are derived virtually from basic_ios<> and define objects that can be used for reading or writing. The classes that are most often used in the Anglo-American language, istream and ostream, are the instantiations for type char.

- The class template **basic_iostream<>** is derived from basic_istream<>, as well as from basic_ostream<>, and defines objects that can be used for writing as well as for reading.

Additional classes are defined for access to files and strings, which are looked at in Sections 8.2 and 8.3.

As has already been explained in Section 4.5.1 on page 196, a number of instances of these classes are predefined. They are listed in Table 8.1. In addition to the objects for streams that handle 'ordinary characters' of type char (cin, cout, etc.), the corresponding objects for the standard channels of wide-character streams are listed.

Symbol	Datatype	Meaning
cin	istream	standard input channel (typically the keyboard)
cout	ostream	standard output channel (typically the screen), buffered
cerr	ostream	standard error output channel (typically the screen), unbuffered
clog	ostream	standard history output channel (typically the screen), buffered
wcin	wistream	standard input channel (typically the keyboard)
wcout	wostream	standard output channel (typically the screen), buffered
wcerr	wostream	standard error output channel (typically the screen), unbuffered
wclog	wostream	standard history output channel (typically the screen), buffered

Table 8.1. Global objects of standard I/O

Purpose of the Stream Buffer Classes

The I/O stream library was designed so that it strictly separates responsibilities. The classes derived from basic_ios 'only' take care of formatting the data[1]. For the actual reading and writing of individual characters, the stream buffer classes are used, which are derived from basic_ios.

Stream buffer classes therefore play an important role if one defines I/O for new devices, redirects streams to other devices or wants to use the character strings in different ways (for example, if one wants to automatically convert all lowercase letters to uppercase letters). Stream buffer classes also take care of the synchronization of simultaneous accesses of several streams to the same device.

---

[1] The formatting is not carried out by the classes themselves, but they delegate special classes, which take into account issues related to internationalization.

In order to enable I/O for special devices, one should therefore not implement classes derived from `basic_ios`. Instead, a special stream buffer class has to be implemented and used by the stream objects derived from `basic_ios`.

Header Files

The definitions of the stream classes are divided into different header files:

- `<iosfwd>`
  This contains the forward declarations of the stream classes.

- `<streambuf>`
  This contains the definition of the base class for the stream buffer, `basic_streambuf<>`.

- `<istream>`
  This contains the definitions of the classes that just support input (`basic_istream<>`), and for the classes that support both input and output (`basic_iostream<>`).

- `<ostream>`
  This contains the definitions of the classes that just support output (`basic_ostream<>`).

- `<iostream>`
  This contains the definitions of the global stream objects, such as `cin` and `cout`.

This division may appear a little strange. In fact, it is sufficient, when using streams for I/O, to only include the header file `<istream>`. Only if the global stream objects are really needed, should `<iostream>` be included. This design has historical reasons. With the use of the global stream objects in a module, special code is necessary that makes sure that these objects are initialized. This code is included by means of `<iostream>`. Because execution of this code adds a certain amount of run-time overhead, one should refrain from including `<iostream>` if possible.

Provided that only the type of the stream class is required in declarations, only `<iosfwd>` should be included. If the operations for reading and writing are required, `<istream>` and `<ostream>` should be included. Only if the global stream objects are used, should `<iostream>` be included.

For special stream features, such as parametrized manipulators, file access or string streams, there are other header files (`<iomanip>`, `<fstream>`, `<sstream>` and `<strstream>`). These are looked at later, with an introduction to the corresponding techniques.

8.1.2 Handling the Stream Status

For the general status of a stream, bit constants are introduced in the class `ios_base`. Although we have already seen this in Section 4.5.3 on page 203, for the sake of completeness, we will briefly look at it again.

Status Bits

The different bit constants are listed in Table 8.2. They are defined as flags (with type `iostate`) in the class `std::ios_base`, and are managed in this class by an internal member.

Bit Constant	Meaning
goodbit	everything is OK, no (other) bit set
eofbit	end of file (EOF)
failbit	error: last process not completed correctly
badbit	fatal error: status not defined

Table 8.2. Bit constants of type `std::ios_base::iostate`

Talking about `ios::goodbit` as a flag it is a bit confusing, because it typically has the value 0 and actually only shows whether another flag is set.

`failbit` and `badbit` are defined as follows:

- `failbit` is set if an operation cannot be executed correctly, but, in principle, the stream is OK. Typical of this are format errors when reading. If, for example, an integer is to be read but the next character is a letter, this flag is set.
- `badbit` is set if something is fundamentally wrong with the stream or characters have been lost. This flag is set, for example, when positioning before the start of a file.

Note that `eofbit` is normally set together with `failbit`, because the condition EOF (end of file) is only seen if the attempt to read further failed.

In addition, on some systems, the flag `ios::hardfail` is included. However, this is not standardized.

Because the flags are defined in the class `ios_base`, they have to be qualified accordingly:

```
std::ios_base::eofbit
```

They can, however, also be qualified by means of `ios`:

```
std::ios::eofbit
```

This is possible because `ios` is an instantiation of the class `basic_ios<>`, which is derived from `ios_base`. Because, formerly, only the class `ios` was provided, this kind of qualification is backwards compatible and is found quite often.

Access to Status Bits

Various member functions (briefly introduced in Section 4.5.3 on page 203) belong to the flags (see Table 8.3).

The first four member functions return a Boolean value that indicates whether particular flags are set. Note that `fail()` yields whether `failbit` or `badbit` is set. This is due to historical reasons and has the advantage that a call for the test is sufficient in the case of an error.

Member Function	Meaning
good()	returns true if everything is OK (ios::goodbit)
eof()	returns true at EOF (ios::eofbit)
fail()	returns true if there are errors (ios::failbit or ios::badbit)
bad()	returns true if there are fatal errors (ios::badbit)
rdstate()	returns the combination of the set flag
clear()	clears all flags
clear(*bits*)	clears all flags and sets *bits* as the status
setstate(*bits*)	sets *bits* as the status

Table 8.3. Member functions for stream status

If clear() is called without an argument, all error flags (including ios::eofbit) are cleared. If an argument is passed, the flags that are passed are set. On page 203, there is a small working example that shows this.

Note that clear() has to be called for every failed stream operation. This is different to the I/O interface of C. There, for example, after a failed attempt to read into an int due to a format failure, one can immediately read the remainder of the line. In the stream classes of C++, failbit is set, which ensures that all following attempts to read fail, until it is explicitly cleared again.

Finally, in order to use streams as Boolean expressions in control constructs, the conversion functions that were introduced in Section 4.5.2 on page 201 are defined (see Table 8.4).

Member Function	Meaning
operator void* ()	returns whether the stream is OK (corresponds to a call of !fail())
operator ! ()	returns whether the stream is not OK (corresponds to a call of fail())

Table 8.4. Conversion operations for streams

Error Status and Exceptions

During standardization, the ability to automatically throw exceptions due to a change of the status bits of a stream was introduced. This means that one can adjust whether a bit, if set, automatically triggers an exception. What bits can trigger exceptions is set and queried with the function exceptions() (see Table 8.5).

Using the following call, all 'errors' for the stream strm automatically throw exceptions:

```
// trigger exceptions for all 'errors'
strm.exceptions (std::ios::eofbit | std::ios::failbit |
                 std::ios::badbit);
```

Member Function	Meaning
exceptions()	returns the bits that automatically trigger exceptions
exceptions(*bits*)	sets the bits that automatically trigger exceptions

Table 8.5. Member functions for triggering exceptions

If, at the moment of this call, one of these bits is already set, the corresponding exceptions are triggered immediately.

Through the passing of 0 or goodbit, the automatic production of stream exceptions can be switched off:

```
// do not automatically trigger exceptions
strm.exceptions(0);
```

The thrown exceptions have type std::ios_base::failure. For this class, it is only defined that an implementation-specific string can be queried using what() (see Section 3.6.3 on page 95).

Note that we are talking about 'exceptions' and not 'errors'. For I/O in particular, there is an important distinction between these terms. Faulty input is common and should be dealt with locally, using the normal data flow. Usually, exceptions should only be triggered for the badbit or if one reads data from a predefined configuration file in which there should not be any read errors.

8.1.3 Standard Operators

The operators >> and << are defined in the classes istream and ostream as standard operators for I/O and are overloaded for all fundamental types, including char*.

The << operator also offers the possibility of writing pointers. If the operator is submitted a parameter of type void*, the address of the pointer is output in a machine-dependent form. The following statement outputs, for example, the content of strings and its address:

```
const char* cstring = "hello";

std::cout << "string: " << cstring << " is at the address: "
          << static_cast<const void*>(cstring)  << std::endl;
```

This can, for example, lead to the following output:

```
String: hello is at the address: 0x10000018
```

This address can also be read using the input operator. It has to be taken into account, however, that addresses are not persistent values in a program. The same object can have a completely different address in a program that has been restarted.

8.1.4   Standard Functions

As well as the standard operators for streams (`<<` and `>>`), other member functions for reading or writing can also be used. The semantics of these functions are discussed for instantiations of the stream classes for `chars` (i.e. using types `istream` and `ostream`). Special aspects, due to the fact that they are functions for `basic_istream<>` and `basic_ostream<>`, are not taken into account.

Member Functions for Input

In the class `istream`, in addition to the `>>` operator, numerous other member functions are defined that are used for reading characters:

- `int get ()`
  returns the character or EOF that is next read. It corresponds to `getchar()` or `getc()` in C. Note that the return value is assigned an `int`. Otherwise, the character with the value -1 or with the value 255 cannot be distinguished from EOF, because EOF is typically defined as the value -1.

- `istream& get (char& c)`
  assigns the next character to the passed parameter c and returns the stream. Its status then gives information about whether the read was successful.

- `istream& get (char* cs, int num, char end = '\n')`
  reads up to $num - 1$ characters, until end, into the character string cs. The character end itself is not read. The end-of-string character '`\0`' is automatically appended. With lines that are too long, the next call of `get()` returns the remaining characters.

- `istream& getline (char* cs, int num, char end = '\n')`
  reads up to $num - 1$ characters, until end, into the character string cs. The character end itself is also read and inserted. The end-of-string character '`\0`' is automatically appended. With lines that are too long, `failbit` is set.

- `istream& read (char* cs, int num)`
  reads num characters into the character string cs. The end-of-string character '`\0`' is not appended. If there are too few characters, `eofbit` and `failbit` are set.

- `int readsome (char* cs, int num`
  reads up to num characters into the character string cs. It returns the number of read characters. The end-of-string character '`\0`' is not appended.

- `int gcount ()`
  returns how many characters were read during the preceding read command.

- `istream& ignore (int num = 1, int end = EOF)`
  skips a maximum of *num* characters, until *end* (character or EOF) appears. In order to skip all characters up to *end*, the expression `numeric_limits<int>::max()` (see Section 9.1.4 on page 531) has to be submitted as *num*.

- `int peek ()`
  returns the next character from the stream, or EOF, without consuming it. During the next read, the character is therefore still available.

- `istream& unget ()`
  puts the character that was read last back into the input stream, so that it is available to be read again next time.

- `istream& putback (char c)`
  puts the character that was read last back into the input stream, so that is available to be read again next time. *c* actually has to be the character that was read last; otherwise `badbit` is set.

With all these functions, whitespaces are not skipped.

Because an upper limit has to be entered, these functions are safer for reading strings than the `>>` operator. However, it is also possible to define a maximum number of characters before reading with `>>` (see Section 8.1.6 on page 487), although this can easily be forgotten.

The implementation of the functions for reading a fraction in Section 4.5.4 on page 208, and of a string in Section 6.1.7 on page 366, contains working examples for different read functions.

Member Functions for Output

In the `ostream` class, in addition to the `<<` operator, some member functions are defined that can be used for the output of characters:

- `ostream& put (char c)`
  outputs the submitted parameter *c* as the next character and returns the stream. Its status then gives information about whether the write was successful.

- `ostream& write(const char* cs, int num)`
  outputs *num* characters of the character string *cs*.

- `ostream& flush ()`
  empties the output buffer by writing all characters that are contained in it.

Tying Input and Output Streams

Input and output streams can be connected together using a special member function:

- `ostream* tie (ostream* os)`
  connects a stream with the submitted output stream *os*.

This has the consequence that if an input operation is called for the stream, the output buffer of the output stream is flushed.

For standard I/O, this is already defined by default:

// tie standard input buffer to standard output buffer
```
std::cin.tie(&std::cout);
```

This ensures that a prompt for inputting is visible before an input value is read:

```
std::cout << "Please input x: ";
std::cin >> x;
```

In fact, before x is read, an implicit `flush()` is called for `std::cout`.

Note that the *address* of an output stream must be passed as a parameter. This ensures that 0 or NULL can be submitted, which cancels an existing coupling:

// cancel coupling of cin *to all output streams*
```
std::cin.tie(static_cast<std::ostream*>(0));
```

The previous coupled stream is returned (a pointer to the output stream, or 0). A call without any parameter is also possible, and returns the current tied stream (or 0).

Examples

The classic filter framework, which simply outputs all the characters that have been read, looks as follows in C++:

```
// io/charcat1.cpp

#include <iostream>

int main()
{
    char c;

    // as long as a character c can be read
    while (std::cin.get(c)) {
        // output characters
        std::cout.put(c);
    }
}
```

Note that, in contrast to the C version, characters that have been read are not tested for EOF and therefore c does not have to be declared as an `int`. This is possible because we read into the passed argument c, so that the return value can be used to test the status of the stream.

As a small improvement, a test can be carried out to see whether the program was actually ended via EOF, and whether the output stream is in a fault-free status:

```
// io/charcat2.cpp

#include <iostream>
#include <cstdlib>

int main()
{
    char c;

    // as long as a character c can be read
    while (std::cin.get(c)) {
        // output character
        std::cout.put(c);
    }

    if (! std::cin.eof()) {
        std::cerr << "read error" << std::endl;
        return EXIT_FAILURE;
    }
    if (! std::cout.good()) {
        std::cerr << "write error" << std::endl;
        return EXIT_FAILURE;
    }
}
```

8.1.5 Manipulators

As was mentioned in Section 4.5.2 on page 199, different manipulators are defined for streams. These are global objects, which, if they are called with the standard input or output operator, manipulate the stream in some way. Table 8.6 lists all standard manipulators from `<istream>` and `<ostream>`. Additional manipulators are provided for formatting. These are introduced in the following sections.

Manipulator	Class	Meaning
flush	ostream	empty output buffer
endl	ostream	output '\n' and empty output buffer
ends	ostream	output '\0' and empty output buffer
ws	istream	skip whitespaces

Table 8.6. Fundamental manipulators

How Manipulators Operate

There is actually a simple trick behind manipulators, which demonstrates how powerful the act of overloading functions can be. Manipulators are nothing more than functions that are called when they are passed to an input or output operator as a second argument.

For the class `ostream`, the output operator is, in principle, overloaded as follows (here, this is pseudo-code for a definition of the class `ostream`; the actual code of the class `basic_ostream<>` is parametrized according to the template parameter):

```
class ostream : ... {
    ...
    ostream& operator << (ostream& (*func)(ostream&)) {
        return (*func)(*this);
    }
};
```

If the `<<` operator is passed a function *func* as its second operand, which takes an `ostream` object as a parameter and returns an `ostream` object, this function is called with the `ostream` object for which the operator `<<` is called.

This sounds rather complicated, but is actually relatively simple. The function (the manipulator) `endl()` is, in principle, defined in the following way (some details are left out, because, instead of `ostream`, the class `basic_ostream<>` is actually used):

```
namespace std {
    ostream& endl(ostream& strm)
    {
        // output newline
        strm << '\n';

        // empty output buffer
        strm.flush();

        // return strm for chaining
        return strm;
    }
}
```

Through the statement

```
std::cout << std::endl
```

the `<<` operator is called with the parameter `std::endl`:

```
std::cout.operator<<(std::endl)
```

Because `std::endl` is a function, this call is converted so that the function passed as an argument is called with the stream as a parameter:

```
std::endl(std::cout);
```

This call finally outputs a line separator and empties the output buffer.

User-Defined Manipulators

It is possible to define manipulators at any time. To do so, as with endl(), only one appropriate function needs to be written.

With the following function, for example, a manipulator for skipping to the end of a line is defined:

```
// io/ignore.hpp

#include <iostream>
#include <limits>

inline
std::istream& ignoreLine(std::istream& strm)
{
    char c;

    // ignore all characters up to the end of the line
    strm.ignore(std::numeric_limits<int>::max(),'\n');

    // return strm for chaining
    return strm;
}
```

The function ignore() skips all characters, up to the line end (see Section 8.1.4 on page 479).

The use of the manipulator is fairly simple:

```
// ignore remainder of the line
std::cin >> ignoreLine;
```

By means of multiple calls, multiple lines can be ignored:

```
// ignore two lines
std::cin >> ignoreLine >> ignoreLine;
```

8.1.6   Format Definitions

For the definition of I/O formats, different members are defined in the ios_base class that define, for example, a minimum field width or the number of positions of floating-point values. In one of these members, a number of format flags are managed as bit constants. Using these format flags, for example, the output of a plus sign can be induced.

Some of these format flags belong together, such as, for example, the flags that activate the octal, decimal or hexadecimal output. In order to simplify the management of these kinds of flags, masks are defined, which manage certain groups of flags.

Setting and Querying Format Flags

For general access to the format flags, the functions that are listed in Table 8.7 are defined.

Member Function	Meaning
setf (*flags*)	sets *flags* as additional format flags and returns the previous status of all format flags
setf (*flags, mask*)	sets *flags* as the new format flag of the group identified by *mask* and returns the previous status of all format flags
unsetf (*flags*)	deletes *flags*
flags()	returns all set format flags
flags (*flags*)	sets *flags* as new format flags and returns the previous status of all format flags
copyfmt (*stream*)	copies *all* format definitions from *stream*

Table 8.7. Member functions for format flags

The functions setf() and unsetf() set and delete flags, respectively. The flags must be combined with the | operator. setf() can be passed a mask that results in all flags being deleted in the appropriate group. For example:

```
// set flags showpos and uppercase
std::cout.setf(std::ios::showpos | std::ios::uppercase);

// only set the flag hex in the group basefield
std::cout.setf(std::ios::hex, std::ios::basefield);

// delete flag uppercase
std::cout.unsetf(std::ios::uppercase);
```

Using flags(), one can retrieve all the flags that have been set and define a new status of set flags. So one can, for example, store a set of flags and later restore it:

```
using std::ios;
using std::cout;

// mark current format flags
ios::fmtflags oldFlags = cout.flags();

// change this and that
cout.setf(ios::showpos | ios::showbase | ios::uppercase);
cout.setf(ios::internal, ios::adjustfield);
...

// restore status of old flags again
cout.flags(oldFlags);
```

One can also change the flags with the manipulators listed in Table 8.8.

Manipulator	Meaning
setiosflags (*flags*)	sets *flags* as format flags (calls setf (*flags*) for the stream)
resetiosflags (*mask*)	deletes all flags of the group identified by *mask* (calls setf (0, *mask*) for the stream)

Table 8.8. Manipulators for format flags

For these manipulators, as with all manipulators with parameters, the header file <iomanip> has to be included. For example:

```
#include <iostream>
#include <iomanip>
...
std::cout << resetiosflags(std::ios::adjustfield) // delete alignment flags
          << setiosflags(std::ios::left);         // set left-aligned flag
```

For almost all format-flag manipulations, there are also special manipulators. As a rule, they are easier to handle and more readable, and should therefore be used when possible.

Field Width, Alignment, and Filling Symbol

For the definition of field width and filling symbol, the member functions width() and fill() are defined (see Table 8.9).

Member Function	Meaning
width()	returns the actual field width for reading and writing
width(*value*)	sets the current field width to *value* and returns the previous field width
fill()	returns the current filling symbol
fill(*c*)	defines *c* as a current filling symbol and returns the previous filling symbol

Table 8.9. Member functions for field width and filling symbol

Using the member function width(), a minimum field width can be defined for an output. However, note that this setting only refers to the output that follows directly, as long as it is not the output of a char. Without parameters, the current minimal field width is returned; with parameters, a new minimal field width is set and the previous one returned. The default value is 0. This is also the value to which the field width is set after a value has been written.

Note that the field width is never used to truncate output. Thus, you cannot specify a maximum field width. Instead, you have to program it. For example, you could write to a string and output only a certain number of characters.

Using the member function `fill()`, a filling symbol can be defined and queried. The default filling symbol is a space.

For alignment within a field, there are three flags. These are defined in the class `ios`, with an appropriate mask, as shown in Table 8.10.

Mask	Flags	Meaning
adjustfield	left	left aligned
	right	right aligned
	internal	left-aligned sign, right-aligned value
	none	right aligned (the default)

Table 8.10. Flags for alignment

In contrast to the field width, filling symbols and alignment remain valid until a new command defines something else.

Table 8.11 shows the effects of the functions and flags during the output of different constants. The underscore is used as a filling symbol.

Alignment	width()	–42	0.12	"Q"	'Q'
left	6	-42___	0.12__	Q_____	Q_____
right	6	___-42	__0.12	_____Q	_____Q
internal	6	-___42	__0.12	_____Q	_____Q

Table 8.11. Examples of alignment

For the `width()` and `fill()` member functions, the manipulators shown in Table 8.12 are defined. In order to make the manipulators available, the header file `<iomanip>` has to be included.

Manipulator	Meaning
setw(*val*)	sets the field width for I/O to *val* (corresponds to `width()`)
setfill(*c*)	defines *c* as the fill character (corresponds to `fill()`)
left	forces left-aligned output
right	forces right-aligned output
internal	forces left-aligned sign and right-aligned value

Table 8.12. Manipulators for alignment

For example, the statements

```
#include <iostream>
#include <iomanip>
...
std::cout << std::setfill('_');
std::cout << std::left << std::setw(8) << "1."
          << std::right << std::setw(8) << 3.14 << std::endl;
std::cout << std::left << std::setw(8) << "2."
          << std::right << std::setw(8) << 7.33 << std::endl;
std::cout << std::left << std::setw(8) << "Sum:"
          << std::right << std::setw(8) << 10.47 << std::endl;
```

produce the following output:

```
1._____3.14
2._____7.33
Sum:_____10.47
```

Using Field Width for Input

You can also use the field width to define the maximum number of characters read when character sequences of type char* are input. If the value of width() is not 0, then at most width()−1 characters are read.

To be on the safe side, width() should always be used if C-strings are read with the >> operator, because otherwise, if there are too many characters, the memory behind the C-string is simply overridden:

```
char buffer[81];
```

// read a maximum of 80 characters as a C-string
```
std::cin >> std::setw(sizeof(buffer)) >> buffer;
```

Better and easier is, of course, the use of a string. In contrast to C-strings, strings can be read without hesitation, because they automatically reserve appropriate memory internally:

```
std::string s;
```

```
std::cin >> s;     // OK
```

Positive Signs and Uppercase Letters

Two format flags influence the output of numbers: showpos and uppercase (see Table 8.13).

Use of the showpos flag forces the output of a positive sign. The flag uppercase defines that, during the output of numbers, uppercase letters are output instead of lowercase ones. This affects integral numbers that are output in hexadecimal form and floating-point values that are output in scientific notation.

Flag	Meaning
showpos	forces the writing of positive signs
uppercase	forces the use of uppercase letters

Table 8.13. Flags for signs and letters of numeric values

For example, the statements

```
std::cout << 12345678.9 << std::endl;

std::cout.setf (std::ios::showpos | std::ios::uppercase);
std::cout << 12345678.9 << std::endl;
```

produce the following output:

```
1.23457e+07
+1.23457E+07
```

Both flags can be set or deleted with the manipulators listed in Table 8.14.

Manipulator	Meaning
showpos	forces the output of a positive sign (sets the flag ios::showpos)
noshowpos	prevents the output of a positive sign (deletes the flag ios::showpos)
uppercase	forces the use of uppercase letters (sets the flag ios::uppercase)
nouppercase	forces the use of lowercase letters (deletes the flag ios::uppercase)

Table 8.14. Manipulators for signs and letters of numeric values

Numeric Base

A group of three flags defines what base is used for I/O of integer values. The flags are defined in the class `ios_base`, with the corresponding mask (see Table 8.15).

Mask	Flags	Meaning
basefield	oct	I/O octal
	dec	I/O decimal (default)
	hex	I/O hexadecimal
	none	output decimal and input in accordance with the leading character of the integral values

Table 8.15. Flags for the numeric base of integral values

A change in base applies to the processing of all integer numbers until the flags are reset. By default, decimal format is used.

If no flag is set for the numeric base (this is not the default), the base of read values depends on the leading characters of the value. If a value begins with 0x or 0X, the number is read as a hexadecimal; if it begins with 0, it is read as an octal; otherwise, it is read as a decimal.

There are basically two ways to switch between these flags:

1. Set a flag and reset the other one:
```
std::cout.unsetf(std::ios::dec);
std::cout.setf(std::ios::hex);
```

2. Set a flag and in the process reset all other flags of the mask automatically:
```
std::cout.setf(std::ios::hex, std::ios::basefield);
```

In addition, manipulators are defined that significantly simplify handling of these flags (see Table 8.16).

Manipulator	Meaning
oct	I/O octal
dec	I/O decimal
hex	I/O hexadecimal

Table 8.16. Manipulators for the numeric base of integral values

For example, the following statements output x and y hexadecimal and z decimal:
```
int x, y, z;
...
std::cout << std::hex << x << std::endl;
std::cout << y << " " << std::dec << z << std::endl;
```

An additional flag, showbase, lets you write numbers according to the usual C/C++ convention for indicating numeric bases of literal values (see Table 8.17).

Flag	Meaning
showbase	if set, indicates the numeric base

Table 8.17. Flags to indicate the numeric base

If the showbase flag is set, octal numbers are written with a leading 0 and hexadecimal numbers are written with a leading 0x (or 0X if ios::uppercase is set).

For example, the statements

```
std::cout << 127 << ' ' << 255 << std::endl;

std::cout << std::hex << 127 << ' ' << 255 << std::endl;

std::cout.setf(std::ios::showbase);
std::cout << 127 << ' ' << 255 << std::endl;

std::cout.setf(std::ios::uppercase);
std::cout << 127 << ' ' << 255 << std::endl;
```

produce the following output:

```
127 255
7f ff
0x7f 0xff
0X7F 0XFF
```

The showbase flag can also be set or deleted with the manipulators given in Table 8.18.

Manipulator	Meaning
showbase	show numeric base (sets the flag ios::showbase)
noshowbase	do not show numeric base (deletes the flag ios::showbase)

Table 8.18. Manipulators to indicate the numeric base

Floating-Point Notation

For the output of floating-point values, there are several format flags and members. The flags listed in Table 8.19 basically define whether the output is given in decimal or exponential representation. They are defined in the class ios, with the appropriate mask. If ios::fixed is set, floating-point values are output with the decimal notation. If ios::scientific is set, the scientific (exponential) notation is used.

Mask	Flag	Meaning
floatfield	fixed	decimal representation
	scientific	exponential representation
	none	use the 'best' of these two notations (default)

Table 8.19. Flags for the representation of floating-point values

For the definition of precision, there is the member function precision() (see Table 8.20).

Without parameters, the precision is returned. With parameters, the passed value is set as the new precision (and the old value is returned). The default value for the precision is 6.

Member Function	Meaning
precision()	returns the current precision of floating-point values
precision(*val*)	sets *val* as the new precision of floating-point values and returns the old precision

Table 8.20. Member function for the precision of floating-point values

If the ios::fixed flag is set, floating-point values are written in decimal representation; if the ios::scientific flag is set, exponential representation is used. The precision set using precision() defines the number of places after the decimal point in both cases. Note that it is not simply cut off, but rounded.

By default, neither ios::fixed nor ios::scientific is set. In this case, the notation used depends on the value written. All meaningful but, at most, precision() decimal places are written as follows: A leading zero before the decimal point and/or all trailing zeros, and potentially even the decimal point, are removed. If precision() places are sufficient, decimal notation is used; otherwise, scientific notation is used.

Using showpoint, we can explicitly request that the decimal point and trailing zeros are written until there are sufficient precision() places (see Table 8.21).

Flag	Meaning
showpoint	forces the output of a decimal point

Table 8.21. Flag for the output of a decimal point

For example of two concrete values, the somewhat more complicated dependencies of the flags and the precision are shown in Table 8.22.

	precision()	421.0	0.0123456789
normal	2	4.2e+02	0.012
	6	421	0.0123457
with showpoint	2	4.2e+02	0.012
	6	421.000	0.0123457
fixed	2	421.00	0.01
	6	421.000000	0.012346
scientific	2	4.21e+02	1.23e-02
	6	4.210000e+02	1.234568e-02

Table 8.22. Examples of the formatting of floating-point values

The output of a positive sign can also be forced for floating-point values, using the showpos flag. Similarly, use the uppercase flag with the scientific notation, forces a large E.

The notation and the precision of floating-point values can also be changed using the manipulators listed in Table 8.23. Because `setprecision` is a manipulator with parameters, the header file `<iomanip>` has to be included.

Manipulator	Meaning
`fixed`	forces decimal notation
`scientific`	forces scientific notation
`setprecision(`*value*`)`	sets *value* as the new value for the precision
`showpoint`	forces the output of a decimal point (sets the flag `ios::showpoint`)
`noshowpoint`	a decimal point is only output if needed (deletes the flag `ios::showpoint`)

Table 8.23. Manipulators for floating-point values

For example, the statement

```
std::cout << std::scientific << std::showpoint
          << std::setprecision(8)
          << 0.123456789 << std::endl;
```

produces the following output:

```
1.23456789e-01
```

I/O Format of Boolean Values

The `boolalpha` flag defines the format that is used to read and write Boolean values. It determines whether a numeric or a textual representation is used (see Table 8.24).

Flag	Meaning
`boolalpha`	if set, textual representation; if not set, numeric representation

Table 8.24. Flag for the representation of Boolean values

If the `boolalpha` flag is not set (this is the default behavior), a numeric representation is used for the input and output of Boolean values. In this case, 0 is used for `false` and 1 for `true`. If a Boolean value is read that is neither 0 nor 1, this is regarded as an error and `failbit` is set in the stream.

If the `boolalpha` flag is set, Boolean values are shown in a textual form. To do so, the textual representation of `true` and `false` that belong to the respective language environment are used. In the standard language environment of C++, these are the character strings 'true' and 'false'; in other language environments, there may be other character strings (for example, 'wahr' and 'falsch' within a German environment).

Special manipulators are defined for the convenient manipulation of this flag (see Table 8.25).

Manipulator	Meaning
boolalpha	forces the textual representation (sets the flag ios::boolalpha)
noboolalpha	forces the numeric representation (deletes the flag ios::boolalpha)

Table 8.25. Manipulators for the representation of Boolean values

For example, using the following statements, the value of the Boolean variable b is written once numerically and once textually:

```
bool b;
...
std::cout << std::noboolalpha << b << " == "
          << std::boolalpha << b << std::endl;
```

Depending of the value of b and the current language environment, the output may read:

```
0 == false
```

General Format Definitions

Two flags are still missing in the list of format flags: skipws and unitbuf (see Table 8.26).

Flag	Meaning
skipws	skip leading whitespaces with >> operator
unitbuf	empty output buffer after every output operation

Table 8.26. Other flags for formatting

The skipws flag is set by default. This causes the >> operator to skip leading whitespaces. This is helpful in order to, for example, automatically skip the separating whitespaces when reading in numeric values. However, this means that, using the >> operator, no whitespaces can be read. In order to make this possible, the flag has to be set.

The unitbuf flag controls the buffering of outputs. If unitbuf is set, outputs are basically written without being buffered. After every output operation, the output buffer is automatically flushed. This flag is normally not set by default, which means that the outputs are buffered. With the standard streams for error outputs, cerr and wcerr, this flag is set automatically in order to force the unbuffered output.

Both flags can be set and unset using the manipulators listed in Table 8.27.

Manipulator	Meaning
skipws	skips leading whitespaces with the >> operator (sets the flag ios::skipws)
noskipws	does not skip leading whitespaces with the >> operator (deletes the flag ios::skipws)
unitbuf	empties the output buffer after every output operation (sets the flag ios::unitbuf)
nounitbuf	does not empty the output buffer after every output operation (deletes the flag ios::unitbuf)

Table 8.27. Manipulators of the other flags for formatting

8.1.7   Internationalization

One can format I/O according to national conventions. One such internationalization (or, in short, $i18n$[2]) is supported via the class std::locale.

Each stream belongs to a language environment via its association with a so-called 'locale' object. The initial locale is a copy of the global language environment attached at the time when the stream was created. It can be queried and changed with the functions listed in Table 8.28.

Member Function	Meaning
getloc()	returns the current locale
imbue(*loc*)	sets *loc* as the current locale

Table 8.28. Member functions for internationalization

The following example shows how these member functions can be used:

```
// io/loc1.cpp

#include <iostream>
#include <locale>

int main()
{
    // use the classic language environment in order to
    // read from the standard input
    std::cin.imbue(std::locale::classic());

    // use a German language environment in order to write data
    std::cout.imbue(std::locale("de_DE"));
```

---

[2] *i18n* is a common abbreviation for '*i*, followed by 18 characters, followed by *n*'.

```
// read and output floating-point numbers in a loop
double value;
while (std::cin >> value) {
    std::cout << value << std::endl;
}
}
```

The statement

```
std::cin.imbue(std::locale::classic());
```

assigns the 'classic' locale to the standard input channel `cin`, which behaves like classic C. The expression

```
std::locale::classic()
```

creates an appropriate object of the class `std::locale`.

The statement

```
std::cout.imbue(std::locale("de_DE"));
```

assigns the locale `de_DE` to the standard output channel. The string `de_DE` stands for 'German in Germany'. The general syntax for locale names is as follows:

language[_*area*[.*character coding*]]

Table 8.29 presents a selection of typical language strings. However, note that these strings are *not* yet standardized. For example, sometimes the first character of *language* is capitalized. Some implementations deviate from the format mentioned previously and, for example, use `english` to select an English locale. All in all, the locales that are supported by a system are implementation specific.

The expression

```
std::locale("de_DE"));
```

is only successful if this locale is supported by the system. If this is not the case, an exception of the type `std::runtime_error` (see Section 3.6.3 on page 95) is thrown.

If everything works, the input is read according to the classic (English) conventions and the output is written according to German conventions. In the example, the loop therefore reads floating-point values in English format and writes them in German format. So, for example, the value read as

47.11

is written as

47,11

Normally, a program only defines locales if, for example, configuration data are read from a file and one has to make sure that this data can be read independently from the current locale (with a German locale, for example, there would be an attempt to read in 47.11 as a floating-point value and to return the value 47, because the point terminats the floating-point value). Instead,

Locale	Meaning
C	default: ANSI-C conventions (English, 7 bit)
ge_GE	German in Germany
ge_GE.88591	German in Germany with ISO Latin-1 encoding
ge_AU	German in Austria
de_CH	German in Switzerland
en_US	English in the USA
en_GB	English in Great Britain
en_AU	English in Australia
en_CA	English in Canada
fr_FR	French in France
fr_CH	French in Switzerland
fr_CA	French in Canada
ja_JP.jis	Japanese in Japan with *Japanese Industrial Standard (JIS)* encoding
ja_JP.sjis	Japanese in Japan with *Shift JIS* encoding
ja_JP.ujis	Japanese in Japan with *UNIX JIS* encoding
ja_JP.EUC	Japanese in Japan with *Extended UNIX code* encoding
ko_KR	Korean in Korea
zh_CN	Chinese in China
zh_TW	Chinese in Taiwan
lt_LN.bit7	ISO Latin, 7 bit
lt_LN.bit8	ISO Latin, 8 bit
POSIX	POSIX conventions (English, 7 bit)

Table 8.29. Selection of names for locales

the locale normally determines the language environment by means of the environment variable LANG. If one submits an empty string to the locale object for initialization, the corresponding object is created:

```
std::locale langLocale("");   // locale by means of LANG
```

Using the member function name(), one can prompt the name of a locale as a string:

```
// output name of the locale
std::cout << langLocale.name() << std::endl;
```

8.1.8 Summary

- By default, stream classes are available for I/O. Classes for input, for output and for input and output are differentiated.
- Numerous functions are predefined for stream classes. Besides the actual I/O operations, these include functions for format definition, accessing status bits, automatic triggering of exceptions and for internationalization.

- Manipulators allow streams to be manipulated in input or output statements. They can also be defined by the user.
- Formatting is controlled not only by member functions, but also by numerous flags and manipulators.

8.2   File Access

This section describes the features of the stream classes that provide access to files.

8.2.1   Stream Classes for Files

The following special stream types are made available for file access:

1. The class template `basic_ifstream<>`, with the two specializations `ifstream` and `wifstream`, are used for read access to files ('input file stream').
2. The class template `basic_ofstream<>`, with the two specializations `ofstream` and `wofstream`, are used for write access to files ('output file stream').
3. The class template `basic_fstream<>`, with the two specializations `fstream` and `wfstream`, are used for files that can have read and write access.
4. The class template `basic_filebuf<>`, with the specializations `filebuf` and `wfilebuf`, are used by other file-stream classes for the actual reading and writing.

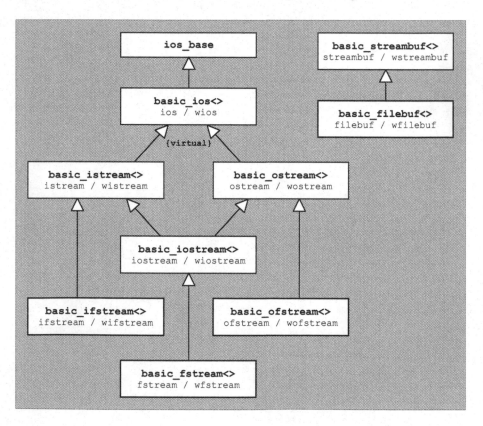

Figure 8.2. Hierarchy of the file-stream classes

These types are defined in the header file <fstream> and are associated with the fundamental stream classes, as is shown in Figure 8.2.

A considerable advantage of the file-stream classes, as compared to the file-access mechanisms of C, is that the files are automatically opened during the declaration of the objects and are automatically closed when the object is destroyed. This is guaranteed by the appropriate constructors and destructors. However, because opening a file can fail, one should check the stream state after the construction of a file-stream object.

8.2.2 Application of the Stream Classes for Files

The following sample program opens the file charset.out in order to output the current character set (all characters with values 32 to 255):

```cpp
// io/charset2.cpp

#include <string>        // for strings
#include <iostream>      // for I/O
#include <fstream>       // for file I/O
#include <iomanip>       // for setw()
#include <cstdlib>       // for EXIT_FAILURE

// forward declarations
void writeCharsetInFile(const std::string& filename);
void printFile(const std::string& filename);

int main()
{
    try {
        writeCharsetInFile("charset.out");
        printFile ("charset.out");
    }
    catch (const std::string& msg) {
        std::cerr << "Exception: " << msg << std::endl;
        return EXIT_FAILURE;
    }
}

void writeCharsetInFile(const std::string& filename)
{
    // open file for writing
    std::ofstream file(filename.c_str());
```

```
      // was the file really opened?
      if (! file) {
          // NO, throw exception
          throw "cannot open file \"" + filename
                + "\" for writing";
      }

      // write character set into file
      for (int i=32; i<127; ++i) {
          // output value as number and character:
          file << "value: " << std::setw(3) << i << "   "
               << "character: " << static_cast<char>(i) << std::endl;
      }

}     // closes file automatically

void printFile(const std::string& filename)
{
      // open file for reading
      std::ifstream file(filename.c_str());

      // was file really opened?
      if (! file) {
          // NO, throw exception
          throw "cannot open file \"" + filename
                + "\" for reading";
      }

      // copy all characters of the file to std::cout
      char c;
      while (file.get(c)) {
          std::cout.put(c);
      }

}     // closes the file automatically
```

In writeCharSetInFile(), the constructor of the class ofstream makes sure that the file whose name was passed is opened with the creation of the object:

```
// open file for writing
std::ofstream file(filename.c_str());
```

With the following query, it is determined whether the status of the stream is OK, and therefore whether the opening was successful:

```
// was the file really opened?
if (! file) {
    // NO, throw exception
    throw "cannot open file \"" + filename
            + "\" for writing";
}
```

Finally, in a loop, all values from 32 to 126 are written, with the appropriate characters:

```
// write character set into file
for (int i=32; i<127; ++i) {
    // output value as number and character:
    file << "value: " << std::setw(3) << i << "    "
            << "character: " << static_cast<char>(i) << std::endl;
}
```

At the end of the function, the file is automatically closed, because the scope of the object is left. The destructor of the class ofstream is defined accordingly.

Similarly, the file submitted for reading is opened in printFile(). Again, if this fails, an appropriate exception is thrown. Otherwise, all the characters are read from the file and are output to the standard output channel cout. The opened file is automatically closed when the function is exited.

8.2.3   File Flags

For the access mode of the file processing there are some flags defined in the ios_base class (see Table 8.30).

Flag	Meaning
in	open for reading (default with ifstream)
out	open for writing (default with ofstream)
app	always append when writing
ate	position at the end of the file after opening
trunc	delete previous file content
binary	do not replace special characters

Table 8.30. Flags for opening files

The binary flag should be set for access to binary files (such as executable programs). By doing so, it is ensured that the characters are read and written as they are. If binary is not set, it is automatically taken into account that, in the world of Windows, the line end is not marked by a newline character, but by the CarriageReturn/LineFeed character sequence (CR/LF).

Without `binary`, therefore, on Windows systems, during the read, the CR/LF character sequence is converted into the newline character, and, during the write, a newline is written as the CR/LF character sequence.

Some implementations provide additional flags, such as `nocreate` (the file must exist when it is opened) and `noreplace` (the file must not exist). However, these flags are not standard and thus are not portable.

The flags can be combined with the | operator. They are then submitted to the constructor as an optional second argument. For example, the following statement opens a file for writing and makes sure that the written text is appended at the end of the file:

```
std::ofstream file("xyz.out", std::ios::out | std::ios::app);
```

Table 8.31 correlates the various combinations of flags with the strings used in the interface of C's function for opening files: `fopen()`. The combinations with `binary` and `ate` are not included. A set `binary` flag corresponds to strings with b appended, and a set `ate` flag corresponds to a seek to the end of the file immediately after opening. Other combinations not listed in the table, such as `trunc | app`, are illegal.

`ios_base` Flags	Meaning	C Mode
`in`	read (file has to exist)	`"r"`
`out`	empty and write (create if necessary)	`"w"`
`out|trunc`	empty and write (create if necessary)	`"w"`
`out|app`	append (create if necessary)	`"a"`
`in|out`	read and write (file has to exist)	`"r+"`
`in|out|trunc`	empty, read and write (create if necessary)	`"w+"`

Table 8.31. Meaning of the flag combinations for opening files

8.2.4   Explicitly Opening and Closing Files

If a file object is produced without it being initialized, no file is opened. However, it can be explicitly opened later using the member function `open()`. Similarly, an opened file can be explicitly closed using `close()`. It can also be queried whether a file is opened or not (see Table 8.32).

Member Function	Meaning
`open(`*name*`)`	opens a file with the default mode of the stream
`open(`*name*`,`*flags*`)`	opens a file with *flags* as a mode
`close()`	closes a file
`is_open()`	returns whether a file is open

Table 8.32. Member functions for explicitly opening and closing files

The following example shows one possible use. It opens all files, one after the other, submitted as parameters in the command line and outputs their contents (this corresponds to the UNIX program cat):

```cpp
// io/cat1.cpp

// header files
#include <fstream>
#include <iostream>
using namespace std;

/* for all passed filenames in the command line
 * - open file, output content and close file
 */
int main (int argc, char* argv[])
{
    // create file stream for reading (without opening a file)
    std::ifstream file;

    // for all arguments from the command line
    for (int i=1; i<argc; ++i) {
        // open file
        file.open(argv[i]);

        // output content of file
        char c;
        while (file.get(c)) {
            std::cout.put(c);
        }

        // clear eofbit and failbit (were set because of EOF)
        file.clear();

        // close file
        file.close();
    }
}
```

Inside the program, the submitted filenames are sequentially opened as file, then output and closed again. Note that, after the output of the contents, clear() is always called. This is necessary because eofbit and failbit are set at the end of the file and these must be cleared before every other operation. open() does not clear these bits. This is also the case if different file is opened.

8.2.5 Random File Access

For positioning in files, C++ provides the member functions listed in Table 8.33.

Member Function	Meaning
`tellg()`	provides a read position
`seekg(`*pos*`)`	sets *pos* as an absolute read position
`seekg(`*offset*,*rpos*`)`	sets *pos* as reading position relative to *offset*
`tellp()`	provides a write position
`seekp(`*pos*`)`	sets *pos* as absolute write position
`seekp(`*offset*,*rpos*`)`	sets *pos* as write position relative to *offset*

Table 8.33. Member functions for positioning in files

For safety, the read and write positions are distinguished between g (stands for 'get') and p (stands for 'put'). The reading position functions are defined in `istream`, while the writing position functions are defined in `ostream`. This does not mean, however, that they can be called for all objects of the `istream` and `ostream` classes. For example, a call to `cin`, `cout` or `cerr` does not make sense. Positioning in files is defined in the base classes because, usually, references to objects of type `istream` and `ostream` are passed as parameters.

The `seekg()` and `seekp()` funstions are called with absolute or relative position statements:

- To handle absolute positions, you must use `tellg()` and `tellp()`. They return an absolute position as a value of type `pos_type`. This value is *not* an integral value, or simply the position of the character as an index. This is because the logical position and the real position can differ. For example, in MS-DOS text files, newline characters are represented by two characters in the file, even though it is logically only one character. Things are even worse if the file uses some form of multi-byte representation for the characters.

  For example:

  // mark current position
  ```
  std::ios::pos_type pos = file.tellg();
  ```
  ...
  // go back to marked position
  ```
  file.seekg(pos);
  ```

  Note that there is a special type for file positions, `std::ios::pos_type`. One can also use `std::streampos` instead. The use of an integral type such as `long`, on the other hand, is not allowed[3]. Thus it is not allowed to use integral values as absolute stream positions.

- For relative values, the offset can be relative to three positions. The corresponding constants are defined by the `ios_base` class and are of type `seekdir`. They are shown in Table 8.34.

---

[3] This was possible in some C++ versions before the standardization.

Constant	Meaning
beg	relative to start of file ('begin')
cur	relative to the current position ('current')
end	relative to the end of the file ('end')

Table 8.34. Constants for relative file positions

For example:

```
// position at the start
file.seekp(0, std::ios::beg);

...

// position 20 characters later
file.seekp(20, std::ios::cur);

...

// position 10 characters before the end
file.seekp(-10, std::ios::end);
```

Note that it is impossible to position before the start of the file or after the end of the file. Otherwise the behavior is not defined.

The following example demonstrates the use of the above functions for positioning by means of a function that outputs the same file twice:

```
// io/cat2.cpp

// header files
#include <iostream>
#include <fstream>
#include <string>

void printFileTwice(const std::string& filename)
{
    char c;

    // open file for reading
    std::ifstream file(filename.c_str());

    // output content of the file for the first time
    while (file.get(c)) {
        std::cout.put(c);
    }

    // clear eofbit and failbit (were set because of EOF)
    file.clear();
```

```
// set read position to the start of the file
file.seekg(0);

// output content of the file for the second time
while (file.get(c)) {
    std::cout.put(c);
}
}

int main(int argc, char* argv[])
{
    // output all passed files in the command line twice
    for (int i=1; i<argc; ++i) {
        printFileTwice(argv[i]);
    }
}
```

Note that, at the end of the file, `eofbit` and `failbit` are set. By doing so, a positioning of the stream is no longer possible. For this reason, `clear()` has to be called before the call of `seekg()`.

8.2.6   Redirecting the Standard Channels into Files

Through the manipulation of the stream buffer, we can redirect I/O within a program. This means that, for example, we can make sure that all outputs to `cout` are not written on the standard output, but to a file instead[4].

The secret is simply to assign another stream buffer to the standard stream:

```
std::ofstream file("cout.txt");   // open file
std::cout.rdbuf(file.rdbuf());    // assign stream buffer to cout
```

By doing so, one can optionally submit all formatting information using `copyfmt()`:

```
std::ofstream file("cout.txt");   // open file
file.copyfmt(std::cout);          // copy formatting flags of cout
std::cout.rdbuf(file.rdbuf());    // assign stream buffer to cout
```

Be careful! If a file stream is destroyed when the scope is exited, the stream buffer is also destroyed. Thus, after the destructions of `file` according to the statements above, `cout` can no longer be accessed. Even the destruction of `cout` at the end of the program is critical. For this

---

[4] In older versions of C++, this was possible by means of a simple assignment, because the objects `cin`, `cout`, and `cerr` had the special type `istream_withassign` or `ostream_withassign`. These types were removed during the standardization, and replaced by the redirection mechanisms described here.

reason, after a redirecting a stream, the status before the redirection should always be restored. The following program shows a complete example:

```cpp
// io/redirect.cpp

#include <iostream>
#include <fstream>
#include <string>

void redirect(std::ostream&,const std::string&);

int main()
{
    std::cout << "first line" << std::endl;

    redirect(std::cout, "redirect.txt"); // redirect cout to redirect.txt

    std::cout << "last line" << std::endl;
}

void redirect(std::ostream& strm, const std::string& filename)
{
    // open file (with buffer) for writing
    std::ofstream file(filename.c_str());

    // save output buffer of the passed stream
    std::streambuf* strm_puffer = strm.rdbuf();

    // redirect output to the file
    strm.rdbuf(file.rdbuf());

    file << "line is directly written to the file" << std::endl;
    strm << "line is written to the redirected stream"
         << std::endl;

    // restore old output buffer of the passed stream
    strm.rdbuf(strm_puffer);

} // closes the file and the redirected buffer
```

The output of the program is as follows:

```
first line
last line
```

The content of the file `redirect.txt` is then as follows:

```
line is directly written to the file
line is written to the redirected stream
```

8.2.7 Summary

- Special stream classes allow I/O in files.
- Special member functions allow positioning in files.
- If a file is read to the end, the `eofbit` and `failbit` flags are set. These must be cleared before further operations on the stream are called.
- The standard channels can be redirected by means of assignment to other stream buffers. Such a redirection should then be reverted.

8.3 Stream Classes for Strings

The mechanisms of the stream classes can also be used for reading from strings or for writing to strings. For example, it may be useful to read in a complete line from a file and then process it. Another example is the formatted writing in a string in order to return an error message with the value of some integral numbers or other objects. Finally, one can also define common type conversions by means of formatted writing into, and formatting reading from, strings.

For the standard compliant environment, there are classes that use `strings` as streams. I will also briefly introduce classes that use C-strings as streams. They are actually out of date, but are still used and have some pitfalls you should be aware of.

8.3.1 String Stream Classes

Similarly to the stream classes for files, there are also stream classes for strings:

- The class template `basic_istringstream<>`, with the specializations `istringstream` and `wistringstream`, for formatting reading from strings ('input string stream').
- The class template `basic_ostringstream<>`, with the specializations `ostringstream` and `wostringstream`, for formatted writing into strings ('output string stream').
- The class template `basic_stringstream<>`, with the specializations `stringstream` and `wstringstream`, for formatted reading from and writing to strings.
- The class template `basic_stringbuf<>`, with the two specializations `stringbuf` and `wstringbuf`, are used by the other string-stream classes for the actual reading and writing.

These types are defined in the header file `<sstream>` and are associated to the fundamental stream classes, as is shown in Figure 8.3.

The most important operation added for string streams is the `str()` function, with which the string value of the string stream can be set or queried (see Table 8.35).

Member Function	Meaning
`str()`	returns the content of the string stream as a `string`
`str(`*string*`)`	sets the content of the string stream to *string*

Table 8.35. Fundamental operations for string streams

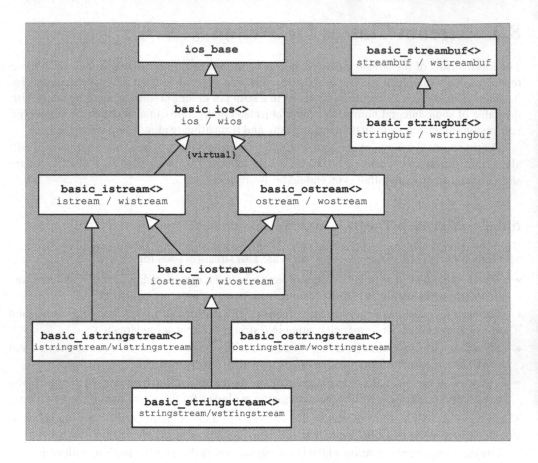

Figure 8.3. Hierarchy of the string-stream classes

Example of Formatted Writing in Strings

The following program shows the use of string streams for formatted writing in streams:

```cpp
// io/sstr1.cpp

#include <iostream>
#include <sstream>

int main()
{
    // create string stream for formatted writing
    std::ostringstream os;

    // write integral value in decimal and hexadecimal forms
```

```
os << "dec: " << 15 << std::hex << " hex: " << 15 << std::endl;

// output string stream as string
std::cout << os.str() << std::endl;

// append floating-point number
os << "float: " << 4.67 << std::endl;

// output string stream as string
std::cout << os.str() << std::endl;

// overwrite the beginning of the string stream with octal value
os.seekp(0);
os << "oct: " << std::oct << 15;

// output string stream as string
std::cout << os.str() << std::endl;
}
```

The output of the program reads as follows:

```
dec: 15 hex: f

dec: 15 hex: f
float: 4.67

oct: 17 hex: f
float: 4.67
```

First, the value 15, in both decimal and hexadecimal formats, is written to the string stream and the string is output. A floating-point value is then written to the string stream, appending it to the previous content. Then the write position is set to the start with seekp(), and the previous content of the string is overwritten by the octal value of 15. As the final output shows, the remaining characters in the string are unchanged. Because the string itself contains a line break after each line (due to the writing of std::endl), and std::endl is written again at the end of every output, the output contains a trailing blank line.

If we want to empty the string of a string stream, an empty string has to be assigned to the stream:

```
std::ostringstream os;   // create string stream
...
os.str("");              // empty string stream
```

Example of Formatted Reading from Strings

We can also read from input string streams:

```cpp
// io/sstr2.cpp

#include <iostream>
#include <sstream>

int main()
{
    // create string that will be read
    std::string s = "Pi: 3.1415";

    // create string stream for formatted reading
    // and initialize it with the string
    std::istringstream is(s);

    // read first string and value
    std::string name;
    double value;
    is >> name >> value;

    // output read data
    std::cout << "Name: " << name << std::endl;
    std::cout << "Value: " << value << std::endl;
}
```

The output of the program is as follows:

```
Name: Pi:
Value: 3.1415
```

8.3.2   Lexical Cast Operator

Using string streams and templates, we can easily implement a new operator for logical type conversions:

```cpp
// io/lexcast.hpp

#include <sstream>
```

```cpp
template<typename TargetType, typename SourceType>
TargetType lexical_cast(SourceType in)
{
    std::stringstream interpreter;
    TargetType out;

    if(!(interpreter << in) || !(interpreter >> out) ||
        !(interpreter >> std::ws).eof()) {
            throw "bad lexical cast";
    }

    return out;
}
```

The first template parameter is the destination type and is explicitly specified (see Section 7.2.4 on page 431). The second template parameter is implicitly determined by means of the passed argument. In the function, the passed argument is written to a string stream and is then read again as a value of the destination type. The last query determines whether there are characters that were not processed during the conversion. This ensures that the string '42.42' is not successfully converted into an int.

The call of this operator could look, for example, as follows:

```cpp
// io/lexcast.cpp

#include <iostream>
#include <string>
#include <cstdlib>
#include "lexcast.hpp"

int main(int argc, char* argv[])
{
    try {
        if (argc > 1) {
            // evaluate first argument as int
            int value = lexical_cast<int>(argv[1]);

            // use int as string
            std::string msg;
            msg = "The passed value is: "
                    + lexical_cast<std::string>(value);
            std::cout << msg << std::endl;
        }
    }
```

```
        catch (const char* msg) {
            std::cerr << "Exception: " << msg << std::endl;
            return EXIT_FAILURE;
        }
    }
```

In the boost repository for supplementary C++ libraries, there is a 'more condensed' version of this operator (see `http://www.boost.org`).

8.3.3 `char*` Stream Classes

The stream classes that provide formatted access to C-strings are only available due to backwards compatibility. They are, however, still used, and, because their usage creates some pitfalls, they will be briefly discussed.

Similarly to the string-stream classes, there are stream classes for type `char*`:

- The class `istrstream` for formatted reading from C-strings ('input string stream').
- The class `ostrstream` for formatted writing to C-strings.
- The class `strstream` for C-strings that are used for reading and writing.
- The class `strstreambuf` as a buffer for `char*` streams.

They are defined in the header file `<strstream>`.

Reading from `char*` Streams

An `istrstream` can be initialized with a string (type `char*`) in two ways: the string can either contain the end-of-string character '`\0`', or the number of characters in the string can be passed as an additional argument.

A typical example is the reading and processing of a name:

```
char buffer[1000];  // buffer for a maximum of 999 characters

// read line
std::cin.get(buffer,sizeof(buffer));

// process line as a stream
std::istrstream input(buffer);
...
input >> x;
```

Writing to char* Streams

A char* stream for writing can either have a dynamic size or be initialized with a buffer of a fixed size. With ios::app or ios::ate, one can append the character written to the string stream to the characters that are already in the buffer.

With the member function str(), the content of the string is provided. However, the following has to be taken into account:

- Provided that the char* stream was not initialized with a buffer of a fixed size, the ownership of the buffer is transferred to the caller of str(). To avoid memory leaks, you have to return the buffer back to the char* stream again, using freeze().
- After the call of str(), the stream is frozen and can no longer be manipulated. By calling freeze(), you can ensure that the char* stream can be manipulated once more.
- str() does *not* append and end-of-string character '\0'. If this is required, it must be explicitly appended using the manipulator std::ends (see Section 8.1.5 on page 481).

The following program shows how char* streams can be used for formatted writing:

```cpp
// io/charstr1.cpp

#include <iostream>
#include <strstream>

int main()
{
    // create dynamic char* stream for writing
    std::ostrstream buffer;

    // write formatted string and append end-of-string character
    buffer << "Pi: " << 3.1415 << std::ends;

    /* output character string
     * - str() freezes the char* stream
     */
    std::cout << buffer.str() << std::endl;

    // cancel the freezing
    buffer.freeze(false);

    // position so that std::ends is overwritten
    buffer.seekp(-1,std::ios::end);

    // write into char* stream further
    buffer << " or also: " << std::scientific << 3.1415
           << std::ends;
```

```
/* output character string
 * - str() freezes the char* stream
 */
std::cout << buffer.str() << std::endl;

// cancel the freezing, so that memory is freed by char* stream destructor
buffer.freeze(false);
}
```

The program has the following output:

```
Pi: 3.1415
Pi: 3.1415
```

Note that the call of `str()` freezes the stream, which means that for further modifications and correct memory management you have to 'unfreeze' the stream:

```
buffer.freeze(false);
```

Note also that `std::ends` is appended, so that the string can be used as a C-string. Because this end-of-string character would terminate the C-string in the middle of the value, is must be overwritten for additional appended characters. By calling

```
buffer.seekp(-1,std::ios::end);
```

the write position is set accordingly.

All these problems do not occur with the string streams introduced in Section 8.3.1 on page 509.

8.3.4 Summary

- Special stream classes allow I/O in strings (type `string`).
- In string streams, one can set both read and write positions explicitly.
- For backwards compatibility, you can also write to and read from C-strings (type `char*`). However, this is a source of trouble and should be avoided.
- Using the user-defined operator `lexical_cast`, one can easily convert types logically.

9

Other Language Features and Details

All language features that have not been explained previously, but play an important role in practice, are introduced in this chapter. In addition to these, I will also provide some further details about the standard library.

To be more precise, this chapter covers details of STL containers (in particular, vectors), numeric limits, smart pointers, function objects, various other aspects of the use of `new` and `delete` operators, function and member pointers, the combination of C++ code with C code, and some additional keywords.

9.1   Additional Details of the Standard Library

In this section, different components of the standard library are discussed in detail. These include vectors and numeric limits. I will also list the operations available for all STL containers and all STL algorithms.

It must be pointed out once more that this book cannot cover all the details of the standard library. It would need a dedicated book to be able to do this. For further details, please refer to my book 'The C++ Standard Library—A Tutorial and Reference' (see bibliography).

9.1.1   Vector Operations

The `vector<>` class was introduced in Section 3.5.1 on page 70, and has been used at various points throughout the book. We now introduce several more possible operations.

Creating, Copying, and Destroying

Table 9.1 lists the constructors and the destructor for vectors. Vectors can be created with or without elements for initialization. In addition, an initial size can be passed without any accompanying elements, in which case the elements are created with their default constructor.

Expression	Meaning
`vector<`*type*`> v`	creates an empty vector
`vector<`*type*`> v1(v2)`	creates a vector as a copy of another vector (all elements are copied)
`vector<`*type*`> v(`*n*`)`	creates a vector with *n* elements, which are created with the default constructor
`vector<`*type*`> v(`*n*`,`*elem*`)`	creates a vector with *n* elements, which are copies of *elem*
`vector<`*type*`> v(`*beg*`,`*end*`)`	creates a vector and initializes it with copies of the elements in the range [*beg*,*end*)
`v.~vector<`*type*`>()`	deletes all elements and frees the memory

Table 9.1. Vector constructors and destructor

A vector can be initialized by another container[1]:

```
std::list<Elem> l;          // l is a linked list of elements
...
// initialize vector v with elements of the list l
std::vector<Elem> v(l.begin(),l.end());
```

---

[1] If the compiler does not support member function templates, you can only pass a container of the same type for initialization.

Comparisons

Table 9.2 lists the comparison operations for vectors.

Expression	Meaning
v1 == v2	returns whether v1 is equal to v2
v1 != v2	returns whether v1 is not equal to v2 (equivalent to !(v1 == v2))
v1 < v2	returns whether v1 is less than v2
v1 > v2	returns whether v1 is greater than v2 (equivalent to v2 < v1)
v1 <= v2	returns whether v1 is less than or equal to v2 (equivalent to !(v2 < v1))
v1 >= v2	returns whether v1 is greater than or equal to v2 (equivalent to !(v1 < v2))

Table 9.2. Comparison operators for vectors

Comparisons with the normal comparison operators are only possible between vectors of the same element type. For comparison of two containers of different classes or types, STL algorithms must be used (see Section 9.1.3 on page 526).

Size and Capacity

To use vectors effectively (and correctly), you should understand how size and capacity work hand in hand. Table 9.3 lists the appropriate operations.

Expression	Meaning
v.size()	returns the current number of elements
v.empty()	returns whether the container is empty (equivalent to size() == 0)
v.max_size()	returns the maximum possible number of elements
v.capacity()	returns the capacity (maximum number of elements without reallocation)
v.reserve(*num*)	enlarges the capacity to at least *num* elements

Table 9.3. Member functions for the size and capacity of vectors

There are three functions that can be used to query the size of vectors:

- `size()`

  Returns the current number of elements in the vector.

  The member function `empty()` checks whether the number of elements is 0 (i.e. the vector is empty).

- `max_size()`

  Returns the highest possible number of elements that a vector can hold. This value is implementation dependent. Because a vector typically manages all elements in a single memory block, there may be limitations placed on some PCs or operating systems. Otherwise, it usually returns the maximum value allowed for an index.

- `capacity()`

  Returns the number of elements that a vector can take without allocating new memory. This value is important for optimizing performance, because a request for new memory (a *reallocation*) invalidates all references to elements. This means that all iterators that refer to elements of a vector become invalid.

  In addition, a request for new memory can be time consuming as all elements from the old memory are copied into the new memory. A reallocation means that a copy constructor and a destructor are called for all elements. The copy constructor copies them into the new memory, and the destructor destroys them in the old memory. This can be quite costly, especially if these operations are not trivial.

It is, of course, useful to avoid requests for new memory. There are several ways of doing this:

- One option is to initialize a vector with a certain number of elements on its creation. This value can be submitted in various ways.

  If no values are passed for initialization, the elements are created with the default constructor:

  ```
  std::vector<Elem> v(5);      // creates a vector with five elements
                               // (five calls to Elem(), the default constructor)
  ```

  This means that a default constructor has to be defined, and if its behavior is non-trivial, this can be quite costly.

- Another option is to reserve space for a certain number of elements. The `reserve()` function is provided for this:

  ```
  std::vector<Elem> v;      // creates an empty vector
  v.reserve(5);             // reserve space for five elements
  ```

The exact way the capacity is handled is implementation dependent. This means that individual implementations can always increase the capacity in ever-increasing steps. However, the language standard states that the capacity of vectors can *never* be reduced (passing a value less than the current capacity to `reserve()` will have no effect). In this respect, it is guaranteed that when elements are deleted, references to the elements in front of the deleted elements remain valid.

Assignments

Table 9.4 lists the different ways of assigning new sets of elements to a vector.

Expression	Meaning
v1 = v2	assigns all elements of v2 to v1
v.assign(*n*)	assigns *n* elements, which are created with the default constructor
v.assign(*n*,*elem*)	assigns *n* elements, which are copies of *elem*
v.assign(*beg*,*end*)	assigns copies of the elements in the range [*beg*,*end*)
v1.swap(v2)	swaps the elements of v1 with those of v2
swap(v1,v2)	same as above (global function)

Table 9.4. Assignment operations for vectors

The assignment operator assigns all elements of a vector to another one. During this operation, depending on the situation and implementation, assignment operators, copy constructors (if the vector increases in size) and destructors (if the vector becomes smaller) are called for the elements.

The forms of the `assign()` function are equivalent to the abilities of the constructors. The assignment of a range can be used to assign an element from another container to a vector [2]:

```
std::list<Elem> l;
std::vector<Elem> v;
...
v.assign(l.begin(),l.end());
```

The `swap()` function offers much better efficiency than the traditional assignment operators. It swaps only the internal data of the containers. In fact, it swaps only the internal pointers that refer to the data. So, `swap()` is guaranteed to have a constant complexity, instead of the linear complexity of an assignment. Therefore, if an assigned object is not needed after the assignment, `swap()` should be used.

Element Access

To gain direct access to the elements of a vector, the operations shown in Table 9.5 can be used.

Note that, except for `at()`, no checks are made to discover whether an appropriate element exists. With an empty vector, calls of `[]`, `front()`, and `back()` therefore result in undefined behavior:

```
std::vector<Elem> v;            // empty!

v[5] = elem;                    // RUN-TIME ERROR: undefined behavior
std::cout << v.front();         // RUN-TIME ERROR: undefined behavior
```

---

[2] Unless a system supports member function templates, elements in the assigned range must be of the same type.

Expression	Meaning
v.at(*idx*)	returns the element at index *idx* (with range checking)
v[*idx*]	returns the element at index *idx* (*without* range checking)
v.front()	returns the first element (*without* checking whether it exists)
v.back()	returns the last element (*without* checking whether it exists)

Table 9.5. Direct access to elements of vectors

This means that the programmer must ensure that the index for an index operator is valid and that the container is not empty when front() and back() are called:

```
std::vector<Elem> v;              // empty!

if (v.size() > 5) {
    v[5] = elem;                  // OK
}
if (!v.empty()) {
    std::cout << v.front();   // OK
}
v.at(5) = elem;                   // ERROR: exception std::out_of_range
```

The at() function, on the other hand, checks the range limits. If there is a violation, an exception of the type std::out_of_range (see Section 3.6.3 on page 95) is generated.

Using Vectors as Ordinary Arrays

The standard guarantees that all elements of a vector can be accessed as an array. This has an important consequence: you can use a vector in all cases in which you could use a dynamic array.

For example, if a C function requires an array of windows, this can be managed using a vector:

```
void raise(Window* window, int number);

std::vector<Window> window;
...

// pass elements as an array
raise(&window[0], window.size());
```

The address of an element can always be used as an array. Therefore, there is usually no longer any need to implement (dynamic) arrays instead of vectors.

Iterator Functions

For indirect access to the elements of the vector, the normal iterator functions (see Table 9.6) are provided.

Expression	Meaning
`v.begin()`	returns an iterator for the first element
`v.end()`	returns an iterator for the position behind the last element
`v.rbegin()`	returns a reverse iterator for the first element of a reversed iteration (therefore the last element)
`v.rend()`	returns a reverse iterator for the position after the last element of a reversed iteration (therefore the position in front of the first element)

Table 9.6. Iterator functions of vectors

The iterators remain valid until an element with a smaller index is inserted or deleted, or the capacity is increased with the addition of new elements or by calling `reserve()`.

Inserting and Deleting Elements

Table 9.7 shows the member functions used to insert and delete elements in vectors.

Expression	Meaning
`v.insert(`*pos*`)`	inserts an element, at the iterator position *pos*, that is created with the default constructor; returns the position of the new element
`v.insert(`*pos*`,`*elem*`)`	inserts a copy of *elem* at the iterator position *pos* and returns the position of the new element
`v.insert(`*pos*`,`*beg*`,`*end*`)`	inserts copies of the elements in the range [*beg*,*end*) at the iterator position
`v.push_back(`*elem*`)`	appends a copy of *elem*
`v.erase(`*pos*`)`	erases the element at the iterator position *pos* and returns the position of the sequence element
`v.erase(`*beg*`,`*end*`)`	erases all elements in the subrange [*beg*,*end*) and returns the position of the sequence element
`v.pop_back()`	erases the last element (without returning it)
`v.resize(`*num*`)`	changes the number of the elements to *num*, whereby, with an enlargement, new elements are created with the default constructor
`v.resize(`*num*`,`*elem*`)`	changes the number of elements to *num*, whereby, with an enlargement, new elements are created as copies of *elem*
`v.clear()`	erases all elements (empties the container)

Table 9.7. Modifying operations of vectors

With all these member functions, it should be remembered that no checks for invalid parameters are carried out. The programmer must therefore ensure that iterators really refer to elements of the vector, that the start of a range is before the end, and that no attempt is made to erase an element from an empty set.

Regarding performance, you should consider that inserting and removing happens faster when

- the capacity was defined large enough on entry;
- multiple elements are inserted with a single operation rather than by multiple operatioons; and
- elements are inserted and removed at the end of the vector.

Inserting or removing elements invalidates references, pointers, and iterators that refer to the following elements. If an insertion causes reallocation, it invalidates all references, iterators, and pointers.

Deleting specific elements is not directly supported. Instead, we can use the following algorithm:

```
std::vector<Elem> v;
...
// erase all elements with the value elem
v.erase(std::remove(v.begin(),v.end(),
                    elem),
        v.end());
```

Here, `std::remove()` removes the elements 'logically' and returns the position of the new end; `erase()` removes the elements 'physically' by reducing the size of the vector.

If just the first element with a specific value needs to be deleted, the above algorithm cannot be used. A possible alternative looks as follows:

```
std::vector<Elem> v;
...
// erase first element with value elem
std::vector<Elem>::iterator pos;
pos = std::find(v.begin(),v.end(),elem);     // find position of the element
if (pos != v.end()) {                        // if found, erase element
    v.erase(pos);
}
```

9.1.2   Common Operations of all STL Containers

Some, but not all, of the vector operations discussed above are available as a common interface to all STL containers. Table 9.8 lists those that are.

Expression	Meaning
ContType<type> c	creates an empty container
ContType<type> c1(c2)	creates a container as a copy of another
ContType<type> c(*beg*,*end*)	creates a container and initializes it with copies of elements in the range [*beg*,*end*)
c.~*ContType<type>*()	deletes all elements and frees the memory
c.size()	returns the current number of elements
c.empty()	returns whether the container is empty (equivalent to size() == 0, but may be quicker)
c.max_size()	returns the maximum possible number of elements
c1 == c2	returns whether c1 is equal to c2
c1 != c2	returns whether c1 is not equal to c2 (equivalent to !(c1 == c2))
c1 < c2	returns whether c1 is less than c2
c1 > c2	returns whether c1 is greater than c2 (equivalent to c2 < c1)
c1 <= c2	returns whether c1 is less than or equal to c2 (equivalent to !(c2 < c1))
c1 >= c2	returns whether c1 is greater than or equal to c2 (equivalent to !(c1 < c2))
c1 = c2	assigns to c1 all elements of c2
c1.swap(c2)	swaps the elements of c1 with those of c2
swap(c1,c2)	same as above (global function)
c.begin()	returns an iterator for the first element
c.end()	returns an iterator for the position behind the last element
c.rbegin()	returns a reverse iterator for the first element of a reversed iteration (therefore the last element)
c.rend()	returns a reverse iterator for the position after the last element of a reversed iteration (therefore the position in front of the first element)
c.insert(*pos*,*elem*)	inserts a copy of *elem* (the return value and the meaning of *pos* are different)
c.erase(*pos*)	erases the element at the iterator position *pos*
c.erase(*beg*,*end*)	erases all elements in the subrange [*beg*,*end*) (and returns the position of the following element)
c.clear()	erases all elements (empties the container)

Table 9.8. Operations common to all STL containers

9.1.3   List of all STL Algorithms

In this section, all algorithms of the STL are listed in order to provide an overview of the library.

All algorithms process a range of elements specified by iterators. This processing can take place with both read and write operations. The algorithms can be divided into different groups: non-modifying, modifying, sorting, etc.

To give algorithms more flexibility you can supply certain auxiliary functions called by the algorithms. Thus, you can use a general algorithm to suit your needs even if that need is very special or complex. For example, you can provide your own search criterion or a special operation to combine elements (see Section 9.2.2 on page 540). For example:

- For algorithms that process elements, conditions can be given for the processing (for example, 'erase all even numbers' or 'find the seventh element with the value 3').
- In the case of numeric algorithms, a specific operation can be defined. For example, the function `accumulate()` can be used to multiply elements.

Some of these algorithms have special versions, the names of which end with '`_if`'. This notation is used for variants of the original algorithm that allow to pass an operation without requiring additional arguments. However, this does not mean that variants of algorithms for operations as arguments always have the ending `_if`. Provided that these are passed with additional parameters, the original name is kept so that the function is simply overloaded.

Another frequently occurring ending in names is '`_copy`'. The `_copy` suffix is used as an indication that elements are not only manipulated but also copied into a destination range. The source range is not modified, then.

Non-Modifying Algorithms

All non-modifying algorithms are listed in Table 9.9. These change neither the sequence nor the value of the elements for which they are called. The algorithms can be used for all containers.

Most important is the `for_each()` algorithm. This allows very complicated actions to be carried out with the elements. An example of its use can be found in Section 9.2.1 on page 538.

Modifying Algorithms

Modifying algorithms change the values of the elements. This may apply to the processed range or a target range of the algorithm. Provided the modification is performed for a target range, and this is not the same as the source range, the source range is not changed. Table 9.10 lists the modifying algorithms.

Note that elements of associative algorithms are constant. This ensures that an element modification cannot compromise the sorted order of the elements. Therefore, you cannot use associative containers as a destination for modifying algorithms.

Algorithm	Functionality
for_each()	calls an operation for every element
count()	counts the elements
count_if()	counts the elements that fulfil a criterion
min_element()	returns the position of the smallest element
max_element()	returns the position of the largest element
find()	searches for a particular element
find_if()	searches for a particular element that fulfils a criterion
search_n()	searches *n* particular values, one after another
search()	searches the first subsequence of particular values
find_end()	searches the last subsequence of particular values
find_first_of()	searches one of several possible elements
adjacent_find()	searches two adjacent elements with particular properties
equal()	tests two ranges for equality
mismatch()	returns the first two different elements of two ranges
lexicographical_compare()	compares two ranges for sorting

Table 9.9. Non-modifying algorithms

Algorithm	Functionality
for_each()	calls an operation for every element
copy()	copies a range
copy_backward()	copies a range backwards
transform()	modifies the elements of one or two ranges
merge()	combines the elements of two ranges
swap_ranges()	swaps the elements of two ranges
fill()	gives all elements a fixed value
fill_n()	gives *n* elements a fixed value
generate()	gives all elements a generated value
generate_n()	gives *n* elements a generated value
replace()	replaces particular values with a new fixed value
replace_if()	replaces values that fulfil a criterion with a fixed new value
replace_copy()	copies a range and replaces elements
replace_copy()	copies a range and replaces elements that fulfil a criterion

Table 9.10. Modifying algorithms

Removing Algorithms

Removing algorithms remove elements from a range. This affects either the processed range or a target range in which the elements that are not removed are copied. Provided that there is a target range, and that this is not equal to the source range, the source is not changed. Table 9.11 lists the removing algorithms.

Algorithm	Functionality
`remove()`	removes elements with a particular value
`remove_if()`	removes elements that fulfil a criterion
`remove_copy()`	copies a range and removes elements with a particular value
`remove_copy_if()`	copies a range and removes elements that fulfil a criterion
`unique()`	removes duplicates, one after the other
`unique_copy()`	copies and removes duplicates, one after the other

Table 9.11. Removing algorithms

Again, as the elements of associative containers are considered as constants, these algorithms cannot be used if the modified range or the target range is (part of) an associative container.

Note that removing algorithms remove elements logically only by overwriting them with the following elements that were not removed. Thus, they do not change the number of elements in the ranges on which they operate. Instead, they return the position of the new "end" of the range. It's up to the caller to use that new end, such as to remove the elements physically (see Section 9.1.1 on page 524).

Mutating Algorithms

Mutating algorithms change the order of elements without altering their value. However, this does not mean that no assignments take place. With every mutation, elements are assigned to one another because the storage of the elements remains stable. Table 9.12 lists the mutating algorithms.

Algorithm	Functionality
`reverse()`	reverses the sequence of elements
`reverse_copy()`	copies and reverses the sequence of the elements
`rotate()`	rotates the elements
`rotate_copy()`	copies and rotates the elements
`next_permutation()`	permutates the sequence in a given direction
`prev_permutation()`	permutates the sequence in the 'other' direction
`random_shuffle()`	mixes up the sequence of the elements
`partition()`	moves certain elements to the front
`stable_partition()`	moves certain elements to the front and keeps relative sequences

Table 9.12. Mutating algorithms

Again, as the elements of associative containers are considered as constants, these algorithms cannot be used if the modified range or the target range is (part of) an associative container.

Sorting Algorithms

Sorting algorithms are a special kind of mutating algorithm because they also change the order of the elements. As a result, the elements are at least partial sorted. The sorting criterion can be submitted as a parameter. By default, elements are compared using the < operator. Table 9.13 lists the sorting algorithms.

Algorithm	Functionality
sort()	sorts elements
stable_sort()	sorts elements but preserves the sequence of elements with identical values
partial_sort()	sorts the first n elements
partial_sort_copy()	copies the first n sorted elements
nth_element()	sorts a certain element
make_heap()	converts a range into a heap
push_heap()	integrates an element in a heap
pop_heap()	removes an element from a heap
sort_heap()	sorts a heap (by doing so, it is no longer a heap)

Table 9.13. Sorting algorithms

Again, as the elements of associative containers are considered as constants, these algorithms cannot be used if the modified range, or the target range, is (part of) an associative container.

In addition to traditional complete sorting, there are also different algorithms that only sort partially. Because sorting is time consuming, it is often worthwhile not to sort all elements if this is not necessary. If, for example, we require the middle element after sorting, or a grouping between the first and the second half of a sorting, the nth_element() function can be used, which processes the container without sorting all elements completely.

Algorithms for Sorted Ranges

As long as one or several ranges are *completely sorted*, the algorithms that are introduced here can be used. There are both non-modifying, as well as modifying, algorithms. Table 9.14 lists the algorithms for sorted ranges.

The advantage of these algorithms is similar to that of associative containers over sequential containers: they demonstrate a considerably improved performance.

The first five sorted-range algorithms in Table 9.14 are non-modifying, as they search only according to their purpose. The other algorithms combine two sorted input ranges and write the result to a destination range. In general, the result of these algorithms is also sorted.

Algorithm	Functionality
binary_search()	returns whether an element is contained
includes()	returns whether all elements of a subset are contained
lower_bound()	returns the first element that is greater than or equal to a value
upper_bound()	returns the last element that is greater than a value
equal_range()	returns a range of elements with a certain value
merge()	combines the elements of two ranges together
set_union()	forms the union set of two ranges
set_intersection()	forms the intersection of two ranges
set_difference()	forms the difference set of two ranges
set_symmetric_difference()	forms the complementary set of two ranges
inplace_merge()	merges two subranges that are directly after one another

Table 9.14. Algorithms for sorted ranges

Numeric Algorithms

A special kind of algorithm is the numeric algorithm. These are listed in Table 9.15.

Algorithm	Functionality
accumulate()	connects all elements
partial_sum()	connects an element with all predecessors
adjacent_difference()	connects an element with its predecessor
inner_product()	connects all operations of two elements of two ranges

Table 9.15. Numeric algorithms

Numeric algorithms are used to numerically combine the elements of one range with another. If you understand the names, you get an idea of the purpose of the algorithms. However, these algorithms are more flexible and more powerful than they may seem at first. For example, as a default accumulate() computes the sum of all elements; but, by a simple redefinition of the combining operation, you could also compute the product of the elements. Similarly, as a default adjacent_difference() returns the difference between an element and its predecessor. By redefining the combining operation, the sum, product or any other conceivable computation can be calculated.

The adjacent_difference() and inner_product() operations can also be used to convert a sequence of absolute values into a sequence of relative values, and vice versa.

The accumulate() and inner_product() algorithms return a value as a result and are, in this respect, non-modifying. The two other algorithms process several values that are written in a target range and are, in this respect, modifying for the target range.

For more details on algorithms, refer to my book 'The C++ Standard Library—A Tutorial and Reference' (see [*JosuttisStdLib*]).

9.1.4 Numeric Limits

The most important implementation details for the numeric fundamental types can be queried using class templates `numeric_limits<>`. These *numeric limits* exist for the following types: `bool`, `char`, `signed char`, `unsigned char`, `wchar_t`, `short`, `unsigned short`, `int`, `unsigned int`, `long`, `unsigned long`, `float`, `double` and `long double`. They are defined in the header file `<limits>` and replace the preprocessor constants defined in the C header files `<climits>`, `<limits.h>`, `<cfloat>` and `<float.h>`.

To define limits, we make use of the class template `numeric_limits<>`. This contains static members that define different numeric properties of the types. Tables 9.16 and 9.17 list the individual members (and the corresponding C constants if available).

Member	Meaning	C constants
is_specialized	the type has a specialization for numeric limits	
is_signed	is signed	
is_integer	is integral	
is_exact	there are no rounding errors (true with all integral types)	
is_bounded	has finite value set (true with all built-in types)	
is_modulo	addition of two positive values can be negative	
is_iec559	conforms to the standards IEC 559 and IEEE 754	
min()	minimal value of the type (has meaning if is_bounded||is_signed)	INT_MIN,FLT_MIN, CHAR_MIN,...
max()	maximal value of the type (has meaning if is_bounded)	INT_MAX,FLT_MAX, CHAR_MAX,...
digits	chars, integers: number of bits (binary digits) floating-point values: number of digits of the mantissa to the base radix	FLT_MANT_DIG,...
digits10	number of digits in the decimal system (has meaning if is_bounded)	FLT_DIG,...
radix	internal number system (of mantissa)	FLT_RADIX
min_exponent	smallest negative integral exponent to base radix	FLT_MIN_EXP,...
max_exponent	largest positive integral exponent to base radix	FLT_MAX_EXP,...
min_exponent10	smallest negative integral exponent to base 10	FLT_MIN_10_EXP,...
max_exponent10	largest positive integral exponent to base 10	FLT_MAX_10_EXP,...
epsilon()	difference between 1 and the smallest value larger than 1	FLT_EPSILON,...

Table 9.16. Members of the `numeric_limits<>` (part 1)

Member	Meaning	C constants
round_style	rounding style	
round_error()	maximal rounding error	
has_infinity	type has value for 'infinity'	
infinity()	representation of 'infinity', if available	
has_quiet_NaN	type has a non-signal-producing value for 'not a number' (NaN) (e.g., for $\frac{0}{0}$)	
quiet_NaN()	representation of non-signal-producing value for NaN, if available	
has_signaling_NaN	type has signal-producing value for NaN (e.g., for $\frac{0}{0}$)	
signaling_NaN()	representation of signal-producing value for NaN, if available	
has_denorm	allows denormalized values (variable number of bits for exponents)	
has_denorm_loss	a loss of precision is identified as a loss of denormalization and not as an inexact result	
denorm_min()	smallest positive denormalized value	
traps	'trapping' is implemented	
tinyness_before	'tinyness' is recognized before a rounding	

Table 9.17. Members of the `numeric_limits<>` (part 2)

The value range of types are, of course, particularly interesting. The following example (which outputs the maxima for some types, with some additional information) shows a possible evaluation of this information:

```cpp
// etc/limits.cpp

#include <iostream>
#include <limits>
#include <string>

int main()
{
    using namespace std;

    // use textual representation for bool
    cout << boolalpha;

    // output maxima of integral types
    cout << "max(short): " << numeric_limits<short>::max() << endl;
    cout << "max(int):   " << numeric_limits<int>::max() << endl;
    cout << "max(long):  " << numeric_limits<long>::max() << endl;
```

```
        cout << endl;

        // output maxima of floating-point types
        cout << "max(float):         "
             << numeric_limits<float>::max() << endl;
        cout << "max(double):        "
             << numeric_limits<double>::max() << endl;
        cout << "max(long double):   "
             << numeric_limits<long double>::max() << endl;
        cout << endl;

        // is char a signed interal type?
        cout << "is_signed(char): "
             << numeric_limits<char>::is_signed << endl;
        cout << endl;

        // are there numeric limits for the type string?
        cout << "is_specialized(string): "
             << numeric_limits<string>::is_specialized << endl;
    }
```

An (implementation-dependent) output look as follows:

```
    max(short): 32767
    max(int):   2147483647
    max(long):  2147483647

    max(float):        3.40282e+38
    max(double):       1.79769e+308
    max(long double):  1.79769e+308

    is_signed(char): true

    is_specialized(string): false
```

The last line of output tells us that there are no numeric limits defined for type std::string. This makes sense, because a string is not a numeric type. Despite this, as one can see, this information can be queried for all types. This is also valid for user-defined types. This is made possible by means of a programming technique used in connection with templates. A common default implementation is defined for all types:

```
    namespace std {
        // general definition of the templates for numeric limits
        template <typename T>
```

```
        class numeric_limits {
          public:
            // generally, there are no numeric limits
            static const bool is_specialized = false;

            ...          // all other members with insignificant values
        };
    }
```

For types for which numeric limits are defined, there is a specialization of the template (see Section 7.3.3 on page 441):

```
    namespace std {
        // specialization of the numeric limits for int
        // - values are implementation specific
        template<> class numeric_limits<int> {
          public:
            // in this case, there are numeric limits
            static const bool is_specialized = true;

            static T min() throw() {
                return -2147483648;
            }
            static T max() throw() {
                return 2147483647;
            }
            static const int digits = 31;
            ...
        };
    }
```

The following code shows a possible complete specialization of the numeric limits for type float. With this, the exact signatures of the members are shown:

```
    namespace std {
        template<> class numeric_limits<float> {
          public:
            static const bool is_specialized = true;

            static float min() throw() { return 1.17549435E-38F; }
            static float max() throw() { return 3.40282347E+38F; }

            static const int digits = 24;
            static const int digits10 = 6;
            static const int radix = 2;
```

```
        static const bool is_signed = true;
        static const bool is_integer = false;
        static const bool is_exact = false;
        static const bool is_bounded = true;
        static const bool is_modulo = false;
        static const bool is_iec559 = true;

        static float epsilon() throw() { return 1.19209290E-07F; }

        static const float_round_style round_style = round_to_nearest;
        static float round_error() throw() { return 0.5F; }

        static const int min_exponent = -125;
        static const int max_exponent = +128;
        static const int min_exponent10 = -37;
        static const int max_exponent10 = +38;

        static const bool has_infinity = true;
        static float infinity() throw() { return ... ; }
        static const bool has_quiet_NaN = true;
        static float quiet_NaN() throw() { return ... ; }
        static const bool has_signaling_NaN = true;
        static float signaling_NaN() throw() { return ... ; }
        static const float_denorm_style has_denorm = denorm_absent;
        static const bool has_denorm_loss = false;
        static float denorm_min() throw() { return min(); }

        static const bool traps = true;
        static const bool tinyness_before = true;
    };
}
```

9.1.5 Summary

- Vectors have a size and a capacity.
- When an element is accessed, vectors do not normally check whether it exists.
- A vector should be used instead of a (dynamic) array.
- Using numeric limits, the properties of numeric types can be evaluated.

9.2   Defining Special Operators

This section looks at the possibility of defining operators for objects so that they behave like pointers or functions.

9.2.1   Smart Pointers

We first introduce objects that behave like 'smart pointers'.

Reasons for Using Smart Pointers

In C++, it is possible to define the * and -> operators for objects. In this way, objects can be given a pointer-like interface. As you implement these operators yourself, the result is the creation of objects that behave like pointers, but that perform more complex, or safer, operations. For this reason, the objects are also called *smart pointers*.

   We have already come across one kind of smart pointer in connection with the STL. Iterators are smart pointers, capable of iterating complex data structures using a simple pointer-like interface (see Section 3.5.4 on page 74).

Smart Pointers and Reference Semantics

One kind of smart pointer is almost always helpful: pointers that manage objects created with new, so that they are automatically deleted when the last pointer to the objects gets destroyed. In this way, reference semantics can be implemented. This means that when copying objects, only the references to them are copied, so that the data of the original and the copy is the same. In this way, you can manage objects that are in multiple STL containers at the same time.

   The following class template defines a smart pointer using reference semantics:

```
// etc/countptr.hpp

#ifndef COUNTED_PTR_HPP
#define COUNTED_PTR_HPP

/* class template for smart pointer with reference semantics
 * - destroys the object that is referred to when the last CountedPtr
 *   that refers to it is destroyed
 */
template <typename T>
class CountedPtr {
  private:
    T* ptr;          // pointer to the actual object
    long* count;     // reference to the number of pointers that refer to it
```

```
public:
    // initialize with ordinary pointer
    // - p has to be a value returned by new
    explicit CountedPtr (T* p=0)
     : ptr(p), count(new long(1)) {
    }


    // copy constructor
    CountedPtr(const CountedPtr<T>& p) throw()
     : ptr(p.ptr), count(p.count) {    // copy object and counter
        ++*count;                             // increment number of references
    }


    // destructor
    ~CountedPtr () throw() {
        release();                   // release reference to the object
    }


    // assignment
    CountedPtr<T>& operator= (const CountedPtr<T>& p) throw() {
        if (this != &p) {        // if not a reference to itself
            release();           // release reference to old object
            ptr = p.ptr;         // copy new object
            count = p.count;     // copy counter
            ++*count;            // increment number of references
        }
        return *this;
    }


    // access to the object
    T& operator*() const throw() {
        return *ptr;
    }


    // access to a member of the object
    T* operator->() const throw() {
        return ptr;
    }

private:
    void release() {
```

```
        ++*count;                    // decrement number of references
        if (*count == 0) {           // if last reference
            delete count;            // destroy counter
            delete ptr;              // destroy object
        }
    }
};


#endif /*COUNTED_PTR_HPP*/
```

You can now create any object using new and give control of it to this kind of pointer:

```
CountedPtr<CPPBook::Fraction> bp = new CPPBook::Fraction(16,100);
```

bp can now be copied and assigned. By doing this, only other references to the object are created, not new objects.

You will notice that the * operator, as well as the -> operator, is implemented. You can therefore access the object using these two types of operator:

```
std::cout << *bp << std::endl; ...  double d = bp->toDouble();
```

If the -> operator is implemented for some classes, something has to be returned for which the -> operator can be called again. If, as here, the -> operator is called for an object of type CountedPtr<CPPBook::Fraction>, this returns the type CPPBook::Fraction*, for which the -> operator is called again.

The following program shows how this class can be used to simultaneously manage objects in multiple STL containers:

```
// etc/refsem1.cpp

#include <iostream>
#include <list>
#include <deque>
#include <algorithm>
#include "countptr.hpp"
using namespace std;

void printCountedPtr(CountedPtr<int> elem)
{
    cout << *elem << ' ';
}

int main()
{
    // type for smart pointer for this purpose
    typedef CountedPtr<int> IntPtr;
```

```
// two different sets
deque<IntPtr> coll1;
list<IntPtr> coll2;

// array of initial ints
static int values[] = { 3, 5, 9, 1, 6, 4 };

/* insert newly created ints in the sets with reference semantics
 * - same sequence in coll1
 * - reversed sequence in coll2
 */
for (unsigned i=0; i<sizeof(values)/sizeof(values[0]); ++i) {
    IntPtr ptr(new int(values[i]));
    coll1.push_back(ptr);
    coll2.push_front(ptr);
}

// output content of both sets
for_each(coll1.begin(), coll1.end(), printCountedPtr);
cout << endl;
for_each(coll2.begin(), coll2.end(), printCountedPtr);
cout << endl << endl;

/* modify elements of the sets in different places
 * - square third value in coll1
 * - negate first value in coll1
 * - set first value in coll2 to 0
 */
*coll1[2] *= *coll1[2];
(**coll1.begin()) *= -1;
(**coll2.begin()) = 0;

// output content of both sets again
for_each(coll1.begin(), coll1.end(), printCountedPtr);
cout << endl;
for_each(coll2.begin(), coll2.end(), printCountedPtr);
cout << endl;
}
```

The program has the following output:

```
3  5  9  1  6  4
4  6  1  9  5  3


-3  5  81  1  6  0
0  6  1  81  5  -3
```

In the boost repository for supplementary C++ libraries, there are several smart-pointer classes (see http://www.boost.org).

9.2.2   Function Objects

It is also possible, and even useful, to define objects that behave like functions. In this case, the '()' operator is defined for the objects. This mysterious-sounding technique will be justified in an example.

An operation can be passed to the STL algorithms for processing. This could, for example, be a function. The following example clarifies this:

```cpp
// etc/transform1.cpp

#include <set>
#include <vector>
#include <algorithm>
#include <iterator>
#include <iostream>

int add10(int elem)
{
    return elem + 10;
}

int main()
{
    std::set<int>    coll1;
    std::vector<int> coll2;

    // insert elements with the values 1 to 9 in coll1
    for (int i=1; i<=9; ++i) {
        coll1.insert(i);
    }
```

```
// output elements in coll1
copy(coll1.begin(), coll1.end(),                          // source: coll1
     std::ostream_iterator<int>(std::cout," "));    // target: cout
std::cout << std::endl;

// transform every element in coll1 to coll2
// - in the process add 10
transform(coll1.begin(),coll1.end(),      // source
          std::back_inserter(coll2),      // target (inserting)
          add10);                         // operation

// output elements in coll2
copy(coll2.begin(), coll2.end(),                          // source: coll1
     std::ostream_iterator<int>(std::cout," "));    // target: cout
std::cout << std::endl;

}
```

In this example, by calling

```
transform(coll1.begin(),coll1.end(),      // source
          std::back_inserter(coll2),      // destination (inserting)
          add10);                         // operation
```

every element from coll1 to coll2 is transformed, and 10 is added by calling the add10()
function. Using add10, the function is passed as an operation to transform() (see Figure 9.1).

The output of the program is as follows:

```
1 2 3 4 5 6 7 8 9
11 12 13 14 15 16 17 18 19
```

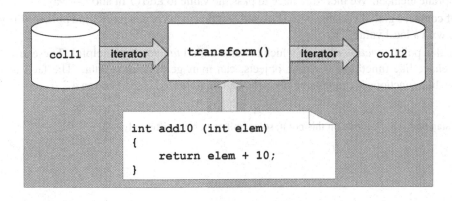

Figure 9.1. Mode of operation of transform()

But what happens if you want to add different values? Provided that these values are established at compile time, a template can be used (compare with Section 7.4 on page 448):

```
template <int W> int add (int elem)
{
    return elem + W;
}

int main() {
    ...
    transform(coll1.begin(),coll1.end(),     // source
              std::back_inserter(coll2),     // destination (inserting)
              add<10>);                       // operation
    ...
}
```

However, it is not currently completely clear whether a template can simply be passed as an operation in this way[3]. In this case, the exact type of the passed operation has to be specified:

```
transform(coll1.begin(),coll1.end(),     // source
          std::back_inserter(coll2),     // destination (inserting)
          (int(*)(int))add<10>);          // operation
```

The expression

```
int(*)(int)
```

denotes a function that receives an `int` and returns an `int`. By means of

```
(int(*)(int))add<10>
```

it is explicitly established that `add<10>` has this type.

But what happens if you find the value to be added at run time? Actually, this value is needed as a second parameter, and `transform()` calls this operation with an argument, namely the appropriate element. We therefore have to pass the value to `add()` in another way.

Of course, a global variable could be used, but this is fairly dangerous and pollutes the global scope with a local value.

At this point, *function objects* (which are also called *functors*) are helpful. These are objects that behave like functions, but, like objects, can manage additional data. The fact, that they behave like functions is implemented via the call operator '`()`' (see Section 4.2.6 on page 166):

---

[3] The standard is not definite on this point, so compilers behave differently.

```
// etc/add.hpp
```

```
// function object that adds the passed value
class Add {
  private:
    int val;       // value to add
  public:
    // constructor (initializes the value to add)
    Add(int w) : val(w) {
    }

    // 'function call' (adds the value)
    int operator() (int elem) const
    {
        return elem + val;
    }
};
```

At run time, we can create such an object, initialized with the value to add, and pass it as operation to the `transform()` algorithm:

```
// etc/transform2.cpp
```

```
#include <set>
#include <vector>
#include <algorithm>
#include <iterator>
#include <iostream>

// include the function object Add
#include "add.hpp"

int main()
{
    std::set<int>    coll1;
    std::vector<int> coll2;

    // insert the elements with the values 1 to 9 in coll1
    for (int i=1; i<=9; ++i) {
        coll1.insert(i);
    }

    // output elements in coll1
```

```
        copy(coll1.begin(), coll1.end(),                    // source: coll1
            std::ostream_iterator<int>(std::cout," "));   // target: cout
        std::cout << std::endl;

        // transform every element in coll1 to coll2
        // - add value of first element to each element
        transform(coll1.begin(),coll1.end(),    // source
                std::back_inserter(coll2),       // target (inserting)
                Add(*coll1.begin()));            // operation

        // output elements in coll2
        copy(coll2.begin(), coll2.end(),                    // source: coll1
            std::ostream_iterator<int>(std::cout," "));   // target: cout
        std::cout << std::endl;
    }
```

The expression

```
    Add(*coll1.begin())
```

creates a temporary object of the Add class and initializes it with the value of the first element of coll1. With

```
    transform(coll1.begin(),coll1.end(),    // source
            std::back_inserter(coll2),       // destination (inserting)
            Add(*coll1.begin()));            // operation
```

this temporary object is passed to transform() as an operation op. Within transform(), the passed operation is called:

```
    template <typename InIter, typename OutIter, typename Operation>
    ... transform (InIter beg1, InIter end1,
                OutIter beg2,
                Operation op)
    {
        ...
        op (currentElement)
        ...
    }
```

If op is a function, this function is called with the current element. If this is a function object, this call is evaluated as

```
    op.operator() (currentElement)
```

Thus, for the object op you call operator '()' with currentElement passed as argument.

9.2.3 Summary

- The operators * and -> can be defined for objects. By doing so, smart pointers can be implemented.
- You can also define the () operator for objects. By doing so, function objects can be implemented.
- Functions and function objects acn be used to define the specific behavior or criterion of an algorithm.

9.3 Additional Aspects of `new` and `delete`

In this section, more special aspects (in addition to the memory-management features introduced in Section 3.8 on page 114) of the `new`, `new[]`, `delete` and `delete[]` operators are introduced.

9.3.1 No-Throw Versions of `new` and `delete`

The `new`, `new[]`, `delete` and `delete[]` operators can be called so that they do not throw exceptions, but instead return 0 or NULL if there is not enough memory.

To do so, `new` has to be passed the `std::nothrow` value as a parameter:

```
CPPBook::Fraction* bp = new(std::nothrow) CPPBook::Fraction(16,100);
if (bp == NULL) {
    std::cerr << "all memory" << std::endl;
    ...
}
```

```
CPPBook::Fraction* flist = new(std::nothrow) CPPBook::Fraction[10];
if (flist == NULL) {
    std::cerr << "all memory" << std::endl;
    ...
}
```

This memory must be freed using `delete` and `delete[]`:

```
delete bp;
delete [] flist;
```

9.3.2 Placement New

If `new` is passed an address of type `void*`, this is understood as a call of `new` in which the memory is already available. By doing so, objects can be initialized in memory that has already been freed. The creation of an object using `new`,

```
CPPBook::Fraction* bp = new CPPBook::Fraction(16,100);
```

can therefore be executed in two steps:

```
// request uninitialized memory
void* p = ::operator new(sizeof(CPPBook::Fraction));
```

```
// initialize memory as an object
CPPBook::Fraction* bp = new(p) CPPBook::Fraction(16,100);
```

You can also separate the destruction and the deallocation of objects into two steps:

```
// clean-up object
bp->~CPPBook::Fraction();
```

```
// free memory
::operator delete((void*)bp);
```

9.3.3   New Handlers

If a request for memory with new fails, under normal circumstances, an exception of type std:bad_alloc is thrown.

You can intervene here. If new cannot reserve memory, a function that throws the appropriate exceptions is called. This kind of function is called a *new handler*.

By using std::set_new_handler(), a new handler can be installed. This function is declared in the special C++ header file <new>.

The new handler is declared as a global function, is called without parameters and has no return value. The following example shows this kind of new handler and its use:

```
// etc/newhdl1.cpp

// header file for the new handler
#include <new>

// standard header files
#include <iostream>
#include <cstdlib>

/* myNewHandler()
 * - outputs error message and exits the program
 */
void myNewHandler()
{
     // output error message on standard error channel
     std::cerr << "out of meemmmoooorrrrrryyyyyyy..." << std::endl;

     // throw appropriate exception
     throw std::bad_alloc();
}

int main()
{
     try {
```

```
            // install your own new handler
            std::set_new_handler(&myNewHandler);

            // and test with endless loops that requires memory
            for (;;) {
                new char[1000000];
            }

            // no computer can have infinite memory
            std::cout << "Yikes, magic!" << std::endl;
        }
        catch (const std::bad_alloc& e) {
            std::cerr << "Exception: " << e.what() << std::endl;
            return EXIT_FAILURE;
        }
    }
```

At the start of the program, the function myNewHandler() is installed as a new handler by passing it to std::set_new_handler()[4]:

```
    std::set_new_handler(&myNewHandler);
```

As there is no difference in C++ (as in C) between a function and the address of a function (the name of a function is seen as its address), the & operator can be omitted:

```
    std::set_new_handler(myNewHandler);
```

Finally, an attempt is made to allocate memory in an endless loop:

```
    for (;;) {
        new char[1000000];
    }
```

Sooner or later, calling new therefore leads to the call of the installed new handler. This is reported with an appropriate error message, and throws an exception:

```
    void myNewHandler() {
        // output error message on standard error channel
        std::cerr << "out of meemmmoooorrrrrryyyyyyy..." << std::endl;

        // throw appropriate exception
        throw std::bad_alloc();
    }
```

---

[4] The internal implementation of set_new_handler() is looked at in more detail in Section 9.4.1 on page 557.

However, this first new handler needs to be rewritten. It may happen that an attempt is made, via a new handler, to request new memory. It is possible that new may be called within the bounds of the output operator <<, or by the exception object being created. This would result in a recursive loop of new handler calls, and the program would eventually crash.

Temporary New Handlers

The std::set_new_handler() function returns the previously installed new handler. This can be used to install new handlers for a restricted control section. The returned new handler is then reinstalled later.

```
// etc/newhdl2.cpp

#include <new>

void f()
{
    std::new_handler oldNewHandler;   // pointer to new handler

    // install new handler and keep old one
    oldNewHandler = std::set_new_handler(&myNewHandler);
    ...
       // call operation with new
    ...
    // install old new handler again
    std::set_new_handler(oldNewHandler);
}
```

The std::new_handler type is simply a function pointer (see Section 9.4.1 on page 557) for a function without parameters and without a return value:

```
namespace std {
    typedef void (*new_handler)();
}
```

New Handlers that Reserve Memory

As a rule of thumb, with commercial programs, it is not enough to simply exit the program if there are errors. Even if there is a lack of memory, clean-up work has to be carried out. However, it is often the case that additional memory is needed for this work. Therefore, it may be useful to allocated memory at the start of the program that is freed if the new handler is called. This behavior could be implemented in a separate module:

```cpp
// etc/newhdl3.cpp

// header file for the new handler
#include <new>

// header file for I/O
#include <iostream>

// forward declaration
static void myNewHandler();

// reserved memory
static char* reserveMemory;

void initNewHandler()
{
    // allocate memory as might be necessary
    reserveMemory = new char[100000];

    // install new handler
    std::set_new_handler(&myNewHandler);
}

static void myNewHandler()
{
    // deallocate reserved memory
    delete [] reserveMemory;

    // output error message on standard error channel
    std::cerr << "out of memory (use emerengy memory)"
              << std::endl;

    // throw appropriate exception
    throw std::bad_alloc();
}
```

In the application program, `initNewHandler()` then only has to be called once at the start.

New Handlers that do not Necessarily Exit the Program

If there is a lack of memory, it is best if it is possible to let the program carry on running. To do this, the new handler can be implemented so that the program is not exited, but tries to carry on running after the call.

If a new handler is called and neither exits the program nor throws an exception, the programs tries to allocate the memory again. The new operator is therefore predefined so that, if no memory can be requested, either `std::bad_alloc` is thrown, or, if a new handler is installed, this is called in a loop, again and again, until either the requested memory is available or the loop is exited via an exception or a program abortion.

A program can therefore install a new handler that does not exit a program, but instead cleans up and frees memory. In the same way, it is possible that the first call of the new handler frees reserved memory and outputs a warning that the memory has been used up. The program, however, runs further and is only then finally exited if the 'reserve memory' is consumed:

```cpp
// etc/newhdl4.cpp

// header file for the new handler
#include <new>

// header filefor I/O
#include <iostream>

// forward declaration
static void myNewHandler();

// reserved memory
static char* reserveMemory1;
static char* reserveMemory2;

void initNewHandler()
{
    // request reserved memory accoring to needs
    reserveMemory1 = new char[1000000];
    reserveMemory2 = new char[100000];

    // install new handler
    std::set_new_handler(&myNewHandler);
}

static void myNewHandler()
{
    static bool firstKiss = true;
```

```
// - first time:  provide reserve memory
// - second time: throw exception
if (firstKiss) {
    // program runs until second call
    firstKiss = false;

    // deallocate first reserved memory for new handler
    delete [] reserveMemory1;

    // output warning on standard error channel
    std::cerr << "Warning: almost out of memory" << std::endl;
}
else {
    // deallocate second reserved memory for new handler
    delete [] reserveMemory2;

    // output error message on standard error channel
    std::cerr << "out of memory" << std::endl;

    // throw appropriate exception
    throw std::bad_alloc();
}
}
```

9.3.4   Overloading `new` and `delete`

The `new` and `delete` operators are predefined in C++ as global operators. However, it is possible to replace these global operators with user-defined versions. A replacement is also possible for a particular class.

By using user-defined implementations, memory management can be optimized for user-defined needs and/or types and special behaviors can be introduced. For example, the following are possible:

- Trace memory management using output statements.
- Reduce the time taken to request memory for many small objects by requesting large blocks in advance.
- Implement automatic memory management (garbage collection).

Overloading Global `new` and `delete`

The predefined `new` and `delete` operators are declared in the language as follows:

```
// new and delete that might throw exceptions
void* operator new(std::size_t size) throw(std::bad_alloc);
void* operator new[](std::size_t size) throw(std::bad_alloc);
void operator delete(void* ptr) throw();
void operator delete[](void* ptr) throw();

// new and delete that might return NULL
void* operator new(std::size_t size, const std::nothrow_t&) throw();
void* operator new[](std::size_t size, const std::nothrow_t&) throw();
void operator delete(void* ptr, const std::nothrow_t&) throw();
void operator delete[](void* ptr, const std::nothrow_t&) throw();
```

By means of user-defined implementations, the memory management can, for example, be redefined for all objects. When doing this, you have to ensure that, for a redefined new, you should always also redefine the corresponding delete.

The new operator gets the size of the object that is to be created as a parameter. The type size_t is used for this, which is defined in <cstddef> as an implementation-specific type. The return type always has to be void* (and not MyClass*). This is because this is not the initialization of an object, but the provision of memory for an object.

The delete operator contains the address of the memory to be freed as a parameter. The return type always has to be void.

The operators declared with nothrow_t, are available for use when new is called with std::nothrow (see Section 9.3.1 on page 546). The corresponding delete operator is called if the memory was successfully requested for an object created with new(std::nothrow), but the constructor of the object threw an exception. In this way, the requested memory is freed again before new returns NULL.

Overloading new and delete in Classes

new and delete can also be implemented individually within separate classes. In the following example, new and new[] are provided for a class MyClass, with an additional output statement:

```
// etc/mynew.cpp

#include <iostream>
#include <cstddef>

void* MyClass::operator new (std::size_t size)
{
    // output message
    std::cout << "call MyClass::new" << std::endl;
```

```
    // call global new for memory of the size size
    return ::new char[size];
}


void* MyClass::operator new[] (std::size_t size)
{
    // output message
    std::cout << "call MyClass::new[]" << std::endl;

    // call global new for memory of the size size
    return ::new char[size];
}
```

Again, note that the return type of new has to be void* (and not MyClass*), because no object is created, but only memory is provided for it.

The scope operator :: inside the implementation operator new ensures that the global operator new is called. Provided that the implementation is not used to redefine the memory management completely, it is always better to redirect it to the global operator. By doing so, it can be ensured that if there is an error, the installed new handler is called, as is expected by the user.

To request memory, size always has to be used. As the new operator is inherited, it can also be called for larger objects of derived classes. It is therefore an error to only provide memory for an object of the appropriate class:

```
    return ::new char[sizeof(MyClass)]; // ERROR
```

It is also incorrect to explicitly call the global new for an object of the class:

```
    return ::new MyClass;                    // ERROR
```

Too little memory is created here, and, in addition, the constructor of the class is called (which should actually happen after the call of new).

Anyone who wants to implement the new operator just for objects of this class has to call the global new for derived classes. To do this, you can simply check as to whether the size of the requested memory corresponds to the size of the object of this class:

```
    void* MyClass::operator new (size_t size) {
        // call global new for derived classes
        if (size != sizeof(MyClass)) {
            return ::new char [size];
        }
        ...
    }
```

However, with derived classes without members, the test fails.

To implement the delete operator for any class so that it outputs additional information, you have to do the following:

```
// etc/mydelete.cpp

#include <cstddef>

void MyClass::operator delete (void* p)
{
    // output message
    std::cout << "call MyClass::delete" << std::endl;

    // call global delete
    ::delete [] p;
}

void MyClass::operator delete[] (void* p)
{
    // output message
    std::cout << "call MyClass::delete[]" << std::endl;

    // call global delete
    ::delete [] p;
}
```

As the example shows, the delete operator contains the address of the memory to be freed as a parameter. The return type always has to be void.

Note that, for both forms of new, the global new for arrays is called. For this reason, the global delete for arrays also has to be called.

A second parameter of the type std::size_t can optionally be declared. This contains the size of the object to be freed:

```
void MyClass::operator delete (void* p, std::size_t size) {
    ...
}
```

new and realloc()

In C++, no operator is provided to explicitly reduce or enlarge memory. This functionality usually has to be realized with new and delete. To use the terminology of C, this means that a realloc() has to be implemented using malloc() and free().

If, however, it is guaranteed by a separate definition that new and delete are implemented internally via malloc() and free(), realloc() can also be called for objects created with new. However, in order to do this, a function such as renew() should be defined so that C and C++ techniques are not confused. In addition, it should be remembered that this function calls the new handler if an error occurs. (Recall that you can set the current new handler using `std::set_new_handler()` (see Section 9.3.3 on page 549).)

I particularly warn against calling `realloc()` directly for objects created with `new`. It normally works, as `new` is typically implemented using `malloc()`, but it is not portable and is very dangerous, as `new()` can be defined differently, which means that the new handler cannot then be used.

9.3.5   The `new` Operator with Additional Parameters

The `new` operator can be overloaded with the declaration of additional parameters. The arguments for these parameters have to be passed in brackets between `new` and the requested type during the call of the operator.

For example, the declaration

```
void* MyClass::operator new (size_t, float, int)
```

enables the following call:

```
new(3.5,42) MyClass
```

The two arguments are passed after the first parameter for the size. Therefore, the following operator is called:

```
MyClass::operator new (sizeof(MyClass), 3.5, 42)
```

The use of additional parameters is not allowed for `delete`.

9.3.6   Summary

- By using `std::nothrow`, it can be ensured that `new` does not throw an exception if there is not enough memory, but instead returns NULL.
- Using *placement new*, objects can be initialized in memory that has already been reserved.
- If no memory can be requested with `new`, a new handler can be defined, which is then called automatically and which executes the appropriate treatment of errors.
- The `new` and `delete` operators can be overloaded.
- When overloading `new`, it has to be taken into account that, if there is an error, an installed new handler will be called.
- You can define separate versions of `new` with additional parameters.

9.4   Function Pointers and Member Pointers

This section shows how pointers to functions and class members can be defined, and how they can be used. Special operators will also be introduced, with which class members can be accessed.

9.4.1   Function Pointers

It is already possible in C to define pointers to functions. Error handlers, for example, are frequently managed in this way.

Error handlers are functions that are installed anywhere, so that they can be called when errors occur. To do so, an error handler is assigned to a function pointer. If an error then occurs, the function to which the function pointer points is called.

An example of these kinds of error handlers are the new handlers introduced in Section 9.3.3 on page 547. A function pointer, as a global variable, points to the function that is called if there is an error:

```
// define type for pointer to new handler
namespace std {
    typedef void (*new_handler) ();
}
```

```
// pointer to current new handler
new_handler myNewHandler;
```

This function pointer can be passed a new handler with the function set_new_handler():

```
new_handler set_new_handler(new_handler newNewHandler)
{
    // store current new handler to restore later
    new_handler oldNewHandler = myNewHandler;

    // install passed function as new new handler
    myNewHandler = newNewHandler;

    // return old new handler
    return oldNewHandler;
}
```

If no memory can be reserved during the call of new, the new handler (if it is installed) is called:

```
// etc/newimpl.cpp
```

```
// possible implementation of operator new
void* operator new (std::size_t size)
{
    void* p;              // pointer for new memory
```

```
                // as long as we do not get new memory,
                // call new handler or throw exceptions
                while ((p = getMemory(size)) == 0) {
                        // no sufficient memory available
                        if (MyNewHandler != 0) {
                                // call new handler
                                (*myNewHandler)();
                        }
                        else {
                                // throw exeption
                                throw std::bad_alloc();
                        }
                }

                // OK, return new memory
                return p;
        }
```

According to the same pattern, functions for any situation can be installed. They are simply held in a function pointer, and are called if and when the appropriate situation arises.

9.4.2   Pointers to Members

If member functions are to be used as parameters, pointers to member functions are required. C++ introduced a pointer to members for this purpose. These always refer to a particular class. Access is possible via operators that were introduced solely for this purpose.

Pointers to Data Members

To declare a pointer to member, the scope operator has to be used in order to specify the class for which the pointer is valid:

```
        // pointer to int members of the class MyClass
        int MyClass::* intPtr;
```

Now the address of an integer member of the class can be assigned to the pointer:

```
        intPtr = & MyClass::xyz;
```

In order to do so, access must be granted to the member (e.g. with the public keyword, or placing the statement in the scope of a member or friend function).

Using the special C++ .* operator, the member can then be accessed:

```
        MyClass obj;
        ...
```

```
// access the member of obj to which intPtr points
obj.*intPtr = 7;
```

If a pointer to an object of the class is used, the special C++ operator ->* can be used:

```
MyClass obj;
MyClass* op = &obj;
...
// for the object to which op points, access the member to which intPtr points
op->*intPtr = 7;
```

Pointers to Member Functions

Pointers to members are predominantly used for the parametrization of member functions. They can be considered as function pointers for classes.

To declare a pointer to a member function, the scope operator has to be used in order to specify the class for the function pointer:

```
void (MyClass::*funcPtr)();
```

In this case, funcPtr is declared as a pointer to a member function of class MyClass that is called without parameters and has void as a return type.

It is recommended here that, as with function pointers, a separate type should be defined, so that the different declarations are easier to maintain and more comprehensible:

```
typedef void (MyClass::*MyClassFunction)();

MyClassFunction funcPtr;
```

After the assignment of a member, the C++ .* operator has to be used for access to the member:

```
MyClass obj;
...
// for obj, call member function to which funcPtr points
(obj.*funcPtr)();
```

As the function call has a higher priority, the expression with the .* operator has to be placed in brackets.

Similarly, the ->* operator is used for pointers to objects:

```
MyClass obj;
MyClass* objPtr = &obj;
...
// for object to which objPtr points, call member function to which funcPtr points
(objPtr->*funcPtr)();
```

A member function can be passed as a parameter in this way, and can be managed in a variable.

The following example demonstrates the use of pointers to member functions:

```
// etc/compptr1.cpp

#include <iostream>

class MyClass {
  public:
    void func1() {
        std::cout << "call of func1()" << std::endl;
    }
    void func2() {
        std::cout << "call of func2()" << std::endl;
    }
};
```

```
// type: pointer to member function of class MyClass
//       without parameter and return value
typedef void (MyClass::*MyClassFunction) ();
```

```
int main()
{
    // pointer to member function of class MyClass
    MyClassFunction funcPtr;

    // object of class MyClass
    MyClass x;

    // pointer to member refers to func1()
    funcPtr = & MyClass::func1;

    // call member function, to which the pointer refers, for object x
    (x.*funcPtr)();

    // pointer to member refers to func2()
    funcPtr = & MyClass::func2;

    // call member function, to which the pointer refers for object x
    (x.*funcPtr)();
}
```

The `func1()` and `func2()` member functions are assigned to the `funcPtr` member pointer one after the other, and called via the same call statement. The output of the program therefore reads as follows:

```
Call of func1()
Call of func2()
```

9.4.3 Pointers to Members for External Interfaces

A working example of the use of pointers to members are interfaces to other processes or language environments in which member functions of objects are to be callable.

The following example shows how, in principle, this is possible:

```cpp
// etc/compptr2.cpp

#include <iostream>

class MyClass {
  public:
    void func1() {
        std::cout << "call of func1()" << std::endl;
    }
    void func2() {
        std::cout << "call of func2()" << std::endl;
    }
};

// type: pointer to member function of class MyClass
//       without parameter and return value
typedef void (MyClass::*MyClassFunction)();

// exported object and exported member function
void* objPtr;
void* objfpPtr;

void exportObjectAndFunction(void* op, void* fp)
{
    objPtr = op;
    objfpPtr = fp;
}

void callMyClassFunc(void* op, void* fp)
{
    // cast types back to original type
    MyClass* myObjPtr = static_cast<MyClass*>(op);
    MyClassFunction* myFuncPtr
                    = static_cast<MyClassFunction*>(fp);
```

```
        // call passed member function for the passed object
        (myObjPtr->*(*myFuncPtr))();
    }

    int main()
    {
        // object of class MyClass
        MyClass x;

        // pointer to member function of class MyClass
        MyClassFunction funcPtr;

        // pointer to member refers to func1()
        funcPtr = & MyClass::func1;

        // export object and member function
        exportObjectAndFunction(&x, &funcPtr);

        // call exported member function for exported object
        callMyClassFunc(objPtr, objfpPtr);
    }
```

In C++, the addresses of objects, as well as the addresses of the member pointers, can be exported as void*:

```
    void exportObjectAndFunction(void* op, void* fp);
    ...
    MyClass x;
    MyClassFunction funcPtr;
    ...
    exportObjectAndFunction(&x, &funcPtr);
```

These addresses can also be used as pointers to members:

```
    void callMyClassFunc(void* op, void* fp) {
        // cast types back to original type
        MyClass* myObjPtr = static_cast<MyClass*>(op);
        MyClassFunction* myFuncPtr
                          = static_cast<MyClassFunction*>(fp);

        // call passed member function for the passed object
        (myObjPtr->*(*myFuncPtr))();
    }
```

Note that the address of a variable that refers to the member function gets exported. Thus you have to make sure that this variable remains valid. It is not possible to export the address of a member function.

9.4.4 Summary

- In C++, pointers to class members can be defined.
- The C++ operators .* and ->* allow parametrized class members to be accessed by objects or object pointers.
- Using pointers to member functions, member functions can be parametrized or can be exported for a call from outside.

9.5   Combining C++ Code with C Code

C++ code can be combined with C code. This is guaranteed in C++.

9.5.1   External Linkage

The interface between C++ and C can only use language features that are available in both languages. In addition, this interface has to be specially 'marked' in C++. This is done using the `extern` keyword. The declaration `extern "C"` declares functions (and also types and variables) that are part of the interface to the language of C. This process is described as *external linkage*.

For example, the following declaration defines the function `foo()` as an interface between C and C++:

```
extern "C" {
    // declaration of the interface between C and C++
    void foo(long, double);
    ...
}
```

It does not matter whether this function is implemented in a C or a C++ module. Therefore, it can be an imported C function or an exported C++ function.

By using `extern "C"`, it is ensured that the function name `foo` remains unchanged as a symbol. Normally, internal symbols for functions consist of information that contains the types of the parameters, as well as the function names. Because of this, it is ensured that a distinction can be made between overloaded functions. This process is described as 'name mangling'.

With the GCC compiler, for example, the declarations

```
void foo();
void foo(long, double);
void foo(const CPPBook::Fraction&);
```

are managed internally as the following symbols:

```
foo__Fv
foo__Fld
foo__FRCQ27CPPBook8fraction
```

The generated symbols are not standardized. For this reason (and for other reasons), it is not usually possible to combine the code of different C++ compilers.

As functions cannot be overloaded in C, name mangling cannot be used there. By using `extern "C"` it is switched off in C++ files.

By means of an appropriate external statement, linkage to other languages is possible. However, this is not guaranteed by the language of C++, but instead depends on the compilers and linkers that are used. As it is usually possible to combine code of a language with C code, this code can always be combined with C++ by using `extern "C"`.

9.5.2 Header Files for C and C++

It is possible to provide header files for use in C, as well as for use in C++. This is supported by the preprocessor constant __cplusplus, which is only defined for C++[5]. For example, a header file might look as follows:

```
#ifdef __cplusplus
extern "C" {
#endif
    void foo(long, double);

    ...
#ifdef __cplusplus
}
#endif
```

Using the preprocessor statements, it is ensured that the statement

```
extern "C" {

    ...

}
```

is only taken into account during a compilation with the constant __cplusplus defined (i.e. a C++ compilation). Otherwise, the functions are declared, as in C or ANSI-C, with parameter prototypes. The standard header files of C are usually implemented in this way for C++.

9.5.3 Compiling `main()`

An important point should be noted. When combining C++ with other code, main() usually has to compiled with a C++ compiler. This is because the constructors of the global C++ objects are called with the call of main(). If main() is not compiled with a C++ compiler, problems may arise. On many systems, there are ways to work around this (e.g. special auxiliary functions for the initialization of the C++ environment). However, this kind of solution is not portable.

9.5.4 Summary

- C code can be combined with C++ code.
- Imported and exported functions (types, variables) have to be declared using extern "C".
- C++ symbols are normally subject to name mangling.
- Binary code of different C++ compilers cannot normally be linked.
- main() should always be compiled with a C++ compiler.
- In C++, the preprocessor constant __cplusplus is defined.

---

[5] In order to avoid name conflicts, constants predefined by the system typically begin with two underscores.

9.6   Additional Keywords

In this section, some additional keywords are introduced.

9.6.1   Unions

A *union* is a data structure in which all members have the same address. Because of this, unions only occupy as much memory as their largest element. Therefore, at any one time, unions can only even contain one of the possible values.

The following unions can, for example, alternatively contain the address of a character or an integral value:

```
union Value {
    const char* addr;
    int         num;
};
```

The language does not manage what kind of value is in a union. If an address is written to a union, it has to be ensured by the programmer that an address is also requested:

```
Value value;

value.addr = "hello";            // assign address to union value
...
const char* t = value.addr;      // query address from union value

value.num = 42;                  // assign number to union value
...
int i = value.num;              // query number from union value
```

Typically, you would mark what is stored in a union in a separate variable or member.

9.6.2   Enumeration Types with `enum`

Enumeration types can also be defined in C++. These are types that can assume different *enumeration values*. For example, this enables you to govern what is in a union:

```
enum ValueKind { Address, Number };

struct Entry {
    ValueKind kind;
    Value     value;
};
```

```
Entry e;

if (...) {
    e.kind = Address;        // assign address to union value
    e.value.addr = "hello";
} else {
    e.kind = Number;         // assign number to union value
    e.value.num = 42;
} ...

const char* t; int i;

switch (e.kind) {
  case Address:
    t = e.value.addr;        // query address from union value
    break;
  case Number:
    i = e.value.num;         // query number from union value
    ...
    break;
}
```

Note that enumeration types and values are valid from the point of their definition to the end of the scope in which they are defined. Thus, to avoid name clashes, you should ensure that enumeration types are not defined in the global naming scope.

Integers can also be assigned to the values of enumeration types:

```
enum Season { Spring=1, Summer=2, Autumn=4, Winter=8 };
```

Without this explicit assignment, the values start would would start from zero.

Enumeration types can take on all values between zero and the greatest integer number rounded up to the power of two. If an enumeration value has a negative value, the same applies (as many bits that are needed in the value range are always used).

Integers can be explicitly converted into enumeration values:

```
enum Range { min = 0, max = 100 }      // range: 0 to 127
Range r;
r = min;            // OK
r = max;            // OK
r = Range(17);      // between min and max
r = Range(120);     // OK, same number of bits as 100
r = Range(200);     // ERROR (undefined behavior)
```

Another example of the use of enumeration lists can be found in Section 6.5.2 on page 420.

9.6.3   The `volatile` Keyword

In order to avoid unsuitable optimizations for a program, functions and variables can be declared with the `volatile` keyword. The exact meaning of such a declaration depends on the compiler.

The general idea, however, is that variables or functions are used in programs in such a way that they play a role outside the scope of the compiler. If usual optimizations would remove these variables or functions, this kind of program would no longer be capable of running.

If, for example, a program only has read access to a resource that is modified outside the program (such as a shared memory segment that is modified by another process), it should be protected with `volatile`:

```
extern const volatile value;
```

Without the `volatile` keyword, the compiler would assume that the value of `value` could not be changed after the first reading, and therefore could optimize further read attempts by just removiong them. By using `volatile`, it is guaranteed that the value of `value` is always reread.

9.6.4   Summary

- Unions are objects that can manage data of different types with the same memory.
- Unions are defined using the `union` keyword.
- Enumeration types and values can be defined using `enum`.
- By using the `volatile` keyword, areas that are not under the control of the compiler can be protected from aggressive optimizations.

10

Summary

Because, for teaching purposes, the language features of C++ have been introduced in stages, the most important features are summarized here. These include useful programming and design guidelines, as well as a comprehensive list of the operators and their properties.

10.1 Hierarchy of C++ Operators

The tables on the following pages contain all the C++ operators. They are designed according to the following principles:

- Horizontal lines separate operators with different priorities. The table is arranged in order of descending priority.
- The column '**Eval.**' defines the order of evaluation among operators with equal priority:
  - L-R denotes that the operators (with equal priority) are evaluated from left to right.
  - R-L denotes that the operators (with equal priority) are evaluated from right to left.
- The last column indicates whether the operator was recently introduced to C++. Operators that are not marked with 'new' are also available in C.

Operator	Meaning	Eval.	
(...)	bracketing		
::	scope resolution, scope assignment		new
.	access to members	L–R	
->	access to members from a pointer (a->b is usually equivalent to (*a).b)		
[...]	array indicing		
fname(...)	function call		
++	postfix increment ('a++')		
--	postfix decrement ('a--')		
type(...)	type conversion (functional notation)		new
static_cast<*type*>(...)	type conversion (logical)		new
const_cast<*type*>(...)	type conversion (remove constancy)		new
dynamic_cast<*type*>(...)	type conversion (downcast, at run time)		new
reinterpret_cast<*type*>(...)	type conversion (reinterpretation of bits)		new
typeid (...)	class ID		new
++	prefix increment ('++a')	R–L	
--	prefix decrement ('--a')		
~	bit complement		
!	logical negation		
+	positive sign		new
-	negative sign		
&	address of		
*	reference to (dereferencing)		
new	create object		new
delete	destroy object		new
new[]	create array of objects		new
delete[]	destroy array of objects		new
(*type*)...	type conversion (cast notation)		
sizeof (...)	size of type or object		
.*	pointer to member access for objects	L–R	new
->*	pointer to member access for pointers		new
*	multiplication	L–R	
/	division		
%	modulo (remainder after division)		
+	addition	L–R	
-	subtraction		
<<	left shift	L–R	
>>	right shift		

Operator	Meaning	Eval.	
<	less than	L-R	
<=	less than or equal to		
>	greater than		
>=	greater than or equal to		
==	equal	L-R	
!=	unequal		
&	bit-wise AND	L-R	
^	bit-wise XOR (exclusive OR)	L-R	
|	bit-wise OR	L-R	
&&	logical AND (evaluated up to first `false`)	L-R	
||	logical OR (evaluated up to first `true`)	L-R	
?:	conditional evaluation	R-L	
=	assignment	R-L	
*=			
/=			
%=			
+=			
-=	'a *op*= b' is equivalent to 'a = a *op* b'		
<<=			
>>=			
&=			
^=			
|=			
,	sequence of expressions	L-R	

10.2 Class-Specific Properties of Operations

The following table shows different properties of class-specific operations and functions that are important in practice.

	is inherited	can be virtual	return type	can be a member	can be a friend	default is generated
default constructor	–	–	–	yes	–	yes[1]
copy constructor	–	–	–	yes	–	yes
other constructor	–	–	–	yes	–	–
destructor	–	yes	–	yes	–	yes
conversion	yes	yes	–[2]	yes	–	–
new, new[]	yes	–	void*[3]	static	–	–[4]
delete, delete[]	yes	–	void	static	–	–[4]
=	–	yes	yes	yes	–	yes
(), [], ->	yes	yes	yes	yes	–	–
op=	yes	yes	yes	yes	yes	–
other operators[5]	yes	yes	yes	yes	yes	–
other member function	yes	yes	yes	yes	–	–
friend	–	–	yes	–	yes	–

[1] If no other constructor is defined.

[2] But returns something.

[3] Returns *type**.

[4] A global operation is predefined for all classes.

[5] Except ., ::, sizeof, .*, ?:, and cast operators, which can't be defined for user-defined types.

10.3   Rules for Automatic Type Conversion

The following list shows what priorities apply to automatic type conversion. The list is ordered with descending priority.

1. Exact agreement or trivial type conversions.
   The following are examples of trivial type conversions:
   - Non-reference <=> reference.
   - Array notation => pointer notation.
   - Variable => constant.
   - Variable => volatile.

2. Suitable function templates without type conversion.

3. Standard conversions containing information:
   - `char, short int, enum => int.`
   - `float => double.`

4. Other standard conversions:
   - Standard conversions of C.
   - Conversions to objects of the base classes (only references and pointers).

5. User-defined type conversions:
   - Constructors with an argument.
   - Conversion functions.

   The following applies:
   - There is a maximum of one self-defined type conversion possible per object (a multiple automatic type conversion is not possible).
   - Any standard conversions are possible before and after.
   - Standard conversions have no influence on priority.
   - Constructors and conversion functions are equivalent.

If nothing matches, it is checked whether there is a suitable function with a variable number of arguments. Otherwise, the call is not possible.

10.4 Useful Programming Guidelines and Conventions

In C++, there are numerous rules that must be observed when using the language. In addition, a number of conventions and de-facto standards have been established when working with C++. The most important programming guidelines and conventions are listed below:

- The file ending for header files should be .hpp (see Section 3.3.5 on page 50).
- The file ending for dot-C files should be .cpp (see Section 3.3.5 on page 50).
- Header files should be enclosed by preprocessor guards that avoid errors as a result of multiple includes (see Section 3.3.7 on page 52).
- using directives should never be used in header files (see Section 3.5.9 on page 90 and Section 4.3.5 on page 176).
- Data members of classes should be initialized using initializer lists, at least if they are not fundamental types (see Sections 4.1.7 and 6.4.2).
- Operators should always be implemented so that they do what is expected of them. As a rule of thumb, the behavior of the operators should be equivalent to the behavior of these operators for fundamental types (see Section 4.2).
- To avoid creating copies when arguments are passed, functions should declare the parameters as constant references (see Section 4.4).
- Constant objects should be declared with the const keyword (see Section 4.4.3 on page 186).
- Member functions that do not change their objects should be declared as constant member functions (see Section 4.4.4 on page 187).
- Input operators should only change an object if the read was successful (see Section 4.5.4 on page 210).
- Input operators of a class should be able to read the format that was written with the output operator of the class (see Section 4.5.4 on page 210).
- Functions for automatic type conversion should be used with care because they can generate unexpected side effects and ambiguity (see Section 4.6.5 on page 229).
- Exceptions should be declared in catch blocks as constant references (see Section 4.7.2 on page 243).
- Classes should at least give the guarantee that an exception will not leak resources or violate invariants (see Section 4.7.10 on page 252).
- Classes with virtual functions should have a virtual destructor (see Section 5.2.5 on page 286).
- When using inheritance, member functions should not be declared as virtual one time and as non-virtual another time (see Section 5.2.2 on page 283).
- When implementing derived classes, the following should be considered (see Section 5.2):
  - Member functions that are not declared as virtual in the base class should not be overridden in derived classes.
  - When overriding member functions of a base class, the parameters must be of the same types.
  - Overridden functions should have the same default arguments.

- During the design of class hierarchies, the following must be taken into account (see Section 6.3):
  - Objects of derived classes should never be subject to any limitations as compared to objects of the base class (as far as either their attributes or their operations are concerned).
  - Any newly added members must not change the meaning of the inherited data members.
- Avoid inheritance (see Section 5.5.5 on page 348).
- The 'rule of three': A class either needs an assignment operator, a copy constructor, and a destructor, or none of these. If one of the three operations is implemented, it must be checked whether the others need to be implemented as well (see Section 6.1).
- A user-defined assignment operator should
  - begin with a query as to whether an object is being assigned to itself;
  - return the object to which another object was assigned as a (constant) reference

  (see Section 6.1.5 on page 362)
- With template code, declarations and implementations should be divided into separate header files (see Section 7.6.1 on page 466).
- Instead of dynamic arrays, STL containers (such as vectors) should be used (see Section 9.1.1 on page 522).
- Names of types and classes should start with uppercase letters.
- Function names, variables, and objects should start with lowercase letters.
- All preprocessor constants should consist entirely of uppercase letters.
- Commercial classes, libraries, and members should always be defined in a separate namespace.
- Programmers should always know what they are doing.

Bibliography

This appendix gives the resources and literature that is referenced in this book and that, in my opinion, is important for a more in-depth introduction to C++. This is not, however, a complete bibliography for C++. An updated version of this bibliography can be found at:
http://www.josuttis.com/cppbook.

Newsgroups

The following newsgroups discuss C++, the standard, and the C++ standard library:

- Tutorial level C and C++ (unmoderated)
    alt.comp.lang.learn.c-c++
- General aspects of C++ (unmoderated)
    comp.lang.c++
- General aspects of C++ (moderated)
    comp.lang.c++.moderated
- Aspects of the C++ Standard (moderated)
    comp.std.c++

These newsgroups are available with the Google newsgroup archive:
    http://groups.google.com

The Standard

[*Standard98*]
ISO
Information Technology—Programming Languages—C++
Document Number ISO/IEC 14882-1998
Available at http://www.ansi.org
ISO/IEC, 1998

[*Standard02*]
ISO
Information Technology—Programming Languages—C++
(as amended by the first technical corrigendum)
Document Number ISO/IEC 14882-2002
ISO/IEC, expected late 2002

About the Language

[*AlexandrescuDesign*]
Andrei Alexandrescu
Modern C++ Design
Generic Programming and Design Patterns Applied
Addison-Wesley, Reading, MA, 2001

[*CargillExceptionSafety*]
Tom Cargill
Exception Handling: A False Sense of Security
C++ Report, November-December 1994
Available at:
  `http://www.awprofessional.com/meyerscddemo/demo/magazine/index.htm`

[*CzarneckiEiseneckerGenProg*]
Krzysztof Czarnecki, Ulrich W. Eisenecker
Generative Programming
Methods, Tools, and Applications
Addison-Wesley, Reading, MA, 2000

[*KoenigMooAcc*]
Andrew Koenig, Barbara E. Moo
Accelerated C++
Practical Programming by Example
Addison-Wesley, Reading, MA, 2000

[*MeyersEffective*]
Scott Meyers
Effective C++
50 Specific Ways to Improve Your Programs and Design (2nd Edition)
Addison-Wesley, Reading, MA, 1998

[*MeyersMoreEffective*]
Scott Meyers
More Effective C++
35 New Ways to Improve Your Programs and Designs
Addison-Wesley, Reading, MA, 1996

[*StroustrupC++PL*]
Bjarne Stroustrup
The C++ Programming Language, Special ed.
Addison-Wesley, Reading, MA, 2000

[*SutterExceptional*]
Herb Sutter
Exceptional C++
47 Engineering Puzzles, Programming Problems, and Solutions
Addison-Wesley, Reading, MA, 2000

[*SutterMoreExceptional*]
Herb Sutter
More Exceptional C++
40 New Engineering Puzzles, Programming Problems, and Solutions
Addison-Wesley, Reading, MA, 2001

[*VandevoordeJosuttisTemplates*]
David Vandevoorde, Nicolai M. Josuttis
C++ Templates - The Complete Guide
Addison-Wesley, Reading, MA, 2002

About the Standard Library and STL

[*AusternSTL*]
Matthew H. Austern
Generic Programming and the STL
Using and Extending the C++ Standard Template Library
Addison-Wesley, Reading, MA, 1999

[*JosuttisStdLib*]
Nicolai M. Josuttis
The C++ Standard Library
A Tutorial and Reference
Addison-Wesley, Reading, MA, 1999

[*LangerKreftIO*]
Angelika Langer, Klaus Kreft
Standard C++ IOStreams and Locales
Advanced Programmer's Guide and Reference
Addison-Wesley, Reading, MA, 1999

Somewhat Outdated but still Helpful

[*EllisStroustrupARM*]
Margaret A. Ellis, Bjarne Stroustrup
The Annotated C++ Reference Manual (ARM)
Addison-Wesley, Reading, MA, 1990

[*StroustrupDnE*]
Bjarne Stroustrup
The Design and Evolution of C++
Addison-Wesley, Reading, MA, 1994

Glossary

This glossary is a compilation of the most important technical terms used in this book. See http://www.research.att.com/~bs/glossary.html for a very complete, general glossary of terms used by C++ programmers.

abstract class
Class for which the creation of concrete objects (*instances*) is impossible or not useful. Abstract classes can be used to combine common properties of different classes in a single type or to define a polymorphic interface. Because abstract classes are used as base classes, the acronym *ABC* is sometimes used for *abstract base class*.

abstract data type
A language-independent description of a data structure using concrete interfaces. For example, we could define a *Stack* abstract data type with three interfaces *push()*, *pop()*, and *is_empty()*. This would include the meaning (effects) of those interfaces, but not their actual implementation or performance characteristics.

ANSI
American National Standard Institute, one national committee that works on the standardization of C++.

attribute
Property or *data member* of a concrete object of a class. Every concrete object of a class uses memory for its attributes. Their values reflect the status of the object.

base class
A class, from which another class inherits properties. Base classes are often *abstract classes*. Base classes are often called *superclasses* in other programming communities.

cast
Name for a explicit type conversion that also exists in C.

class
Description of a category of objects. The class defines a set of characteristics for any object. These include its data (*attributes*, *data members*) as well as its operations (*methods*, *member functions*). In C++, classes are structures with members that can also be functions and are subject to access limitations. They are declared using the keywords `class` (or `struct`).

class template
A template of a class that is parametrized for different types or values. Actual classes can be generated by substituting the template parameters by specific entities. Class templates are also described conceptionally as 'parametrizable classes.'

collection class
Class that is used to manage a group of objects. In C++, collection classes are also called *containers*.

concrete class
A class, from which concrete objects (instances) can be created (as opposed to an *abstract class*).

constant member function
A member function that can be called for constant and temporary objects because it does normally not modify members of the object it is called for.

constructor
Member function of a class that is called during the creation of an object of the class and is used to bring the newly created object into a useful initial state.

container
See *collection class*.

conversion function
Special member function that defines how an object of a class can be converted to an object of another type. It is declared using the form `operator` *type*`()`.

copy constructor
Function that is called if a new object is created as a copy of an existing one. This happens in particular with the passing of parameters and return values if no references are used. In C++ a default copy constructor is predefined for every class that copies memberwise. It can be replaced by a user-defined implementation.

data member
Attribute of an object or a member that is not a member function. Every concrete object of a class uses memory for its data members with values that reflect the status of the object.

declaration
A C++ construct that introduces or reintroduces a name into a C++ scope. See also *definition*.

default constructor
Constructor that is called when a new object is created without any arguments for initialization.

definition
A *declaration* that makes the details of the declared entity known or, in the case of variables, that forces storage space to be reserved for the declared entity.

derived class
A class that inherits the properties of another class (called the *base class*). Semantically this is often a 'concretion' of the base class. Base classes are often called *subclasses* in other programming communities.

destructor
Function that is called for an object of a class if it is destroyed.

dot-C file
A file in which *definitions* of variables and noninline functions are located. Most of the executable (as opposed to declarative) code of a program is normally placed in dot-C files. They are the files that are used a *translation units* to get compiled (and linked) to object files, libraries, or executable programs. Usually, they include *header files*, in which usable constants, functions, classes, etc., are declared. They are named *dot-C* files because they are usually named with a .cpp suffix (although, other suffixes such as .C, .c, .cc, or .cxx are also used).

encapsulation
Design concept which limits the access to things or objects. By means of this restriction, an object can only be manipulated using a well defined interface. By doing so, interfaces can be verified better and inconsistencies can be avoided. C++ supports the encapsulation by means of special access keywords.

function template
A template of a function that is parametrized for different types or values. Actual functions can be generated by substituting the template parameters by specific entities. Function templates are also described conceptionally as 'parametrizable functions.'

header file
A file that contains *declarations* of variables and functions that are referred to from more than one translation unit, as well as *definitions* of types, inline functions, templates, constants, and macros. Header files are meant to become part of a *translation unit* through a #include directive. They are usually named with a .hpp suffix (although, other suffixes such as .h, .H, .hh, or .hxx are also used). They are also called *include files*.

include file
See *header file*.

inheritance

Reduction of a type or a class (*derived class*) to another type or class (*base class*) by defining only the properties that are added (or modified). Inheritance makes it possible for common properties of different kinds of objects to be combined and to be implemented only once. By doing so, the base class is supporting abstraction. The base class is the generic class that defines the common properties that can be used to derive many more concrete variants.

initializer list

A comma-separated list of expressions enclosed in braces used to initialize objects (or arrays). In constructors, the values that are entered can be used for the initialization of members of a class or for the call of the constructor of a base class.

instance

The term *instance* has two meanings in C++ programming: The meaning that is taken from the object-oriented terminology is *an instance of a class*: An object that is the realization of a class. For example, in C++, std::cout is an instance of the class std::ostream. The other meaning is *a template instance*: A class, a function, or a member function obtained by substituting all the template parameters by specific values. In this sense, an *instance* is also called a *specialization*.

ISO

International Organization for Standardization, the international committee that works on the standardization of C++.

iterator

An object that knows how to traverse a sequence of elements. Often, these elements belong to a collection (see *collection class*).

member

Element of a class. A member can be a *data member* (*attribute*) that has an object of the class and reflects the status of the object, or a *member function* (*method*) that describes which operations can be called for an object of the class. A special case is that of static members that do not describe properties of individual objects but properties of the whole class (data that is shared by all objects).

member function

Function that can be called for an object of a class. It is declared as a member in the class structure. It can also be called a *method*, which is the corresponding general object-oriented term.

message

Object-oriented name for the call of an operation for an object. The call is seen as a message that is sent to the object and leads to a reaction. In C++, a message is a call of a *member function*.

method

Object-oriented name for the implementation of an operation that can be called for an object of a class. In C++, a method is called a *member function*.

multiple inheritance
The capability that a class can be derived from more than one *base class*.

object
Central term of object-oriented programming. An object is an information carrier that represents different data that has a certain status (value) and provides an interface to perform operations. An object can therefore represent abstractions of any kind, such as a process or a football game, for example. An object is simply 'something' that is of interest, is described, and plays a part in a program. The properties of objects (the data that they represent and the operations with which they can be executed) are described in classes.

pointer
Object or variable that contains a program address and therefore points to something else in the program. A pointer is, for example, the address of a function or object to which indirect access can then be made.

polymorphism
The ability for the same operation to be called for different kinds of objects that, according to the object, leads to different reactions. In object-oriented terminology, this means that different kinds of objects can receive the same message, but are interpreted differently because the classes have different methods for the message. In C++, there is the ability for different objects to be managed under a common class/type so that the same function call may result in different operations depending on the actual class/type of the object/value. The common class/type can be implemented as a *base class* ('dynamic polymorphism') or as a *class template* ('static polymorphism').

reference
A 'second name,' that can be given to an existing object. References are used in particular when parameters and return values are passed in order not to produce copies ('call-by-reference'). In addition, 'reference' is also used if something 'refers' to something else (which might be a reference in the sense of a 'second name' or a pointer).

source file
Header file or *dot-C file*.

specialization
The process or result of substituting template parameters by actual values so that actual classes or functions are generated.

structure
Composition of different members into one common, complete object. Structures offer the option of abstraction (for example, an engine, the body work, four wheels, and so on being combined and managed as a car).

subclass
See *derived class*.

superclass
See *base class*.

template
A template of a function (*function template*) or a class (*class template*) that is parametrized for different types or values.

translation unit
The code that is compiled as the result of preprocessing a *dot-C* file. That is, it is a *dot-C* file with all the header files and standard library headers it #includes, without the program text that is excluded by conditional compilation directives such as #if or #ifdef.

whitespace
The common name for the standard spaces under C, C++ and UNIX. These characters are new-lines, blank spaces, and tabulator characters.

Index

Note: Bold page numbers indicate major topics; italic page numbers indicate examples.

A

E

N

P

S